THE THEOLOGY OF

Paul Tillich

THE THEOLOGY OF
Paul Tillich

EDITED BY
CHARLES W. KEGLEY

The Pilgrim Press

New York

The first edition, edited by Charles W. Kegley and Robert W. Bretall, was published by The Macmillan Company in 1952.

Library of Congress Cataloging in Publication Data
Main entry under title:

The Theology of Paul Tillich.

　　Bibliography of the publications of Paul Tillich: p. 395.
　　Includes indexes.
　　1. Tillich, Paul, 1886–1965—Addresses, essays, lectures.
I. Kegley, Charles W.
BX4827.T53T48　　1982　　　230'.092'4　　　82–301
ISBN 0–8298–0499–4 (pbk.)　　　　　　　　AACR2

Grateful acknowledgment is hereby made for permission to quote from the following published works of Paul Tillich:

The Interpretation of History. Copyright 1936 by Charles Scribner's Sons; copyright renewed 1964 by Paul Tillich (New York: Charles Scribner's Sons, 1936). Reprinted with the permission of Charles Scribner's Sons.

The Shaking of the Foundations. Copyright 1948 by Charles Scribner's Sons; copyright renewed 1976 by the Estate of Paul Tillich (New York: Charles Scribner's Sons, 1948). Reprinted with the permission of Charles Scribner's Sons.

The Protestant Era. Reprinted by permission of The University of Chicago Press. Copyright 1948 by The University of Chicago Press.

Systematic Theology (Volume I). Reprinted by permission of The University of Chicago Press. Copyright 1951 by The University of Chicago Press.

Appreciation is also expressed to the editors and publishers of the many periodicals and journals from which the contributors have gathered additional insights into the thought and writings of Professor Tillich.

The Pilgrim Press, 132 West 31 Street, New York, New York 10001

CONTENTS

INTRODUCTION TO THE SECOND EDITION

THE thought and writing of Paul Tillich remain an important influence in contemporary theology and philosophy. There is ample reason to believe that he will be the object of increasing study and debate in the decades ahead. Indeed, Tillich can now be said to be guaranteed a central role in the history of philosophy and theology.

Since Tillich's death in 1965, a new generation of scholars, teachers, students, and public has appeared. This enlarged edition of *The Theology of Paul Tillich* enhances the possibility of greatly improved theological and philosophical study. In the exchange between Tillich and his interpreters and critics, this book discusses, illuminates, clarifies, even settles issues still prominent today. The basic format of an intellectual autobiography, analytical essays on aspects of Tillich's thought and work, and Tillich's reply to the essays provide an interchange of ideas new readers will find surprising and stimulating.

This edition of *The Theology of Paul Tillich* is published to coincide with the twenty-fifth anniversary of the founding of the United Church of Christ, the American denomination in which Tillich held his ministerial standing. It contains a major new and extended assessment of Tillich's thought by a distinguished theologian, Langdon Gilkey of the University of Chicago. Also included is an updating of their original essays by two contributors, James Luther Adams and Charles Hartshorne.

Finally, Robert P. Scharlemann has rendered a valuable service by bringing up-to-date the bibliography of Tillich's writings available in English. Such an update is long overdue.

It is with sadness that I note the death of Robert Bretall, co-editor of the first edition of this book. I profoundly regret the passing of this distinguished author, editor, philosopher and life-long friend.

CHARLES W. KEGLEY

BAKERSFIELD, CALIFORNIA

INTRODUCTION

A s we enter the second half of the twentieth century, religion and theology are less likely to be neglected by thinking men. Whatever may be the causes of the present-day return to religion, the fact remains that religious thinking has again become intellectually respectable. As against the climate of a generation and more ago—when the notion of a "Christian intellectual" was almost a contradiction in terms—we now see religiously minded men—motivated in their thinking by basic religious and theological assumptions—taking a more and more prominent and commanding place in the world of thought.

The Library of Living Theology is dedicated to the furthering and the clarification of this phenomenon of our times. Granted that religion and theology are again in the forefront of thought and life, and that they are once more "respectable," *which* religion is best, *which* theology is the most valid? There is much vigorous discussion, but little general agreement. Certain trends may be seen—for example, the swing away from humanism and liberalism—but these are only straws in the wind, and in any case prove nothing about *validity*. Neither the good nor the true can be derived from the "is."

In 1939 Professor Paul Arthur Schilpp, of Northwestern University, set out to clarify the issues in contemporary philosophy through a series of books entitled *The Library of Living Philosophers*. His idea was original and unique: to devote each volume in the series to the thinking of a single living philosopher, and to include in each (1) an intellectual autobiography; (2) essays on different aspects of the man's work, written by leading scholars; (3) a "reply to his critics" by the philosopher himself; and (4) a complete bibliography of his writings to date. This philosophical series—now numbering eight volumes—has met with universal acclaim. The editors of the present series gladly acknowledge their debt to Professor Schilpp, not only for the general plan of the volumes, but also for valuable criticism and friendly advice in planning this series. Our aim, quite simply, is to do for present-day theology what he has done and is continuing to do so well for philosophy.

A note on the use of the word "theology" is in order. In the Christian tradition "theology" has usually meant *dogmatic* theology, that is, a systematic account of God, man, immortality, and the like, based either on the Bible (Biblical theology) or on the creedal standards of a given church (Confessional theology). Within the last fifty or seventy-five years, however, the term has been extended to include the rather different theologies constructed by the liberal theologians in the tradition of Schleiermacher and Ritschl— theologies based not on authoritative revelations or Church councils, and thus "once for all delivered," but on changing human experience and even on empirical, scientific knowledge. In America the leading representative of this empirical theology was probably the late Douglas Clyde Macintosh; today it is being carried on in a somewhat different way by Henry Nelson Wieman. For this liberal "theology of religious experience," the term "theology" is not clearly distinguishable from "philosophy of religion."

The Library of Living Theology will remain neutral on this issue of terminology. For us "theology" will include theologies of both types: subject and essayists will be selected from representatives of both schools of thought, as well as from points of view which cannot properly be ranged under one banner or the other. Paul Tillich, the subject of our first volume, is probably a good example of the last-mentioned type of "subject."[1]

At this point the question may be asked, whether we intend to confine ourselves to *Christian* theology, or perhaps to theology within the Western Judaeo-Christian tradition. The answer to this question is No. We begin with writers who stand firmly within this tradition simply because they represent the most vigorous theological thinking that is being done today. Quite apart from any natural prejudices we Westerners may have, it is simply the case that outside the Western framework theology is almost dormant today, or at

[1] See his distinction between "kerygmatic" and "apologetic" theology in *Systematic Theology*, I, 3–8.

least quiescent,[2] whereas within that framework it is very much alive.[3] The choosing of subjects for the various volumes of the *Library* will be governed as far as possible by this criterion of "aliveness," capacity for creativity and individuality of thought. If these qualities should appear in a Buddhist or Mohammedan philosopher, for example, we shall gladly consider him as a possible "subject" of a future volume.

The *Library of Living Theology* will thus be catholic in character, that is, in the correct sense of the word: universal. It might be called religious and theological in its subject matter, philosophical in its method and basic approach. Its editors happen to represent just this union of religious and philosophical interests; they are at home in the "borderland" between philosophy and religion, and they feel the desirability of promoting clarification and mutual understanding in this embattled region. The *odium theologicum* is well known, and asserts itself today as in the past. Perhaps a certain amount of "fighting spirit" is essential to a good discussion, and *in this sense* our aim is to provide a real battleground for some of the keenest intellects of our day. It is only through rigorous and unrestrained freedom of discussion that clarification can result. With clarification should come sympathetic understanding of positions other than one's own. At the very least it should call for a refusal to dismiss these positions and those who uphold them with the conveniently opprobrious tags of "liberal," "modernist," "fundamentalist," "neo-orthodox," and the like. These tags may be useful in a rough way, but as applied to almost every great thinker of our time—and certainly to those who are to be subjects of this series—they will, upon examination, reveal inadequacies and a fundamental inability to grasp the true "inwardness" of the man's thought. In view of these considerations, *The Library of Living Theology* may serve as an agency not only of enlightenment, but also of mutual understanding and good will.

The choice of Paul Tillich as the subject for this first volume will come as no surprise to those who are acquainted with his work. The adjective "great," in our opinion, can be applied to very few thinkers

---

[2] An exception to this statement might be found in the work of the Indian philosopher-mystic, Sarvepalli Radhakrishnan, who is to be the subject of a forthcoming volume in Professor Schilpp's series.

[3] Professor Tillich, in his work cited above, pp. 15–18, has suggested a radical reason for going further and *identifying* "theology" with "Christian theology."

of our time, but Tillich, we are far from alone in believing, stands unquestionably amongst these few. No one conversant with theological and philosophical issues who has glimpsed the monumental outlines of the *Systematic Theology*, for example, can fail to be impressed with its depth, its symphonic structure, and its integrity. With Dewey, Whitehead, Russell, and Santayana stands a man whom future generations probably will pronounce no whit their inferior either dialectically or in his grasp of the philosophical requirements of our time, but whose feet are planted solidly upon Christian soil, rooted in the Word of God. His name is Paul Tillich.[4]

Though the expression is subject to misinterpretation, there is a sense in which Tillich's work constitutes a kind of Protestant "Summa" for our time. We are aware that Professor Tillich himself (in his *Systematic Theology, I*, vii, 59) disclaims any intention of writing a "Summa," indicating rather that he presents a "system." In the very nature of the case, Protestantism can have no "Summa," for "the Protestant principle" precludes anything like finality. Yet in a given historical situation presumably there can be a work which most fully gathers up the strands of all that is best in secular thought, and unites them with the truths of God's self-disclosure. Augustine, Aquinas, Calvin, and Schleiermacher, for instance, tried to accomplish something like this, and in some important respects the theological thought of Paul Tillich has the same marks.

There is another aspect of Tillich's work, however, which should not be overlooked—an aspect in which he comes closer to Augustine than to any of the other writers mentioned. This is the element of the imagination—that which helps to make a great theologian a great preacher. There is an emotional and volitional depth in Tillich's writing which is inherent in the thought itself—thought that vibrates beneath the surface of the abstractions and gains all the more power because of this tension. These seeming abstractions themselves are charged with emotion. What could be more abstract than "Being"? But in this "theology of the New Being" the abstract metaphysical term becomes filled with emotional and volitional content—a content which stems partly from our Christian inheritance, but mostly from that very "existential disruption" of our time, in which we feel ourselves separated from all that religion has meant by "salvation,"

---

[4] The statement of Georgia Harkness, to the effect that what Alfred North Whitehead is to American philosophy, Paul Tillich is to American theology, is well known.

"regeneration," and "eternal life." This probably is what makes Tillich preeminently an apostle to the skeptics, the "intellectuals," and the disillusioned of our era; but it is also what makes his philosophy in a sense classical, because the "intellectuals" are only those who feel more deeply and more coherently what the masses obscurely feel. Thus, in the published sermons of the subject of this first volume—for example, the ones gathered together under the title *The Shaking of the Foundations*—we find a remarkable combination of simplicity and profundity. These stirring and beautiful sermons would not be easy to match in any age; and there is evidence that their appeal is not limited to the "wise and prudent," although the message may be directed especially to them in the sense that Tillich identifies himself always with the "disinherited"—intellectually as well as materially—of our supposedly Christian culture.[5]

Any minister who cannot derive inspiration and a wealth of suggestions from such sermons as "The Escape from God," "The Depth of Existence," "The Yoke of Religion," "Born in the Grave," "You Are Accepted," and "Behold, I Am Doing a New Thing" (to mention only a few that we know are favorites) has probably ceased to think, or (what amounts to the same thing) has become so wedded to a dogmatic and formalized statement of Christian truth that he cannot minister to the real needs of thinking people in our secular world. Against such a "hardening of the arteries" in Christian theology Tillich comes as a most welcome stimulant. The channels are relaxed, and again the lifeblood begins to flow.

Yet this is only half of the truth. According to Karl Barth the message (kerygma) must be "thrown at those in the situation—thrown like a stone." Tillich does not wholly agree; but much of the power of his own work comes precisely from the fact that, on the one hand, he stands where the skeptic, the secularist, the enemy of Christianity

[5] The editors have been informed by one of the essayists of two recent instances in which the timeliness and meaning of Professor Tillich's printed sermons have dramatically borne fruit in experience. We cite these two instances as evidence that seemingly abstract ideas can have concrete meaning. One was the case of a Negro convict who was given a copy of *The Shaking of the Foundations*. After prolonged study of it, and following his release from prison, he stated that he was able to discover thereby what is meant by the assertion that one must "die to live." He has since begun his education for the Christian ministry.

The other instance was that of a brilliant young man who, with a fatal disease, spent the last months of his life pondering the message of this book, and finding in it, as he said to his family and friends, his first insight into the meaning of the Christian faith for one facing death.

stands, seeing all that he sees and feeling all that he feels of revulsion against "the shams of Christendom" and of justified rebellion
against the enslaving "yoke of religion"; on the other hand, he stands
in the promised land where the Christian has always stood, and he
speaks out of the depth in which the divine promises are received in
the face of life's disruptedness.

Nothing is demanded of you—no idea of God, and no goodness in your-
selves, not your being religious, not your being Christian, not your being
wise, and not your being moral. But what is demanded is only your being
open and willing to accept what is given to you, the New Being, The
Being of love and justice and truth, as it is manifest in Him Whose yoke
is easy and Whose burden is light.

. . . . You are accepted, accepted by that which is greater than you, and
the name of which you do not know. Do not ask for the name now; perhaps you will find it later. Do not try to do anything now; perhaps later
you will do much. Do not seek for anything; do not perform anything; do
not intend anything. Simply accept the fact that you are accepted! . . .
After such an experience we may not be better than before, and we may
not believe more than before. But everything is transformed. In that moment, grace conquers sin, and reconciliation bridges the gulf of estrangement.[6]

Here is a modern evangelicalism whose significance and applicability in preaching—especially to the "unsaved," the religiously
illiterate, and the alienated—are almost unlimited. This aspect of
Tillich's work has not been treated by the contributors to the
present volume.

The evangelical note, moreover, rings out free from any hint of
fundamentalism or fideism. Tillich's position on the perennial
question of the relation between reason and revelation—a position of great simplicity, although of the utmost philosophical
sophistication, and summed up in his "method of correlation"[7]
—seeks not only to provide an answer to the extremes of rationalism (the primacy of reason over faith) and fideism (the primacy
of faith over reason), but at the same time to render intelligible and defensible a mediating position which many consider
rooted in Biblical theology. In the thirteenth century and again in
the sixteenth, Christian thinkers believed that they could show that
philosophy is capable of giving positive answers to its questions—

---

[6] The Shaking of the Foundations, pp. 102, 162.
[7] Systematic Theology, I, 60–65.

answers which, when properly understood, are not in conflict with
revealed knowledge but supplementary to such knowledge. Today
we are in a different situation. On the one hand, natural science
has practically routed philosophy in its "quest for certainty"; on the
other hand, we are more suspicious than ever of revelation, not so
much because it pretends to come from a source superior to our
natural reason, but rather because, with the abdication of philosophy, it does not seem to make contact with reason at any point;
and also because, interpreted and presented in a rigid, unimagina-
tive way, its content has seemed at many points to be at variance
with the findings of the natural sciences. Profound skepticism both
of philosophy and of revelation; the realization that science gives us,
not certainty but at least "reliable knowledge"; and yet the emptiness, the "waste land" left by this skepticism in the minds and hearts
of men, together with the dim awareness that psychologically this
emptiness must be filled by something—by demonic forces born out
of anxiety, if not by Love—such is the climate of thought and feeling
in which we of the mid-twentieth century find ourselves.

What, indeed, can meet the requirements of this situation? An
increasing number of our abler minds—as the essays of this volume
suggest—are fairly near to saying that the answer is in the kind of
"systematic theology" developed by Paul Tillich, employing, as it
does, the method of correlation in which the philosophical question
is paired with the theological answer stemming from revelation.
According to this view it is recognized that "philosophy cannot
answer ultimate or existential questions *qua* philosophy";[8] that the
function of philosophy is to raise these ultimate questions rather
than to answer them; and that in so far as it does claim to give a
final answer to these questions, it falls into antinomies and conflicts
which can be resolved only on the basis of a "New Being" overcoming the estrangement and contradictions of our existence. Yet it
is important to have the questions asked, and the Christian answer
is really an answer *to* these questions. At the same time this theological answer is presented in a way which frees it from all taint
of obscurantism, irrationalism, and even "supranaturalism." What
is "supernatural" from the standpoint of estranged and disrupted
existence is essentially natural, and no conflict with empirical science
is possible.[9] "The new being means that the old being has not yet

[8] *The Protestant Era*, p. xxvi.
[9] *Ibid.*, p. 18.

destroyed itself completely. . . ."[10] Formally, the difference between Tillich's "Protestant synthesis" and that of Scholasticism is the difference between a correlation of negative and positive (question and answer, philosophy and theology, reason and revelation) and a correlation of two positives (natural knowledge and revealed truth); actually the gulf is much wider—between a prescientific *Weltanschauung* claiming finality for itself, and one which is everywhere cognizant of science and its implications, and which above all claims no such finality.[11]

One of the chief aims of this first volume is to establish a new pattern of theological discussion which will be serviceable in the future. The form or structure will remain the same; the content will vary as forthcoming volumes are devoted to the thought of the preeminent minds of our age who have already agreed to be "subjects," for example, Reinhold Niebuhr, Emil Brunner, and Karl Barth.

CHARLES W. KEGLEY

DEPARTMENT OF PHILOSOPHY AND RELIGION
WAGNER COLLEGE
NEW YORK CITY

ROBERT W. BRETALL

DEPARTMENT OF PHILOSOPHY AND PSYCHOLOGY
UNIVERSITY OF ARIZONA
TUSCON, ARIZONA

[10] *The Shaking of the Foundations*, p. 101.
[11] *The Protestant Era*, pp. 162–163, 176–177, and *passim*.

I

AUTOBIOGRAPHICAL REFLECTIONS
OF PAUL TILLICH

AUTOBIOGRAPHICAL REFLECTIONS

I. EARLY YEARS

BECAUSE autobiographical sketches have appeared as introductions of two of my former books, *The Interpretation of History* and *The Protestant Era,* I feel somewhat embarrassed in attempting the same assignment a third time; but it must be done because it is required by the structure of the present series. So I have decided to add to the factual information about the events of my life certain reflections, some of which may be taken as implicit answers to the questions and criticisms raised by my colleagues who have produced the substance of this volume.

The fact that I was born on the 20th of August, 1886, means that a part of my life belongs to the nineteenth century, especially if one assumes the nineteenth century to end (as one should) with August 1, 1914, the beginning of the First World War. Belonging to the nineteenth century implies life in relatively peaceful circumstances and recalls the highest flourishing of bourgeois society in its productive grandeur. It also implies aesthetic ugliness and spiritual disintegration. It implies, on the one hand, revolutionary impulses directed against this self-complacent period, and on the other hand, a consciousness of the Christian humanist values which underlie even the antireligious forms of this society, and which made and make it possible to resist the inhuman systems of the twentieth century. I am one of those in my generation who, in spite of the radicalism with which they have criticized the nineteenth century, often feel a longing for its stability, its liberalism, its unbroken cultural traditions.

My birthplace was a village with the Slavic name Starzeddel, near Guben, a small industrial town in the province of Brandenburg, at the Silesian border. After four years my father, a minister of the Prussian Territorial Church, was called to the position of super-intendent of the diocese of Schönfliess-Neumark. Superintendent was the title of the directing minister in a group of parishes, with functions similar to those of a bishop, but on a smaller scale. Schönfliess was a place of three thousand inhabitants, in eastern Brandenburg. The town was medieval in character. Surrounded by a wall, built around an old Gothic church, entered through gates with towers over them, administered from a medieval town hall, it gave the impression of a small, protected, and self-contained world. The environment was not much different when, from my twelfth to fourteenth year, I stayed as a pupil of the humanistic *Gymnasium,* and as a boarder of two elderly ladies, in Königsberg-Neumark, a town of seven thousand people with the same kind of medieval re-mains, but bigger and more famous for their Gothic perfection.

These early impressions may partly account for what has been challenged as the romantic trend in my feeling and thinking. One side of this so-called romanticism is my relationship to nature. It is expressed in a predominantly aesthetic-meditative attitude toward nature as distinguished from a scientific-analytical or technical-con-trolling relation. It is the reason for the tremendous emotional im-pact that Schelling's philosophy of nature made upon me—although I was well aware that this philosophy was scientifically impossible. It is theologically formulated in my doctrine of the participation of nature in the process of fall and salvation. It was one of the reasons why I was always at odds with the Ritschlian theology which establishes an infinite gap between nature and personality and gives Jesus the function of liberating man's personal life from bondage under the nature within us and beside us. When I came to America, I found that Calvinism and Puritanism were natural allies of Rit-schlianism in this respect. Nature is something to be controlled morally and technically, and only subjective feelings of a more or less sentimental character toward nature are admitted. There is no mystical participation in nature, no understanding that nature is the finite expression of the infinite ground of all things, no vision of the divine-demonic conflict in nature.

When I ask myself about the biographical background of this so-called romantic relation to nature, I find three causes which prob-ably worked together in the same direction. First, I find the actual communication with nature, daily in my early years, in my later years for several months of every year. Many memorable instances of "mystical participation" in nature recur in similar situations. A second cause of the romantic relation to nature is the impact of poetry. The German poetic literature, even aside from the romantic school, is full of expressions of nature mysticism. There are verses of Goethe, Hölderlin, Novalis, Eichendorff, Nietzsche, George, and Rilke which never have ceased to move me as deeply as they did when I first heard them. A third cause of this attitude toward nature came out of my Lutheran background. Theologians know that one of the points of disagreement between the two wings of the Continental Reformation, the Lutheran and the Reformed, was the so-called "Extra Calvinisticum," the doctrine that the finite is *not* capable of the infinite (*non capax infiniti*), and that consequently in Christ the two natures, the divine and the human, remained outside each other. Against this doctrine the Lutherans asserted the "Infra Lutheranum"; namely, the view that the finite *is* capable of the infinite, and consequently that in Christ there is a mutual indwelling of the two natures. This difference means that on Lutheran ground the vision of the presence of the infinite in everything finite was theologically affirmed, that nature mysticism was possible and real, whereas on Calvinistic ground such an attitude is suspect of pantheism and the divine transcendence is understood in a way which for a Lutheran is suspect of deism.

Romanticism means not only a special relation to nature; it means also a special relation to history. To grow up in towns in which every stone is witness of a period many centuries past produces a feeling for history, not as a matter of knowledge, but as a living reality in which the past participates in the present. I appreciated that distinction more fully when I came to America. In lectures, seminars, open houses, and personal conversations with American students I found that an immediate emotional identification with the reality of the past was lacking. Many of the students here had an excellent knowledge of historical facts, but these facts did not seem to concern them profoundly. They remained objects of their intellect, and almost never became the elements of their existence. It is the European destiny to experience in every generation the wealth and the tragedy of historical existence, and consequently to think in terms of the past, whereas America's history started with the loss both of the burden and of the richness of the past. She was able to think in terms of the future. It is, however, not only historical consciousness generally which was emphasized by the romantic school; it was the special valuation of the European Middle Ages through which romanticism was deeply influential in the intellectual history of the last one hundred years. Without this influence I certainly would not have conceived of the idea of theonomous periods in the past and of a new theonomy in the future.

Two other points of biographical significance ought to be mentioned in connection with the years in Schönfliess and Königsberg. The first is the effect which the early life in a parish house had upon me, standing as I did with a confessional Lutheran school on one side and on the other a beautiful Gothic church in which Father was a successful pastor. It is the experience of the "holy" which was given to me at that time as an indestructible good and as the foundation of all my religious and theological work. When I first read Rudolf Otto's *Idea of the Holy,* I understood it immediately in the light of these early experiences, and took it into my thinking as a constitutive element. It determined my method in the philosophy of religion, wherein I started with the experiences of the holy and advanced to the idea of God, and not the reverse way. Equally important existentially as well as theologically, were the mystical, sacramental and aesthetic implications of the idea of the holy, whereby the ethical and logical elements of religion were derived from the experience of the presence of the divine, and not conversely. This made Schleiermacher congenial to me, as he was to Otto, and induced both Otto and myself to participate in movements for liturgical renewal and a revaluation of Christian and non-Christian mysticism.

Existence in a small town in eastern Germany before the turn of the century gave to a child with some imaginative power the feeling of narrowness and restrictedness. I have already referred to the surrounding wall as a symbol of this. Movement beyond the given horizon was restricted. Automobiles did not exist, and a secondary railway was built only after several years; a trip of a few miles was an event for man and beast alike. The yearly escape to the Baltic Sea, with its limitless horizon, was the great event, the flight into the open, into unrestricted space. That I have chosen a place at the Atlantic Ocean for the days of my retirement is certainly due to these early experiences. Another form of escape from the narrowness of my early life came in making several trips to Berlin, the city in which my father was born and educated. The impression of the big city was somehow similar to that of the sea: infinity, openness, unrestricted space! But beyond this it was the dynamic character of the life in Berlin that affected me, the immense amount of traffic, the masses of people, the ever changing scenes, the inexhaustible possibilities. When, in the year 1900, my father was called to an important position in Berlin, I felt extreme joy. I never lost this feeling; in fact, it was deepened when I really learned of the "mysteries" of a world city, and when I became able to participate in them. Therefore I always considered it a good destiny that the emigration of the year 1933 brought me to New York, the largest of all large cities.

Still deeper in their roots and their effects than the restrictedness in space and movement were the sociological and psychological restrictions of those years. The structure of Prussian society before the First World War, especially in the eastern part of the kingdom, was authoritarian without being totalitarian. Lutheran paternalism made the father the undisputed head of the family, which included, in a minister's house, not only wife and children, but also servants with various functions. The same spirit of discipline and authority dominated the public schools, which stood under the supervision of the local and county clergy in their function as inspectors of schools. The administration was strictly bureaucratic, from the policeman in the street and the postal clerk behind the window, through a hierarchy of officials, to the far-removed central authorities in Berlin—authorities as unapproachable as the "castle" in Kafka's novel. Each of these officials was strictly obedient to his superiors and strictly authoritative toward his subordinates and the public. What was still lacking in discipline was provided by the army, which trespassed in power and social standing upon the civil world and drew the whole nation from earliest childhood into its ideology. It did this so effectively in my case that my enthusiasm for uniforms, parades, maneuvers, history of battles, and ideas of strategy was not exhausted until my thirtieth year, and then only because of my experiences in the First World War. But above all this, at the top of the hierarchy, stood the King of Prussia, who happened to be also the German emperor. Patriotism involved, above all, adherence to the king and his house. The existence of a parliament, democratic forces, socialist movements, and of a strong criticism of the emperor and the army did not affect the conservative Lutheran groups of the East among whom I lived. All these democratic elements were rejected, distortedly represented, and characterized as revolutionary, which meant criminal. Again it required a world war and a political catastrophe before I was able to break through this system of authorities and to affirm belief in democratic ideals and the social revolution.

Most difficult to overcome was the impact of the authoritarian system on my personal life, especially on its religious and intellectual side. Both my father and mother were strong personalities. My father was a conscientious, very dignified, completely convinced and, in the presence of doubt, angry supporter of the conservative Lutheran point of view. My mother, coming from the more democratic and liberal Rhineland, did not have the authoritarian attitude. She was, however, deeply influenced by the rigid morals of Western Reformed Protestantism. The consequence was a restrictive pressure in thought as well as in action, in spite (and partly because) of a warm atmosphere of loving care. Every attempt to break through was prevented by the unavoidable guilt consciousness produced by the identification of the parental with the divine authority. There was only one point at which resistance was possible; namely, by using the very principles established by my father's authoritarian system against this system itself. And this was the way I instinctively chose. In the tradition of classical orthodoxy, my father loved and used philosophy, convinced that there can be no conflict between a true philosophy and revealed truth. The long philosophical discussions which developed belong to the most happy instances of a positive relation to my father. Nevertheless, in these discussions the break-through occurred. From an independent philosophical position a state of independence spread out into all directions, theoretically first, practically later. It is this difficult and painful break-through to autonomy which has made me immune against any system of thought or life which demands the surrender of this autonomy.

In an early polemic between Karl Barth and myself, he accused me of "still fighting against the Great Inquisitor." He is right in asserting that this is a decisive element of my theological thought. What I have called the "Protestant principle" is, as I believe, the main weapon against every system of heteronomy. But Barth must have realized in the meantime that this fight never will become unnecessary. History has shown that the Great Inquisitor is always ready to reappear in different disguises, political as well as theological. The fact that I have equally often been accused of neo-orthodoxy and of old liberalism is understandable in view of the two strong motives I received in the years under discussion: the romantic and the revolutionary motives. The balance of these motives has remained the basic problem of my thought and of my life ever since.

II. PREWAR YEARS

In the year 1900 we moved to Berlin. I became a pupil at a humanistic *Gymnasium* in Old Berlin, passed my final examinations in 1904, and was matriculated in the theological faculties of Berlin, Tübingen, and Halle. In 1909 I took my first, in 1911 my second theological examination. In 1911 I acquired the degree of Doctor of Philosophy in Breslau, and in 1912 the degree of Licentiat of Theology in Halle. In the latter year I received ordination into the Evangelical Lutheran Church of the province of Brandenburg. In 1914 I joined the German Army as a war chaplain. After the end of the war I became a *Privatdozent* of Theology at the University of Berlin, the beginning of my academic career. Reviewing these fifteen years of preparation, interrupted and at the same time completed by the war, I find abundant material for philosophical reflection. But I must restrict myself to some observations about the impact of these years on my own development.

In Königsberg, as well as in Berlin, I was a pupil in a "humanistic *Gymnasium*." A *Gymnasium*, compared with American institutions, consists of high school plus two years of college. The normal age for finishing the *Gymnasium* is eighteen. A humanist *Gymnasium* has as its central subjects Greek and Latin. My love of the Greek language was a vehicle for my love of the Greek culture and especially the early Greek philosophers. One of my most enthusiastically prepared and best received courses had as its subject matter the pre-Socratic philosophy. The problem of the humanistic education is its relation to the religious tradition which, even without a special religious instruction, is omnipresent in history, art, and literature. Whereas in the United States the basic spiritual conflict is that between religion and scientific naturalism, in Europe the religious and humanistic traditions (of which the scientific world view is only a part) have been, ever since the Renaissance, in continuous tension. The German humanistic *Gymnasium* was one of the places in which this tension was most manifest. While we were introduced into classical antiquity in formal classes meeting about ten hours a week for about eight years, we encountered the Christian tradition at home, in the church, in directly religious instructions in school and outside the school, and in indirect religious information in history, literature, and philosophy. The result of this tension was either a decision against the one or the other side, or a general skepticism or a split-consciousness which drove one to attempt to overcome the conflict constructively. The latter way, the way of synthesis, was my own way. It follows the classical German philosophers from Kant to Hegel, and remained a driving force in all my theological work. It has found its final form in my *Systematic Theology*.

Long before my matriculation as a student of theology, I studied philosophy privately. When I entered the university, I had a good knowledge of the history of philosophy, and a basic acquaintance with Kant and Fichte. Schleiermacher, Hegel, and Schelling followed, and Schelling became the special subject of my study. Both my doctoral dissertation and my thesis for the degree of Licentiat of Theology dealt with Schelling's philosophy of religion. These studies seemed more to foreshadow a philosopher than a theologian; and indeed they enabled me to become a professor of philosophy of religion and of social philosophy in the philosophical faculties of Dresden and Leipzig, a professor of pure philosophy in Frankfurt, a lecturer in the philosophical departments of Columbia and Yale, and a philosopher of history in connection with the religious-socialist movement. Nevertheless I was and am a theologian, because the existential question of our ultimate concern and the existial answer of the Christian message are and always have been predominant in my spiritual life.

The fifteen years from 1904 to 1919 have in various ways contributed to this decision. My experiences as a student of theology in Halle from 1905 to 1907 were quite different from those of theological student Leverkühn in Thomas Mann's *Doctor Faustus* in the same period. It was a group of great theologians to whom we listened and with whom we wrestled in seminars and personal discussions. One thing we learned above all was that Protestant theology is by no means obsolete, but that it can, without losing its Christian foundation, incorporate strictly scientific methods, a critical philosophy, a realistic understanding of men and society, and powerful ethical principles and motives. Certainly we felt that much was left undone by our teachers and had to be done by ourselves. But this feeling of every new generation need not obviate the gratefulness for what it has received from its predecessors.

Important influences on our theological existence came from other sides. One of them was our discovery of Kierkegaard and the shaking impact of his dialectical psychology. It was a prelude to what happened in the 1920's when Kierkegaard became the saint of the theologians as well as of the philosophers. But it was only a prelude; for the spirit of the nineteenth century still prevailed, and we hoped that the great synthesis between Christianity and humanism could be achieved with the tools of German classical philosophy. Another prelude to the things to come occurred in the period between my student years and the beginning of the First World War. It was the encounter with Schelling's second period, especially with his so-called "Positive Philosophy." Here lies the philosophically decisive break with Hegel, and the beginning of that movement which today is called Existentialism. I was ready for it when it appeared in full strength after the First World War, and I saw it in the light of that general revolt against Hegel's system of reconciliation which occurred in the decades after Hegel's death, and which through Kierkegaard, Marx, and Nietzsche has become decisive for the destiny of the twentieth century.

But once more I must return to my student years. The academic life in Germany in these years was extremely individualistic. There were no dormitories for students, and very few and impersonal activities for the student body as such. The religious life was almost completely separated from the life of the churches, chaplains for the students did not exist and could hardly be imagined. The relation with the professors and their families was sporadic and in many cases completely absent. It is this situation which made the fraternities in Germany much more important than they are in this country. My membership in such a fraternity with Christian principles was not only a most happy but also a most important experience. Only after the First World War, when my eyes became opened to the political and social scene, did I realize the tremendous dangers of our prewar academic privileges. And I look now with great concern at the revival of the fraternities in post-Hitler Germany. But in my student years the fraternity gave me a communion (the first one after the family) in which friendship, spiritual exchange on a very high level, intentional and unintentional education, joy of living, seriousness about the problems of communal life generally, and

Christian communal life especially, could daily be experienced. I question whether without this experience I would have understood the meaning of the church existentially and theoretically.

III. POSTWAR YEARS

The First World War was the end of my period of preparation. Together with my whole generation, I was grasped by the overwhelming experience of a nation-wide community—of the end of a merely individualistic and predominantly theoretical existence. I volunteered, and was asked to serve as a war chaplain, which I did from September, 1914, to September, 1918. The first weeks had not passed before one's original enthusiasm disappeared; after a few months I became convinced that the war would last indefinitely and ruin all Europe. Above all, I saw that the unity of the first weeks was an illusion, that the nation was split into classes, and that the industrial masses considered the Church as an unquestioned ally of the ruling groups. This situation became more and more manifest toward the end of the war. It produced the revolution, in which imperial Germany collapsed. The way in which this situation produced the religious-socialist movement in Germany has often been described. It is also commented on in this volume. I want, however, to add a few reflections. I was in sympathy with the social side of the revolution even before 1918, the side which soon was killed by interferences of the victors, by the weakness of the socialists and the necessity of their using the army against the communist, further by inflation and the return of all the reactionary powers in the middle of the twenties. My sympathy for the social problems of the German Revolution has roots in my early childhood which are hard to trace. Perhaps it was a drop of the blood which induced my grandmother to build barricades in the Revolution of 1848, perhaps it was the deep impression of the words of the prophets against injustice and the words of Jesus against the rich; all these were words which I learned by heart in my very early years. But whatever it was, it broke out ecstatically in these years and is still a reality, although mixed with resignation and some bitterness about the division of the world into two all-powerful groups between which the remnants of a democratic and religious socialism are crushed. It was a mistake when the editor of the *Christian Century* gave to my article in the series "How My Mind Changed in the Last Ten Years" the title

"Beyond Religious Socialism." If the prophetic message is true, there is nothing "beyond religious socialism."

Another remark must be made here regarding my relation to Karl Marx. It has always been dialectical, combining a Yes and a No. The Yes was based on the prophetic, humanistic and realistic elements in Marx's passionate style and profound thought, the No on the calculating, materialistic, and resentful elements in Marx's analysis, polemics, and propaganda. If one makes Marx responsible for everything done by Stalin and the system for which he stands, an unambiguous No against Marx is the necessary consequence. If one considers the transformation of the social situation in many countries, the growth of a definite self-consciousness in the industrial masses, the awakening of the social conscience in the Christian churches, the universal application of the economic-social method of analysis to the history of thought—all this under the influence of Marx—then the No must be balanced by a Yes. Although today such a statement is unwelcome and even dangerous, I cannot suppress it, as I could not suppress my Yes to Nietzsche during the time in which everything which deserves a No in him was used and abused by the Nazis. As long as our thought remains autonomous, our relation to the great historical figures must be a Yes and a No. The undialectical No is as primitive and unproductive as the undialectical Yes.

In the years after the revolution my life became more intensive as well as extensive. As a *Privatdozent* of theology at the University of Berlin (from 1919 to 1924), I lectured on subjects which included the relation of religion to politics, art, philosophy, depth psychology, and sociology. It was a "theology of culture" that I presented in my lectures on the philosophy of religion, its history and its structure. The situation during these years in Berlin was very favorable for such an enterprise. The political problems determined our whole existence; even after revolution and inflation they were matters of life and death. The social structure was in a state of dissolution, the human relations with respect to authority, education, family, sex, friendship, and pleasure were in a creative chaos. Revolutionary art came into the foreground, supported by the Republic, attacked by the majority of the people. Psychoanalytic ideas spread and produced a consciousness of realities which had been carefully repressed in previous generations. The participation in these movements created manifold problems, conflicts, fears, expectations, ecstasies, and despairs, practically as well as theoretically. All this was at the same time material for an apologetic theology.

It was a benefit when, after almost five years in Berlin, my friendly adviser, the minister of education, Karl Becker, forced me against my desire into a theological professorship in Marburg. During the three semesters of my teaching there I met the first radical effects of the neo-orthodox theology on theological students: cultural problems were excluded from theological thought; theologians like Schleiermacher, Harnack, Troeltsch, Otto, were contemptuously rejected; social and political ideas were banned from theological discussions. The contrast with the experiences in Berlin was overwhelming, at first depressing and then inciting: a new way had to be found. In Marburg, in 1925, I began work on my *Systematic Theology,* the first volume of which appeared in 1951. At the same time that Heidegger was in Marburg as professor of philosophy, influencing some of the best students, existentialism in its twentieth century form crossed my path. It took years before I became fully aware of the impact of this encounter on my own thinking. I resisted, I tried to learn, I accepted the new way of thinking more than the answers it gave.

In 1925 I was called to Dresden and shortly afterward to Leipzig also. I went to Dresden, declining a more traditional theological position in Giessen because of the openness of the big city both spatially and culturally. Dresden was a center of visual art, painting, architecture, the dance, opera, with all of which I kept in close touch. The cultural situation was not much different when, in 1929, I received and accepted a call as professor of philosophy at the University of Frankfurt. Frankfurt was the most modern and most liberal university in Germany, but it had no theological faculty. So it was quite appropriate that my lectures moved on the boundary line between philosophy and theology, and tried to make philosophy existential for the numerous students who were obliged to take philosophical classes. This, together with many public lectures and speeches throughout Germany, produced a conflict with the growing Nazi movement long before 1933. I was immediately dismissed after Hitler had become German chancellor. At the end of 1933 I left Germany with my family and came to this country.

In the years from 1919 to 1933, I produced all my German books and articles with the exception of a few early ones. The bulk of my literary work consists of essays, and three of my books, *Religiöse Verwirklichung, The Interpretation of History,* and *The Protestant Era,* are collections of articles which themselves are based on addresses or speeches. This is not accidental. I spoke or wrote when I was asked to do so, and one is more often asked to write articles than books. But there was another reason: speeches and essays can be like screws, drilling into untouched rocks; they try to take a step ahead, perhaps successfully, perhaps in vain. My attempts to relate all cultural realms to the religious center had to use this method. It provided new discoveries—new at least for me—and, as the reaction showed, not completely familiar to others. Essays like those on "The Idea of a Theology of Culture," "The Overcoming of the Concept of Religion in the Philosophy of Religion," "The Demonic," "The Kairos," "Belief-ful Realism," "The Protestant Principle and the Proletarian Situation," "The Formative Power of Protestantism," and, in America, "The End of the Protestant Era," "Existential Philosophy," "Religion and Secular Culture"—these were decisive steps on my cognitive road. So were the Terry lectures which I delivered at Yale in October, 1950, under the title "The Courage to Be." This method of work has the advantages referred to, but it also has its shortcomings. There is even in a well organized work such as my *Systematic Theology* a certain inconsistency and indefiniteness of terminology; there is the influence of different, sometimes competitive motives of thought, and there is a taking for granted of concepts and arguments which have been dealt with in other places.

The first volume of *Systematic Theology* is dedicated "to my students here and abroad." *The Protestant Era* could have been dedicated "to my listeners here and abroad." That is, to the numerous nonstudent audiences to whom I spoke in addresses, speeches, and sermons. Looking back at more than forty years of public speaking, I must confess that from the first to the last address this activity has given me the greatest anxiety and the greatest happiness. I have always walked up to a desk or pulpit with fear and trembling, but the contact with the audience gives me a pervasive sense of joy, the joy of a creative communion, of giving and taking, even if the audience is not vocal. But when it becomes vocal, in periods of questions or discussions, this exchange is for me the most inspiring part of the occasion. Question and answer, Yes and No in an actual disputation—this original form of all dialectics is the most adequate form of my own thinking. But it has a deeper implication. The spoken word is effective not only through the meaning of the sentences formulated, but also through the immediate impact of the personality behind these sentences. This is a temptation because one can use it for methods of mere persuasion. But it is also a benefit, because it agrees with what may be called "existential truth"; namely, a truth which lives in the immediate self-expression of an experience. This is not true of statements which have a merely objective character, which belong to the realm of "controlling knowledge"; but it is valid of statements which concern us in our very existence, and especially of theological statements which deal with that which concerns us ultimately. To write a system of existential truth, therefore, is the most difficult task confronting a systematic theologian. But it is a task which must be tried again in every generation, in spite of the danger that either the existential element destroys systematic consistency or that the systematic element suffocates the existential life of the system.

IV. AMERICAN YEARS

To begin life anew in the United States at forty-seven years of age and without even a minimum knowledge of the language was rather difficult. Without the help of colleagues and students at Union Theological Seminary and the assistance of German and American friends it might easily have been disastrous. It is now over eighteen years that I have taught at the seminary, and because in two years I shall reach the required retirement age, I want to take this occasion to say what Union Seminary has meant to me.

It was first of all a shelter at the moment when my work and my existence in Germany had come to an end. The fact that shortly after my dismissal by Hitler I was asked by Reinhold Niebuhr (who happened to be in Germany that summer) to come to Union Seminary prevented me from becoming a refugee in the technical sense. Our family arrived in New York on November 4, 1933. At the pier we were received by Professor Horace Friess of the philosophy department of Columbia University, who had asked me in Germany to give a lecture in his department. Ever since 1933 I have been in close relation to the Columbia philosophers, and the dialectical conversation across Broadway (the street separating Columbia and Union) has never ceased, but rather has developed into an intensive cooperation. It was Union, however, that took me in as a stranger, then as visiting, associate, and full professor. Union Seminary was not only a shelter in the sense of giving a position and an apartment; it was also a shelter in the sense of affording a community of life and work. The seminary is a closely knit community of professors and their families, of students, often likewise with their families, and of the staff. The members of this fellowship meet one another frequently in elevators and halls, at lectures, in religious services and social gatherings. The problems as well as the blessings of such a community are obvious. For our introduction into the American life all this was invaluable, and it was also important for me as a counteraction against the extreme individualism of one's academic existence in Germany.

Union Seminary, moreover, is not an isolated community. If New York is the bridge between the continents, Union Seminary is the lane of that bridge, on which the churches of the world move. A continuous stream of visitors from all countries and all races passes through our quadrangle. It is almost impossible to remain provincial in such a setting. The world-wide outlook theologically, culturally, and politically is one of the things for which I am most grateful. The cooperation of the faculty has been perfect. During seventeen years at Union Seminary I have not had a single disagreeable experience with my American colleagues. I regret only that the tremendous burden of work prevented us from enjoying a more regular and more extensive exchange of theological ideas. The work at the seminary is first of all a work with students. They come from all over the continent, including Canada. They are carefully selected, and their number is increased by exchange students from all over the world. I loved them from the first day because of their human attitude toward everything human (including myself); their openness for ideas, even if strange to them, as my ideas certainly were; their seriousness in study and self-education in spite of the confusing situation in which they found themselves in a place like Union Seminary. The lack of linguistic and historical preparation produced some difficulties, but these were overbalanced by many positive qualities. Union Seminary is not only a bridge between the continents, but also a center of American life. Its faculty, therefore, is drawn into innumerable activities in New York and in the rest of the country, and the more so the longer one is on the faculty. It is obvious that in spite of the great benefits one can derive from such contacts with the life of a whole continent, the scholarly work is reduced in time and efficiency. Beyond all this, Union Seminary gives to its members a place of common worship. This was a new experience for me, and a very significant one. It provides for the faculty an opportunity to relate theological thought to their own and to the general devotional life of the Church. It creates for the students the possibility of experiencing this relation of thought to life and thereby of judging the one in the light of the other. It placed upon me the obligation of expressing myself in meditations and in sermons as well as in the abstract theological concepts of lectures and essays. This adds in a profound way to the thanks I owe to Union Theological Seminary.

In this way I came into relationship with other important groups and institutions. Immediately after my arrival I was received into what is now the Theological Discussion Group and into the American Theological Society. I want to express my thanks to the members of these groups for what the continuous discussion with them has meant and still means to me. It was in this fashion that I studied American theology—the way of the dialogue, which is, indeed, the dialectical way. After several years I was asked to join the Philosophy Club, whose monthly meetings I almost never missed, and which gave me a dialectical introduction into the American philosophical life in its manifoldness and intensity. Full semester, summer, and even full year courses in different universities and departments provided for other personal and scholarly introductions into American academic life and thought. At the same time cooperation with the Federal Council of Churches in refugee work, participation in the ecumenical conference in Oxford, addresses and discussions in all kinds of religious meetings, regular preaching obligations, membership in Church committees, apologetic courses, and the like, brought me into an active relation with the life of the churches in this country and beyond its borders.

For external and practical reasons it became impossible to maintain the relationship to artists, poets, and writers which I enjoyed in postwar Germany. But I have been in permanent contact with the depth-psychology movement and with many of its representatives, especially in the last ten years. The problem of the relation between the theological and the psychotherapeutic understanding of men has come more and more into the foreground of my interest, partly through a university seminar on religion and health at Columbia University, partly through the great practical and theoretical interest that depth psychology has aroused in Union Seminary, and partly through personal friendship with older and younger analysts and counselors. I do not think that it is possible today to elaborate a Christian doctrine of man, and especially a Christian doctrine of the Christian man, without using the immense material brought forth by depth psychology.

The political interests of my postwar years in Germany remained alive in America. They found expression in my participation in the religious-socialist movement in this country; in the active relation I maintained for years with the Graduate Faculty of Political Sciences at the New School for Social Research, New York; in my chairmanship of the Council for a Democratic Germany during the war; and in the many religio-political addresses I gave. In spite of some unavoidable disappointments, especially with the Council, politics remained, and always will remain, an important factor in my theological and philosophical thought. After the Second World War I felt the tragic more than the activating elements of our historical existences, and I lost the inspiration for, and the contact with, active politics.

Emigration at the age of forty-seven means that one belongs to two worlds: to the Old as well as to the New into which one has been fully received. The connection with the Old World has been maintained in different ways: first of all through a continuous community with the friends who had left Germany as refugees like myself, whose help, criticism, encouragement, and unchanging friendship made everything easier—and yet one thing: namely, the adaptation to the New World, more difficult. But it is my conviction, which has been confirmed by many American friends, that a too quick adaptation is not what the New World expects from the immigrant, but rather the preservation of the old values and their translation into the terminology of the new culture. Another way of keeping contact with the Old World was the fact that for more than fifteen years I have been the chairman of the Self-help for Emigrees from Central Europe, an organization of refugees for refugees, giving advice and help to thousands of newcomers every year, most of them Jews. This activity brought me into contact with many people from the Old World whom I never would have met otherwise, and it opened to view depths of human anxiety and misery and heights of human courage and devotion which are ordinarily hidden from us. At the same time it revealed to me aspects of the average existence in this country from which I was far removed by my academic existence.

A third contact with the Old World was provided by my political activity in connection with the Council for a Democratic Germany. Long before the East-West split became a world-wide reality, it was visible in the Council, and with many tragic consequences. The present political situation in Germany—as distinguished from the spiritual situation—has lost nothing of this character. I see it as thoroughly tragic, a situation in which the element of freedom is as deeply at work as is the element of fate, which is the case in every genuine tragedy. This impression was fully confirmed by my two trips to Germany after the Second World War. I lectured at several German universities, in 1948 mainly at Marburg and Frankfurt, in 1951 mainly at the Free University in Berlin. Of the many impressions these visits gave me, I want to point only to the spiritual situation in Germany, which is open, surprisingly open, for the ideas which are discussed in this book. An evidence of this is the speed with which my English writings now are being translated and published in Germany. This way of returning to Germany is the best I could imagine, and it makes me very happy.

But in spite of these permanent contacts with the Old World, the New World grasped me with its irresistible power of assimilation and creative courage. There is no authoritarian system in the family—as my two children taught me, sometimes through tough lessons. There is no authoritarian system in the school—as my students taught me, sometimes through amusing lessons. There is no authoritarian system in the administration—as the policemen taught me, sometimes through benevolent lessons. There is no authoritarian system in politics—as the elections taught me, sometimes through surprise lessons. There is no authoritarian system in religion—as the denominations taught me, sometimes through the presence of a dozen churches in one village. The fight against the Great Inquisitor could lapse, at least before the beginning of the second half of this century.

But beyond this I saw the American courage to go ahead, to try, to risk failures, to begin again after defeat, to lead an experimental life both in knowledge and in action, to be open toward the future, to participate in the creative process of nature and history. I also saw the dangers of this courage, old and new ones, and I confess that some of the new ones have begun to give me serious concern.

Finally, I saw the point at which elements of anxiety have entered this courage and at which the existential problems have made an inroad among the younger generation in this country. Although this fact constitutes one of the new dangers, it also means openness for the fundamental question of human existence: "What am I?" the question which theology and philosophy both try to answer.

Looking back at a long life of theological and philosophical thought, I ask myself how it can compare with the world of our predecessors in the last generations. Neither I myself nor anybody else can answer this question today. One thing, however, is evident to most of us in my generation: We are not scholars according to the pattern of our teachers at the end of the nineteenth century. We were forced into history in a way which made the analysis of history and of its contents most difficult. Perhaps we have had the advantage of being nearer to reality than they were. Perhaps this is only a rationalization of our shortcomings. However this may be, my work, although humanly speaking not yet finished, has come close to its end. The criticism contained in this book shows its limitations; but that it has been judged as worthy of such criticism is honor and joy. And it is the reason for profound gratitude to all those who have worked on it in the spirit of scientific criticism and personal friendship.

PAUL TILLICH

UNION THEOLOGICAL SEMINARY
NEW YORK CITY

II

ESSAYS OF INTERPRETATION
AND CRITICISM OF
THE WORK OF PAUL TILLICH

1

Langdon Gilkey

TILLICH:
THE MASTER OF MEDIATION

1

TILLICH:
THE MASTER OF MEDIATION

THIS contemporary article will seek to answer the query, What has proved important in Tillich's thought since his death in 1965? His thought has remained influential or significant: read and reread, discussed, criticized, appealed to, and followed in whole or in part. While many of the great theological systems of the first half of this century are now more of historical than contemporary interest, Tillich's is one with which we continue to wrestle, perhaps in disagreement with him, perhaps in agreement, or, usually, in a combination of both. His influence also penetrates the many fields associated with or adjacent to philosophy and religion such as philosophy of science, of language, of existence, art criticism, psychology and therapy, studies of culture, social theory.

On the other hand, as many observers have remarked, there is no Tillichian "school"; that is, a self-conscious community of thinkers who pattern their thought on his and seek deliberately to extend, make more coherent, and defend the basic categories of his system. While there unquestionably is still a Whiteheadian school, a Thomist school, a Lonergarian school, and as there were once Barthian and Bultmannian schools, Tillich is without such an explicit band of followers. Yet he remains in the forefront of our intellectual scene as a massive and widespread influence pervading and reshaping much of our thinking.

The ground of this persistent and massive influence—besides the obvious points that his thought is at once original and provoking and yet (unlike Barth's) available in a reasonably limited corpus— is, I think, that the passage of time has shown that Tillich's thought elegantly represents a *mediating* position. Tillich loved polarities and saw almost everything in their terms; that is, in terms of opposites in vast and precarious tension that potentially (and necessarily) form a creative unity. It might please him to hear that rather than providing one option in our present scene (though there are one or two Tillichians), the main role of his thought has been to provide a point—on a surprising number of different axes—where seemingly opposite positions come into a tense, comprehensible, relation, a point in relation to which they become polarities. The scope and tensive unity of his thought is such that it has the capacity to make contact with, to "touch," and to relate itself to almost every sort of position in a variety of areas. In this sense, he continually mediates all over the place, and for this reason he interests and stimulates so many different thinkers in so many areas.

Whether one is a philosopher (analytic or speculative) or a Biblical theologian, whether one is an ontologist or an existentialist, interested in forms of personal angst or social liberation, in public arguments or deep personal experiences, in cultural analysis or doctrinal issues, in language analysis or experience, in humanism or the transcendent, in hermeneutics or speculation, in mysticism or in rationality, in the religions of the world or in the Christian message, people find Tillich significantly *there* or, so to speak, "next door." Possibly he will be too much with "them over there" rather than "with us over here," but still be the nearest to us than all of "them"! To philosophers, he is the most sensible and bearable of the religious thinkers and certainly of the Biblical theologians; to the latter he is the most religious and theological of the philosophers, to Protestants the most Catholic of "us," to Catholics the most nearly Catholic of "them." To students of religion, therapeutic theorists, sociologists, and art critics Tillich is "the only theologian we can or wish to read." He mediates not by bringing them all into his unity, but by standing "next to" or "within sight of" almost everyone. Thus, even if there are few Tillichians, his influence is widespread. Whitehead said "existence never takes a holiday from metaphysical categories." Tillich, in that sense, is almost metaphysical. If he doesn't appear on a bibliography in almost every humanistic field, one feels he should be there. That is not true of many other genuinely great and widely influential thinkers.

The reason for this power to mediate between opposing positions in a wide number of areas of interest and of thought lies in the character as well as the originality and profundity of his thinking

rather than because he is a systematic thinker. Tillich's thought
mediates, in the sense that it uncovers significant unities between
diverse areas of life and importantly touches all of them. Most great
philosophers—and here Tillich is a philosopher to the core—in the
classical tradition have done this. Tillich is unique in that he not
only mediates *philosophically* (on the basis of culture) the various
facets of life, but also mediates *between* culture and religion, philosophy and theology. He is both philosopher and theologian, "on
the boundary" between culture and religion, standing in both and
viewing each from the center of the other. Unlike other philosophers,
he brings to culture a religious or theological interpretation of the
elements of culture, as well as a philosophical interpretation of religion and theology. Such mediation has been rare.

As a theologian, he has genuine philosophical wisdom on a number of cultural issues, and yet as a philosopher he brings to his
analysis a theological profundity, a religious interpretation of things
and events that few philosophers can manage. This role of mediation between cultural life and religion gives his thought its uniqueness, its near-universality of relevance, and its unceasing ability to
illuminate the obscure corners of our existence. Only those for whom
a religious interpretation of anything is anathema or those who view
any theoretical interpretation of religion as blasphemous find Tillich
empty of all interest.

The foundation for this unique mediating role in the system itself
is its basic equation: Being Itself equals God. Or, in less cryptic
language, the *ground* of finite being, and so of all ordinary cultural
and historical experience (when the latter is truly understood), is
the same as the referent of religious concern and faith (when truly
interpreted), God. The ground of culture and the ground of religion
are in the end the same. And more: a proper religious analysis of
culture will uncover that sacred ground of culture (theology of
culture), and a proper cultural (philosophical) analysis of religion
will uncover and manifest that ground or referent of religion (philosophical theology). Thus, not only are cultural and religious institutions (e.g., states, artistic and scientific communities, churches)
deeply associated, but cultural expressions and activities on the one
hand and religious realities on the other are interrelated. Finally,
cultural thought or self-interpretation (science, psychology, social
theory and philosophy) and reflection on religion (theology) are
"correlated." Works (literary, artistic, philosophical), acts, proposi-

tions, and theories in culture have an essential relation to religion because they depend on and express, for Tillich, a "religious import" or "religious substance"; in turn, religious acts, communities, propositions, symbols and theories have relevance to culture and its modes of discourse because they inevitably are expressed and enacted in particular cultural form. Students in diverse academic fields discover Tillich as that single theologian most relevant and interesting to their own area of concern. On their subject matter, and especially on its religious ground and its religious implications, Tillich is novel and stimulating because of the way he viewed and interpreted the width of common experience. In the end, it is an expression of the relationship to God, the ground of all being and meaning.

If the persistent influence of Tillich is related to the mediating character of his thought—and to the truth or insight that such interrelating of diverse, opposing polarities brings with it—then we can clarify his present importance by locating and describing the most significant areas of mediation that his thought accomplishes. To me, there are three of these: (1) the interrelation of culture and religion (theology of culture), (2) the more specific interrelation of philosophy and religion, resulting in theology (method and correlation), and (3) those aspects of his systematic theology in which important and currently relevant mediation takes place: ontology and religion, Catholicism and Protestantism, Christianity and other religions, estrangement and hope in history.

CULTURE AND RELIGION

Tillich is unique not only in seeking (as a philosopher) to unite in one coherent conceptual analysis all the various aspects of culture (as Whitehead and Dewey did), or in seeking that unity in the unconditioned ground of culture (as did Hegel), but in viewing that ground as the object of *religion*, as fully manifest only through religion (in response to revelation), and explicable only by means of religious symbols and through reflection on religion (theology). This "correlation," interrelation or "mode of cooperation" methodologically between culture and religion on the one hand and between the substantial analysis, interpretation and understanding of culture and of religion on the other, runs through all of Tillich's thought. In each case, the finite represents an essentially valuable and coherent, but a religiously transcended, realm. There is being (finitude) and the infinite ground of being (God), there is reason (the culture-producing power) and the depth of reason (revelation), there is culture and the religious substance of culture. This is, therefore, a religious analysis of cultural life; that is, one based on a religious relation to and understanding of what is regarded as the foundational center of culture's life, its religious substance.

Moreover, the negative theme characteristic of most high religions that a serious derangement, estrangement or "fall" has taken place, also characterizes Tillich's analysis and differentiates him radically from most philosophers, especially Dewey and Whitehead. In fact, this differentiation from "essentialist" philosophy reaches a climax in his interesting reversal of Hegel. Whereas for Hegel, cultural history exhibits the rationality of a gradual synthesis into a higher unity, for Tillich that history exhibits estrangement in its inexorable unraveling of an original unity into a self-destructive disunity; it moves from an original creative theonomous synthesis, through the ambiguous thesis of autonomy to the nemesis and destruction of heteronomous antitheses. (See especially *The World Situation.*) His religious and theological analysis of culture is based not only on the religious apprehension of the immanent holy and the sacred ground (creation), but on the particular symbol or myth of the fall, an expression of our estrangement from that sacred ground. Without such a dialectical (positive and negative) analysis based on the symbols (creation and fall) of a particular religious tradition—a theology of culture as opposed to a philosophical analysis of religion—Tillich (after World War I) believed that the true situation of culture and of reason within it could not be understood.

To most theologians, this analysis is too concerned with culture and too dominated by philosophical procedures and categories to be legitimate. To almost all philosophers, this analysis as philosophical is comprehensible, but is not quite acceptable. Its premises are neither those of cultural common sense nor are they demonstrable; it is far too religious, too dependent on strange religious myths, and it is unquestionably too gloomy, One may remark that the only things in its favor are the clear facts of our historical present! The current situation in Western culture, even more than his own situation (Germany during and after World War I, in the 1920s and 1930s) warrants this sort of theoretical mediation between the cultural and the religious, this theological dialectic of affirmation, negation, and reaffirmation.

Tillich's affirmation of the creativity, value, and integrity of culture is remarkable for a theologian. Here his deep indebtedness to the German *Aufklärung* reveals itself: culture (as culture) is not essentially fallen, a kingdom of Satan, nor merely a "natural" and preliminary level of value. On the contrary, it is the creation of ontological reason, of reason in touch with its depth. In its own way, each culture represents an apprehension of the unconditioned power and the meaning that are the divine. He defines culture as that which reason, essential reason, produces. (He also defines reason as the culture-producing power of human beings.) Thus, culture, as the product of essential reason, has an unconditioned depth or import and embodies an unconditioned meaning; yet, as the product of reason, it has its own autonomous integrity. Culture sets its own canons, procedures, and norms; it produces autonomously its own creative works, and it judges or assesses them by its own autonomous criteria. The divine is the *ground*, not the controller, of human culture-producing power. The meaning, quality, and value of culture's works are immanent within them, not extrinsic to them. This is one important meaning of Tillich's category of *theonomy* as descriptive of a creative culture.

This analysis of culture sharply distinguishes itself from many secular analyses of culture in two divergent ways. In the first place, it regards all creative culture as rational, as the product of creative reason and therefore as potentially unified and coherent: art, morals, law, government, economic and social structures, arts of healing, and practices of religion. If reason and the rational are associated exclusively with scientific, technological, or organizational reason (with the laboratory, the academy, the corporation), then much of culture is irrational, the product of instincts, emotions, arbitrary preferences, fantasy, unexamined tradition, habits, chance arrangements. As a consequence, reason and rational discourse are excluded from many areas essential to culture's actual life, a situation Tillich regarded as arid and dangerous.

On the other hand, this entire rational panorama is for Tillich also saturated with the "depth of reason," with what transcends and yet is in union with reason, with an unconditioned import, meaning and value that provide the *eros*, the purpose, the commitment, the integrity, and the responsibility (in essence the "vitality") necessary for any form of rational creativity, for creative cultural life. This latter transcendent dimension is strange to most contemporary analysis, although a number of sociological interpretations of society and philosophical interpretations of science and of the scientific community have uncovered many of these unexpected aspects of ultimacy (of the "religious") as foundational for the life of wider cultures and specialized communities. For Tillich, culture essentially is separated neither from the rational nor from the religious. It is both humanistic and religiously based. A theonomous culture is created and penetrated by human reason and also by the infinite divine ground of reason. Thus, while culture is a rational and human creation, it is also an aspect of the work of Providence, an effect of revelation in its most general sense, and a constituent element in the Kingdom or the final and perfected form of divine creation.

Understanding culture positively as the creation of reason offends many theologians. Tillich's equally-definite assessment of the negativities of culture, of its estrangement and, therefore, its path to injustice and self-destruction, has seemed to others, a number of philosophers and social theorists, far too gloomy, "typsiche deutsche Weltschmerz," or possibly the idiosyncratic consequence of four "upsetting" years as a German army chaplain. In any case, it was typical of Tillich to view history dialectically, as evidencing on the one hand the career of creative reason inspired by its ground—and thus ever full of new possibilities (*kairoi*)—but also evidencing an apparently inexorable process of unraveling, a progressive disunity, separation and conflict, resulting in the end in catastrophic nemesis which then may lead to a new *kairos* and to new possibilities. Further, he was convinced (against secular analysts) that the basic forces or factors at work in this dialectical process could only be understood by a religious and a theological analysis (theology of culture), and (against the optimistic rationalists among the latter) that the history of the culture stemming from the Enlightenment, our own culture, illustrates this dialectical unraveling process. The facts of our present seem to bear him out.

For Augustine and for Tillich, the loss of the unifying ground of life results in a disunity, a separation from one another of the interrelated facets and aspects of life. God is the principle of unity and harmony, separation from God the cause of disunity, disharmony, and a final consequent loss of being (reality) and meaning (value). And as did Augustine, Tillich applied this fundamental principle of interpretation to individual and to social or historical existence. Thus, he sees Enlightenment culture beginning with a powerful assertion of the autonomy of reason against the heteronomy, the absolute and yet uncreative authority, of the now alien and external religious powers of the receding medieval world. This was, however, an autonomy with theonomous elements. It assumed the ultimate identity of Reason and Nature, of the rational, the good and the beautiful, and so of objective and subjective, of reality and value, of cognition, morals, and art. As a consequence, the "rational" stood not only for that which is true (the result of the rational cognitive processes of science) but also for that which is just (the result of rational and radical politics) and that which is beautiful (the harmonious and the orderly). In that theonomous unity (that is, through the exercise of ontological reason), the power and meaning of modern culture were nurtured.

Reason, however, in its self-conscious autonomy, has slowly cut itself off from its ground and gradually has lost these theonomous elements; as a result, fatal separations in cultural life have taken place. Reason has become "technical reason," solely concerned with cognition, manipulation and organization; it has become divorced from consideration of ends, from both the good and the aesthetic. Human subjectivity thus shrinks to a process of rational calculation, seeking to control and organize unordered and undirected desires; thought is separated from its objects, and becomes either sceptical or manipulative; reality becomes mechanical and vacuous, dominated by a meaningless fate; and inner spirit becomes irrational and subjective, ultimately empty, determined by outside forces and unreal to itself. Therefore, a technological culture, dominated by a scientific and technological definition of reason, objectifies its world and infinitely subjectifies its persons. Communion with nature is only achieved by manipulation and exploitation, communion with one another only by the creation of primitive communities that further submerge persons into a new heteronomy.

For Tillich, autonomy in history (in existence) is not self-sustaining. Inexorably it dissolves itself—or it dissolves the hidden unities on which its power is based—and then in order to save itself, it creates against itself a new heteronomy that smothers all autonomy and creativity. The development of scientific and humanistic German culture into the emptiness of the Weimar and the ideology of the Third Reich provided, of course, Tillich's actual model. But, unfortunately, the problems he there discerned have progressively characterized the whole of the post-Enlightenment West with its manipulation and exploitation of nature, its new sense of industrial fatedness and loss of strong inwardness, and its ever-present and threatening ideologies.

Central to Tillich's interpretation of culture is that there are extra-scientific and extra-technological elements of cultural life that are crucial to its existence. These elements are represented by the foundations of its customs, norms, law, institutions and values or aims in life, as well as its religion (its ultimate concerns). These elements are characterized and upheld by deep emotion, commitment and loyalty (*eros*), and they structure and shape the ends, purposes, meanings, and values (the object of *eros*) that constitute and direct every culture's life. When reason is seen as merely scientific and technical, these elements in turn become irrational; that is, they are seen as emotive, arbitrary "preferences," as merely subjective, or possibly as only self-interested. In the laboratory and the academic life, such irrational elements are controlled by scientific commitment, by adherence to procedures, and so on. In society at large, they represent a continuing powerful, foundational presence and potential danger. In any case, they do not and will not go away —however they may be banished from the rationality of the self-interpretation of the culture. They need to be penetrated by reason (they are its creations) and unified among themselves, with scientific cognition, and in relation to the depths of reason; that is, in terms of the fundamental mythical and cultic structures of the society's life (for example, such symbols as democracy, freedom, a free society). Unless this unifying process in thought, social legislation, political life, and custom takes place, these elements will form themselves irrationally and heteronomously into a new and destructive unity, into a false or demonic substance, also unconditional, holy, mythical and cultic.

Tillich, therefore, would hardly be surprised that in our advanced technical society, the religious would return in a multitude of unexpected forms. In our isolated, precarious, and vulnerable life, fundamentalism and charismatic possession, religious cults, and a concern for the occult have manifested themselves anew as powerful responses to the threatening forces and the debilitating emptiness of an industrial and technological culture. Correspondingly, in the public sphere such nontechnical and nonscientific elements as participation in community, loyalty, and commitment to its myths and cults, ideologies of class, race, and especially nation, reappear in potent form as bearers of oppressive and dangerous heteronomy.

The realms of value and of the sacred, even if banished in principle from the academy, are never in fact banished. They return, given new force through the coherence, unity, and ultimacy provided by a unified ideology, to take over the culture and even the rational elements within it. Science, technology, and a rational industrial society, which once saw themselves as conquering and eradicating the religious, now become its servants. In so doing, they become instruments of the demonic.

The central theme at work in this analysis is the *interdependence* or *interpenetration* of the autonomous elements of culture with the religious elements. As unconditioned meanings and commitments make the creative autonomy of a culture possible, so heteronomous meanings and commitments can render any culture demonic. More specifically, they can hallow with an unconditioned value the unjust and oppressive economic and political structures of a culture's life, and they can unify the culture around an exclusivist and fanatical mythos. The religious substance of the culture, its forms of ultimate concern and of ultimate meaning, can render dangerous, as well as creative, culture's existence in history. Correspondingly, the specifically religious elements, forces or communities (churches) exhibit the same potential ambiguity. They can become trivial or heteronomous. In either case, they pose a danger to their own health and to that of culture.

As trivial, the churches merely follow the culture's mythos and concentrate on their own separated sacred realm, when they should be challenging the culture's injustice and its complacent and possibly heteronomous myths (as in the religious socialist protest against capitalism and as in Tillich's resistance to Nazism). As heteronomous, the churches can unite with the national myths to annihilate all autonomously creative cultural life (as in the Moral Majority). The culture needs desperately, therefore, on the one hand a political criticism of its injustice, as Tillich embodied in his early career. On the other hand, culture needs a rational and a religious critcism of its ultimate presuppositions if it is to be whole and healthy. The first (the rational critique) is to render these mythic elements "rational" and so to set these religious dimensions within creative relationships to the autonomous elements of the culture's life; and the second (the religious critique) is to criticize the demonic tendencies of that religious substance and to give it a firmer and more creative grounding in the depth of reason, in Being Itself or God.

Socialism should be religious as well as theoretical. Correspondingly, religion needs desperately and equally the rational and moral
critique of culture so that it is not esoteric, trivial, and irrelevant
nor heteronomous. Culture and church depend on each other and
equally need each other and the critique that each gives to the
other. In fact, their separation manifests the "fall" of each from its
true essence. Their unity manifests the fulfillment of each in theonomy, or, in eschatological terms, in the Kingdom.

PHILOSOPHY AND RELIGION

A more specialized issue within the general relation of culture
and religion is the relation of philosophy to religion and questions
of philosophical and theological method. Here, too, Tillich is negatively and positively mediating: negatively as disliked by philosophers for seeming, after a lot of rhetoric, to abandon philosophy
and to reduce it to a mere instrument of theology; negatively by
theologians for abandoning theology by subordinating it to philosophical questions, categories, and norms. Positively, I will argue
first that Tillich, partly because of the way he described his famous
method of correlation, is frequently misunderstood as giving philosophy only a preliminary, question-asking role in significant truth.
Second, when it is sorted out, his position is genuinely a mediating
one between philosophical and theological thinking (provided, of
course, that the latter is recognized at all). He recognizes the essential dependence of each upon the other and the role of each if either
is to complete itself—much as culture and religion need each other
to be what they essentially are.

Tillich always regarded himself fully as much a philosopher as a
theologian and always defended philosophy as an essential, legitimate, and exciting vocation. Probably he was more deeply shocked
and offended by any belittling of philosophy than of revelation or
theology (he understood the "why" of the latter!), whether by
empiricist and positivist philosophers ("nominalists," he called
them), or by religious enthusiasts. He saw himself as representing
the classical tradition in philosophy as one who regarded philosophy
as a first-order form of knowing, and not merely as the analyst of
the claims to know of other disciplines. The latter represented to
him, of course, the reduction of reason to technical reason and so
the immediate dissolution of the unity of cultural life. Philosophy,
then, was an aspect of cognitive reason, the ability of mind to grasp

the structures of given reality, to interpret them in terms of universals, and, thus, to help guide and unify noncognitive aspects of reason (the "shaping" of reality embodied in the practical activities of culture in economics, law, political life, education, literature, and the arts). Since these active, shaping aspects of cultural life also represent powers of "reason," they, too, represent principles and structures about which we can and should think. Philosophy, therefore, has the widest possible range; coextensive, so to say, with the extent of culture itself. It is cognitive of the structures of given finite reality as the unifying discipline of the cognitive sciences, analytical of the structures of cultural activity, and normative in expressing the obligations and ends inherent in these structures and activities. Unlike the British empirical tradition and Kant, Tillich believed that an ontology, a metaphysical "science" of given reality, was possible. A philosophy of art, law, society, and morals was possible and relevant because the structures of finite being (the objective *Logos*) could be known by philosophical reason (ontological reason or the subjective logos).

For Tillich, this philosophical understanding and analysis of the structure of being is not only possible but essential for the health of culture and religion. Without such an ontological analysis spanning the separate disciplines of inquiry and the separate aspects of culture, no unity of cultural discourse or of individual life is possible; no rational discussion or discrimination of over-arching and unifying ends or meanings is possible—and so, anxiety, irrationality, and heteronomy hover nearby. Without understanding the structures of being (of self, community, temporality, and history), no understanding of the existential anxieties, derangements, possibilities, and obligations of personal and communal life is possible.

We are subject, then, to unknown and arbitrary terrors and have no inward (for Tillich, autonomous) way of dealing with them. Finally, without such analysis, it is not possible to penetrate and render as coherent as possible the unconditional dimensions of culture: the depth of reason, the sacred and the holy, the realm of myth and cult—that vision of ultimate being, meaning, and value which provides the import or the religious substance that permeates, animates and directs all of culture's autonomous life. While in significant ways transcendent to the subject-object realm where cognitive and analytic reason is at home, this realm nevertheless represents for Tillich the depths of reason, in union with reason and so available in its own manner to reason. This penetration of reason into the realm of transcendence is crucial for him; otherwise, there can be no unity of autonomy with its own transcendent elements (there is heteronomy), and there can be no rational criticism of the religious dimensions of a culture's life. Such interpenetration is necessary for the culture and for its religious communities, for philosophy, and for theonomous religion.

In any case, Tillich had the utmost respect for philosophy. Its aim is to understand the *structures* of being as given in experience (*Systematic Theology*—ST—I, 20, 22, 230). Critical of tradition, of authority, of any heteronomous claims, it thrives on distance as well as on commitment and participation. It pursues its task of understanding, "whatever the consequences" to dearly-cherished views and represents, he once said, "the infinite courage to carry an interpretation out to the end in the face of all the evidence and in the face of all that one might desire *not* to be the case." It must consistently refuse to introduce alien and heteronomous authorities into its discussion. Representing autonomous creative reason, philosophy appeals only to its own norms: common experience and rational coherence (ST, I, 23). Tillich always believed (or believed he believed) that any argument about the structures of finite being (reason, human being, society, history and so on) was a philosophical and not a theological argument, one that could be adjudicated by purely empirical and/or rational warrants.

For Tillich, however, philosophy—and finite reason—is by no means omnicompetent. It is itself dependent, as is all of finite being, on something beyond itself, something which grounds its powers and gives meaning to their exercise, on what Tillich calls the "depth of reason" (ST, I, 79–80). Philosophy thinks from this depth on its basis. From it comes its apprehension of unity with its world, its courage, self-confidence, commitment, and hope. Without this participation in its unifying ground, reason shrinks to technical reason and becomes vulnerable to the return of this "depth" in its demonic forms. Culture lives from its religious substance and expresses it and cannot itself, therefore, produce it as one of its own artifacts. Philosophy thinks from its depth and cannot itself think to it. Without that depth, it becomes technical reason and cannot "think" at all.

This dependence on its depth for its own essential exercise or possibility represents, for Tillich, the inescapable finitude of reason, its confinement to the subject-object realm, to its given world of nature, history, and the self, to ordinary or common-level experience. It means that a "natural theology," a proving of "God" on the basis of thought about the world, history, or the self, represents, for Tillich, a "category-mistake," a confusion of what is the depth and ground of thought with what is within the subject-object realm of thought and so can be concluded by it. It is to mistake God for "a being," an object of thought, instead of the ground or depth of thought (ST I, 205). Here, despite his earlier disagreement with Kant about the general possibility of ontology, he is in agreement with him on the impossibility of proving God from ordinary experience.

Reason, furthermore, is finite and incapable of establishing its own ground; it is also in estrangement (ST, I, 81ff.). Its powers are not only transcended by its own depth but are separated from that depth. As a consequence, they are unable to unify and order themselves, to establish and heal themselves. Tillich is, in certain significant respects, a humanist. However, with regard to the capacity of human powers, including that of reason, to overcome their own deepest problems, he is adamant that this is not possible. Human capacities, like human finitude itself, can be rescued only from beyond themselves if they would fulfill or realize themselves. If some new theonomy appears out of the nemesis of autonomy and heteronomy, it is a manifestation of a new *kairos*, a new uncovering of the ground of being and meaning, the appearance of the Eternal Now in the midst of the moments of time (cf. *The Religious Situation*, Introduction), an historical turn that can only be called "revelation." To be sure, a *kairos* can be expected and anticipated. It appears as a challenge to and a demand on us, a demand for criticism of the present, for assessment of its needs, for creative thought and action into the new. But, such creative historical work is a response to a *kairos*, not the cause of its appearance. A *kairos* bringing in a new creative theonomy is the basis of a new cultural life, not the result or consequence of cultural life.

Tillich is very clear on the point that reason is fulfilled in revelation; that is to say, the "answers" to its own antinomies and contradictions are received there. In seeking to become and fulfill itself in the face of its destructive antinomies, reason seeks for its own ground, it "asks for revelation" (ST, I, 93–94, 105). In the reception of revelation, unity with that ground is provided. In cultural and

historical life in the appearance of a new theonomy, an historical
kairos, the possibility of ontological reason, is once again given to
us. Culture lives from its religious substance, from the manifestation (*kairos*) of the ground, power and meaning of being that
establishes that culture's life. Correspondingly, philosophy, as the
epitome of cultural reason, lives from its relation with its own depth
via that cultural *gestalt* or religious substance. Every great epoch
of philosophy expresses and so lives from the religious substance
of its culture insofar as it depends as a condition for its own possibility on the unity of thought and being, subject and object, of
reality and value, apprehended in that culture's creative life.

With this understanding of the relation of culture and the religious, Tillich's insistence that "religion provides the answers to
philosophy's questions" makes sense. It is not that Tillich thought
that, descriptively speaking, philosophers do not provide answers,
or should not provide them. He loved the pre-Socratics, Plato,
Plotinus and Spinoza, as well as Schelling, Schopenhauer and
Nietzsche. It is that fundamental answers a given philosophy may
offer represent theoretical expressions of the most fundamental presuppositions implicit in the religious substance of the philosopher's
culture. They function, therefore, as the basis rather than the conclusion of his or her thought. In this he would agree with Hegel,
Collingswood and Whitehead (to name a few), except that he
prefers to view the presupposed and given substance which metaphysics expresses as religious in character. These presuppositions
form the religious element in a given philosophy corresponding to
the religious substance of the culture, or, as he also put it, "the
mystical *apriori*" (ST, I, 9) at the base of every philosophy. The
philosopher is, consequently, a "hidden theologian" (ST, I, 25), not
as one dependent on the particular religious tradition (though that
may be), but as a participant in the culture's ultimate presuppositions, its ultimate concerns, and its establishing and healing answers
to those concerns (ST, I, 24–25, 230ff.). Without such participation,
Tillich believes, the philosopher could neither be nor think as a
philosopher. Thus does *Logos* (the power of thought, especially of
philosophical thought) have a "fate," or live from a *kairos* (cf.
The Protestant Era, "Philosophy and Fate"). It is dependent on and
relative to the historical culture in which it thrives.

For Tillich, then, both religion (that is, the community explicitly
centered about a given religious tradition or relevation) and philos-

ophy (representing the self-interpretation of a culture) are unable to complete themselves without the other. As in the relation of culture and religion, they are mutually dependent from start to finish. Without the help of philosophy, religious reflection is unable to proceed. It is unable to express reflectively the "existential estrangement" of human beings and unable to express reflectively and meaningfully—in terms of cultural self-understanding—the symbolic answers of the religious tradition. Religious traditions or communities separated from philosophy become esoteric, meaningless, and, in the end, heteronomous. Without religion and reflection on its symbols, philosophy cannot reach or uncover its own ground, or ponder reflectively its own deepest questions. It can merely express the inadequate and frequently demonic "answers" enshrined in its cultural heritage or ideology. It is continually subject to the destructive dialectic of scepticism and relativism on the one hand and of absolutism on the other.

Correlation is the way Tillich viewed this pattern of interdependence and cooperation, the combined and cooperative procedure to which both philosophy and religion are naturally prone. In correlation, each is implied and called for by the needs of the other—and is the way in which, therefore, each fulfills itself through its partnership with the other. Correlation is the methodological expression of fulfilled ontological reason, of theonomous reason, of thought and *eros*, rationality and faith—in short, of the union of reason with its own creative depth and ground, of "true philosophy." Tillich is not saying that philosophers are helplessly bewildered vacuities who go around only asking questions and that theologians pass out answers to impoverished cultural theorists as John D. Rockefeller passed out dimes to impoverished small boys, although some of his phrasings can sound that way. Systematic theology, whose method is that of "correlation," represents for Tillich the culmination and fulfillment of philosophy as well as the actualization of reflection on a religious tradition. As culture is completed when its religious substance expresses the central *Kairos* of *kairoi* (in theonomy), so the thought of culture is completed when it is grounded in and informed by "final revelation," when it transcends itself in becoming "theology." How, then, does this cooperative method proceed?

It begins with philosophy, the analysis of the ontological structure of finitude, an enterprise in which philosophy is at home and of which it clearly is capable (ST, I, 20, 22, 230). The reason for this philosophical beginning for reflection on religion follows from Tillich's most fundamental principles. The first of these is the distinction between religion and reflection on religion, between religion and theology. Religion consists negatively of existential anxieties, problems, crises, and positively of existentially-received "answers" or resolutions. It involves an experienced answer to an ultimate concern, but it does not necessarily involve a theoretical understanding of itself. However, to reflect on religion involves such theory, and this is theology. Now (the second basic principle) since ultimate concerns (religion) relate to our being and our nonbeing and so to the existential awareness of our being and our nonbeing (ST, I, 12–14), so reflection on religion requires reflection on the structure of our being and the crises (the shocks of nonbeing) that structure is heir to. We understand what is going on in "religious" ultimate concern about our being and our nonbeing by understanding the structure of our being, especially the meaning of that structure. The first task, therefore, is to uncover the structures of finite being: of reason, of finitude, of spirit, of history. This is the task of philosophy and it could, in principle, proceed indefinitely, taking up problem after problem in epistemology, in cosmology, ontology, or metaphysics. In principle, Tillich believed this to be possible as well as important for the cultural and for the religious community. But he did not carry it out, for he was by vocation a theologian, and, I suspect, this is where his real interests lay.

The theologian, says Tillich, is interested in the meaning of being (ST, I, 20, 22, 230): that is, in its ultimate concerns, its crises and dilemmas, its answers and its resolutions ("theology is soteriology" [ST, I, 24]). Thus, at this point we move from the philosophical task of analyzing the structure of finite being to the theological task of investigating the meaning latent in that same structure of finitude, a structure now philosophically discriminated. Our own structure, says Tillich, is that of finite freedom; the meaning of that structure ("finitude felt from the inside") is, he says, anxiety (ST, I, 191–92)—or, as he should have said in this connection, "wonder and anxiety." Thus in a "theological analysis of our finitude" we look at the affirmations and the dangers lurking in the self-world correlation (this is the central category), at the affirmations and anxieties implicit in the categories of time, space, causality and substance. We examine the antinomies and contradictions possible because of the polarities and at the crucial issues for our existence implied by the infinite-finite synthesis that is human being. By this philosophical/theological (that is to say, first structure, *then* meaning) analysis, we uncover the "questions" (dilemmas, crises, threats) involved in our being—the negative side of our ultimate concerns—to see reflectively what constitutes the desperate situation we experience existentially in being human. We then see what constitutes "salvation," what the received answers of religion mean. Philosophical/theological analysis uncovers reflectively the ultimate questions that our finitude and our existence pose. In turn, theology will reflectively express the answers received through participation in the revelation present within a given religious tradition. Theological analysis in union with philosophical analysis, therefore, asks the question.

"Answers" on the level of our actual existence are received existentially within a community of faith, by participation in its life and by participation in its symbols, its message. Such existential ("religious") answers give us courage, self-acceptance, self-criticism, self-affirmation, serenity, purpose, confidence, and love. They are summed up by faith and love and made possible by being "grasped by the ground of our being," which is most fundamentally what Tillich meant by participation, by faith, and by the experience of grace. This is the "ecstasy" within which dependent revelation is received in a particular religious tradition. It is communicated through the media of dependent revelation, especially Word, sacrament, and the "symbolic" character of the transformed lives (saints) in the community (ST, I, 116–17, 126–28). As the basic meaning of "question" is existential dilemma or impasse, so the basic meaning of "answer" is existential participation in the New Being received through the medium of tradition. However, we are at this point discussing reflection, theory (theology is a theoretical discipline), not actual existence. Thus, just as in our question phase we did not analyze our own personal situation (though preaching and counselling well might) but the "cultural self-interpretation of our epoch" (its philosophical understanding of itself [ST, I, 4]), so now we concentrate on the theoretical or reflective component (or bearer) of the answer, of the experience of grace; namely, the symbolic content of the religious tradition within which this participation occurs, its message, gospel, or teachings.

In the answering section of theology, therefore, the religious symbols constituting the "message" are set anew into theoretical form, into the form of philosophical or theological understanding. Theology is the theoretical task of interpreting the symbols of its tradition in the light of the questions of human existence to which these symbols "have been found" existentially to be an answer, or the answer. The "finding" or experiencing of participation and healing is presupposed and not established through the enterprise of theology (ST, I, 9, 23–24, 117, 129).

The symbol or category "revelation" is interpreted theologically as the answer to the dilemma of reason (which is the way it was experienced and received), as the appearance of the depth of reason. "God" is interpreted theologically as the answer to the questions or dilemmas of our finite freedom, as the ground and power of being. Jesus the Christ as the appearance of the New Being is the answer to the dilemmas of our estranged existence. Since the dilemmas are the negative meanings of our ontological structure, the answers to these dilemmas are understood in terms of that ontological structure. They are answers to its dilemmas, and so are meaningful to us. Thus are the religious symbols, experienced as effective on the existential level of religion, transposed on the theoretical level (theology) into the ontological categories relevant to our finitude.

There is, however, this substantial difference[1]: the answer comes

---

[1] There are other differences in linguistic style from purely philosophical discourse in the system as a whole. In the case of the analysis of existence (Vol. II, Part III, Section I), Tillich does not proceed "philosophically" since estrangement is not an aspect of essential structure and so philosophically uncoverable. Rather, as in the "answers" of the other parts, he proceeds with the help of a religious symbol (the Fall), and he recognizes that he is analyzing a "half-way myth" (ST, II, 29–31). Correspondingly, the answer to the estrangement of structure (the New Being and the Kingdom) are likewise initiated via the help of symbols expressive of a revelational correlation. His interpretation here is likewise an ontological interpretation of a "half-way myth," though he does not seem explicitly to have recognized this point. Thus the role of myth in Tillich's philosophical theology is considerable, as the role of myth in expressing the religious substance of culture had already indicated.

Myth, or "half-way myth," explicates both the central dilemmas of estrangement and the received answers to those ultimate dilemmas—in fact, the center of "religion" and thus of the Christian religion, its Kerygma or "message." Again we see how, despite the philosophical form of his theology, Tillich's thought is centered on revelation and on its decisive center in the appearance of the New Being. Certainly the central thrust of his interpretation of individual and social-historical existence is dependent on revelation as well as on the philosophical analysis of finitude. Only the permanent and unchanging relations to finitude, helpless in itself, from beyond itself. It comes from the depths of reason (and so a mystery to it [ST, I, 108–09]), from the infinite ground of self and world, from the prius of subject and object, from that which transcends the finite realm. These ontological categories are used symbolically (analogically) and not "properly," "literally" or "univocally" (ST, I, 155–56; II, 9–10), as in most contemporary philosophical theologies (for example, in Process theology). Tillich's theology is ontological through and through, based on the correlation he perceives between our ontological structure and our religious dilemmas and answers. However, he uses constructively these ontological categories derived by a philosophical/theological analysis of finitude to speak to God analogically (symbolically). He presupposes revelation and its ecstatic reception as the basis for that speech and for the symbols that are thus ontologically interpreted. It can be assumed that this form of ontological/ analogical/ecstatic speech (theology) is as relevant to the analysis of the mythical and cultic elements of culture (its religious substance) as to those elements of an explicitly religious community since myth and cult (however "distorted") express the depth of reason in all cultural life (ST, I, 80–81). In this sense, "theology" is a cultural, public discipline for Tillich, as well as one designed for a religious community. Culture and religion go together throughout historical life. In any case, let us note that as theological analysis joined with a predominantly philosophical analysis to uncover theoretically the questions of our finitude and our existence, so here a philosophical (ontological) analysis joins with a theological (a symbolic understanding of religious symbols) on the answering side.

One brief word on symbol. This crucial category has very wide use in Tillich's thought: linguistic, philosophical, especially religious, theological, and ethical. Since he dealt with it cryptically at best in those contexts, it seems unclear and even inconsistent to many commentators as well as nonsensical to those for whom there is nothing transcendent to talk about, nor (even if there were) any possibility of our talking intelligibly about it. Tillich assumes that there is something transcendent to talk about and that we can and do (and do so all the time). He uses, in the first instance, the word

---

of God to the world are, therefore, purely "symbolic-ontological" discourse; all else (and that is most of the system: estrangement, judgment, revelation, New Being, Christ, ecclesia, Spiritual Presence, Kingdom) is actually "mythical-symbolic-ontological."

"symbol" to refer to the medium or vehicle with which such speech, if responsible and intelligible, goes about its task. Symbol is ordinary language used in a self-transcending way to refer beyond the ordinary (ST, I, 123, 131).

Tillich's usage, however, is much wider than the linguistic/philosophical/theological. Symbol (or "medium") means at the most fundamental level the finite in its creative relation to its divine ground, as manifesting through itself, in its fulfilledness and "transparency," that ground, that is, as the medium or vehicle or hierophony of the divine (ST, I, 118ff., 123, 177, 133ff.). Through some aspect (excellence or power) of a particular finite creature, aspects or sides of the infinite ground can manifest themselves. Thus, mountains, the sea, sky, lightning, heroes, states, and ruler (king, father, mother) are symbols of the divine—as are or can be words and concepts if they are set in a religious/revelatory/ecstatic context. As the symbol participates in the ground in order to manifest that ground through itself, so do we in turn participate through the symbol in the divine ground. A statue of the Buddha may be merely an aesthetic object to me and I participate in and through it only "secularly." It can become a *symbol* of the Buddha Essence to another who participates religiously in or through it. Participation here means communion or union with the symbol and (more to the point) union through the symbol with the transcendent. It occurs in an aesthetic relationship (as opposed, say, to a mere seller or buyer) with regard to an ethical obligation or an ideal, in a personal relationship between persons, in a political relationship to a group (consider flags, capitols, presidents, leaders) and, most deeply, in a religious relationship. In each, let us note, the unconditioned ground is present through the symbol (as beauty, as good, as value, and so on). In each, our participation through it in turn changes, stabilizes, heals and recreates us. And, most important, the participation by the symbol itself is what enables the symbol to manifest the ground it participates in; that is, enables it to manifest power and grace outward to others and to establish communion between these other creatures and their divine ground. Here the symbol becomes hierophany or "sacrament," a visible sign of an invisible grace.

Granting this range of meanings for symbol, it is clear why Tillich says that a symbol is "true" in this religious usage when, and only when, it communicates the divine ground in which it participates

(ST, I, 105, 128). In this sense, too, humans can also become the most powerful of all symbols insofar as they participate in the divine ground, are therefore "transparent to it," and empowered to manifest it to others. The ultimate criterion for a symbol is given by this highest and most decisive instance of it. Such a decisive symbol is, therefore, the locus of "final" revelation, that creaturely medium through which the divine decisively manifests itself, its power and its meaning. This is, for Tillich, Jesus as the Christ: that symbol who, by pointing beyond itself to its ground, was totally transparent to it and so unsurpassably communicated it (ST, I, 132–33, 150–52). This final and decisive symbol, therefore, becomes the religious center, the ethical norm, as well as the theological criterion, for all else: for the divine itself, for authentic humanity, for church, for the religious substance of culture, for the process and goal of history (ST, I, 137). When Tillich speaks of symbol, he has all of the above in mind, especially the universal, relevant religious/ethical implications centering about the Christ figure. With this rich and varied set of references, it is not surprising that his rather brief allusions to symbols should seem to a later age, itself saturated with technical and specialized discussions about the uses and interrelations of words, incomplete and confusing.

FOUR ISSUES

In this concluding section, I will deal with four examples of the way Tillich's mode of thought spans subjects usually separated and unites disciplines of inquiry generally unrelated to one another.

1. To American students the strangest aspect of Tillich's thought —and possibly one reason why there has been no "school"—is his pervasive and central ontological analysis of religion. Ultimate concern has to do with our being and our nonbeing. As a consequence, reflection on religion (on ultimate concern) must be ontological; that is, first of all, reflection on the structures of our being and the forms of their estrangement, and, second, if the religious answers are to fit the problems they address, an interpretation of divine grace in relation to those structures, and their healing. This was the theoretical reason by which he legitimated his naturally philosophical or ontological mode of thinking about anything at all! Today, his analysis strikes many students as odd, almost eerie. To the two predominant backgrounds of current American Protestantism, evangelicalism and Ritschlian liberalism, religion is primarily moral.

Religion, for most of us, has to do with the state of our souls, not of our bodies, and it has to do essentially with our moral spiritual state. Even the issues of faith or belief are felt to be moral issues, and the clearly ontological question of eternal life seems dependent on the moral state of our souls. Tillich found this viewpoint judgmental, heteronomous, moralistic, limited, unreflective, "petit bourgeois." He could barely find words with which to describe it or those he took to be its theological sources, Calvin and Ritschl. Tillich did not wish to exclude the moral, but he set it within a larger ontological context as the only way in which it could be understood and its terrors could be borne. It was this modality of thought (or, possibly, of piety) that separated him more than anything else from his good friend, Reinhold Niebuhr (for whom the terrors of morality were to be borne via the divine *agape*).

In any case, Tillich's mode of ontological analysis resulted in an extraordinary widening of the scope of the religious, and of the relevance and meaning of religious and theological categories. If religion concerns the structures of our finitude as well as our thoughts, intentions and actions, many deep problems of being human and many forms of renewal suddenly become relevant religiously: the body, its decay, and its health; the organism and its temporality, its growing old and having to die; the person and his or her space; the self and its power to affirm itself, to "be"; the ineradicable contingency of our existence; the loss of community and consequent loneliness; the sense of the emptiness, and the terrible anxieties that accompany each of these sorts of issues.

They are experiences devastatingly characteristic of modern culture. Together, they constitute a large part of what Tillich meant by our epoch's "meaninglessness" (ST, I, 48–502). They are not directly "moral" problems, though their threatening and disintegrating power frequently forces us, Tillich reminds us, to become immoral. Clearly they are, at base, "religious" since they are unquestionably of ultimate concern, and they have been addressed by great and powerful forms of religion. A large part of Tillich's uncanny power to communicate to ordinary people in his sermons and lectures (I recall one lady saying, "I didn't understand a word of what he said, but he was certainly talking about me!") lay in his sensitivity to and reflection on the anxieties and sufferings inherent in our finitude, characteristic of the totality of our being. He could magisterially relate these sufferings to the promises and symbols of faith. It also accounts for the idiosyncratic character of Tillich's analysis of estrangement: it is precisely an analysis of the suffering experienced by the sinner, rather than (as in Niebuhr) an analysis of the injustice perpetrated on and experienced by the victim of the sinner (cf. especially ST, II, 59–79). For Tillich, estrangement is the separation from our divine ground. It entails, therefore, a progressive ontological as well as moral deterioration of the self and its world that is terrible to go through. Tillich set his penetrating eyes on this consequence of sin. This is ontological. It is also existential and religious *ontology*—and that was new and powerful. It described things our whole culture is undergoing. Finally, to provide as the basis of theological reflection an ontological analysis of the self, of, so to speak, its conditions of being at all, and to offer modes of interpreting the basic anxieties of its finitude and of its ways of losing itself, related Tillich's thought immediately to medicine and the entire range of the arts of healing, to depth psychology and therapy, to sociology, anthropology, and the history of religions. Had he lived longer, it surely would have related him to modes of religious healing and of meditation common now.

2. Another area of Tillich's thought is a mediating or bridge position; namely, what we now call ecumenical theology and especially ecclesiology, the understanding of the church. Tillich is unquestionably the "most Catholic" of Protestant theologians. One might even say that to "Biblical" Protestants, he is the "most Protestant" of Catholic theologians. This mediating stance is evident to most Protestant students (cf. the ontological character of his theology, his emphasis on the presence of the holy, on different modes of mediation of that presence, on the sacraments, and on liturgy, on tradition and tradition's interpretation of the message). Nevertheless, Tillich is frequently misunderstood by Catholic readers. They note that, like many of his Protestant contemporaries, he is wary of the demonic possibilities of the church (cf. Barth, Niebuhr, and so forth).[2] He was extremely critical of the Chalce-

---

[2] One must recall that in the generation of 1910–30 the church, both Catholic and Protestant, remained an impressive and potentially menacing social, political and spiritual power. It was effectively capable of sanctifying, blessing and furthering destructive social forces, as it did in World War I and in the Nazi period. This is less the case in 1980, though it briefly surfaced again in Tübingen. With the rise of the Moral Majority, it may well reappear powerfully again.

donian Christological formula and of Thomistic theology; he distinguished, though he never separated, revelation from the religious response of the community; he emphasized the Protestant principle and was very critical of the Roman Catholicism of his own day as "heteronomous." While our hypothetical present-day Catholic might in fact thoroughly agree with most of these negative assessments of the pre-Vatican II Roman Church, he or she tends to suspect that these arguments indicate an "anti-Catholic bias" whenever they emanate from a Protestant contemporary of that Catholic world.

Tillich criticized traditional Catholicism for its lack of the Protestant principle of self-criticism. It is important to note, however, that he is equally critical of Protestantism for its lack of Catholic substance (cf. the essays in *The Protestant Era*). No social community, for Tillich, can exist without a spiritual center, a "religious substance": an apprehension of and participation in the unconditioned power and meaning on which that culture's creative life is based, a meaning penetrating its cognitive, its artistic, its moral, its political and social institutions, and its vocations; a participation structured by the symbols and myths of the community enacted and reenacted in, and so experienced through, its important rites. Correspondingly, no religious community can continue to be without a spiritual substance (or presence), the continuation of "dependent revelation" through the media of that dependent revelation (in the Christian case, Word, sacrament, and "saints") through which each generation participates once again in the originating revelation (the New Being in Jesus as the Christ) on which the community was founded. This holy spiritual substance (dependent revelation received via the media) is the "Catholic substance" of the church. There can be no church without it. The weakness of Protestantism is that it has lost, or tends to lose, this substance, the presence of the holy. Its relation to the original event has become too verbal, too intellectualistic, too conscious. It became doctrinal and moral, possibly adequate to bourgeois classes, but in the end leaving the church empty of genuine content. While grace is personal, and Protestantism was right to insist on this point, grace overleaps the personal and the conscious. It relates also to the physical, the subconscious, the communal levels of our life else it hardens into heteronomous orthodox doctrine or softens into humanistic moralism. The return of the Catholic substance, qualified by a Protestant principle of self-criticism, is essential for the health of the church. No one else in the 1920s predicted so helpfully the promise of a new Catholicism, or what present Protestants see that they need from the Catholic Church.

Clearly, the fundamental model for this view of a theonomous society and of a theonomous church is the New Being as it is manifested in Jesus as the Christ (cf. ST, I, 132–156). Surprisingly, Tillich's sociology, his understanding of history and his ecclesiology turn out to be "Christomorphic" in their methodology. The New Being in Jesus as the Christ is characterized by unbroken unity with God, "transparency" to the divine. He was, as noted, the paradigmatic "symbol" communicating with unconditioned power the divine power and meaning present in him. But equally, and as the condition of that symbolic power, Jesus pointed beyond himself to the source of that power. He refused to arrogate the power to himself and, as a consequence, he sacrificed himself ("all that was Jesus about him," ST, I, 134–136) in order to be the Christ.

In this dialectic of presence and yet of self-criticism and self-sacrifice lies the root of the ecclesiology of Catholic substance and Protestant principle, and of Tillich's sociology of religious substance and of the rational/theological criticism of that substance; in fact, his entire scheme of theonomy, autonomy, and heteronomy. Thus both society and church "fall" when they fail to unite these two elements and so to embody this Christological model. Society becomes void of substance (the implications of an autonomous, technological culture) and so subject to heteronomy (making itself and its ideology absolute). Church, in turn, becomes void of spiritual substance (empty, doctrinaire, or humanistic) or heteronomous (pointing to itself as absolute). Furthermore, just as society and church alike represent "estranged existence in history" or the "Fall," so the historical careers of Protestantism and Catholicism, when they separate from each other, equally represent that more fundamental estrangement from the divine ground and from the New Being. Correspondingly, Protestantism and Catholicism in union with each other express essential aspects of the New Being. Together, each represents aspects of the continuation of the Incarnation or of the Spiritual Presence essential to renewed historical life. Ideally, Catholicism represents the symbol of the Incarnation of the New Being into historical existence as present to each generation, and Protestantism represents the symbol of the cross, the self-sacrifice of the true medium, as the necessary condition of that full spiritual presence in history. One could hardly find today a more mediating position between these two historic notions of the church.

3. Tillich, as he ruefully predicted, did not live long enough to attempt the mediation between Christianity (and Western culture) and the other religions of the world. Nevertheless, more than any other theologian of the century, he enunciated principles helpful in that new and radical task. During his later years, the sun was setting on the long day of the West's dominance, and much that Tillich said of other religions reflects (though not nearly as sharply as did the thoughts of most of his contemporaries) the lingering glow of that innate sense of the superiority of Western culture and religion characteristic of that now vanished epoch: its emphasis on (and pride in) individuality, autonomy, personality, history, science, democracy. However, unlike most of his neo-orthodox or philosophical contemporaries, Tillich had an uncany sense of what was to come in the near future: the reappearance of those older, non-Western traditions in grace and in power among us, and so the problem of the situation of Christianity and of Western culture among these other traditions.

More than any theologian of his time, he felt the presence of grace (of truth and of healing power) in other religions, and he began to express this awareness theologically. More than any philosopher of his time, he felt the relativity of the Western consciousness and of Western culture and Christianity as theoretical, moral and social entities. Thus, the problem of relativism was always an essential one for him. Unlike most of those who then and now have faced the same problem, he knew no easy answer. He refused to say, with the neo-orthodox, that the divine Word transcends culture, and so the gospel of Christ is nonrelative and universal ("message always appears in a relative situation"). He refused to say, with most philosophers, that, while religions are obviously "positive" and so culturally relative, Western science and Western philosophical modes of thinking are clearly universal ("logos always appears in a historical kairos"). Thus, while his final explicit attempts to resolve these new and radical issues were preliminary, as he recognized, he did enunciate several principles that seem potentially capable of mediating in this area, too.

Unlike many twentieth-century theologians who emphasized estrangement, revelation and the decisiveness of the event of Christ, Tillich also was deeply concerned with religion as a universal human phenomenon. As we have seen, his own theological and cultural analysis begins with religion on the human or "subjective" side as ultimate concern, on the "objective" side as response to the continual, powerful, threatening, and healing presence of the holy, of unconditioned power and meaning. Thus, he offers a sympathetic and universally applicable interpretation of religion, of its relation to human being and existence, of its relation to society and to history, and to the structures and depths of being. It is also true that his understanding of religion transcends the limits of either a moral, a kerygmatic or even a sacramental understanding of religion. He included the whole range of significant religious phenomena: rites, sacraments, rules and taboos, myths, doctrines, clergy and hierarchy, not to mention religion's ambiguous relations to community, state, law, academy, and history. Such a definition—or one, at least, like it in scope—is essential for any assessment of religions as historical and human phenomena, for any understanding at all of the relative validity and power of religions, and, in fact, for any sort of cultural interpretation whatsoever. Clearly, any philosophy or theology of religions will depend on some such understanding of the basic category, religion, itself.

Tillich's own understanding of the origin of religion is that it arises as (1) a response to the continuing presence of the creative divine ground in human life, and (2) as a response to the universal presence of the New Being (ST, II, 80, 86–87). Religions arise, for Tillich, not from neurosis, social maladjustment or "projection," but from awareness of, experience of, and response to the divine, "God" as creator, preserver, and redeemer. Such an interpretation can be the basis for a theological interpretation of other religions that acknowledges and celebrates the truth, power, and grace resident within them.

In the eyes of many historians and philosophers of religion concerned with mediation between diverse religions and diverse cultures, a definite Christological standpoint (and Tillich's theology is Christomorphic) immediately scuttles any such mediation and returns us to Christian absolutism and exclusivism. This is not the case with Tillich, and I question that initial assumption in general. First, a Christologically-centered theology can (as Barth's is) be universalist, or at least open, on the question of salvation. Tillich's surely is that (cf. ST, II, 147). Secondly, a high Christology is not the only expression of the absolutization of a particular tradition, although it also can be that. A thinker also can absolutize Western modes of thought, science, psychology, sociology, anthropology, and philosophy. For example, the move from a Christological theology to a metaphysically-centered theology merely represents, or may represent, a move from a Western religious parochialism (which Western intellectuals recognize) to a Western intellectual or philosophical parochialism (which the latter usually do not recognize). From the perspective of most post-Enlightenment academics, while Christianity is incurably historical and particular, Western science and thought are universally solid. From the perspective of another religion or culture, however, each of these two is equally Western, strange, attractive-repellent, infinitely dubious. For instance, to a Christological theology and to most modern philosophies, astrology, Karma, the "higher consciousness," "identity with the divine" are symbols or concepts that are simply false; to conservative Christian apologists, these represent religious error, if not idolatry; to most Western academics, they represent primitive myth or ideology, and while they are perhaps charming, interesting, and harmless, they are certainly untrue. The idea that universality is to be achieved theologically may be arrogance; the idea that it is achieved through Western philosophy or science is optical illusion. Or else it is as dogmatically assertive that "at last in the West we now know the way the world really is," as was any religious orthodoxy. And the religious effort to achieve universality by means of a common "perennial" or "esoteric" mystical center to all religions, and so to all legitimate cultures, can also be parochial, dependent on the insistence that one form of religion alone is legitimate and so represents a position exclusive of other nonmystical forms of religion.

Even in comparison with most present-day thinkers attempting to mediate theoretically between religions, Tillich almost alone saw the relativity of given forms of religion and of given forms of culture, even of a scientific, linguistic, technological, and pragmatic culture. For him, the Christian revelation is received in a relative situation and its message always interpreted in and through a particular historical and cultural situation. Every cultural philosophy expresses a *kairos*, a particular and relative form of originating theonomy.

Yet he also understood (from Augustine) the impossibility of an ultimate relativism. Existential ultimate concerns are too pressing to be fobbed off with an indifferent relativism of affirmation and of understanding. All thought of any sort, however practical and empirical, depends upon a presupposed stance and a presupposed structure of understanding. For Tillich, we all stand somewhere and must do so. To do so is relative to its time and place. His own attempt to mediate this dilemma of inevitable relativism and yet of an inescapable relation to the unconditioned is, therefore, profound, original, instructive, and possibly fruitful.

His solution is both religious (existential rather than theoretical) and revelational (based on the appearance of the divine and not on the transcendent and universal powers of a certain form of cultural rationality)—an unusual solution for the problem of the encounter of competing religions. It begins, as most of his thought does, Christomorphically. As he reiterated, without revelation reason is hopelessly finite and estranged, determined, parochial. Without the criticism given it by revelation (as well as by philosophy), religion tends to become demonic. In Jesus as the Christ, the bearer of the New Being, there has appeared one in continual unity with the universal divine ground and therefore (and the "therefore" is crucial) one who points beyond himself by negating himself, that is, "all that is finite (Jewish) about himself" (ST, I, 134–36). This principle of transcending the self by means of a *negation* of the finite and particular attributes or characteristics of the self is Tillich's principle for achieving transcendence of the limited in every realm: for transcending the Jewish, or the first century, situation; for transcending a closed ecclesiastical tradition and opening out to the world; for transcending "God" to the God beyond God; for transcending Western Christianity in the name of more universal forms of Christianity. It does not achieve the universal; nothing finite can do that. But it continually points to it and opens us out to it. It is, as he frequently noted, one application of his expanded principle of justification by faith. Even more, it is his central Christological principle.

In the question of the relation of Christianity to other religions, it is intriguing. In this wider context, to stand somewhere—which we cannot avoid—and really to stand somewhere authentically in relation to God, requires that we be willing to negate the particularity of the place where we stand and be open to "places." This is not to leave or to abandon that "standing place" for with any other place absolutism will reenter. A self-negating, and continually self-negating, particularism, if religious, if related to ultimacy (and not,

say, to universal metaphysical categories which are culturally relative) is, therefore, the only human path or way to universality. Or,
as Kierkegäard might say, it is the only way an existing individual
can be in real relation to infinity and eternity without comical self-
delusion. This is an interesting, if probably for most, too unmystical
or untheoretical a possibility.

4. The final area of important mediation is one where fruitful
further work on Tillich might be undertaken. This is the mediation
between religion and theology as "politically liberating enterprises,"
directed essentially at social and historical transformation on the
one hand, and religion and theology as resolving inward, personal,
existential problems and providing theoretical, even philosophical,
interpretations of culture, of life, and of destiny on the other. There
is little question that mediation between these two extremes is
currently revelant, as it was when Tillich began his career. Throughout his life, Tillich suffered under and struggled against the separation of these two interpretations of religion.

Tillich's personal life mediated these two emphases, even if his
later thought never brought them together to his own complete
satisfaction. The first fifteen years of his career within Germany
were almost entirely devoted to political and "liberationist" theology,
to the establishment of the community of "Religious Socialists" and
to the theoretical elaboration and defense of its principles. It was
largely because of his prominence in this radical political activity
(the group was religious but also Marxist-socialist), and because of
his strongly moral social convictions (he protested not so much the
Nazi attack on theology as their exclusion of Jews from German
universities), that Tillich was removed from his professorship and
forced to leave Germany. As he said once later in my hearing (having been told frequently by Barthian critics, that his theology of
culture and his method of correlation represented an "accommoda-
tion to culture"), "Barth had a more useful theology for making
war on the Nazis [quite an admission!]—but I left on an earlier
train than he did. He returned home to Switzerland while I was
expelled into a strange, terrifying new world—and [with a twinkle],
anyway, my interpretation of theology is right!"

In America, Tillich was hesitant to do "political theology." There
were several reasons for this. One was the presence of his deeply-
admired friend, Reinhold Niebuhr, on the same theological faculty.
When asked about political matters, Tillich would smile and say,

"When you have a living genius in these things right here, ask him!" Niebuhr would laugh, and Tillich would be silent. More privately, he said that his own thought, like that of so many European intellectuals, had been so saturated with Marxist perspectives that it was hard for him to "rethink it" and start again. That is, his religious socialist views tended (as his early works show) to see "bourgeois society" as the sole source responsible for most of Western culture's ills. "And then, you see, the leading bourgeois power unexpectedly has rescued me, given me a home, a place, security, work, freedom and respect. What is an anti-bourgeois Theoretiker, then, to say?" He said frequently that before he came, he had not appreciated sufficiently either the significance of the political dimension of society, and so the necessity of political democracy, nor had he understood, as he later came to, the political vulnerability of socialism. Thus he looked forward, he said once, to a new synthesis (possibly a new *kairos*) of socialist insight into economic tyranny and into the necessity of just distribution and the common good, with the democratic insight into political tyranny and the necessity of individual freedom and self-constitution. Meanwhile, his own interests and the concerns of his theological writing moved to the questions of reason and faith, philosophy and theology, existence in an industrial, technological culture, and "in-house" theological issues—represented by his writings in America and by the vast mediating achievements referred to already in this article. With the exception of the brief later work *Political Expectation*, he never really brought together (as he would have if he had lived to encounter the liberation theologies) his own experience of socialist radicalism and of democracy, nor the relation of the political theology of his early period with the existential/ontological theology of the *Systematic Theology*.

Like many theologians of the European 1920s, Tillich had a dim view of the prospects of European culture. The essentials of that view have been more than validated by our social experience since his death. As a consequence, the sense of decline of our cultural life has deepened. Unlike the liberals and many liberationists, Tillich was no progressivist. In that, he was surely right. On the other hand, as his various works on history (especially ST, III) show, Tillich represented by no means a pessimistic view of history as a whole; he regarded it as under the guidance of the divine providence and as renewed continuously by the presence of the New

Being (the Spirit). Confidence in the appearance of a new *Kairos* (even if it was not the one he had expected) formed a powerful and persistent note in his view of history.

No one who has absorbed Tillich's vision of the unconditioned and living divine power and meaning, permeating and renewing, as well as judging, all creaturely life and historical existence, could feel ultimate despair and discouragement about the future—even in the face of the nemesis of technological culture as Tillich pictured it, or of the sorry facts of our present. Again, Tillich did not live to mediate between the realism of his own cultural analysis and the hope latent in his theological vision of history and its divine ground. Of all the mediating tasks left for his children and grandchildren, perhaps this will turn out to be the most important.

LANGDON GILKEY

THE DIVINITY SCHOOL
UNIVERSITY OF CHICAGO
CHICAGO, ILLINOIS

2

Walter M. Horton
TILLICH'S ROLE IN CONTEMPORARY THEOLOGY

2

TILLICH'S ROLE IN
CONTEMPORARY THEOLOGY

CONTEMPORARY theology has followed roughly parallel lines of development in Continental Europe, in the British Isles, and in America. In all three areas a liberal theology based upon German idealistic philosophy was widely influential at the turn of the century and up to the time of the First World War. In all three areas the wars and social convulsions which have followed one another so swiftly since 1914 have broken down the idealistic identification between the Kingdom of God and modern Western culture, and begun a process of theological reorientation. The break with idealistic liberalism is most radical in Continental theology and least radical in American theology; but all along the line, in varying degrees, a characteristic shift in emphasis has taken place: from reason to revelation, from divine immanence to divine transcendence, from human dignity to human frailty, from Christ the example to Christ the Savior, from progress to crisis, from time to eternity.[1]

Paul Tillich is one of the principal architects of the new theological structure that has been erected on the ruins of idealistic liberalism. Both in Europe and in America (since national socialism made him an exile) he has stood close to the chief designers of our new theological patterns. As an associate of Karl Barth in the "dialectical theology" movement, and later as a critic of Barth, he left a mark upon Continental theology which years of absence have not

---

[1] For a more detailed description of the theological trend in America, England, and the Continent, see my *Realistic Theology* (New York and London: Harper & Brothers, 1934), *Contemporary English Theology* (New York and London: Harper & Brothers, 1936), and *Contemporary Continental Theology* (New York and London: Harper & Brothers, 1938).

obliterated. In America he has been the colleague and close friend of Reinhold Niebuhr, who has been chiefly instrumental in diverting American theology from idealistic to realistic lines. If Niebuhr excels him in polemical vigor and practical strategy, he excels Niebuhr in constructive power and theoretical comprehension. Since Tillich's influence upon Protestant thought in Europe and America has been so important, the quickest way to determine his rôle in contemporary theology will be to compare him with other Protestant thinkers in both areas. Yet he needs to be related to Catholic thought too, if his full significance is to be grasped. No Thomist and no Scholastic, he nevertheless shows a concern to relate theology to all knowledge and all culture which reminds one more of St. Thomas than of any contemporary Protestant thinker.

Our study of Tillich will therefore fall into three sections: (1) his place in Continental Protestant theology; (2) his place in American Protestant theology; (3) his relation to Catholic theology.

I. TILLICH'S PLACE IN CONTINENTAL PROTESTANT THEOLOGY

The term "neo-orthodox" is becoming canonical to designate the position of Karl Barth and other contemporary theologians who undertake to correct modern theology by going back to the Protestant Reformers. Since Tillich owes much to Luther, and since he undoubtedly considered himself an associate of Barth in the early days of the "dialectical theology,"[2] this would seem to entitle us to pin the label "neo-orthodox" on him, too. But before adopting a term that would in this case be very misleading, let us first consider whether it properly describes the whole "dialectical" group, and then consider the special place of Tillich within and beyond the "dialectical" group.

Otto Piper, in his book on *Recent Developments in German Protestantism* (1934), described the "theology of the younger generation," following World War I, as differing generally from prewar theology, but divided into two contrasting trends, "the conservative type" and "the progressive theology." Althaus and others represented the first trend; Barth, Tillich, and Piper himself the second. While the "progressives" shared with the "conservatives" a new concern for men's practical problems in a dangerous age, a new

---

[2] Cf. his article in *Kant-Studien*, XXVII (1922), where he speaks (p. 447) of his "spiritual comradeship" with Barth and Gogarten in a theology of "paradox" to which they and he had independently been led.

sense that the Bible and the traditional creeds contain "God's living word to the reader,"[3] a new central emphasis upon doctrine and a new responsibility to the Church, they did not share the conservatives' attitude toward society and the state as veritable instruments of divine Providence—an attitude which later played into the hands of national socialism.

It is far more appropriate to consider Tillich as a "progressive" than as an "orthodox" of any kind. His autobiographical introduction to *The Interpretation of History* points out that "precisely in the protest against the Protestant orthodoxy (even in its moderate form of the nineteenth century) I had won my way through to autonomy."[4] Barth once protested that Tillich's fear of an orthodox Inquisition in Protestantism was unnecessary; Tillich's comment was, "The 'Grand Inquisitor' is about to enter the Confessional Church, and strictly speaking, with a strong but tight-fitting armor of Barthian supranaturalism."[5] This fear of a new orthodoxy was one of the causes of his eventual break with Barth. If Barth is a "progressive," what shall we call Tillich! What demands explanation is why so liberal a mind ever was led to approve the "dialectical theology" movement in the first place, and to participate in its sharp attack on liberal Protestantism.

Tillich makes it very clear that he has never completely repudiated liberalism, either in the economic-political sense[6] or in the theological sense. For liberal theology's contribution to Biblical and historical criticism he remains grateful, while turning against the humanistic pride of certain idealistic doctrines. Even the idealistic element in liberalism, however, is not wholly rejected: "I am an idealist," he confesses, "if idealism means the assertion of the identity of thinking and being as the principle of truth."[7] But under the impact of the tragedy of the First World War, together with the criticisms of Kierkegaard, Marx, and Nietzsche, he came to reject decisively the idealists' claim "that their system of meaningful categories portrays reality as a whole."[8] Idealism supposes it possible to pass in an unbroken line from the spirituality of the self, the intelligibility of the world, the meaningfulness of culture, the general

[3] Piper, *op. cit.* (London: Student Christian Movement Press, 1934), p. 64.
[4] *The Interpretation of History*, p. 25.
[5] *Ibid.*, p. 26.
[6] *Ibid.*, p. 29.
[7] *Ibid.*, p. 60.
[8] *Ibid.*, p. 61.

development of religion, to the ultimate reality who is God Himself; but this philosophy of religion makes God relative to self and world, religion relative to culture, and revelation relative to general history of religion. A true philosophy of religion must protest against all such relativism, and seize upon *ultimate concern for Unconditioned Being* as the essential element in religion. When we approach the Unconditioned, our concepts necessarily become broken and para- doxical. To compare or liken the Unconditioned Being to any con- ditioned reality—even to make it first and greatest in a series of any sort—is to destroy the idea of the Unconditioned. "There is therefore no way from self to God"; but by the way of "systematic paradox" one may pass from God to self, from God to world without losing religion in culture or revelation in general history of religion.[9]

Some of Barth's most basic ideas appear unmistakably in the early essay of Tillich from which we have just quoted: Kierkegaard's "in- finite qualitative distinction" between temporal and eternal reality; "no way" to cross this gulf from the manward or earthward side, whether by "natural theology" or by some other form of *Nebenord- nung;* necessity of revelation from the divine side, inevitability of paradox when divine revelation is expressed in human thought and human language. Tillich has never repudiated these Barthian ele- ments in his thought; indeed, he has maintained them with a *logical rigor* that makes him unique among contemporary German theo- logians, as Otto Piper points out;[10] but from the first his theological method has differed from Barth's, and the divergence has gradually become a matter of open and conscious dissent. What is the essen- tial difference between them?

Tillich's most succinct criticism of Barth runs as follows: "a dia- lectic theology is one in which 'yes' and 'no' belong inseparably together. In the so-called 'dialectic' theology they are irreconcilably separated, and that is why this theology is not dialectic. Rather, it is paradoxical, and therein lies its strength; and it is supernatural, which constitutes its weakness."[11]

This compact statement in English harks back to a rather de- tailed German discussion between Tillich, Barth, and Gogarten, which ran through several numbers of *Theologische Blätter* in

[9] See *"Die Ueberwindung des Religionsbegriffs in der Religionsphilosophie,"* Kant-Studien, XXVII, 446–469.

[10] Piper, *op. cit.,* p. 136.

[11] "What is Wrong with the 'Dialectic' Theology?" *Journal of Religion,* XV (1935), 127–145.

1923–1924, nearly a dozen years earlier, when the dialectic theology was still young. Tillich begins by saying that he stands with Barth, with Kierkegaard and Pascal, with Luther and Augustine, John and Paul, against every "immediate, unparadoxical relation to the Unconditioned" which turns the unapproachable divine Majesty into a finite idol. But a fully dialectic conception of the relationship between God and nature, God and spirit, God and history, would preserve a constant balance between the No of divine judgment and the Yes of divine grace.

Barth and Gogarten fail to do this. They find nature so irrational that the order of creation can no longer be discerned in it, man's spirit so perverted that the image of God is lost, history so meaningless that it all bears the "minus sign" of alienation from God— and then in Jesus Christ, and in him alone, they find the unexpected, unprepared Yes which overcomes the otherwise universal No of judgment and rejection. Tillich, on the contrary, finds God revealed as well as concealed, present in grace as well as in judgment, throughout the length and breadth of nature, spirit, and history. He maintains that every negative judgment, such as Barth so sweepingly passes on the whole temporal order, presupposes and implies a positive judgment without whose light no judgment at all could be passed. Everything in nature, spirit, and history is capable of revealing God, if reverently referred to its Unconditioned Ground and Source, though everything becomes demonic if deified without qualification. "Faith is not affirmation of the absurd, but grows on the basis of the invisible process of revelation which secretly runs through history and has found its perfect expression in Christ."[12] In a rejoinder to Barth's answer to this, Tillich makes bold to add that he sides with Schleiermacher and Hegel against Barth in their attempt to overcome the "profane autonomy" of secular culture and find God's traces everywhere, though he joins with Barth in denouncing the pantheistic idolatry of their direct unparadoxical way of seeing God's presence in the finite.[13]

In his *Systematic Theology* Tillich approaches the definition of his relation to Barth from another angle. All theology, as he sees it, has two principal tasks: to state the eternal Christian message and to relate it to the existing cultural situation. Barth's "kerygmatic"

---

[12] "Kritisches und Positives Paradox," *Theologische Blätter*, II (1923), 263–269.
[13] *Ibid.*, p. 295.

theology performs the first of these tasks admirably. Without identifying the message with some frozen formula from the past, or with the very words of Scripture, Barth has been able to recover (for a generation that had lost it) the great recurrent refrain that runs through all Scripture and Christian teaching. He maintains his position with self-criticism and humor, and with great willingness to vary his phraseology. But he refuses, as though it were treason, the apologetic task of interpreting the message to the contemporary situation. "The message must be thrown at those in the situation—thrown like a stone."[14] Tillich is convinced, on the contrary, that it is the unavoidable duty of the theologian to relate the Christian message to the cultural situation of his day. Barth persists in dodging this duty, thus falling into a "supranaturalism" that "takes the Christian message to be a sum of revealed truths which have fallen into the human situation like strange bodies from a strange world."[15]

Tillich's method of correlation, the basis of his whole theology, is expressly designed to avoid this pitfall without falling back into idealistic liberalism. It recognizes that "man cannot receive answers to questions he never has asked," and that he "has asked . . . in his very existence . . . questions which Christianity answers"; so it begins each topic with a philosophic analysis of some aspect of man's actual existence, ending with a question to which the Christian revelation gives a symbolic and paradoxical but finally adequate answer: Reason and Revelation, Being and God, Existence and Christ, Life and the Spirit, History and the Kingdom of God.[16] On the first or apologetic side of his thought, he is indebted to Kierkegaard's existential philosophy, as on the second or kerygmatic side, he is indebted to Kierkegaard's doctrine of paradox; but by correlating the two sides, point by point, he gives his thought a rational comprehensiveness unknown to Kierkegaard and impossible for Barth. Incidentally, he proves that an existential thinker can have a system—in spite of the *Unscientific Postscript*—though not of the closed Hegelian type.

To make Tillich's place in contemporary Continental Protestantism stand out with due clarity, one more relationship needs to be

---

[14] *Systematic Theology*, I, 7.

[15] *Ibid.*, p. 64. In discussion I have heard Tillich blame the influence of this Barthian supernaturalism for destroying all hope of an alliance between Protestantism and the labor movement, which might possibly have prevented the rise of Nazism.

[16] *Ibid.*, pp. 65–67.

examined: his firm opposition to the "German Christian" compromise with national socialism. His personal friend Emanuel Hirsch became an ardent adherent of this movement, hailing the Nazi revolution as a "holy storm," a "power full of blessing," in which "the work of the Almighty Lord" was to be seen, and in whose *Weltanschauung* "Germans of Evangelical faith should find their sustaining natural historic dwelling place."[17] Karl Barth and his allies, standing on the platform of the Barmen Declaration, had a simple defense against such a Nazified Christianity as Hirsch's: they denied that the Christian God was to be found anywhere outside the Bible. Tillich was on Barth's side against Hirsch, but for much more complicated reasons. In fact, Hirsch's identification of God's present will with national socialism bore an embarrassing resemblance to Tillich's doctrine of *kairos*, which identified God's present will with social democracy. From his exile in America, Tillich wrote a long open letter to his German Christian friend, in which he carefully dissociated the authentic doctrine of *kairos* from Hirsch's twisted version of it.

At many points Hirsch was startlingly close to the favorite doctrines of Tillich and the religious socialists. He spoke of the crisis of "autonomous" reason, the conflict with "demonic" forces, the importance of the "boundary situation"; and if he did not use the Greek term *kairos*, he spoke of the "religious meaning of our historic moment" in language that Tillich himself might have used.[18] In spite of all these similarities, there was a deep difference between Hirsch's discernment of the hand of God in national socialism and Tillich's discernment of it in social democracy. It was not simply a matter of political judgment, as Tillich was careful to show, but involved the fundamental distinction between a *priestly, sacramental* attitude toward modern political movements, and a *prophetic, eschatological* attitude. The New Testament doctrine of *kairos*, to which the religious socialists gave a new application, is thoroughly prophetic and eschatological. It sees the "fullness of time" (*kairos*) in which Christ came as a time of fulfillment, a time of judgment, and a time of promise yet to be fulfilled. To find a special instance of *kairos* in the rise of the labor movement and the convergence of forces between religious socialism and secular social

[17] *Theologische Blätter*, XIII (1934), 313.
[18] *Ibid.*, p. 309.

democracy was not to make socialism coordinate with New Testament revelation, nor to suspend the Christian duty of prophetic criticism against the "demonic" elements in socialism. Hirsch, on the contrary, was giving his unqualified, "unbroken" support to national socialism, as though the year 1933 brought a new revelation comparable to the year 33; and he condemned everything connected with the Weimar Republic as though it were downright sinful. The "belief-ful realism" of the religious socialists never condemned the Age of Wilhelm or adored the Age of Social Democracy with any such priestly, sacramental, undiscriminating enthusiasm.[19]

Hirsch was surprised to find his friend taking sides with Barth against him, on theological grounds, and inclined to consider that this was only a screen for a basically political difference. Tillich did not deny his political opposition to Nazism, for which he was already suffering exile; but in a second open letter he insisted that he, Barth, and Hirsch occupied three clearly distinct positions on the greatest theological issue of the day—the relation between divine and human activity in history—an issue as important for us as the issue of Christ's divine and human natures was for the post-Nicene Fathers. Hirsch and Barth represent two untenable positions on this great issue: "'Chalcedonian' confusion of the divine with the human" (Hirsch, analogous to the Monophysites) and "'Chalcedonian' division between the two" (Barth, analogous to the Nestorians). What Tillich and the religious socialists intended with their doctrine of *kairos* was to relate the Kingdom of God to human politics more intimately than Barth's Godless universe permitted, while firmly refusing to consecrate any political order as though it were "unbrokenly" divine and immune to criticism. This second letter contains a solemn (and, as events proved, badly needed) warning about the danger of exempting any political régime—above all, a totalitarian régime—from prophetic criticism, whether by deifying it with Hirsch or by profaning it with Barth. Hirsch's doctrine of the "two kingdoms" limits the Church's sphere to the inner life of the individual, and gives over the political and social orders to the uncriticized authority of the State. "Barth also removes them from criticism, but he renders them profane at the same time, and places them under objective norms which consciously or unconsciously contain an element of prophetic criticism. Hirsch gives them explicitly re-

[19] *Ibid.*, pp. 311–314.

ligious consecration, and therewith waives all right to criticize the demons that possess them."[20]

We have followed Tillich through three stages of dialectic Yes and No in his relation to Barth. When we first catch sight of him, he is agreeing with Barth in a doctrine of God as the Unconditioned Being approachable only through paradox. Next we find him negating Barth's radical negation of all extra-Biblical sources of theology. Finally, we see him turning back a degree toward Barth, while still opposing his purely "kerygmatic" approach to theology, when he encounters Barth's diametric opposite in Emanuel Hirsch. These three stages should suffice to define Tillich's relation to contemporary Continental theology. If Barth is neo-orthodox, Tillich is not; if Hirsch represents the nemesis of liberalism (as unfortunately he does to some extent), he also helps to make clear why Tillich cannot be a liberal, but prefers to live on the "boundary" between liberalism and neo-orthodoxy.

II. TILLICH'S PLACE IN AMERICAN PROTESTANT THEOLOGY

Tillich appeared on the American scene during the great economic depression of 1929–1935, a time as decisive and creative for American Protestant thought as the years immediately after World War I had been for Continental Protestantism. Idealistic liberalism, which broke down in Europe after 1914, remained vigorous in America through the First World War and through the decade of prosperity that followed the war. Fundamentalist attacks during the years 1920–1925 failed to unseat the liberals from their place of leadership in the major denominations, and left liberal theology more self-confident after the attacks than before. Barth and Brunner were not unknown in America during those confident years, but they were regarded as victims of a postwar psychosis peculiar to decadent Europeans. After 1930, however, American liberals became conscious that their faith in human ability, their at-homeness in a smiling world, and their hope of progress toward a veritable Kingdom of God on earth were largely relative to a particular social order which showed alarming signs of breaking down and cracking up. In a mood of great humility, they became aware of their idealistic utopian illusions, and in search of a more durable basis for their faith they listened with new attentiveness to voices from Europe.

[20] See Tillich's short letter, "Um was es geht," in *Theologische Blätter*, XIV (1935), pp. 117–120, for the above quotations.

It was under the sponsorship of the Niebuhr brothers that Tillich became known to Americans. Richard Niebuhr's translation of *The Religious Situation,* with an interpretative introduction, was the initial step; presently Tillich appeared in person as a colleague and close associate of Reinhold Niebuhr at Union Theological Seminary. The Niebuhrs were then making their first big impact on American theology—prophets of doom were mounting in the theological market as stocks were falling in Wall Street—and Tillich was vaguely felt to be somehow connected with this impact. His earliest public lectures, delivered in a formidable German accent, created an impression which might be described as "respectful mystification." (It was hours later that I realized, after first listening to him, that the word "waykwoom," many times repeated, and the key to the whole lecture, was meant to represent the English word "vacuum.")

What actually penetrated and stuck in the American mind, in those early days, was just the two blessed words "belief-ful realism." What a mighty, subtle, closely concatenated, all-embracing system lay behind them we are only now beginning to realize. But realism of every sort was gaining the ascendancy in those difficult days: Steinbeck's literary realism, Niebuhr's political-economic realism, Whitehead's "provisional realism" in philosophy, and the "religious realism" of a whole group of writers who published a symposium in 1931. Tillich's term "belief-ful realism," derived from the realm of art,[21] fell into combination with all these other realisms, and helped the growth of a general trend toward objectivist rather than subjectivist thinking, toward God-centered rather than man-centered thinking—a movement wherein thinkers of many different types found themselves temporarily comrades in a broad united front. His book *The Religious Situation,* to which this term is the key, did much to make this trend and this movement more self-conscious. Thus at his first appearance in America, Tillich found himself adopted and praised by many who had hardly begun to understand him.

Broad united fronts seldom last very long. The realistic united front, into which Tillich was so speedily accepted, soon showed signs of internal dissension. As previously in the case of the dialectic theology, Tillich felt himself in conscience bound to define his differences as well as his agreements with other American "realists."

[21] *The Interpretation of History,* p. 16.

I believe that nothing brings out his position with greater clarity than a study of his relationship with the empirical theology and religious naturalism of Henry Nelson Wieman. Wieman's objectivistic, realistic, theocentric trend, developed in opposition to religious humanism and idealistic liberalism, is as decisively marked as the parallel trends in Barth or Tillich; but the radical empiricism of his approach—a heritage from James, Dewey, and D. C. Macintosh—makes him as difficult for European theologians to appreciate as Barth is for most Americans. Let us see how Tillich has reacted to this thoroughly American *enfant terrible;* if he passes the Wieman test it will be as good as taking out his theological naturalization papers!

Tillich had the advantage of a personal encounter with Wieman as early as 1935, when he and Wieman and Reinhold Niebuhr were lecturers at a ten-day seminar on religion at Fletcher Farm, Proctorsville, Vermont, chaired by Gregory Vlastos and conducted with friendly informality. A high point in the conference was a three-cornered discussion on the nature of God, in which all the lecturers took part. Wieman said "that Dr. Tillich was at the same time more monistic and less realistic than he . . . pluralistic at the human level and monistic at the transcendent level." Over against this, Wieman sought to maintain "an ultimate pluralism whereby God was in no way responsible for evil . . . with no statement as to the ultimate outcome of the struggle between it and good and as opposed to God, not merely an instrument of God for good"[22] Tillich in reply "commented upon Dr. Wieman's complete break with the Christian tradition and Greek philosophy, and characterized his position as in direct line with Zoroastrianism . . . the plurality of powers and the duality of good and evil. . . . God was a duality and at the same time ultimate, which was a contradiction in terms." Christian belief in God's omnipotence, added Tillich, was a necessary guarantee of men's "ultimate transcendent security" and God's "ultimate transcendent commandment." A God about whom men must decide "would not be God."[23]

It is probable that neither of the two understood the other very fully at this first meeting. Wieman promptly rejected Tillich's interpretation of him, insisting that one may adhere to the Christian and Greek traditions without accepting any particular kind of meta-

[22] *Informal Report of a Seminar on Religion,* p. 53.
[23] *Ibid.,* p. 55.

physics. A few years later, in *The Growth of Religion* (1938), Wieman grouped Barth, Brunner, Niebuhr, and Tillich together as "neo-supernaturalists." In his review of this book, Tillich rejected Wieman's interpretation of all four, while also objecting to the grouping. "What we all have in common," he says, "is simply the attempt to affirm and to explain the majesty of God in the sense of the prophets, apostles and reformers—a reality which we feel is challenged by the naturalistic as well as the fundamentalistic theology." This affirmation does not put God "outside" the natural world, as Wieman claims, even in the case of Barth. "The unconditioned character of the divine, emphasized more by Barth than by anyone else, destroys the 'side by side' of the Divine and the natural. With respect to myself, I only need point to practically all my writings and their fight against the 'side by side' theology even if it appears in the disguise of a 'super.' The Unconditioned is a qualification of the conditioned, of the world and the natural, by which the conditioned is affirmed and denied at the same time."[24] In other words, if even Barth is not a supernaturalist in the sense attributed to him by Wieman, still less is Tillich—who charges Barth with supernaturalism in another sense—to be described by this term. The Divine, as he sees it, does not inhabit a transcendent world *above nature;* it is found in the "ecstatic" character of *this* world, as its transcendent Depth and Ground. (Pupils of Wieman who have recently studied with Tillich have been so impressed with this feature of his teaching that they have described him as a religious naturalist.)

If these preliminary jousts between Wieman and Tillich have failed to define the difference between them clearly, there is nevertheless an important difference to be defined. For a more adequate statement of it, we must refer to the discussion of theological empiricism in Tillich's *Systematic Theology*. Against Barth, and in partial agreement with Schleiermacher, he gives an important place to experience in his theological method; but he thinks that Wieman and other recent adherents of the empirical method "made it a kind of fetish, hoping that it would 'work' in every cognitive approach to every subject"; whereas any adequate theological methodology should be "derived from a previous understanding of the subject of theology, the Christian message."[25]

[24] *Journal of Religion*, XX (1940), 69–72.
[25] *Systematic Theology*, I, 34.

Theological empiricism, says Tillich, is an ancient and honorable tradition in Christian thought, going back to St. Augustine by way of the early Franciscan theologians. Subordinated in Thomism, Scotism, and Protestant orthodoxy, "the principle of experience reappeared in full strength in Continental Pietism and Anglo-American Independentism, Methodism, and Evangelicalism . . . and found classical theological expression in Schleiermacher's theological method."[26] It is unfair to treat Schleiermacher's appeal to the "feeling of absolute dependence" as a purely subjective approach to theology; actually he meant something very similar to Tillich's "ultimate concern about the ground and meaning of our being"; but when he tried to derive all the contents of his system from the Christian "religious consciousness," he ignored the fact that Christianity centers in a historic event given *to* experience, not derived *from* it. "Experience is not the source from which the contents of systematic theology are taken, but the medium through which they are existentially received."[27]

American theological empiricism is distinguished from Schleiermacher's "by its alliance with philosophical empiricism and pragmatism." Its ruling concept is "mere experience" rather than specifically religious or Christian experience, so it tends to arrive at a philosophy of religion detached from historic Christian theology. The term "experience" in this school of thought has three distinguishable senses. (Wieman uses it in all three meanings.)

1. *Ontological.* "Reality is identical with experience," so that "nothing can appear in the theological system which transcends the whole experience." This results in a religious naturalism that excludes "a divine being in the traditional sense" from theology, replacing God with "special experiences or a special quality of the whole experience," such as Wieman's "uniting processes." Tillich thinks this type of empiricism does not actually derive its results from experience in general, but from a special religious experience enabling the theologian to select the divine aspects of experience. "In spite of its circular reasoning"—inevitable in all religious thought—"empirical theology of this type has made a definite contribution to systematic theology. It has shown that the religious objects are not objects among others but that they are expressions of a quality or dimension of our general experience," much as the "phenomeno-

[26] *Ibid.,* p. 41.
[27] *Ibid.,* p. 42.

logical theology" of Rudolf Otto has done in Continental Protestant thought.[28]

2. *Scientific.* Here "experience" implies objective experimental testing like that employed in the empirical sciences. Macintosh and Wieman have claimed that theology is an "empirical science" in this sense; Tillich finds the claim entirely groundless. Theology does not deal with objects that can be "discovered by detached observation" or "tested by scientific methods of verification," which always eliminate the personal equation. "The object of theology can be verified only by a participation in which the testing theologian risks himself in the ultimate sense of 'to be or not to be.'" Without such an existential participation Wieman's "creative process" and Bright-man's "cosmic person" are nonreligious concepts; with it, they are no longer "scientific" concepts.[29]

3. *Mystical.* "Experience by participation" is the meaning "se-cretly presupposed by the ontological as well as by the scientific concept of experience." Tillich has great respect for it, and expressly admits it to his theological method; but he denies that it can be a source of primary revelation by itself, as Schleiermacher implied, and as the American empiricists imply in a more radical sense. He disagrees with Barth's exclusion of mystical experience, whether Christian or non-Christian, from the proper sources of theology; but he describes it as a *receptive medium* for the appreciation and inter-pretative transformation of primary revelation rather than a *pro-ductive source* of revelation. Trust of experience as the primary source of religious truth is based on a doctrine of man which over-confidently asserts the unbroken unity of the human spirit with the divine Spirit. "Even the saint must listen to what the Spirit says to his spirit, because the saint is also a sinner."[30]

Tillich's place in American Protestant theology might be briefly summarized by saying that he stands "on the boundary" between Barth and Wieman on the issue of theological empiricism, as in Europe he stood between Barth and Hirsch on the issue of *kairos.* Since empiricism has been so strong in American theology, not only among idealistic liberals but also among their realistic critics, it seems as though any position to the right of consistent empiricism must be some form of Barthian neo-orthodoxy. Tillich proves that

[28] *Ibid.,* pp. 42–43.
[29] *Ibid.,* p. 44.
[30] *Ibid.,* pp. 45–46.

one may be a severe critic of uncontrolled empiricism without denying the importance of the empirical factor in theology. As a more or less close associate of Wieman in the empirical theology movement of the early thirties, I have been helped by Tillich toward a new theological orientation in which historic revelation counts far more, but the empirical approach is not therefore abandoned. Wieman himself now lays more stress on unique historic events as determinants of religious truth,[31] without ceasing to be an empiricist.

My principal reservation about Tillich's theological method—one in which I think Wieman would join—has to do with his absolute rejection of theology's claim to be called "scientific" in the empirical-science sense. Against the claim of theology *as a whole* to be scientific, I find his arguments very strong; but my contention has been, and still is, that a *part* or *phase* of theology should be scientific. As a particularly clear example, I would cite that part of theology where the doctrines of man, sin, and (personal) salvation overlap with the field of mental hygiene. There are "dependable factors" (Macintosh) on which man's personal good or ill observably depend. Pure and applied psychology are most important for theology at this point. This does not mean that psychological or other scientific concepts can ever replace theological concepts, which are inevitably the product of an "existential participation" going beyond the "detached" scientific attitude, as Tillich makes clear. But once framed, theological concepts can be clarified and verified, to an important degree, by detached observations of the scientific type. The theologian is a better theologian if he occasionally and temporarily turns scientist. Scientific research now going on into the actual results of pastoral counseling, with control groups to indicate what happens *without* such counseling, ought to yield valuable contributions to systematic as well as to practical theology. Tillich himself grants that practical theology, which is interdependent with systematic theology, contains "technical," "nontheological" material drawn from psychology, sociology, and

[31] Cf. my contribution to the Macintosh symposium on *Religious Realism* (New York: The Macmillan Company, 1931) with my contribution to the Baillie and Martin symposium on *Revelation*, ed. John Baillie and Hugh Martin (London: Faber and Faber, Ltd., 1937), and compare any of Wieman's earlier books with the chapter on Religion in *The Source of Human Good* (Chicago: The University of Chicago Press, 1946). But do not overlook the footnote in this chapter where Tillich's transcendence of experience is specifically rejected.

other scientific sources. This implies that science pertains to some parts of theology, and therefore indirectly to the whole.

III. TILLICH'S RELATION TO CATHOLIC THEOLOGY

While Tillich is definitely committed to the service of the Protestant movement, we should be overlooking a uniquely significant part of his rôle if we made no mention of his relationship to Catholic thought. Here, as in so many other respects, Tillich has always lived "on the boundary" between rival trends in Christendom, far out on a promontory, feeling the pull of the sea and the land, and fully content with neither. Against Roman Catholic "heteronomy" (authoritarianism) he felt in his early youth "a protest which was at once both protestant and autonomous"; but this opposition did not extend to Catholic doctrine or worship; and once in his life he seriously thought of becoming a Catholic. This was in 1933, when the Protestants had not yet reacted to the Nazi challenge as firmly as the Catholics, and the only two choices seemed to be "Christian or heathen Catholicism, the Roman Church or national heathenism in Protestant garb."[32] Since the German Protestant Church did not finally go heathen, he did not desert it; but he has fought the evils of Protestantism tirelessly, declaring that the end of the "Protestant era" is in sight unless they are conquered. His conception of ideal Christianity has always included the principle of Catholicism as well as the principle of Protestantism, that is, priestly-sacramental elements as well as prophetic-eschatological.

It will be enough to conclude this essay with a brief personal confrontation between Tillich and a contemporaneous Catholic, so as to place him in relation to Catholic thought. There is no Catholic thinker with whom he has had such persistent relations as he has had with Barthian neo-orthodoxy or American theological empiricism; but a German-American Jesuit, Gustave Weigel, of Woodstock College, has written a remarkably discerning review of *The Protestant Era* which may help us to see Tillich's theology from the Catholic angle.[33]

"There is something Thomistic about this brilliant thinker," says Father Weigel, "not in the sense that he subscribes to the more

[32] *The Interpretation of History,* pp. 24–25.
[33] "Contemporaneous Protestantism and Paul Tillich," *Theological Studies,* XI (June, 1950).

characteristic Thomistic theses—he rejects many of them violently —but in the sense that he is moved by the same feeling for unity and completeness in his vision of the real. . . . He has made luminous that strange thing, Protestantism, to which he is passionately attached." He has done so by reducing it to its essential principle, "explicitly a protest against idolatry in any form and implicitly a complete surrender to God as the basis of all reality."[34] Father Weigel finds that by thus reducing Protestantism to one far-reaching principle, and building his system organically around it, he has made it possible for a Catholic to "read his book and in spite of its non-Catholic emphases and positions find himself at home because of its method." Nor is the principle thus clarified wholly alien to Catholicism. "It is true to say that the Catholic Church lives on protest. However, the protest must be one that will make the Church more Christian and not dissolve her into amorphous impotence. . . . Is not Tillich's half-hearted recognition of the fact that Catholicism has better preserved the substance of Christianity than Protestantism a protest against unlimited protest?"[35]

Both the appreciation and the criticism of this Catholic reviewer point to important elements in Tillich's position, which he himself recognizes. To begin with the criticism, Tillich *whole*-heartedly insists that without Catholicism's maintenance of the "holiness of being," Protestantism's "holiness of what ought to be" would wither away; without the sacraments, the authority, the symbolism, the mysticism, and the rational sweep of Catholic Christianity (best represented for him in the Eastern Orthodox and Anglican churches), Protestantism would have no soil in which to thrive.[36] He does not really identify Protestantism with true "theonomous" Christianity; he presents it as a needed reaction to the demonic "heteronomy" into which Catholicism degenerates. (Catholicism, in turn, is a needed reaction against the "autonomy" of degenerate Protestantism.) As for the "feeling for unity and completeness" our Catholic observer appreciates in Tillich, this reflects his strong conviction that Protestantism should try to achieve a "formal clarity, consistency and philosophical strictness," and a correlation of revelation with reason, analogous to that of Catholic theology at its

[34] *Op. cit.*, pp. 185–187.
[35] *Ibid.*, pp. 199, 195.
[36] See his article in *The Protestant Digest*, III (1941), 23-31, on "The Permanent Significance of the Catholic Church for Protestantism."

best.[37] Both of these "Catholic" elements in Tillich's thought are of great significance for defining his rôle in contemporary theology. The first makes him a great potential leader in the formulation of a theology for the ecumenical movement. The second furnishes a promising basis for cultural reconstruction.

1. A THEOLOGY FOR THE ECUMENICAL MOVEMENT

At the Amsterdam Assembly of the World Council of Churches, the "deepest difference" between the member churches was defined as the difference between the more "catholic" churches stressing the extension of the Incarnation through unbroken apostolic succession, and the more "protestant" churches, which minimize the importance of institutional continuity, finding the marks of the true Church in the prophetic preaching of the Word or the ever renewed witness of the Spirit. In the defining of this difference, and the approach to a resolution of it through friendly conference of the opposing parties, Karl Barth played a leading and quite irenic rôle at Amsterdam; but the ecclesiology expounded in his Amsterdam paper, and in other recent writings, is so intransigently Protestant, so far toward the extreme left wing of Protestantism, that it makes any real reconciliation between the Catholic and Protestant principles seem inconceivable. Barth's services to the ecumenical movement have been very great; his theology has established a middle ground between orthodox and liberal Christians so that they can communicate. An extraordinary proportion of the ecumenical leaders in Europe are Barthians. But at the juncture now reached in the movement, when the Catholic-Protestant issue needs to be thought through to a constructive solution, Barth's theology offers no hope of such a solution.

With Tillich it is otherwise. Institutional Catholicism may inevitably clash with institutional Protestantism; but there is no inevitable clash, to his way of thinking, between the "sacramental" principle of Catholicism and the "prophetic" principle of Protestantism. Each becomes "demonic" without the other; both together are needed to constitute the principle of true "theonomous" Christianity. Should Tillich become active in the ecumenical movement, or should his disciples play some such leading rôle in it as Barth's disciples have played, a doctrine of the true Church might be

[37] *Ibid.*, pp. 30–31.

worked out that would be equally acceptable to Anglo-Catholics and Congregationalists—and perhaps eventually to Roman Catholics and Quakers! If Tillich had been at Amsterdam, he might have offered a more precise definition of "our deepest difference," in terms of "holiness of being" and "holiness of what ought to be," than the delegates present were able to formulate; and he might have shown how each of these essential forms of holiness presupposes and requires the other for its own completion. The task remains unaccomplished, but the call is clear for Tillich or his disciples to attempt it.

2. A THEOLOGY FOR CULTURAL RECONSTRUCTION

Modern culture as a whole is in a disintegrated state. The medieval synthesis has been disrupted, both as a unity of mind and as a unity of society. In the universities (now become multiversities) the fields of learning have become so autonomous that they are no longer mutually comprehensible, no longer parts of an intelligible whole. In Western society at large, economics and politics, art and science have become "lost provinces" united by no common cultural core, controlled by no general principles of faith or morals.

Educators and sociologists who address themselves constructively to this agonizing problem of cultural disruption are almost forcibly driven into the camp of the Catholic neo-Thomists. The Catholic Church has never abandoned her cultural concern, never permitted her frame of reference for the fields of learning and the departments of human living to be broken up. In our own day philosophers like Maritain and sociologists like Christopher Dawson have freshly related the Catholic frame of reference to the new knowledge and new problems of the age in such a way as to offer a really constructive "alternative to chaos." There is almost no other alternative that seems to offer any hope of escape. The cultural synthesis attempted by Schleiermacher, Hegel, Troeltsch, and other liberal Protestants has ended in cultural relativism; neo-orthodoxy, reacting against this relativism, has tended to abandon the cultural problem altogether—though Brunner has lately returned to it in his Gifford Lectures on *Christianity and Civilization*. In the absence of any adequate Protestant alternative to the neo-Thomist cultural synthesis, educators and social thinkers have been confronted with a painful dilemma: to go Catholic or stay in chaos! Robert Hutchins, at the University of Chicago, did not hesitate to surround himself with neo-Thomist advisers; but many of his faculty fled further into chaotic autonomy rather than risk involvement in Catholic authoritarianism. With all due appreciation of the services rendered by neo-Thomist thought in the modern cultural crisis, it must be said that it is nothing less than tragic to have neo-Thomism presented as the *only* alternative to chaos.

If there is one Protestant theologian capable of stepping into this breach, it is Paul Tillich. He has never abandoned his cultural concern, inherited from Troeltsch and liberal Protestantism. His teaching at Frankfurt was so much concerned with art, science, economics, politics, and general culture that hostile critics frequently charged him with deserting his job as a philosopher of religion. (I talked with one of these critics on a visit to Frankfurt, not long after Tillich had left.) One of his early writings, still untranslated, bears the striking title "On the Idea of a Theology of Culture." He has given much attention throughout his life to the proper ordering of the fields of learning. The "central proposition" of his philosophy of religion was, "Religion is the substance of culture, culture is the expression of religion."[38] One of the five main divisions of his essays collected in *The Protestant Era* is devoted to "Religion and Culture." Finally, in his *Systematic Theology*, he has presented a correlation of reason and revelation which resembles Thomism in the "unity and completeness" of the "vision of the real" it presents, as Father Weigel rightly notes, but which offers a real alternative to Thomism as a cultural framework because of its altered "existential" conception of the nature of reason and the nature of revelation. No modern man need fear that in fleeing to Tillich from the autonomous chaos of modern culture he will be capitulating to some new "heteronomy," some revamped medieval authoritarianism. Tillich regards the revolt of modern man as a justified and needed revolt, and he endeavors to preserve the proper independence of each field of learning, as well as the independence of each segment of society from undue coercive control. His ideal of a truly "theonomous" culture is one in which freedom and order are united. This ideal needs to be powerfully presented, if modern culture is not to flee from chaos into tyranny.

We have presented Tillich, in his own words, as a thinker standing always "on the boundary" between opposing views: between

[38] *The Protestant Era*, p. xvii.

Barth and Hirsch, between American empirical theology and European dialectical theology, between Protestantism and Catholicism. This portrait is true, but we might easily misconstrue it so as to get a false impression of Tillich's rôle in contemporary theology. We might conclude that he is a typical "mediating theologian." He himself invites us to this conclusion, for he consciously and gladly accepts the task of "mediating" as an essential part of his theological task, derived from his teacher Martin Kaehler.[39] But the constant temptation of the mediating theologian is to be a mere middleman, exchanging the thoughts of others, interpreting them sympathetically, building out of them a purely "eclectic" body of teaching with no firm central principle of its own. This is why the term "mediating theologian" has derogatory connotations.

In Tillich's case this temptation—to whose fearful strength I can testify from long experience—is firmly resisted. When he stands "on the boundary" between two opposing views, he listens sympathetically to both parties, and the conflict between them becomes a conflict in his own soul; but he does not solve the conflict simply by "steering a middle course" or by "extracting the least common denominator" or by any other mechanical expedient. He locates the major issue in each conflict, and thinks down to rock bottom, until he finds a basis on which a comprehensive solution can be erected, and into which bits of truth from each side can be fitted, but from which the errors and excesses of both are firmly excluded. Then he relates the solutions of various problems to one another in a comprehensive framework, so that they mutually support one another. It is a marvel that interests as diverse as his can be united in one mind without pulling it apart. He has known deep mental pain for the greater part of his life. Yet now that we begin to see the outlines of his system, it is evident that despite all inward stresses and tensions, it actually does have the tensile strength to hang together! The advent of such a system is something to celebrate. It does not happen every day.

Let us do with his system that which it invites us to do: test it by sharp criticism at every apparent point of weakness. It will yield on matters of detail, and improve itself under criticism. In its main lines it is now fixed, and only time will destroy it, as all things finite must expect to be destroyed in the end. Before it perishes, it

[39] *The Protestant Era*, p. xiii.

will have furnished a dwelling place for multitudes of homeless modern minds, and it will have contributed to the reform of the modern Church and the reintegration of modern culture.

WALTER MARSHALL HORTON

DEPARTMENT OF PHILOSOPHY OF CHRISTIANITY
THE GRADUATE SCHOOL OF THEOLOGY
OBERLIN COLLEGE
OBERLIN, OHIO

3

Theodore M. Greene
PAUL TILLICH AND OUR
SECULAR CULTURE

3

PAUL TILLICH AND OUR SECULAR CULTURE

PAUL TILLICH is, I am convinced, the most enlightening and therapeutic theologian of our time. He analyzes our conscious problems and our unconscious needs more profoundly, and he shows us
how these problems can be solved and these needs satisfied more
constructively, than any recent or contemporary thinker. His critique
of historical Christianity would, if taken seriously, provoke revolutionary changes in the Church and in present-day theology. No less
significant is his diagnosis of our secular culture and his affirmative
answer to the recurrent question: How can we, with complete integrity, reinterpret religion and, through such reinterpretation,
recapture the spiritual and cultural vitality which modern secularism has so largely lost?

Tillich's theological impact upon Protestantism has not been so
violent as that of Karl Barth. He has not spoken with the prophetic
eloquence of Reinhold Niebuhr. As a philosopher, which he is, he
has not exhibited the originality of Bergson or Whitehead, and he
will never enjoy the popularity of John Dewey. As a philosopher-
theologian, which he is preeminently, he lacks the persuasive lucid-
ity and sweet reasonableness of William Temple. Yet he speaks
to our age from a more illuminating historical perspective, with
greater catholicity of interest and deeper sympathetic understanding, more creatively and imaginatively, than any of these philosophers and theologians.

His writings include many earlier articles and monographs in
German and many more recent articles in various American journals. Two books, translated into English under the titles *The Religious Situation* and *The Interpretation of History,* are unhappily
out of print, but a volume of sermons, *The Shaking of the Foundations,* and a volume of essays, entitled *The Protestant Era,* as well

as the first volume of his two-volume magnum opus, *Systematic Theology,* are available.

I get from these writings the impression not of a completed composition, but of a careful charcoal sketch on a very large canvas. This sketch reveals Tillich's lifelong preoccupation with basic problems and indicates the direction in which he so persistently presses for their solution. It exhibits amazing compositional complexity and balance. It also records a wealth of penetrating insights into his vast and varied subject matter, that is, the whole of nature, man and God—insights which justify the assurance that the sketch could be worked into a finished composition. Yet, to push my pictorial metaphor one step further, one feels that part of Tillich's provocative power derives from the fact that his thinking is still incomplete, still in process. In this respect it is reminiscent of Leonardo's unfinished "Adoration of the Magi" or of one of Cézanne's unfinished still lifes. His careful articulation of basic forms and structures, with just enough detailed elaboration to guide further inquiry and application, frees and stimulates the imagination of the individual reader to fill in his own details and work out his own practical applications. Tillich himself would welcome this response. It is not his desire to impose upon anyone a stifling monolithic system demanding total acceptance. It is rather his hope that his analysis may provide the honest and independent thinker with a basic framework within which he can do his own creative and responsible thinking.

It is hard for the layman to comprehend Tillich's thought in all its sweep and power. His writing is difficult for several reasons. The reader is initially bewildered by the number and variety of problems, secular and religious, which are dealt with. Unless he is unusually well read, he is also baffled by the wealth of historical, philosophical, and theological learning which is presupposed in Tillich's epigrammatic allusions to the cultures of other centuries, to the major philosophical systems of the West, and to countless theological controversies and doctrines through the ages. Tillich's generous use of technical terms, some of them original, is a further initial hazard, though finally a great aid. His thought is difficult primarily, however, because of the profundity of his insights and the revolutionary power of his diagnoses and prescriptions.

The revolutionary nature of his thinking expresses itself at times in statements that are paradoxical and shocking. One is brought up sharp when one hears a Christian theologian declare that he does

not believe "that God exists," or that "the first word . . . spoken by
religion to the people of our time must be a word spoken against
religion."[1] The assertion that "nobody can understand the character of the present world revolution who has not been prepared
for it by the Marxian analysis of bourgeois society"[2] sounds dangerously communistic at a time when all acquaintance with, or interest in, Russian ideology is politically suspect. Such statements as
these, which occur in Tillich's writings with stimulating frequency,
are baffling and disconcerting until one understands them in the
context of a philosophy which is fundamentally liberal and anti-
totalitarian, profoundly religious rather than secular, and basically
Christian. In long-range terms Tillich's thought is, in intention and
achievement, conservative of the best in our Hebraic-Christian,
Greco-Roman, democratic-scientific tradition. Its final effect is
affirmative, not negative, constructive rather than iconoclastic.

In short, Tillich notably exemplifies his own basic methodological
principle, which he calls the "Protestant principle," both in its affirmative and its negative aspects, its Yea as well as its Nay. He declares
his opposition to all absolutizing of the relative, that is, to all idolatry, and also to all relativizing of the Absolute, that is, to all forms
of relativistic nihilism. But, simultaneously, he gives his unswerv-
ing support to all genuine human creativity and discovery—in art
and science, theology and religious ritual, political organization
and social action. He rebukes the churches and the theologians for
their perennial opposition to secular effort and their repeated failure
to incorporate valid secular insights into their thinking. He wel-
comes all the positive achievements of modern science (including depth psychology), modern art (even in its most tortured experiments), and modern philosophy (even when it is explicitly
unreligious or anti-Christian). Yet he insists that a culture which
is merely secular is a culture which has lost, or is in process of
losing, its ultimate anchorage and orientation, and is therefore
doomed to meaninglessness and futility. Its only hope lies, he is
convinced, in a radical reorientation to God—not to a God who is
"one among other existent beings," and whose existence is merely
"problematical," but to the God who is encountered whenever man
feels "ultimate concern," and who is most adequately conceived

[1] *The Protestant Era*, p. 185.
[2] *Ibid.*, p. 260.

of as the "Ground and Abyss" of all reality, all meaning, all power and vitality.

This, in very general and preliminary terms, is Tillich's larger perspective and thesis. The other essays in this volume will explore in some detail various facets of his synoptic system. I shall address myself in this essay primarily to the import of his thinking for our secular age and its many urgent problems.

II

What are the chief anxieties and perplexities of modern man? How do man's abiding needs manifest themselves in the contemporary scene? One of Tillich's chief contributions is his historically oriented answer to these questions.[3]

The early and high Middle Ages were "theonomous" periods, theonomy being defined as "a culture in which the ultimate meaning of existence shines through all finite forms of thought and action; the culture is transparent, and its creations are vessels of a spiritual content."[4] The later Middle Ages, in contrast, were "heteronomous," where heteronomy is defined as "the attempt of religion [or any other institutionalized power] to dominate autonomous cultural creativity from the outside."[5] The Renaissance revolted against this ecclesiastical heteronomy and, at its triumphant best, exemplified man's responsible self-reliance and creativity, his faith in reason's ability to discover objective truth, beauty, and goodness, and to relate himself meaningfully to a meaningful reality. Gradually, however, man lost his faith and increasingly limited reason to the scientific study of nature and to its exploitation of nature in modern technology. In thus cutting its ties with "its ultimate ground and aim," technological civilization gradually became "exhausted and spiritually empty." What were once vital communities became groups of lonely competitive individuals, of "hollow men" (to use Eliot's famous phrase), whose lives had largely lost meaning for themselves and for others. This period of "technical" reason is the period of ruthless and exploitative bourgeois capitalism, of irresponsible individualism and proletarian misery. The intolerable slavery to

[3] See particularly his essay in *The Christian Answer*, ed. H. P. Van Dusen (Scribner's, 1945); see also *The Protestant Era*, pp. xvi ff.

[4] *The Protestant Era*, p. xvi.

[5] *Ibid.*

which the proletarian masses were subjected, particularly in Russia and on the European continent, led finally to their revolt and to the totalitarian answer to their longing for economic security and a cohesive community. This answer, however, has proved to be a new heteronomy, a twentieth century secular domination of man's autonomy by a tyrannical absolutistic state, resulting not in a free community but in a "compelled" society.

Western culture has thus, in Tillich's analysis, encountered three different "faces" of the Leviathan, his symbol for the recurrent institutionalized threat to human freedom—the ecclesiastical face in the late Middle Ages, its technological face in more recent centuries, when the machine, created by man to serve him, threatens to become a devouring monster, and its contemporary political face in the totalitarian state, Fascist, Nazi, and Communist. Reason, in turn, has functioned in these successive eras, first "theonomously," in humble recognition of its finitude, then "autonomously," in self-complacent self-reliance, then "technically," with great exploitative skill but in spiritual bankruptcy, and, finally, as "planning" reason, directed to the regimentation and indocrination of the masses, and with equal disregard for reverent religious dedication and for responsible human initiative.

This historical evolution has, of course, followed a different pattern and has proceeded at a different tempo in England, in the several European nations, in Russia, and in the United States. Russia plunged almost overnight from a feudalistic into a totalitarian culture, overleaping the intervening stages of autonomous culture and belatedly developing its technology under the aegis of the communistic state. Western Europe and England witnessed the flowering Renaissance autonomy and the slow development of technology in a laissez-faire economy and an evolving democratic state. Italy and Germany have lived through their respective violent and short-lived nationalistic totalitarianisms. England has taken the halfway socialistic step within a healthy democratic framework. We in this country have taken a small step in the direction of socialism in our "New Deal" and in its contemporary echo, the "Fair Deal." Our proletarian problem, though grave in most industrial and in some rural areas, has never been as acute as it has been in England, on the European continent, and particularly in Russia.

The entire West, including Russia, however, has fallen prey to what Walter Lippmann called the "acids of modernity," and to what Eliot has so vividly described in *The Wasteland* and the *Four Quartets.* "It is," says Tillich, "not an exaggeration to say that today man experiences his present situation in terms of disruption, conflict, self-destruction, meaninglessness and despair in all realms of life. This experience is expressed in the arts and in literature, conceptualized in existential philosophy, actualized in political cleavages of all kinds, and analyzed in the psychology of the unconscious."[6] This is the actual cultural situation to which theology must address itself if it is to speak to modern man intelligibly and helpfully. Our cultural predicament would be hopelessly tragic were it not for the possibility that our spiritual impoverishment may become for us what St. John of the Cross and other Christian mystics have called "the dark night of the soul"—the stage of despair and penitence in which human arrogance is at least temporarily beaten down, and in which man once again acknowledges his finitude and turns for help to the Unconditioned which alone can satisfy and sustain him.

The man of today . . . is aware of the confusion of his inner life, the cleavage in his behavior, the demonic forces in his psychic and social existence. And he senses that not only his being but also his knowing is thrown into confusion, that he lacks ultimate truth, and that he faces, especially in the social life of our day, a conscious, almost demonic distortion of truth. In this situation in which most of the traditional values and forms of life are disintegrating, he often is driven to the abyss of complete meaninglessness, which is full of both horror and fascination.[7]

But, Tillich continues, this

vacuum of disintegration can become a vacuum out of which creation is possible, a "sacred void," so to speak, which brings a quality of waiting, of "not yet," of a being broken from above, into all our cultural creativity. . . . This is the way—perhaps the only way—in which our time can reach a theonomous union between religion and culture.[8]

This, then, is Tillich's analysis of the challenge of our times. Our "loss of an ultimate meaning of life" results finally in the loss both of personality and of community. Our loss of personality expresses itself in an "oscillation between a cynical and a fanatical surrender to powers the nature of which nobody can fully grasp or control,

---

[6] *Systematic Theology,* I, 49.
[7] *The Protestant Era,* p. 202.
[8] *Ibid.,* p. 60.

and the end of which nobody can foresee."[9] The cynic despairs of objective values and, no less, of reason's ability to discover them even if they were real and awaited discovery. He therefore resigns himself, in the spirit of modern positivism, to the ultimate irrationality of all human belief and effort, purpose and resolve. The fanatic, no less skeptical, and with no more justification, is driven by his loneliness and emptiness to try to forget his despair in a passionate loyalty to, and a frenzied participation in, *any* cause, movement, or experience capable of producing in his tortured soul a fleeting intoxication. Both of these escapist devices result in the disintegration of personality.

This loss of personality is inevitably accompanied by the loss of community:

> Only personalities can have community. Depersonalized beings have social interrelations. They are essentially lonely, and therefore they cannot bear to be alone because this would make them conscious of their loneliness, and, with it, of the loss of the meaning of life. The striking "lack of privacy" [in our contemporary culture] is not an expression of community but of the lack of community. And there is no community because there is nothing to have in common. . . . Cultural remnants of earlier periods are used to cover up our cultural nakedness.[10]

What will suffice to cure us of this mortal illness? Not the revival of an ancient ecclesiastical heteronomy, Catholic or Protestant, nor any new secular political heteronomy, Communist or Fascist—no regimenting tyranny forcing salvation upon us from without! Our only hope is the creation of a new and authentic theonomy, a spiritual reconstruction, in which secularism and religion *both* purge themselves of arrogance and mutual disdain, and conjointly undertake their common task of revitalizing *in contemporary terms* man's innate capacity for responsible and creative initiative and his inborn proclivity, now largely atrophied, to reverence the God who transcends all finitude and complements his human finitude.

> A new theonomy is not the negation of autonomy, nor is it the attempt to suppress it and its freedom of creativity. . . . Heteronomy imposes an alien law, religious or secular, on man's mind. . . . It destroys the honesty of truth and the dignity of the moral personality. It undermines creative freedom and the humanity of man. Its symbol is the "terror" exercised by absolute churches or absolute states. . . . Theonomy does not stand against

[9] *Ibid.*, p. 263.
[10] *Ibid.*, p. 264.

autonomy as heteronomy does. Theonomy is the answer to the question implied in autonomy, the question concerning a religious substance and an ultimate meaning of life and culture.[11]

Only the very complacent and optimistic secularist today is likely to dispute Tillich's diagnosis of our contemporary predicament, and only the very complacent churchman will care to defend the Church against the charges of dogmatism and self-righteousness. The questions which will most urgently present themselves to all thoughtful liberals, with or without churchly affiliation, are these: Has Tillich been able to reinterpret God and religious belief, man and human reason, reality, finite and ultimate, in such a way as to make the concept of a new theonomy meaningful and plausible? Can faith and reason be so reinterpreted as to make honest and informed religious dedication possible? Can a belief in God as the Source and Ground of all our being be reconciled with a belief in human freedom, initiative and responsibility? Can the central claims of Christianity be made credible in the light of modern science and modern philosophical reflection? Can the Church be revitalized and thus enabled to revitalize our culture? To answer these questions we must examine, however cursorily, Tillich's account of God and man's knowledge of Him, of Christianity and the Church.

Before attempting this summary, however, we must make clear Tillich's methodological approach to these problems, and particularly his account of "participation" and "detachment" as complementary attitudes, *both* of which are essential for genuine religious comprehension.

III

The contemporary dispute over religion is to a considerable extent a dispute over the presuppositions and method of "objective" inquiry leading to valid conclusions. Both parties to the dispute agree that genuine knowledge is, in some sense, "objective" and rational. No one denies that the charge, repeatedly voiced by John Dewey and other naturalists, that theistic belief is "private" and "irrational" would, if correct, invalidate the theist's claim to real knowledge of the Deity. The crucial questions are, therefore: What are the criteria of "objective" knowledge? and How can "privacy" be transcended and "irrationality" be avoided?

Modern positivism answers these questions by an appeal to sci-

[11] *Ibid.*, p. 46.

ence and scientific method. Scientific knowledge is "objective," and the scientific method of inquiry is valid because the scientist's approach to the world of nature is impersonal and free from all emotional involvement. His attitude throughout is that of the impartial "spectator," not that of a participating "agent" with a personal stake in the outcome of the inquiry. His findings are therefore public and verifiable by others, not private and unsharable; they are unemotional and rational, not colored by emotional concern.

Tillich recognizes the value of such scientific detachment. He insists, however, that problems which concern us as human beings cannot be understood or solved, or even discussed intelligently, in this impersonal and detached way. Before undertaking an analysis of the contemporary historical scene, for example, he pauses to examine the nature and presuppositions of fruitful analysis:

> An analysis seems to be a matter of scientific detachment, of disinterested spectatorship. . . . But in such an analysis [that is, of the "storms of our times"] . . . still another element is contained, an element of personal involvement—in spite of scientific detachment—an element of valuation and decision, or, as it is called today, an "existential" element. Something that concerns our whole existence, our economic and political, cultural and religious existence, cannot be discussed as if we were unconcerned spectators.[12]

His first point, then, is that "involvement" is inevitable whenever issues of human concern are being investigated. His second point is that such involvement, far from making the inquiry invalid and its results subjective, is a necessary condition of genuine objectivity in these areas. He is as much committed to the need for objectivity as are the most militant positivists; he is as violently opposed to subjectivism and irrationalism as they are. His purpose is rather to discover the nature and preconditions of valid objective insight in all areas of human concern and particularly when man's concern is "ultimate," that is, religious.

> There are objects for which the so-called "objective" approach is the least objective of all, because it is based on a misunderstanding of the nature of its object. This is especially true of religion. Unconcerned detachment in matters of religion (if it is more than a methodological self-restriction) implies an a priori rejection of the religious demand to be ultimately concerned. It denies the object which it is supposed to approach "objectively."[13]

[12] *Ibid.*, p. 238.   [13] *Ibid.*, p. xi.

No epistemology, then, is adequate unless it is appropriately geared to its proper object. "Technical" realism has a restricted validity in being adequate to the "controllable" character of natural phenomena. "Mystical" realism provides us, as we shall see, with a precious and irreplacable encounter with Divinity, but it leaves us blind to God's self-revelation in history. "Historical" realism enables us to comprehend the historical scene, yet only superficially because its perspective is so exclusively anthropocentric. Only what Tillich calls a "belief-ful or self-transcending realism" is capable of revealing to us the pattern *and* the import of nature and history in the ultimate perspective of man's ultimate concern.

Such belief-ful realism is not, in Tillich's view, the product of involvement alone, in opposition to detachment. It is rather the result of participation *and* detachment in fruitful combination.

The issue is brought to its sharpest focus in the contrast between "kerygmatic theology," that is, the theology which is "confessional" in claiming to expound the Christian message of the eternal *logos* made flesh in "Jesus as the Christ," and a philosophy obedient to "nothing in heaven and earth" except the "universal *logos* of being as it gives itself to the philosopher in experience." Tillich sees no ultimate conflict even here, if what the kerygmatic theologian proclaims is indeed true:

The Christian claim that the *logos* who became concrete in Jesus as the Christ is at the same time the universal *logos* includes the claim that wherever the *logos* is at work it agrees with the Christian message. No philosophy which is obedient to the universal *logos* can contradict the concrete *logos*, the Logos "who became flesh."[14]

Where does this leave us? Not in a state of hopeless and irreconcilable conflict between the complete detachment of philosophy and science, on the one hand, and the complete involvement of theology, on the other hand, but rather in what Tillich regards as a healthy and mature state of tension, both in philosophy, in so far as it is vital, and in theology, in so far as it is reflective. *Both* detachment and involvement are necessary for significant insight into those dimensions of reality which are of major human concern. Genuine objectivity in these realms of experience can be achieved only by a dialectical swing back and forth between active belief-ful participation and dispassionate criticism.

I have, of course, barely indicated the nature of this very com-

[14] *Systematic Theology,* I, 28.

plex and controversial problem and Tillich's detailed treatment of it. His analysis is much too rich and involved to permit of any brief summary that is at all adequate. Yet his basic methodological approach to the problem of religious knowledge has, I hope, been indicated at least in bare outline. To understand religion we must participate in it with full venturesome commitment, but we must *also* interpret it as critically and honestly as we can, drawing richly upon all relevant secular knowledge. To understand Christianity we must enter into "the circle" of Christian faith, but we must *also* interpret this faith in historical perspective and with philosophical rigor. Only thus can we achieve an understanding of ourselves and our "world" which is both relevant to our ultimate concern and intellectually honest, a systematic theology that is both "liberal" and "orthodox." In summarizing his own position at the close of his Introduction to *The Protestant Era* Tillich makes clear to what extent the "Protestant principle," which he makes his own, is both liberal and orthodox.

It is liberal in its insistence (*a*) that Holy Scripture be studied "with the critical methods of historical research and with a complete scientific honesty"; (*b*) that "Christianity cannot be considered in isolation from the general religious and cultural, psychological and sociological development of humanity"; and (*c*) that Protestant theology must be stubbornly rational in its opposition to "holy superstitions, sacramental magic, and sacred heteronomy." But, simultaneously, liberal Protestantism, as Tillich conceives of it, must be orthodox (*a*) in regarding "Scripture as Holy Scripture, namely, as the original document of the event which is called 'Jesus the Christ' and which is the criterion of all Scripture"; (*b*) in insisting upon "the infinite distance between God and man, and the judgment of the Cross over and against all human possibilities"; and (*c*) in acknowledging "that man in his very existence is estranged from God, and that a distorted humanity is our heritage."[15] Is such a position as this liberal or orthodox, he asks, and answers that it is neither one to the exclusion of the other. It is, at least in intention, both. "Liberal" Christianity takes on, in Tillich, an affirmative meaning and a positive context which earlier forms of Christian liberalism lacked; it simultaneously exhibits an open-minded receptivity to secular knowledge and philosophical criticism which Christian orthodoxy and neo-orthodoxy have seldom exhibited. In short, Til-

[15] *The Protestant Era*, pp. xxvii-xxviii.

lich seems to me to give our secular age an account of religion and Christianity which it can accept, if it will, with complete intellectual and moral integrity.

IV

I have devoted the first part of this essay to some of Tillich's basic attitudes rather than to his analyses of our major secular activities because these analyses follow from his fundamental position and lose much of their significance when they are taken in isolation. I very much wish, however, that I had the space in which to explore his most illuminating discussions of history, of recent and contemporary social and political movements, of modern psychology, of art, ancient and modern, and of the symbolic nature of all theological use of language. All I can attempt, in the remaining pages, is to give an indication of the ways in which Tillich exemplifies, in his own thinking, the Protestant "openness" to secular insights and achievements in all these fields of human creative endeavor and, simultaneously, his forthright prophetic Nay to all secular claims, explicit or implicit, to humanistic self-sufficiency.

1. We have noted his insistence on historical orientation and the imperative need for "existential" decision on all matters of human import. We have also referred to his analysis of the historical development of our culture since the early Middle Ages. His more inclusive interpretation of history as such is based on his philosophical and theological conviction that history is a process which is essentially forward-moving and unrepetitive (thus rejecting all cyclical interpretations of history), and that the pattern which is thus unfolded is determined partly by "destiny" and partly by man's own individual "freedom." By "destiny" he means in this context a certain inevitability in the course of events over which individual men and women have no control, and to which they must therefore adapt themselves as best they can. This uncontrollable inevitability is what the ancient Greeks called "fate," but what Christians, through faith in divine Providence, are able to regard as a manifestation of a "saving fate," that is, of Grace. "God reveals himself not only *in* history but also *through* history as a whole."[16]

This leads Tillich to the formulation of his powerful concept of *kairos*, the "right time" (in contradistinction to *chronos*, chronological time). *Kairos*, as he uses it, has a general, a special and a

16 *Ibid.*, p. 22.

unique sense. In its general sense it refers to "every turning point in history in which the eternal judges and transforms the temporal." In its special sense, "as decisive for our present situation, it is the coming of a new theonomy on the soil of a secularized and emptied autonomous culture." In its unique and universal sense it is, "for Christian faith," the appearing of Jesus as the Christ.[17]

History, so viewed, is a series of successive contemporary situations, of historical "presents," which the men and women of each contemporary generation must accept as the given historical matrix of all their individual activities. This means that some human activities, individual and corporate, are possible in one age and not in another. It therefore means that to be really alive and free one must function realistically in one's contemporary social and historical setting. This in turn means that no political philosophy or program of social reform, no art, no theology or religious ritual, can be either meaningful or effective unless it is right for its time, that is, obedient to the *kairos* of its particular historical period. But the Christian will also be able to see the whole course of history, including his own period, in the light of Jesus the Christ as the unique *kairos,* the eternal criterion for all historical evaluation and the everlasting promise that history will be redeemed in God's own good way and time.

2. Tillich's analysis and assessment of the present world situation reflect this *kairos* orientation. He takes far more seriously than we Americans are inclined to do the creation of the proletarian situation out of the social exploitation of ruthless bourgeois capitalism and the challenge of this situation to all liberal democrats and to the Church. We dare not, he insists, be complacent regarding our capitalistic economy or our present forms of political democracy. We must recognize their many assets, but we must also think and act as radically as the times may dictate in the direction of political, economic, and social reform. Tillich himself, while still in Germany in the 1920's, took an active part in the religious-socialist movement, and he is still in sympathy with its basic principles and platform. Yet, characteristically, he takes pains to guard against any doctrinal approval of this or any other practical program as *the correct* Christian answer to man's historical predicament.

Religious socialism should . . . avoid considering socialism as a religious law, by appealing to the authority of Jesus or to the primitive Christian

[17] *Ibid.,* pp. 46–47.

community. There exists no direct way from the unconditional to any concrete solution. The unconditional is never a law or a promoter of a definite form of the spiritual or social life. The contents of the historical life are tasks and ventures of the creative spirit. . . . What we are confronted with is never and nowhere an abstract command; it is living history, with its abundance of new problems whose solution occupies and fulfils every epoch.[18]

3. Tillich's approach to modern science, notably modern depth psychology, might be anticipated from the general tenor of his thought. Theologians, he is convinced, have much to learn from the psychological explorations of the inner and unconscious self and from the therapeutic maxim of psychoanalysis which dictates "acceptance of one's own conflicts when looking at them and suffering under their ugliness without an attempt to suppress them and to hide them from one's self."[19] Psychology, in turn, has no less to learn from the Christian distinction between psychopathic fears, which are in principle removable by psychiatric and psychoanalytical treatment, and that far more ultimate anxiety over one's inevitable death and over the perpetual threat of the meaninglessness of existence which is man's inescapable mortal lot, and which can be cured only by a religious "acceptance of the divine grace which breaks through the realm of law and creates a joyful conscience."[20]

The basic principle here invoked is simple, however difficult may be its concrete application in individual cases. Therapeutic psychology is like surgery which gets rid of a diseased organ but relies on "nature" to heal the wound and on nourishing food to restore the patient's vitality. Psychiatry and psychoanalysis are invaluable in the diagnosis of frustrations and suppressed fears and also in their removal. In and of themselves, however, as scientific techniques, they are powerless to induce in the recovering patient that affirmative orientation to one's fellow men which is the essence of morality and that orientation to the Unconditioned which is the essence of religious dedication. Only a psychology become "theonomous," or a religious ethic coupled with scientific knowledge and skill, can heal man's basic illness radically and completely.

4. Tillich's sympathetic understanding of modern art is not surprising. His interpretation of nature, animate and inanimate, as having a "life" of its own, and as therefore inviting our love, respect,

---

[18] *Ibid.*, p. 51.   [19] *Ibid.*, p. 149.
[20] *Ibid.*, p. 149.

and admiration rather than our contemptuous and callous exploitation, enables him to express and defend that loving and respectful
handling of the media of art which has characterized all sensitive
creative artists in every culture. "Technical" reason, in its anti-
sacramental trend, for example, forces upon houses, furniture, and
all kinds of objects of our daily use forms which are "not derived
from their inherent power and practical meaning." It imposes "from
the outside" shapes and decorative ornaments "which do not express
the true nature of the material of which they are made . . . or the
purpose for which they are produced." What is needed is a new
realism sensitive to both medium and social function.

Many of the spiritual leaders in architecture and the applied arts have
realized this situation, and they are trying to rediscover the inherent
power and beauty of the materials they use and of the products they
create. They want to unite themselves with things, not in order to exploit
them but in an attitude of devotion and in the spirit of *eros* [or what the
eighteenth century called "natural piety"].[21]

Art, however, to be significant, must not merely honor the medium
and, in applied art, the intended utilitarian function; it must also
be expressive of man's spiritual insights and aspirations. Hence the
inadequacy of aestheticism, of mere " 'art for art's sake,' which disregards the content and meaning of artistic creations for the sake
of their form."

Aestheticism deprives art of its existential character by substituting
detached judgments of taste and a refined connoisseurship for emotional
union. No artistic expression is possible without the creative rational form,
but the form, even in its greatest refinement, is empty if it does not express a spiritual substance.[22]

Tillich's whole conception of art is well summarized in a short
German article published in 1931.[23] All art, he there argues, should
express man's ultimate concern. Art, to be authentically religious,
must avoid all mechanical imitation of older styles, however vital
they may have been in their own time, as well as all mechanical
reliance on a subject matter that has religious associations. It must,
instead, be *alltäglich*, touching everyday life and not just religiously
sanctified days *("kein heiliger Bezirk!")*; it must be contemporary,

21 *Ibid.*, p. 123.
22 *Systematic Theology*, I, 90.
23 In *Kunst und Kirche*, No. 1, 1931.

not imitative of older forms or symbols; it must be functionally "real" in its handling of the medium in question; above all, it must be truthful, expressive of complete moral, intellectual, and spiritual integrity. Tillich values such truthfulness to the point of preferring that modern art which expresses our contemporary despair to art which expresses a too easy and therefore not wholly sincere religious affirmation. "One often gets the impression that only those contemporary cultural creations have greatness in which the experience of the void is expressed. . . ."[24]

5. This approach to art is echoed and worked out in great detail by Tillich in his treatment of symbolism and his demand that theologians develop symbols appropriate to the contemporary scene and intelligible to modern man. He analyzes painstakingly the symbolic and metaphorical nature of all the traditional concepts which Christian theologians have traditionally employed in their attempts to describe the God of Jesus as the Christ. Every one of these—Father, Creator, omniscient, omnipotent, and so forth, must be taken not literally but symbolically, as pointing beyond their ineradicably anthropomorphic meanings to the mysterious Unconditioned who is God himself. They are all human "projections." But (to take this metaphor seriously as a metaphor) they are projections *on* something, namely, the "realm of ultimate concern," that is, the Deity himself.[25] They can therefore throw light not merely on the nature of man and his hopes and fears, as well as his cultural background (which they always do), but also on the nature of God himself as he reveals himself to man.

Anthropomorphic symbols are adequate for speaking of God religiously. . . . Nothing is more inadequate and disgusting than the attempt to translate the concrete symbols of the Bible into less concrete and less powerful symbols. Theology should not weaken the concrete symbols, but it must analyze them and interpret them in abstract ontological terms.[26]

This does not relieve the theologian or the religious poet or the philosopher, however, of the obligation to create new symbols[27]

---

[24] *The Protestant Era*, p. 60.
[25] *Systematic Theology*, I, 212.
[26] *Ibid.*, p. 242.
[27] Cf. *Systematic Theology*, I, 78–80. "While only a metaphorical description of the depth of reason is possible, the metaphors may be applied to the various fields in which reason is actualized. In the cognitive realm the depth of reason is its quality of pointing to truth-itself, namely, to the infinite power of being and of the ultimately real, through the relative truths in every field of knowledge.

in each generation, so that the language in which God and his world are thought about and described may be a language that is "transparent," a *Gestalt* of Grace, for the generation then alive.

I can best conclude this essay with two final quotations from Tillich. The first is from the Preface to his *Systematic Theology*. "My ardent desire," he writes, "is that [my students, here and in Germany] shall find in these pages something of what they expect—a help in answering the questions they are asked by people inside and outside their churches." I am very confident that not only those who have been students of Paul Tillich, but all who will take the trouble to study his writings, will derive very great help in answering the questions which reflect their ultimate concern. The other passage I should like to quote are his concluding words in the Introduction to *The Protestant Era*.

There is . . . after the second World War . . . a general feeling that more darkness than light is lying ahead of us. An element of cynical realism is prevailing today, as an element of utopian hope [prevailed after the first World War]. The Protestant principle judges both of them. It justifies the hope, though destroying its utopian form; it justifies the realism, though destroying its cynical form. In the spirit of such a realism of hope, Protestantism must enter the new era, whether this era will be described by later historians as a post-Protestant or as a Protestant era; for, not the Protestant era, but the Protestant principle is everlasting.

THEODORE M. GREENE

DEPARTMENT OF PHILOSOPHY
YALE UNIVERSITY
NEW HAVEN, CONNECTICUT

In the aesthetic realm the depth of reason is its quality of pointing to 'beauty-itself' . . . through the creations in every field of aesthetic intuition. In the legal realm the depth of reason is its quality of pointing to 'justice-itself,' namely, to an infinite seriousness and an ultimate dignity, through every structure of actualized justice. In the communal realm the depth of reason is its quality of pointing to 'love-itself,' namely, to an infinite richness and an ultimate unity, through every form of actualized love. This dimension of reason, the dimension of depth, is an essential quality of all rational functions. It is their own depth, making them inexhaustible and giving them greatness."

4

Theodor Siegfried

THE SIGNIFICANCE OF PAUL TILLICH'S THEOLOGY FOR THE GERMAN SITUATION

4

THE SIGNIFICANCE OF PAUL TILLICH'S
THEOLOGY FOR THE GERMAN
SITUATION*

O UR subject compels us to deal with the whole of the unusually rich work of Tillich, systematically as well as historically. This is difficult, and will certainly lead to some omissions and subjective distortions, but it is not impossible. For it is *one* basic principle from which the manifold lines of Tillich's thought have developed through three decades of systematic elaboration. Although even now—as we confidently hope—the end of this development has not been reached, one can already see the astonishing harmony between the starting point and the final state of his work.

More than thirty years ago (in 1919), Paul Tillich read to the Berlin branch of the Kant-Gesellschaft a paper on "The Idea of a Theology of Culture."[1] It was a program for further elaboration in philosophy of religion as well as in theology. The term "theology of culture" was created by Tillich in a moment in which the so-called "liberal theology" stood before its catastrophe, denounced by many, including Tillich himself, as a surrender of the Christian message to cultural trends. Of course, the desire to see all the cultural functions in a religious perspective is as old as Christianity. The medieval theologians, in their all-embracing "Summae," fulfilled the want in a classical way. The Reformers gave it a new impetus through their doctrine of the "two realms," which liberated the secular realm

---

* This essay by Prof. Siegfried was translated, condensed, and adapted to the theological situation in the English-speaking world by the Editors in close concurrence with Prof. Tillich.

[1] "Über die Idee einer Theologie der Kultur," in *Religionsphilosophie der Kultur: Zwei Entwürfe,* by G. Radbruch and P. Tillich (Berlin: Kant-Gesellschaft, 1920), Philosophische Vorträge, No. 24.

102

from ecclesiastical control and related it directly to God as an expression of his creative power. This is the basis of the idea of a "theonomous culture" which plays such a rôle in Tillich's thought. German classical philosophy elaborated this idea, and liberal theology (from Schleiermacher to Harnack and Troeltsch) followed its lead. The difference between Tillich, on the one hand, and idealism and liberal theology, on the other, was from the very beginning his emphasis on a radical criticism of culture as such, and not only of particular manifestations of man's cultural life. The Yes and No of the Unconditional over against everything human was understood in its full depth, according to the interpretation of the Unconditional not only as the ground, but also as the abyss of everything finite. In this point Tillich is only partly at odds with the liberal theology, for liberals like Wobbermin and Harnack have seriously warned of the optimism of the late nineteenth century, and have pointed to the critical function of Protestantism in a world of unavoidable fragments and distortions. If, nevertheless, they themselves seemed to be unduly optimistic, this was because in the background of their feeling and thinking stood the certainty of God's forgiving grace. But it remained in the background, whereas Tillich has brought it again into the foreground. He has placed the latent assumption of liberal theology into the center of his thought, thus saving it from being suffocated by the sand of merely cultural activities. There is another point of difference, however, between Tillich and the dominating Ritschlian brand of liberal theology. Whereas in the school of Ritschl ontology was taboo, Tillich has always tried to relate theology and ontology; furthermore, he has elaborated an ontology of his own in order to show how all realms of reality are translucent to the divine ground of being and meaning. The cultural spheres, through their specific means of expression, point immediately to this divine ground. This gave Tillich the possibility of distinguishing between cultural and ecclesiastical theology, thus overcoming the traditional split between a sacred and a profane sphere. The holy, according to this vision, is a dimension in everything real, and not a section within reality. The much-criticized distinction between cultural and ecclesiastical theology is necessary because the symbols of traditional religion cannot be missed in the religious life itself and are needed to give interpretative concepts even to the theology of culture. Nevertheless, it is fortunate that the *Systematic Theology* of 1950 has overcome that earlier dualism.[2] Its subject is the "New Being" in the picture of Jesus as the Christ, and it tries to relate this new reality to all forms of human existence, that is, to the whole of culture. It tries to unite the acceptance of the religious tradition with the participation in the actual situation of our period. But even this was somehow anticipated in the paper of 1919, in which Tillich demanded

the universal human community . . . which includes all cultural activities and their religious substance, whose teachers are the creative philosophers, whose priests are the artists, whose prophets are the seers of new personal and social ethics, whose bishops are the leaders toward new goals in the life of society whose deacons are the executives of a new economic order.[3]

In these words the central theme of religious socialism, the expectation of a New breaking into the Old at the hour of destiny (*kairos*), and the significance of Protestantism for this event are indicated, though not yet developed.

Thus the paper on "The Idea of a Theology of Culture" proved to be a significant prelude to the work which was to follow. In accordance with the main emphases of this essay, and in the light of the consequent publications, we shall concentrate on four subjects: (I) Religious Socialism, (II) the Philosophy of Religion, (III) Systematic Theology, (IV) the Protestant Principle.

I. RELIGIOUS SOCIALISM

The spiritual shock produced by the catastrophes of the First World War drove members of the older as well as the younger generation in Germany to look for a radical reorientation in all realms of life. This is true of the liberal theologians who much earlier had created the Evangelical Social Congress, and who, at this critical moment, tried to transform it into a tool for a democratic and social renewal. Men like Rade, the editor of *Die Christliche Welt* (the German counterpart of *The Christian Century*), Adolph Harnack, Ernst Troeltsch, and Rudolf Otto belonged to their group. But the younger generation, of whom Tillich was one of the leaders, reached beyond the limited goal of a political and social reform. The reality and power of the socialist movement grasped their imagination. They joined the attacks on the bourgeois world and did so just at the moment in which the socialist movement, after having been

[2] See *Systematic Theology*.
[3] Über die Idee, etc." pp. 45 ff.

excluded in imperial Germany from any participation in political responsibility, was obliged to take over the full responsibility in the most tragic moment of German history. They wanted to enter into a moral and intellectual solidarity with the socialist movement, both in its criticism and its creative efforts. Religious socialism, according to Tillich's formulation of it, is first of all an attempt to interpret the socialist movement—its reality and its ideas—in religious terms. This program demanded a thorough theological discussion of some central concepts of Marxism, above all that of class struggle and that of ideology (including the atheistic emphasis of Marxism). A religious interpretation of the class struggle was not without antecedents; thirty-five years ago the great German sociologist Max Weber had shown that after the dissolution of the personal relation between master and servant in the competitive society, the struggle of labor against capital is justified from a Christian point of view. Moreover, fifteen years ago the Swiss leader of religious socialism, H. Kutter, had powerfully pointed to the prophetic character of the socialist fight against the supremacy of the bourgeois class, and above all against the bourgeois church. In the same spirit Tillich asserted that the situation of the class struggle cannot be overcome without the instrument of the class struggle. A new order must be brought about, an order in which the class struggle itself will disappear.

Even more important, and certainly more difficult to deal with, was the Marxist concept of "ideology." Ideology in Marxism designates the intellectual "superstructure" which men build on the basis of the economic social "substructure." It includes law and morals, metaphysics, art, and religion. If a society is split, the ideologies are also split, and each group uses its special ideology as an instrument in the class struggle. Ideologies are produced unconsciously; they mirror the deepest trends of a group: its strivings, its life instincts, and its will to power. Conscious arguments and decisions are rationalizations of these unconscious or half-conscious drives. Thinking expresses being; it is bound to the being, which it expresses. Tillich accepted the insight implied in this analysis, that life is a whole, and that the intellectualistic separation of pure thought from the life processes is impossible. He also accepted the truth in Marx's concept of ideology, that the controlling ideas of a period are expressions of the life of a group and not of isolated individuals, however great they may be.

But if this is the case, the question of truth—philosophical as well as theological—arises forcefully. If every thought is the expression of a particular social situation, how are valid norms, theoretical as well as practical, possible? Is the doctrine of ideology not the most radical form of relativism and skepticism, undermining even its own validity? And what about the atheistic consequences connected with Marx's doctrine of ideology? To the last question Tillich answers: Atheism can be a religiously justified protest against idolatry, for instance, against the use of religion for the purpose of maintaining class supremacy. But he applies the same criterion also against the attempts of Marxism to extricate the socialist movement from the criticism of having an ideology. Such an attempt is declared to be utopian. It absolutizes the proletariat, denying its finitude and estrangement and separating it from the general human predicament. It is idolatrous, just as is the idolatrous use of the belief in God by bourgeois ideology. In this way the true and the false application of the idea of ideology are distinguished.

All this, however, does not answer the question of how it is possible to make a contrast between true and false if the concept of ideology is accepted. In order to answer this fundamental question, Tillich introduces the concept of the "*kairos.*" It is taken from the New Testament, especially from the message of Jesus concerning the kingdom of God as being "at hand," that is, both here and not yet here. But it is generalized by Tillich for the interpretation of other moments of history, for example, the moment after the First World War, which by many Germans of the younger generation was considered to be a concrete *kairos,* a moment in which eternity breaks into time and new creative possibilities appear.

Let us first ask: What has remained of the idea of the *kairos* today, after the socialist rebirth which Tillich thought was destroyed by the two totalitarian powers which called themselves socialist, first Nazism, then Communism, both of which threaten the substance of Christianity and humanity? Tillich had already, at the time he elaborated the idea of *kairos,* asked himself with great concern: "Was not everything just romanticism, intoxication, utopia?" Perhaps it was, in so far as it contained a judgment about the special situation. But within the concrete analysis—which may have been erroneous—a principle of universal validity was discovered; namely, the importance, the limits, and the decisive character of every historical moment. And in this idea two later ideas are anticipated, the concept of the New Being which breaks into history, and the eschatological interpretation of history which centers around the proposition that "nothing is in the *eschaton* which is not in history." So the doctrine of the *kairos* proved its fertility even if its concrete application to the moment after the First World War was mistaken.

In the doctrine of the *kairos* and its far-reaching consequences, the basic difference of Tillich's dialectical thinking from that of Karl Barth and his friends is manifest. Barth has described his attitude to the world in a well known image. Before the brackets which enclose all life stand a plus and a minus sign with equal validity, so that no decision is possible. Judgment and grace bracket the whole of life without entering it concretely and without permeating it actually. History is not able to receive the transhistorical. In a permanent struggle with this attitude, Tillich, in spite of his acceptance of the dialectical No, insisted on the openness of reality generally, and of history especially, for the transcendent, in judgment and grace. He early foresaw the destructive consequences of Barth's negative dialectics, particularly in the conservative Lutheran atmosphere of Germany. Religious indifference toward the political realm makes this realm an easy prey for authoritarian and totalitarian powers, and wrongly gives an easy conscience to those who side with these powers. The conflict between Barth and Tillich has a philosophical background. Barth—following in this respect the neo-Kantian Ritschlian tradition—denies the possibility that the unconditional can appear in the conditioned, and delivers the world of the finite to the unbreakable laws of physics. Tillich, fortunately, was strongly influenced by Schelling, and was able to speak of a dynamic immanence of the transcendent in world and history. But ultimately it was not the accident of their philosophical education but basic religious decisions which drove Barth in the one direction, Tillich in the other. For, as Tillich shows in his *Systematic Theology,* behind every creative philosophy lie ultimate religious decisions.

If the *kairos* doctrine is carried through specifically, many difficulties arise. The question was: In view of the radical No of the divine judgment over everything finite, how can man's creative impetus be preserved? Is man's creativity not reduced to meaninglessness by the dialectical No? Tillich answers with the concept "*Gestalt* of Grace" (*Gestalt* = form, structure). In a "*Gestalt* of Grace" the unconditional breaks into the conditional. It is not a

reality alongside other realities, not a thing which could be seen
and grasped; but it is manifest for the intuition of faith in nature
and history, in the depth of people's souls, and in the structures of
the social life, but above all in the Church, in its message and its
sacraments. The participation in such *"Gestalten* of Grace" makes
creative action possible, in spite of the radical No both of prophetic
and of rational criticism. For the *Gestalt* precedes the critique,
giving it norm and power. (It is an interesting remark of Tillich's
that the prophetic criticism, which presupposes a *Gestalt* of Grace,
is itself the root and strength of all rational criticism.) But one must
ask: If the *Gestalt* of Grace is not identical with anything finite,
not even with the Christian Church—if, on the contrary, all religious
forms, including the Church, stand under the radical No of the
divine judgment—how, then, is action possible? How can the Protestant be active if he knows that everything he may achieve is
subjected to a radical No? Only when, in the *Systematic Theology,*
the New Being was described as the actuality of love, was the final
answer found. But in the meantime a problem, dealt with by Tillich, showed the unsuccessful wrestling with the question of Protestant action. It was the problem of personalism. In his essay on
"The Idea and the Ideal of Personality," he fights against the ideal
of the closed or rounded personality.[4] He emphasizes that personality is open both for the holy and for the demonic. Open it should
be for the impact of the divine; open for the neighbor and the community in unity with whom it alone can come to fulfillment; open
for the realities of the world which it should not transform into
mere objects; open for the deep things of the soul, out of which
consciousness grows. All this was an anticipation of the doctrine of
love in Tillich's later works. But at this early time he was not able
to solve the problems of ethics as related to the Protestant principle.

Summing up the distinction between Barth and Tillich, one can
say that whereas Barth puts the whole of reality into the brackets of
a Yes and No, and accepts in a positivistic way the world in its
estrangement from God, Tillich drives, on the basis of the same
Yes and No, toward what he calls *Gläubiger Realismus* (Belief-ful
or Self-transcending Realism), discussed in *The Protestant Era*
under the title "Realism and Faith." On his way to this concept,
Tillich spoke of the "transcendent meaning" of all cultural forms,

[4] See *The Protestant Era,* Chap. VIII.

and he distinguished between those in which this "meaning" is manifest and those in which it is hidden. But this emphasis on the "meaning" of cultural forms could easily be interpreted as an attempt to avoid their transformation and to evaluate personal and social activities only as ways of witnessing to their transcendent fulfillment. Of course, the actual analysis offered by Tillich and his friends in the *Blätter für Religiösen Sozialismus,* and his concept of *Religiöse Verwirklichung* (Religious Realization) should exclude such an understanding. It was the introduction of the concepts of "historical realism" (in *The Protestant Era*) and of the "New Being" (in the *Systematic Theology*) which made this misunderstanding impossible. The New Being, creating and shaping both community and personality, is the fulfillment of what is potential in nature and history. In the New Being reality is not only transparent, but also fulfilled. Finitude is more than a pointer to the infinite, it is the plane on which the presence of the infinite is expected and demanded. The New Being unites creation and ultimate fulfillment, the beginning and the end.

II. PHILOSOPHY OF RELIGION

Tillich's *Philosophy of Religion* (in Dessoir's *Lehrbuch der Philosophie,* Vol. II, 1925) gives the systematic foundation of many later views, expressed above all in his work *Religiöse Verwirklichung.*[5] The *Philosophy of Religion* represents a turning point in the discussion of the idea of religion. It has not lost its significance even today, especially in two respects: first, it does not start with an analysis of the religious consciousness and its contents, but points from the very beginning to the presence of the unconditional within the conditioned. It does not understand religion as a mental function alongside others but as a quality in all mental functions and contents of reality. With reference to the first point: Neo-Kantianism, in its defense against positivism and materialism, had tried to discover the structures of the mind in which rational thinking and acting are rooted. The idea of God was treated as a presupposition of the human consciousness, but the question of its reality remained unanswered. Ernst Troeltsch and Rudolf Otto tried to transcend this subjectivistic foundation of the philosophy of religion. Tillich followed them and made a further step in the same direction: his doctrine of the immediate presence of the unconditional in mind

[5] Berlin: Furche-Verlag, 1929.

and reality beyond the cleavage between subject and object is a partial return to classical German philosophy. It transcends the Kantian foundation to which Troeltsch and Otto still held. From this follows the second point mentioned before, the interpretation of the unconditional as the creative ground of all mental functions, and consequently of religion as present in the whole life of mind and of culture. It is natural that this doctrine was sharply attacked by people who felt that it undermined genuine religion. But it is also understandable that others felt it to be a liberating break-through in a double direction: the captivity of religion within the limits of human consciousness seemed to have been broken; further, the whole breadth of life was now seen in the light of the unconditional; the division of a secular and a religious sphere was overcome.

Tillich has described the unconditional as the ground and the abyss of being and meaning. As the abyss, the unconditional is the unexhaustible depth in which everything finite disappears; as the ground the unconditional is the creative bearer of everything finite, the source of its being and meaning. Out of the abysmal character of the unconditional follows the divine No, the judgment over everything finite which claims to be infinite. It follows the Cross as the central symbol of the divine self-manifestation and the prophetic struggle against every religion, even Christianity, when the latter puts itself in the place of the unconditional. Out of the unconditional as ground follows the divine Yes, the affirmation of the finite as a potential medium of the infinite. It follows the primacy of grace which makes the prophetic criticism possible. It follows the openness for the world, for nature and history. It follows the all-inclusiveness of grace. In these formulations of the *Philosophy of Religion*, answers are given which sometimes surpass later statements, while at the same time preparing for them.

At this point some problems which are important for Tillich's understanding of religion must be discussed. The first is the question of a normative religion. Tillich derives a normative idea of religion from a comparison of the sacramental, the mystical, and the prophetic types of religion. A synthesis of them, as given in Christianity, is considered as the criterion of every religious reality. The history of religion is interpreted as a development of these types, driving from all sides to the Christian synthesis. But is it not possible to see the historical movement driving in a quite different direction? Moreover, is this not the attitude of the religions and quasi religions which are in competition with Christianity? Although Tillich is open to all forms of religious realizations, he has not shown the foundation of his normative concept in a convincing way.

The same is true of his dealing with the notion of "doubt." In his pamphlet *Rechtfertigung und Zweifel* (Justification and Doubt)[6] he drives the doubt to the point at which it becomes the doubt of itself as doubt, This is good "aporetics" (method of dealing with inescapable cognitive conflicts), but it does not help one who is in the situation of radical doubt to overcome the existential foundations of, and the logical arguments for, his doubt. Only if they are taken seriously in their special weight can the tension of doubt be dissolved.

It is the combination of objective analysis and existential participation which characterizes Tillich's method. While in the two problems just discussed Tillich falls short of his own methodological ideal, that ideal is fully realized in his discussion of the demonic and of creaturely suffering. The demonic is a structure of reality, but it is at the same time a matter of moral responsibility. It unites an objective-ontological and a personal-existential element. In the same way the problem of suffering, the famous question of theodicy, is solved in a humble yet profound way by an objective analysis on the basis of the personal experience of suffering and solidarity with the suffering of the others. Existential concern and objective explanation are united. When, finally, Tillich speaks in his *Systematic Theology* about the theological circle as the horizon within which the theologian has to work, he does not eliminate the quest for objective analysis.[7] For the theological circle is centered in Jesus as the Christ, who, as the manifestation of the divine Logos, unites concreteness with universality. In spite of the existential elements in his thought, Tillich has, in distinction from Barthianism and existentialism, never denied the principle of methodological rationality.

III. SYSTEMATIC THEOLOGY

The *Systematic Theology* is the summary of Tillich's whole work. All the different elements, developed before, are shaped into a

[6] In *Vorträge der theologischen Konferenz* (Giessen: Töpelmann, 1924).
[7] See p. 16 in Vol. I.

powerful systematic edifice, whose center is the paradox of the
New Being appearing under the conditions of existence. It is a paradox, but it is *not* something irrational; it involves no logical contradiction. For God works through the Logos. The New Being is
paradoxical because it transcends all human expectations and possibilities. It enters the context of ordinary experience but it cannot
be derived from it. This point of view shows the polar contrast of
Tillich's thought to that of Barth and his school. Methodologically,
the difference is that Tillich affirms reason and experience in theology while Barth denies them; materially, the difference is that
Tillich speaks of the new reality in which man participates with
his whole being and in all his functions, while Barth starts with
the "Word of God," which stands against man. Tillich develops
a theology of regeneration over against a theology of eternal crisis.
This enables him to be universal in the subjects drawn into his system, similar to what the medieval "Summae" tried to do. There is
no realm to which theology does not have something to say from
its own point of view, be it science or history, psychology or medicine. All become fertile for theology, and theology gives to all of
them a new dimension. The theologian never interferes with the
autonomous work of the scholar in any realm. No contradiction
between the knowledge of revelation and scientific knowledge of
any kind is possible, because they lie on different levels. This thesis
(which undoubtedly will arouse an excited debate, especially in
Germany) is necessary for Tillich because he does not accept the
Barthian idea of a closed time of salvation of which we hear only
by report (the event of Jesus Christ). But the New Being is a past
and present reality in which we, and everything that exists, participate, though fragmentarily and by anticipation and in a continuous
fight with possible and actual demonic distortions.

Tillich's *Systematic Theology* speaks the language of the modern
man. It tries to be open, both to tradition and to the present. It
succeeds in this effort in a unique way. The problems and anxieties,
the cleavages and conflicts of human existence as experienced in
our period—all are discussed in his theology. This enables him to
show the vitality of old Biblical conceptions such as new creature,
life, spirit, truth, thus liberating them from their dogmatic captivity.

In his discussion of existentialism, Tillich gives a thorough
analysis of the relationship of essence and existence which belongs
to the most important sections of his first volume. He tries to over-

come the uprootedness of existentialism by pointing to the essential structures of being which are present and creative even in the most disrupted forms of existence. In this he follows the Thomist and Neo-Thomist tradition (as in the work of Gilson and Mounier). On the other hand, he deviates from it by emphasizing the "structure of destruction" within existence and the impossibility of regaining our essential wholeness except through the healing power of the New Being.

Tillich defines human nature essentially as "finite freedom." This does not contradict his agreement with Luther's doctrine of the existential servitude of man's will. On the contrary, as in Luther, the first is the condition of the second. But by defining man as finite freedom he has some advantages in present-day discussion. Against the naturalistic denial of the self he restates its dignity and its danger. Against the existentialist absolutizing of man's freedom he emphasizes its finitude and its dependence on the divine creativity. Against the theological positivism of Ritschl and Barth he stresses the cosmological basis of man's being. Against the neoorthodox denial of any point of contact between God and man he finds this point of contact in man's nature as finite freedom. Against the exclusive emphasis on pure grace he points to the divine imperative which addresses itself to human freedom. All this certainly means a change of emphasis as over against Luther. While Luther had to fight with human arrogance and the belief in man's power to reach God, the breakdown of this belief and the widespread nihilism of our age have placed before Tillich a quite different task. The different language used by him, therefore, is not "heretical" in comparison with Luther's language, but it is the adequate tool for a changed situation.

There is, however, a point at which it seems to me that Tillich has surrendered his methodological coordination of reality and revelation: namely, in his Christology. His thesis that it is not the historical Jesus as elaborated by historical research but the Biblical picture of Jesus as the Christ with which systematic theology has to deal seems to eliminate at least *one* reality—the historical (and as such the historically problematic) Jesus from the media of revelation. Is this methodologically justified and religiously tolerable? I do not think so.[8]

8 It was editorially impossible to include Prof. Siegfried's very long and careful arguments about this point in the framework of the present book. They were

In spite of this difference, an important common basis between Tillich's and my own position is given: the affirmation of the extreme situation which is present latently or openly in every moment of man's existence, the affirmation of the New Being and its healing power, the affirmation of the world as transparent to the divine and as the medium in which the New Being realizes itself, the affirmation of the Church as the community of the New Being. All this is an answer, and, as I believe, the most adequate answer to the question raised by the German situation. It shows how it is possible to find within the limits of finitude, and in a situation of disruption and chaos, true and essential humanity.

IV. THE PROTESTANT PRINCIPLE

The whole work of Tillich has a definitely Protestant character. The emphasis on grace as the *prius* of action and thought, the unity of regeneration, judgment, and justification, the idea of the *kairos* as a divine manifestation out of which political and social transformation follow—all this is essentially Protestant. But above all it is Tillich's doctrine of the ultimate situation which shows the Protestant character of his thought. Grace appears at the boundary line of existence in the moment in which man is delivered to nothingness and despair. This makes the ultimate situation ambiguous. It is, on the one hand, the place of a complete loss of self; it is, on the other hand, the place where man can find his true being. Therefore Tillich can agree with Nietzsche, Freud, and the existentialists in their analysis of the human predicament, and he can agree with the reformers in their emphasis on the reality of grace as the foundation not only of the religious, but also of the secular realm. Beliefful realism is an eminently Protestant principle precisely because it relates every religious element to a secular one and vice versa. In this sense Tillich agrees with Schleiermacher that "the Reformation goes on," and has not been completed with the creedal statements of the Reformation age, as old and new orthodoxies assert. The problem of present-day Protestantism is the fact that Protestantism arose in correlation with the rise of bourgeois society, and that the freedom of the Christian was correlated with the freedom of the citizen. Today the bourgeois forms of life, especially its indi-

---

available, however, to Prof. Tillich, who intends to deal with them in the Christological section of the second volume of his *Systematic Theology* more fully than he could in the "Reply to Critics" in this book. The Editors.

vidualism, are in a state of disintegration. Will Protestantism be drawn into the same disintegration? This question is the subject of *The Protestant Era*. The concepts of love as the power of reunion and the New Being as the basis of a community are supposed to answer the question of future Protestantism. The central position of the New Being in Tillich's thought shows once more its difference from Karl Barth's solution, and it shows that Protestantism cannot be judged alone by the expression it has found in the neo-orthodox theology. Roman Catholics, in their discussion with Protestants, have during the last decades referred almost exclusively to Barth and his followers as the representatives of Protestantism. Consequently, they have claimed the ideas of grace, universality, and affirmation of culture as the property of Catholicism. But Protestantism is not identical with any of its historical forms. The expression given to it in Tillich's theology, therefore, must fully be taken into account in every interconfessional discussion.

The relation of the Protestant principle to the Protestant reality leads to a series of questions which can only briefly be indicated. The first is the question of the orders of political life, seen in the light of the principle of love and the idea of the New Being. Tillich follows Luther's intuition of the relativity of all social orders. But he applies his principle also to the feudal-paternalistic order, which Luther thought to be valid for his time and beyond his time; he also applies it to the bourgeois-capitalistic order, which he criticizes in the name of religious socialism. At the same time he tries to find an immovable principle of ethics which unites absoluteness with openness for all historical relativities. This he finds in the nature of love. Love makes the positivism of law—in political as well as in the juridical sense—impossible, because it cannot accept any social state of things as lying beyond its criticism. Whether supranatural or rational or historical absolutism, love undercuts them by its permanent criticism of everything given. But love goes beyond criticism. It creates leading ideas, middle concepts between its own absolute validity and the demands of the concrete situation. Such middle concepts (a term taken from American and English authors on Christian social ethics) have regulative power for a special group in a special situation, but they have no absolute validity (socialism was always considered by Tillich to be such a mediating idea). They are necessary for educational and organizational reasons, but they are not exempt from the criticism of the

Protestant principle. It is an urgent question in the present German situation as to which mediating concepts should be used and how they should be related to the Christian message. For instance, are the "rights of men" to be elaborated from a secular as well as from a religious point of view?

The second question to be discussed in the light of the Protestant principle is that of autonomy. Tillich, in agreement with Paul's letter to the Romans and with Kant, defines autonomy as the ability of man to discover the universal law of theoretical and practical reason in himself without dependence on heteronomous authorities. But in view of the distortion of men's autonomy in his state of estrangement, Tillich demands a theonomy which transcends autonomy as well as heteronomy. He sees the remnants of a theonomous foundation even in such secular institutions as political democracy, and he—like other American visitors to Germany—has interpreted democracy in its deepest meaning as mutual openness, involving recognition of the dignity of every human being *as* human, and recognition of tolerance and sociability. However, the question to be asked of Tillich (and, as we hope, to be answered by Tillich) is: How can one unite the necessary elements of authority with autonomy or theonomy? It is the relation of trust and authority which demands an answer in the light of the Protestant principle. Is there an authority which is not heteronomously distorted? Is there a theonomous authority? The answer Tillich gives points not to doctrinal statements but to the cultus. According to him, the cultus gives an ultimate meaning to the daily life; it gives a set of symbols understandable to the primitive as well as to the sophisticated mind. "Protestant formative power" is at work wherever reality is transformed into an active expression of a gestalt of grace."[9]

The third and last question to which I want to point is that of the Protestant churches in the light of the Protestant principle. According to Tillich, their future is dependent on their theological openness toward the theoretical problems of the present situation in contrast to a theology of restoration and confessional isolation; it is dependent on their ethical openness toward the social problems of today in contrast to the attempt to identify the Christian message with a special political or economic structure; it is dependent on their acceptance of free groups which find a common

⁹ *The Protestant Era*, p. 219.

liturgical and sacramental expression of their actual problems in distinction from an archaistic restitution of obsolete forms of the past.

It would be extremely important if these and the other basic ideas of Tillich's theology gained influence in the present German situation. It could mean a revitalization of Protestantism in itself and in its relation to the world.

THEODOR SIEGFRIED

DEPARTMENT OF THEOLOGY
THE UNIVERSITY OF MARBURG
GERMANY

5

George F. Thomas
THE METHOD AND STRUCTURE
OF TILLICH'S THEOLOGY

5

THE METHOD AND STRUCTURE
OF TILLICH'S THEOLOGY

I<small>N</small> the Preface to his *Systematic Theology* Tillich tells us that his purpose is "to present the method and the structure of a theological system written from an apologetic point of view and carried through in a continuous correlation with philosophy." Obviously, a complete treatment of the method and structure of his system would require an analysis of all parts of the system. Since only the first half of the system has been published, this is impossible. But Tillich has given us in the Introduction a description of the method and structure of his system as a whole, and in Parts I and II he has given us enough applications to enable us to understand the general character both of the method and of the structure determined by it.

The method is intelligible only if the *apologetic point of view* is always borne in mind. Tillich tells us at the outset that a theological system must serve two quite different needs, "the statement of the truth of the Christian message, and an interpretation of this truth for every generation,"[1] and that it is very difficult to satisfy both of these demands. For example, fundamentalism does not concern itself sufficiently with the "situation" to which theology must speak, while apologetic theology since the Enlightenment has often been tempted to surrender the truth of the Christian message in order to find common ground with those outside the Church. Despite the dangers, however, kerygmatic theology which "emphasizes the unchangeable truth of the message (*kerygma*)" must be completed by apologetic theology which speaks to the special "situa-

[1] *Systematic Theology*, I, 3. Succeeding references in this essay to page numbers of quotations from *Systematic Theology*, I, will be given in parentheses after the quotations.

tion," if it is not to become narrow and irrelevant. On its side, apologetic theology must be "based on the *kerygma* as the substance and criterion of each of its statements," if it is not to lose its Christian character.

There can be no doubt that, while his systematic theology combines apologetic and kerygmatic elements, Tillich is primarily an apologetic theologian. As Barth is probably the greatest living representative of kerygmatic theology, Tillich is probably the outstanding representative of apologetic theology at the present time. However, this does not mean that he neglects the kerygmatic element; it means only that the whole of his systematic theology is written "from an apologetic point of view."

How seriously he takes the kerygma, or "message," of Christianity is shown by his insistence that the theologian must work within the "theological circle." Whereas the philosopher of religion is "general and abstract" in his concepts, the theologian seeks to be "specific and concrete," entering the theological circle "with a concrete commitment" and "as a member of the Christian church." Tillich, however, qualifies this statement in a rather perplexing way. "Every theologian," he says, "is committed *and* alienated, he is always in faith *and* in doubt, he is inside *and* outside the theological circle. Sometimes the one side prevails, sometimes the other; and he is never certain which side really prevails. Therefore one criterion alone can be applied: a person can be a theologian as long as he acknowledges the content of the theological circle as his ultimate concern" (10). Doubtless this is simply a strong assertion of the fact that, under the conditions of human existence, faith is bound to be assailed by doubt. Unfortunately, the language suggests that the faith or commitment of the theologian does not need to be settled and strong but may be completely vacillating. However, when Tillich adds that a theologian needs only to be "ultimately concerned with the Christian message, even if he is *sometimes* inclined to attack and to reject it" (10) he makes it clear that he is thinking only of an occasional struggle with doubt and that a definite commitment to the theological circle is required.

There are two "formal criteria" of every theology. "The object of theology is what concerns us ultimately. Only those propositions are theological which deal with their object insofar as it can become a matter of ultimate concern for us" (12). The value of this first criterion is that it enables us to distinguish between "ultimate" and "preliminary" concerns. Thus it prevents us from confusing theo-logical questions with scientific, historical, political, or other ques-tions which have to do with our relation to the world of existence, and safeguards the "Protestant principle" that nothing relative should be raised to the level of the absolute and made an object of ultimate concern. The second "formal criterion" of every theology is that "only those statements are theological which deal with their object insofar as it can become a matter of being or not-being for us" (14). For only that which has "the power of threatening and saving our being," "the structure, the meaning and the aim of exist-ence," is of ultimate concern to us.

These two "formal criteria of every theology" are an expression of Tillich's *existentialist approach* to theology. It is this approach which largely determines his method of seeking in theology for answers to the questions raised by man's situation. It may profit-ably be contrasted with the approach of the Catholic theology of Aquinas. According to Aquinas, "sacred doctrine or theology is not a practical but a speculative science."[2] Though it deals with practi-cal matters, it does so in a secondary way, since "it is more concerned with divine things than with human acts."[3] Though Tillich also would hold that theology is primarily interested in truth about God, it is practical in the sense that it is motivated not by a purely theoretical interest but by a practical one, that is, man's ultimate concern with that which threatens or saves him. A result of this is that, while he is far more metaphysical than most Protestant theo-logians, he does not attempt, as Aquinas does, to answer every pos-sible question man's reason can ask. His "system" is not a "summa." In contrast with Protestant orthodoxy, he does not start with the answers of the Christian message but with an analysis of the human situation. As a result, the terms in which the answers are given are determined by the nature of the questions far more than in Protestant orthodoxy. Thus his existentialist approach has substantial advan-tages over that of Catholic or of Protestant orthodoxy. By starting with the human situation, it makes man more aware of his need; and by stating the Christian message in terms of that need it shows man that the message is not being arbitrarily imposed upon him. In a time like ours, when the optimism of man about himself has been so rudely shaken and he has become a prey to anxiety, a real-

[2] *Summa Theologica*, Q. 1, a. 4.
[3] *Ibid.*, Q. 1, a. 4.

istic analysis of his existence may be the most fruitful starting point for a presentation of the Christian message. That is why the doctrines of man and history have been so central in recent Christian theology.

But the fact that the existentialist approach to theology may be natural and fruitful in a time when man is looking for an ultimate source of security and meaning should not blind us to the danger involved in it. It seems obvious that when the two "formal criteria" of theology require us to restrict theology to that which is "a matter of ultimate concern" to us, there is a danger that theology will become anthropocentric. Is it really true that for religion, especially a "high" religion like Christianity, God is a matter of ultimate concern *only* because He has "the power of threatening or saving our being"? Certainly God has this power, and men have always turned to Him to deliver them from threats to the meaning of their existence. For God is the ultimate Being upon whom men are "absolutely dependent" not only for their creation and preservation, but also for their redemption from evil. To Christians God is not a metaphysical principle such as the Prime Mover of Aristotle; He is the Father who loves His children and saves them from sin and death. Therefore if a man "believes in" God but feels no real need of His saving power, it is doubtful whether he can be regarded as a Christian. Thus the fact that we have an ultimate concern with God as the Power who can save us from the threat of nonbeing is beyond question.

But we may question whether our ultimate concern with God is due *solely* to the fact that He can save us. In Christianity is there not also a concern for God for His own sake? If not, what can be meant by the first commandment, "Thou shalt love the Lord thy God"? It may be replied that Jesus calls upon us to love God in response to His antecedent love for us. "We love him because he first loved us," that is, because He has shown through His love for us that He is the Source of our good. But there is no evidence that the prophets and psalmists always thought of men as loving God solely because they depended upon Him for their true good. Though they often show their gratitude for His acts of deliverance in the past and His blessings in the present, they also praise Him as holy, majestic, and mighty. By virtue of what He is, He is to be accorded glory and honor. Under the influence of existentialism and its preoccupation with man, are we to forget that "man's chief end is to glorify God and to enjoy Him forever"? As Rudolph Otto has shown, the experience of God as "the holy" is the basis of all religion. Perhaps men feel "awe" before Him as the mysterious and transcendent "Other" before they turn to Him for salvation from the threat of nonbeing. Doubtless it is true that men are prevented from giving glory and praise to God so long as they are alienated from him by their sin, and that they must be reconciled to Him before they can overcome their excessive self-concern enough to love Him. This may be what Tillich has in mind in his "formal criteria." But these criteria should be formulated in such a way as to take account of the fact that man's salvation is not merely *from* threats to his being but also *to* love and fellowship with God.

Tillich makes some interesting suggestions about the *organization* of theology which we must consider briefly before dealing directly with his method. The first of these has to do with "natural theology," which constituted a section of systematic theology in the classical tradition and has been largely replaced since Schleiermacher by an autonomous philosophy of religion. Neither of these ways of dealing with natural theology is satisfactory, Tillich argues. The main reason for this negative judgment is that the "autonomous" reason cannot prove the existence of God. Tillich suggests that the theologian should take the philosophical element in natural theology "into the structure of the system itself, using it as the material out of which questions are developed" (30). Thus its claim to give an answer to the question of the existence of God is rejected, but it is given a secondary place in the analysis of the situation.

The second suggestion is that apologetics, which in traditional theology had been partly included in the section on natural theology and in modern theology had been identified with philosophy of religion, should be regarded as "an omnipresent element and not a special section of systematic theology" (31). This is required, of course, by the combination of kerygmatic and apologetic elements in Tillich's systematic theology, and its validity will be determined by the fruitfulness of that combination. Those who think that kerygmatic theology should be the whole rather than a part of systematic theology will naturally reject the idea that the apologetic element should be "omnipresent." Others who believe that apologetics has some value for those outside the Church may think that the purity of the kerygma, or message, can be preserved only by keeping apologetics separate from systematic theology. Final judgment on this matter may be reserved until we have seen how successfully Tillich combines apologetic and kerygmatic elements in the second volume. If he can show that distinctive doctrines of the Christian message, such as the Incarnation, can be presented more effectively as "answers" to the "questions" implied in the human situation, and that their purity is not lost in the process, the inclusion of apologetics as an "omnipresent element" will be justified. On the other hand, if the inclusion of the apologetic element seems to obscure or distort the distinctive Christian doctrines, it will be unjustified. Tillich is well aware that the attempts of modern apologists have often led to a surrender of important aspects of the kerygma and the intrusion of alien philosophical ideas into systematic theology. It must be added that some of the readers of his first volume will wonder whether his own use of categories and principles derived from a metaphysical analysis of "Being" in his presentation of the doctrine of God does not lead him also into these dangers. But that question falls outside the scope of this essay.

The third suggestion about the "organization of theology" is that "an 'existential' theology implies ethics in such a way that no special section for ethical theology is needed" (31). The reason given for this is that "the ethical element is a necessary—and often predominant—element in every theological statement" (31). This is highly dubious. It is true that Christian ethics rests upon a theological foundation, and the attempt by some Protestant liberals to state the principles of Christian ethics in independence of that foundation has led to a misunderstanding of them. Christian ethics has been identified with "the ethical teachings of Jesus," and little attention has been paid to the interpretation of morality by Paul, Augustine, Luther, and others in the history of the Church. Therefore the recent tendency of neo-orthodox theologians to reject an independent Christian ethics is understandable. But this does not mean that Christian ethics should be taken back "into the unity of the system" and not even be treated as a "special section" of systematic theology.

Two reasons may be offered for this assertion. First, while it may be true that "an ethical element is a necessary element in every theological statement," adequate treatment cannot be given to the special problems of Christian conduct unless separate attention is paid to them. This is true not only with respect to the "social application" of the principles, but also with respect to the principles themselves. Problems such as the relation of *agape* to "natural" and "revealed" law, the qualities and virtues fostered by *agape,* and the relation of *agape* to the necessity of restraining evil are too complex and difficult to be treated incidentally, even in an occasional long excursus, by the systematic theologian. Secondly, the primary interests and abilities of the systematic theologian are seldom, if ever, those required of one who is to deal thoroughly with the problems of Christian ethics. The closest relations of a systematic theologian of the type Tillich describes are usually with historical theology and philosophy. He may or may not be sufficiently familiar with the history of Christian ethics from its beginnings in the New Testament to the present time. Naturally, his competence in ethics will be deeply affected by these facts. Even more important, however, his primary interest and effort are usually directed toward the problems of belief rather than of practice. Whether he is a kerygmatic theologian or at once an apologetic and kerygmatic theologian like Tillich, this is bound to be the case. Just as there is nothing to prevent a philosopher whose primary interest has been metaphysics from making a contribution also to ethical theory, so a systematic theologian *may* also make a contribution to Christian ethics. But there is no assurance of this. Even if, like Luther, he speaks on occasion about ethical issues, he is likely to touch only on those which are bound up closely with his theological position, to deal with them only in broad and general terms, and to say nothing about many other important ethical issues.

Tillich admits that "reasons of expediency may, nevertheless, justify the preservation of departments of Christian ethics" (31). This may indicate that he is aware of the necessity of dealing somewhere with the special problems of Christian ethics directly and comprehensively. But more than "reasons of expediency" require this. The importance of the subject, the peculiar character of problems of conduct, and the special qualifications required for dealing with these problems effectively are all involved. The plain truth is that Christian ethics has seldom been treated by systematic theologians with the seriousness it deserves. The paucity of books in Christian ethics on a level comparable to the many books in theology is perhaps a sufficient proof of this and a warning that Christian ethics should not be swallowed up by systematic theology.

Up to this point we have been considering Tillich's view of the *nature* and *organization* of systematic theology. We must now deal more directly with his conception of *method*. In addition to the question concerning "the method of correlation," the following questions are considered: What are the *sources* (in the sense of the materials) of systematic theology? Is *experience* one of the sources, and if not, what is its rôle? What is the *norm* or criterion by which the sources are to be interpreted? What is the function of *reason?* In what sense should systematic theology be *systematic?* We shall first state Tillich's answers to these questions, and then make some critical remarks about them.

1. The *sources* of systematic theology are many and complex. Tillich sharply rejects the claim of neo-orthodox Biblicism that the Bible is the *only* source, on the ground that the Biblical message could not have been understood and cannot be received without the preparation for it in religion and culture. This view rests upon his strong belief in "universal revelation" and in the fulfillment of all religions by the "final revelation" in Jesus as the Christ. However, the Bible is the *basic* source, because "it is the original document about the events on which the Christian Church is founded" (35). The Biblical material is made available to the systematic theologian by the Biblical theologian who does not present "pure facts" but "theologically interpreted facts" (35).

In addition to the Bible, the sources are Church history, including historical theology, and the history of religion and culture. Thus there is an "almost unlimited richness" in the sources of systematic theology. But there are "degrees of importance" in this immense material, corresponding to its "more direct or more indirect relationship to the central event on which the Christian faith is based" (40).

2. What is the rôle of *religious experience* in systematic theology? It is the "medium," says Tillich, through which the sources come to us. The early Franciscans realized the importance of personal "participation" in spiritual realities, but Schleiermacher went too far in trying to "derive all the contents of the Christian faith from what he called the 'religious consciousness' of the Christian" (42). On this point Tillich is closer to the Protestant Reformers than he is to the Evangelicals who "derived new revelations from the presence of the Spirit" or to the theological empiricists for whom experience is "the main source of systematic theology" (45). He holds that "Christian theology is based on the unique event Jesus the

Christ," and that "this event is given to experience and not derived from it" (46). He admits that, in the process of receiving, experience colors and even transforms what is given to it, but holds that the transformation must not be intended. At the same time he adds that the influence of the medium "should not be so small that the result is a repetition rather than a transformation" (46).

3. The variety of the sources and the indefiniteness of the medium make it necessary to have a *norm* to guide the theologian. Tillich points out that in every period a norm has been employed. For example, for the Roman Church the norm was "salvation from guilt and disruption by the actual and sacramental sacrifices of the God-man," for Luther "justification by faith" and the authority of the Bible. Tillich holds that "man experiences his present situation in terms of disruption, conflict, self-destruction, meaninglessness, and despair in all realms of life" (48), and asks the question of "a reality in which the self-estrangement of our existence is overcome" (49). Therefore the "norm" of theology for our situation should be "the 'New Being' in Jesus as the Christ" (50).

4. In what sense should systematic theology be *rational* in character? Though reason is not the "source" of theology, it has an important rôle. The theologian must clarify the meanings of terms in relation to their various connotations ("semantic rationality"), using philosophical terms whenever he finds them helpful (55–56). He must follow the principles of meaningful discourse formulated by logic ("logical rationality"). He must not suppose that dialectical thinking is opposed to logic, for "dialectics follows the movement of thought or movement of reality through Yes and No, but it describes it in logically correct terms" (56). Similarly, the use of paradox does not involve logical contradiction. Thus the Incarnation is a paradox not because it is a logical contradiction but because of "the fact that it transcends all human expectations and possibilities" (57). Finally, theology must adopt a definite method and carry it through ("methodological rationality"). Theology must take the form of a "system." Tillich defends the necessity of systematic thinking by pointing out that a system does not have to be deductive, that it does not "close the doors to further research," and that it does not "stifle the creativity of the spiritual life" (58–59).

We shall now offer a few critical remarks on these points in order.

1. One of the sources of strength in Tillich's theology is his recognition of the variety and complexity of the *sources* of theology.

Radical Biblicists not only fall into the "self-deception" mentioned by him; they also cut themselves off from the insights of the past and present theologians of the Church. Anyone familiar with the history of Christian thought can learn much not only from the great thinkers of the Church, but also from thinkers of the second rank or from heretics like Tertullian and Meister Eckhart, who have stated an aspect of the truth in extreme but vivid fashion. Moreover, the thinking of any contemporary theologian has been largely shaped, often unconsciously, by the thinking of the past. The greatest danger of the radical Biblicist, perhaps, is that he unconsciously brings to his interpretation of the Bible theological ideas and emphases he has derived from his own denomination or from his favorite teacher or from one strand of historical theology. If a theologian's understanding of the Christian message is not to be narrow and provincial, he must make use of the *whole* of historical theology rather than of a small *part* of it. One of the sources of Tillich's strength is that he knows the history of Christian thought so thoroughly and is able to use it so effectively.

Though one must heartily approve the principle that the Bible is not the only source of systematic theology, there are times when one wishes that Tillich would refer more often to it. He is right in maintaining that the language of the systematic theologian need not be exclusively Biblical, and that philosophical terms should be used whenever necessary. But if the Bible is the "basic source" of systematic theology, one would think that more frequent references to it would be appropriate, especially in presenting the "answers" of the Christian message. Not only can the language of the Bible often give more vivid and moving expression to a theological doctrine than the abstract language of philosophy; but also reference to the Biblical basis of a doctrine gives greater assurance of its Christian character. If the Bible is the "basic source," why should it not be used more explicitly? Is not Tillich's failure to refer to it more often likely to lead some of its readers to deny that at crucial points his theology is really based upon the Bible?

2. Tillich's view that *experience* is only the "medium" through which the sources are received is directed against the view of Reformation "enthusiasts" and extreme Liberals who speak as if a wholly "new" revelation may come to men through religious experience and may transcend the revelation through Christ. Thus it protects the "final revelation" of "New Life in Jesus as the Christ" and makes

consistency with that revelation the test of the validity of any further revelation. As Paul says, "No one speaking by the Spirit of God ever says 'Jesus be cursed!' and no one can say 'Jesus is Lord!' except by the Holy Spirit."[4] To this extent the denial that experience is an "independent source" of systematic theology must be accepted. But does not Tillich go too far in saying that it is not a "source" but only a "medium"? He admits that the act of "receiving" the sources "transforms" them. He also insists that, while the transformation must not be too great, it must not be so small as to result in a mere "repetition." Does not this imply that, while no wholly "new" revelation, discontinuous with the "final revelation" in Christ, can be admitted by systematic theology, a religious experience might give rise to a revelation of an aspect of Christian truth which was not fully recognized in the past? If so, such a religious experience might be regarded more naturally as a "source" than as a "medium."

That this is more than a mere possibility is shown by the fact that as a result of developing experience, there have been in Christian history "revelations" of aspects of Christian truth which were not clearly understood by the Christians of earlier periods, for example, the importance of a social application of Christian ethics in the late nineteenth and twentieth centuries. If one believes that the Holy Spirit has been active in the lives of Christians to guide them into new truth, there is no reason why these should not be called "revelations." To guard against misunderstanding, however, we should use one of Tillich's distinctions and call these "dependent" rather than "original" revelations. "An original revelation," says Tillich, "is a revelation which occurs in a constellation that did not exist before. . . . In a dependent revelation the miracle and its original reception together form the giving side, while the receiving side changes as new individuals and groups enter the same correlation of revelation" (126). Perhaps Tillich is prevented from saying that religious experience can be a source of theology by mediating "dependent" revelations because of his view that revelation can come only in an "ecstatic" experience and his recognition that the religious experience of theologians is not usually "ecstatic." But may not even a systematic theologian have an occasional experience of an "ecstatic" character? "The Spirit bloweth where it listeth."

3. What are we to say about Tillich's *norm* of systematic theol-

[4] I Cor. 12:3 (RSV).

ogy, "New Being in Jesus as the Christ"? He is surely right in holding that it is impossible to make use of the many materials of systematic theology unless there is some criterion to serve as a guide. He is also right in maintaining that different periods and thinkers in the history of Christian thought have made use of different criteria. Moreover, the Biblical character of his own "norm" is obvious, for St. Paul speaks of "a new creation" (Galatians 6:5), "a new being," and "a new state of things" (II Cor. 5:17). The Gospel was "good news," a message of hope and salvation. It may well be that the greatest need today, when Christians as well as others have become disillusioned and are threatened with despair, is to recall to men the message that God transforms the lives of those who are in Christ. Thus "New Being in Jesus as the Christ" is clearly a primary theme of Christianity.

However, it is dubious whether this theme should be regarded as *the* "norm" of systematic theology to the exclusion of other themes. Tillich asserts that the "question" asked by men today "is *not*, as in the Reformation, the question of a merciful God and the forgiveness of sins; *nor* is it, as in the early Greek church, the question of finitude, of death and error; *nor* is it the question of the personal religious life or of the Christianization of culture and society. It is the question of a reality in which the self-estrangement of our existence is overcome" (49. Italics mine). Does Tillich really mean that all of these questions but the last are unimportant to man in our time? Does he mean that *other* "norms," such as "justification by faith," can be *replaced* by his "norm" of the "New Being"?

4. For all that Tillich has said about the rôle of *reason* in theology the writer of this essay has nothing but praise. A strong defense of reason against uncritical attacks is balanced by a clear recognition that the Christian message was "received" by reason rather than "produced" by it. In my opinion his position offers the best way of avoiding both rationalism and irrationalism. However, I shall raise a question later about his view of the use of reason in the philosophical analysis of the "situation."

We have postponed our consideration of the *method of correlation* in order to see it in the wider context of Tillich's method as a whole. We have seen that his reason for employing the "method of correlation" is that he wishes to combine kerygmatic with apologetic theology. But it is also a method peculiarly congenial to a man who is both a philosopher and a theologian, who is both theo-retical and practical in his interest.

"The method of correlation," says Tillich, "explains the contents of the Christian faith through existential questions and theological answers in mutual interdependence" (60). The analysis of the "situ-ation" and the development of the "questions" constitute a "philo-sophical task." Though this task is carried out by the theologian, he does it as a philosopher, and what he sees "is determined only by the object as it is given in his experience" (64). Tillich insists upon the importance of this analysis of the situation. But it is important to note that the "answers" cannot be inferred from the "questions" but must be provided by the Christian message. "They are 'spoken' to human existence," he says, "from beyond it" (64), that is, from the "final revelation" in Jesus as the Christ. However, if the *content* of the Christian answers is derived from revelation, in their *form* "they are dependent on the structure of the questions which they answer" (64). For example, "if the notion of God appears in sys-tematic theology in correlation with the threat of non-being which is implied in existence, God must be called the infinite power of being which resists the threat of non-being" (64). Thus Tillich repudiates both the naturalistic view that the answers can be de-veloped out of human existence itself and the supernaturalistic view that the Christian message is "a sum of revealed truths which have fallen into the human situation like strange bodies from a strange world" (64).

We can understand better the "method of correlation" if we look briefly at an example of its application: the "question" of Reason and the "answer" of Revelation. Under the conditions of existence, Tillich says, reason falls into "self-destructive conflicts" with itself. The polarity of "structure" and "depth" within reason produces a conflict between "autonomous" and "heteronomous" tendencies, and this conflict leads to "the quest for theonomy." The polarity between "static" and "dynamic" elements within reason leads to a conflict between "absolutism" and "relativism." This leads to "the quest for the concrete-absolute." The polarity between "formal" and "emo-tional" elements produces a conflict between "formalism" and "ir-rationalism." This leads to "the quest for the union of form and mystery." "In all three cases," Tillich remarks, "reason is driven to the quest for revelation" (83). Also a dilemma arises between "con-trolling" knowledge and "receiving" knowledge. "Controlling knowledge is safe but not ultimately significant, while receiving knowledge can be ultimately significant, but it cannot give certainty." This "dilemma" leads to the quest for revelation which gives a truth which is both certain and of ultimate concern (105).

The "final revelation" in Jesus as the Christ, Tillich argues, gives the "answers" to these "questions" by overcoming the conflicts within reason. It liberates and reintegrates reason and thus fulfills it (150). For example, it liberates reason from the conflict between absolutism and relativism by presenting a "concrete absolute." "In the New Being which is manifest in Jesus as the Christ," says Tillich, "the most *concrete* of all possible forms of concreteness, a personal life, is the bearer of that which is *absolute*, without condition and restriction" (150). The absoluteness of the revelation in Christ is shown by "the complete transparency and the complete self-sacrifice of the medium in which it appears" (151). Again, the final revelation in Christ overcomes the conflict between the formal and the emotional elements in reason through the participation of the whole of a person's life in it and the consequent bringing together of all the elements of reason.

The principle involved in these conflicts and their resolutions is the need of reason to be healed. "Actual reason needs salvation," says Tillich, "as do all the other sides of man's nature and of reality generally. Reason is not excluded from the healing power of the New Being in Jesus as the Christ. Theonomous reason, beyond the conflict of absolutism and relativism, of formalism and emotionalism—this is reason in revelation" (155). The "essential structure" of reason is not denied by the final revelation; it is "re-established under the conditions of existence, fragmentarily, yet really and in power" (155).

We have described the "method of correlation" and illustrated its application by reference to the correlation of the "question" of Reason with the "answer" of Revelation. The *structure* of Tillich's whole system is determined by his use of this method. "The method of correlation," he says, "requires that every part of my system should include one section in which the question is developed by an analysis of human existence and existence generally, and one section in which the theological answer is given on the basis of the sources, the medium, and the norm of systematic theology" (66).

Since the form of the "answers" is determined by the philosophical analysis of the situation, the way in which that analysis is conceived is crucial for any evaluation of the "method of correlation." What is Tillich's *view of philosophy* and its relation to theology? Though both philosophy and theology deal with the structure of reality, they deal with it from different perspectives. "Philosophy deals with the *structure* of being *in itself*," says Tillich; "theology deals with the *meaning* of being *for us*" (22). This basic difference is the source of other differences. The philosopher, like the scientist, tries to maintain a "detached objectivity" toward being; the theologian is "involved in" it, looking at it with passion and love and commitment. Again (22, 23), the philosopher "looks at the whole of reality" in seeking the structure of being; the theologian "must look where that which concerns him ultimately is manifest," at "the logos manifesting itself in a particular historical event" (23). Finally, the philosopher deals with the categories of being "in relation to the material"; the theologian deals with them in relation to "the quest for a 'new being'" (24). For the primary interest of the philosopher is theoretical; the primary interest of the theologian is "existential" or "soteriological."

Tillich acknowledges that there is "convergence" between the philosopher and the theologian. For the creative philosopher also has an ultimate concern, whether he is fully conscious of it and admits it or not. "He is a theologian," says Tillich, "to the degree in which his existential situation and his ultimate concern shape his philosophical vision" (25). But the "divergence" remains because "the philosopher does not intend to be a theologian," and "tries to turn away from his existential situation, including his ultimate concern, towards pure reality" (25). The conclusion Tillich draws from this divergence between philosophy and theology is that there can be neither conflict nor synthesis between them. There can be no *conflict* between the philosopher as such and the theologian as such. When the theologian enters the philosophical arena, he must enter it as a philosopher; only as a philosopher can he be in conflict with another philosopher, that is, he must make his appeal to reason alone.

There can be no *synthesis* of philosophy and theology for the same reason: there is no "common basis" on which they could meet. There fore there can be no such thing as a "Christian philosophy." Indeed, the ideal of a "Christian philosophy" is a self-contradictory one, because it denotes "a philosophy which does not look at the universal *logos* but at the assumed or actual demands of a Christian theology"

(28). Of course, any Western thinker may be a "Christian philosopher" in the sense of one whose thinking has been in some measure shaped by the Christian tradition, but an "intentionally" Christian philosopher is a contradiction in terms because the philosopher must "subject himself" to nothing but being as he experiences it.

Now Tillich is certainly right in holding that the philosophical enterprise is destroyed when a philosopher "subjects himself" to theology. The philosopher must follow the truth as it is disclosed to him. But Tillich begs the question as to the relation between philosophy and theology when he asserts that the philosopher seeks the truth only in "the whole of reality," "the universal *logos* of being," and never looks for it in any particular place. For there is nothing to prevent a philosopher from finding the key to the nature of reality in a concrete manifestation, a particular part of reality. Indeed, every creative philosopher must take as his starting point some part or aspect of reality which seems to him to provide the clue to an understanding of reality as a whole. He begins with a "vision" of reality in which this part or aspect appears as dominant, and then works out his philosophy under the guidance of his vision.

Now the philosopher who is a Christian does not differ from other philosophers in starting with a belief which he takes as the key to reality. He differs from them only in that his "vision" is the love of God as manifested in Christ. He finds the key to reality in particular historical events. This does not mean that, having found the key in a *particular* place, he should cease to look at the *universal* structure of being. As a philosopher, it is his task to inquire into the structure of being as a whole. But the fact that he has found the key enables him to look at the structure of being with a clearer understanding of it. His faith does not take the place of his reason, but opens his reason to a dimension of reality hitherto invisible to it and thus enables it to perform its philosophical task more completely. Moreover, his philosophy is "intentionally" Christian in that it is the work of a person who is conscious that his faith has brought him new light as well as new life, and is resolved to look at the structure of being in that light. Of course the Christian philosopher does not close his eyes to light from other sources, for example, science and morality, as if Christianity had a monopoly of truth. His intention, both as a Christian and as a philosopher, is to seek truth wherever it may be found, even if it should require him to reexamine and reformulate his Christian convictions.

The main reason Tillich rejects the possibility of such a Christian philosophy is that he thinks philosophy must approach the structure of being with detachment and without existential concern. For it is only on this supposition that philosophy has to be restricted to the purely "critical" task of analyzing the structure of being without reference to its meaning for us. Yet Tillich himself admits that the creative philosophers have been moved by an ultimate concern, and hence have been in a sense theologians. If so, the distinction between philosophy and theology is relative, not absolute. As a matter of fact, this seems to be Tillich's view also. In conversation he has said that his sharp distinction between them is based upon "extreme cases," that is, cases of philosophers who are not also theologians and theologians who are not also philosophers. These "extreme cases" being regarded as limits that are only approached by actual philosophers and theologians is an aid to theoretical analysis, but should it be normative for our view of philosophy?

This argument may be supported by a consideration of Tillich's own philosophical thinking. Could his philosophical analysis of the human situation and the "questions" implied in it have been made by anyone but a Christian? Could it have been made, for example, by a naturalist or a Platonic idealist? It seems clear to me that at a number of points it could not. It is true that his analysis of "Being" and of the contradictions involved in man's "existence" is deeply influenced by non-Christian philosophers from Parmenides to the existentialists. But at crucial points it also shows the influence of his Christian faith. Again, his Christian faith manifests itself in the way the "questions" implied by the philosophical analysis are stated. For example, in reason the conflict between "autonomy" and "heteronomy" leads to the "question" of "theonomy," he says, and the "anxiety" due to the finitude of existence leads to the "question" of "God" as the ground of meaning and courage. Naturalistic philosophers, in contrast, can see nothing wrong with the "autonomy" of reason, and cannot understand why the "anxiety" of finite man should cause him to seek an "escape from reality" in religious faith.

Tillich might admit that in fact only a philosopher influenced by the Christian tradition would be likely to think as he does on these matters, but he might also insist that he would cease to be a philosopher if he tried to be "intentionally" Christian in his thinking. But unless it is supposed that the Christian faith must distort rather than clarify man's vision of reality, it is difficult to see why. Clearly,

Tillich does not suppose this. On his view reason needs "salvation" from its inner conflicts, and it is "saved" and "fulfilled" rather than destroyed by the final revelation in Christ. Moreover, he asserts that no philosophy which is obedient to the universal *logos* can contradict the concrete *logos*, the Logos who became flesh. If so, may we not also say that "no philosophy which has been developed from a basis of faith in the concrete *logos* can contradict the universal *logos*"? Thus if the revelation in Christ "saves" and "fulfills" the reason and if Christ is a manifestation of the "universal *logos*," it is difficult to see why a philosophy based upon faith in Christ should distort the vision of reality.

Therefore if a "Christian philosopher" is not one who merely rationalizes dogmas accepted on authority, but one who tries to look at the structure of being from the perspective of the Christian faith, Tillich is primarily a "Christian philosopher," and there is no reason why he should not "intentionally" be one. Of course, he is a "Christian philosopher" primarily in the first half of each part of his book, that is, where he analyzes the existential "situation" and develops the "questions" implied in it. In the second half of each part he is a "Christian theologian." Is it not because his analysis of the "situation" *is* largely that of a Christian *philosopher* that his "answer" as a Christian *theologian* is relevant to it? Thus the fruitfulness of the "method of correlation" depends upon the enlightenment of the philosophical reason by the Christian faith. If this enlightenment has not come to a philosopher, his analysis of the human situation will lead him to raise questions quite different from those which can be answered by the Christian message. The "final revelation" in Christ not only provides us with the "answers" but also makes us aware of our real situation and of the "questions" we ought to ask.

In short, the main difficulty with Tillich's "method of correlation" and with the "structure" based upon it is that he seems to allow to philosophy in its analysis of the human situation an "autonomy" which is not rooted in "theonomy." Only the "theonomous," the "saved" reason, according to his own view, can be expected to see the truth of the situation clearly and profoundly. Only such a reason can properly formulate the "questions" to which the Christian message gives the "answers." This would not be very important if the possibility of a "Christian philosophy" were the only issue at stake. But another issue is involved: Can a philosophical reason which has not been fully "converted" by the Christian faith correctly formulate the "structure" and "categories" of Being and raise the deepest "questions" implied in existence? If not, will not the Christian "answers," whose form is determined by the nature of the "questions," be distorted or obscured?

It is beyond the scope of this essay to consider whether, in applying his method, Tillich himself has given a correct analysis of the "situation," raised the right "questions," and presented the "answers" in the most adequate way. These matters have to do with the content rather than with the method and structure of his theology. But I must at least express a doubt as to whether he has always escaped the danger mentioned in the preceding paragraph. I shall give only one example. "God," says Tillich, "is the answer to the question implied in being," a question which arises in "the shock of possible non-being" (163). This is the "question" raised by philosophy. What is the "answer" given by theology? "The being of God is being-itself," says Tillich. "The being of God cannot be understood as the existence of a being alongside others or above others. If God is *a* being, he is subject to the categories of finitude, especially to space and substance. Even if he is called the 'highest being' in the sense of the 'most perfect' and the 'most powerful' being, the situation is not changed" (235). Several inferences are drawn from this. For example, he states that the question of the existence of God can be neither asked nor answered, for God is "above existence." Again, while "man cannot be ultimately concerned about anything that is less than personal," to speak of a "personal God" means only that God is the ground of everything personal and that he carries within himself the ontological power of personality. He is not a person, but he is not less than personal.

It seems to me that in the Christian message, "God" means "*a* being," not "being-itself." He is, of course, not a being "alongside" others, but He *is* a being "above others." Therefore "existence" *can* be predicated of Him, though not the contingent finite existence of His creatures. He is a concrete individual, though an individual without the limits of finite individuals. He is not merely "the ground of everything personal"; He *is* personal Himself. If this is the Christian view, I wonder whether Tillich's statement of it has not been weakened at points by the intrusion into his thinking of an impersonal philosophy alien to the spirit of Christianity.

Despite this doubt, as well as the other difficulties raised in this essay, I strongly suspect that his two-volume work will be regarded as the greatest systematic theology from the apologetic point of view in our generation.

GEORGE F. THOMAS

DEPARTMENT OF RELIGION
PRINCETON UNIVERSITY
PRINCETON, NEW JERSEY

6

David E. Roberts
TILLICH'S DOCTRINE OF MAN

TILLICH'S DOCTRINE OF MAN

I. THE PLACE OF THE DOCTRINE IN TILLICH'S SYSTEM

The doctrine of man is clearly central in Paul Tillich's theology. Each of the five parts of his system begins with an analysis of human existence (and existence generally) as the basis for developing a theological question. Taken together, these passages constitute an integral interpretation covering (1) human rationality, (2) human finitude, (3) human sin, (4) man's living unity, and (5) human destiny. The content of the five corresponding answers —Revelation, God, Christ, the Holy Spirit, and the Kingdom of God—cannot be derived from the questions, but their form is conditioned by the fact that they must be relevant to the manner in which the questions are being asked. Thus this essay has to scrutinize one segment of Tillich's thought, while depending upon the rest of the volume to fill in the total setting. The chief justification for such a procedure—apart from limitations of space—is that the view of man we shall examine underlies all Tillich's writings, not only his *Systematic Theology*. A clear understanding of it is an indispensable precondition for grasping what he has to say about political, cultural, psychological, and ethical problems.

II. A COMBINATION OF OBJECTIVE AND EXISTENTIAL THINKING

Is this view one which any thinking person would have to arrive at, quite apart from Christian revelation? No. Then are the dice loaded? Is man being induced to ask questions about himself in such a way that only Christian revelation can provide adequate answers? Tillich's reply is that everyone, at least implicitly, has a doctrine of man which incorporates theological questions and ultimate concern about the answers. No one can avoid viewing himself in the light of whatever answers may come to him. Hence no one can arrive at an interpretation of man that is both neutral and complete simultaneously. An anthropology can incorporate neutral findings, such as those provided by the sciences and philosophy; but if it is limited to such findings it is incomplete because existential concern has been excluded.

Thus his own interpretation, in each of its five sections, combines neutral and existential factors. The former have to do with the structure of being, and reason is the final judge as to the adequacy of this part of the analysis. The latter have to do with the meaning of being *for us,* and the questions which arise in this connection involve unconditional concern. This position is obviously open to attack from two sides. First, from those who believe that it is possible and proper to construct a wholly objective interpretation of man, and who feel that its validity is undermined as soon as personal religious commitment is allowed to influence it. Secondly, from those who hold that a Christian interpretation of man should be developed exclusively on the basis of revelation, without introducing concepts derived from philosophy or the sciences.

III. THE LIMITATIONS OF OBJECTIVITY

So far as the first criticism is concerned, Tillich acknowledges, of course, that the sciences and philosophy can study man objectively—including his religious commitments. Nor does he wish to put any restrictions upon what they may discover by means of their chosen methods. The limitation to which he calls attention is intrinsic to these methods themselves. They avowedly aim at a kind of detachment which will not be swayed by personal, social, and historical conditions; and the value of their findings is directly connected with the extent to which they succeed in maintaining such a perspective. But they are therefore different from that self-knowledge which comes to man only from within personal concern, its passions, fears and loves. That man is thus concerned about the structure, meaning, and aim of his life is a fact—an empirical fact, if you like. But to try to note it from the outside, simply as an item of information, is to fail to deal with it as it is. Such concern is a datum of human experience; but the datum cannot be viewed without distortion unless its self-transcending character is taken seriously. Objectivity is a virtue in the sciences (which deal with things) and in philosophy (which deals with rational principles); but it becomes a question-begging vice, which excludes in advance the only appropriate way of dealing with a crucial portion of the evidence, when one discusses personality and interpersonal relationships. Objective methods demand that one keep oneself out of the picture; but theological questions are of such a nature that they place the self and the meaning of life directly at stake.

The neutral side of Tillich's anthropology leaves his system open to receive objective findings as they are discovered. He resists the sciences and philosophy only at the point where these disciplines cease to remain themselves and become cryptotheological in the process of attempting to exclude theology. Nevertheless, his system is not completely open because it is committed to the assumption that the content of Christian revelation genuinely answers the questions which man asks *qua* human being; it genuinely answers the ultimate concern which underlies *all* the religious and cultural questing of the race—past, present and future.

A completely open approach involves assuming that human religious experience is the only possible source and content of theology. This in turn presupposes that man is undistortedly united with, or even identical with, the divine; the divine comes to fruition as the religious consciousness of man. Against such a point of view Tillich seeks to show that existential distortion (sin) has so broken the affinity between the human and the divine, that revelation comes *to* man and, in part, *against* him, instead of *from* him. The issue can thus be stated quite succinctly. In the one case true answers to religious questions are produced by human experience; in the other case they are given to human experience. But this issue cannot be settled by an appeal to open experience. For one thing, the former alternative is by no means presuppositionless; it represents a definite decision. Furthermore, the question cannot be handled merely by an appeal to future results; for unless one has some criterion for judging fresh experience, it is impossible to know how the future has turned out, once it has arrived. There must be an interplay between structural norms (ontological, anthropological, and theological) and fresh experience; and concerning the former, everyone must take a stand somewhere. The organizing center for an interpretation may be "the democratic process" or "the creative potentialities of man"; but no matter what center is chosen, it cannot be objectively demonstrated—partly because it is the expression of ultimate concern, and partly because all value-arguments presuppose its acknowledgment before they can have any point. Tillich's view of Christian revelation takes a stand upon something that is in this sense indemonstrable, but it is not antirational; and in so far as his doctrine of man does justice to existential concern there is good ground for holding that it is less arbitrary and more complete than theories which purport to be purely objective. Moreover, as we shall see, the neutral side of his interpretation, as well as the existential side, is implicated in his rejection of indiscriminate "openness." He holds that the structural characteristics of human nature are universal.

Perhaps it might be urged, however, that a naturalistic interpretation can be developed without equating the human religious consciousness with the divine. Here man gives himself the only bona fide answers, not merely theoretically, but by means of ethical activity, through his interrelationship with Nature (instead of God). The structures and processes on which he bases his answers "transcend" him in the epistemological sense of being objective to him, but not in the axiological sense of being superior to him. Tillich's approach to such an issue suggests that the reaching of bona fide answers involves the overcoming not merely of intellectual errors, but of inner conflicts. Human existence is meaningful in an ultimate, instead of a provisional, sense only in so far as one can live in the truth instead of merely knowing about it. What enables man ever to move toward such integration? It cannot be simply the empirical self. At this point naturalistic writers usually speak of latent human potentialities. But these potentialities are not ungrounded. If we cite an interrelationship between man and certain potentialities in Nature, then this interrelationship *is* axiologically superior to what the empirical self has succeeded in actualizing at any point up to that of perfect integration. Thus the creative forces are supraindividual, though they work in and through the individual. It is very dangerous to equate them with social or group forces inasmuch as no individual can reach maturity and autonomy if he derives the meaning of his existence exclusively from social processes; under some circumstances he reaches his own highest development only by resisting such processes. The "natural and human potentialities" turn out to be the basis on which one seeks to correct psychological and social maladjustments and to remove individual and group illusions. But the concept remains defective until something is done to answer the question, "potentialities of or for what?" And, in any event, the concept is functionally equivalent to "the divine." In so far as one claims to have reached bona fide answers on such a basis, is it not accurate to say that they have been given to him at least as much as he has given them to himself? And is it not true that the more seriously one sees the need for drastic changes in the psychological and social conditions the human race confronts, the more he needs some means of expressing the fact that man is, in important respects, estranged from an essential goodness which can be thought of as potentially his only because it transcends as well as includes him?

At a time when some forward-looking psychologists, anthropologists, and sociologists are seeking to move toward a unified interpretation of man (which in the end will have to include ethical and metaphysical problems), Tillich's approach takes on special importance. For he is closely in touch with these efforts and sympathetic toward them. Therefore he is in a favorable position to answer those who assume that they can develop an adequate doctrine of man without considering theological questions (except for purposes of phenomenological description or empirical research).

IV. THE LIMITATIONS OF "REVELATION ALONE"

Now let us examine his reply to the second criticism, which holds that a Christian interpretation of man should be developed exclusively on the basis of revelation. It is that the theologian cannot avoid ontological questions about man, and that he therefore cannot afford to ignore the light which objective findings can throw upon these questions. He agrees that the norm of systematic theology is given to the Church at that point where it is confronted by revelation; it is not produced by reflection of any kind, philosophical or theological, and it is given as a reality (the New Being, the picture of Jesus as the Christ) instead of as an ideal or as a concept. But Tillich explicitly parts company with Karl Barth by admitting that God's self-manifestation is dependent upon the way man receives this manifestation. This means that the reception of revelation is conditioned by human existence; and we are in no position to construct a doctrine of revelation-in-itself apart from reception of it. The only way to avoid such an acknowledgment is to insist that what receives revelation is something present to human existence but not in human existence. Some may interpret this as meaning that the connection between revelation and human existence is dialectical; but for Tillich it means that no connection has been established, and that such a theology is moving in a Docetic-Monophysite direction. For him the dialectic is encountered where question (human existence) and answer (revelation) meet. The fact that man *can* ask about this unity shows that the link between essential human goodness and God has not been completely destroyed. The fact that man *must* ask about it shows that he is estranged from such unity. Theology is dialectical because it is caught in the conflict between essence and existence. If there were no conflict, man would already be in the Kingdom of God instead of in history. But if the essential goodness of man were totally destroyed, then the conflict would be totally insoluble, for there would be no basis in human nature for a recovery of unity between reason and revelation, the finite and the infinite.

V. THE CONTRAST BETWEEN TILLICH AND THOMISM

Tillich's rejection of the Thomist solution, which in a sense stands between the two opposed camps just discussed, can be indicated quite briefly. Where he regards the positive link between the divine and the human as furnishing the possibilities for a *correlation between questions and answers,* Thomism tries to regard it as furnishing a basis for *two sets of answers*—natural and revealed theology. Tillich denies (*a*) that natural theology can furnish answers, and (*b*) that the answers of revelation are supernatural truths.

VI. RELATIONS BETWEEN PHILOSOPHY AND THEOLOGY

After this glimpse of how his doctrine of man stands in relation to its chief contemporary competitors, let us ask how he goes about combining the neutral and the existential ingredients which are blended in all five sections. The possibility of this combination rests upon the possibility of a general combination between philosophy and theology. We cannot take time to comment upon his insistence, against logical positivism and other antimetaphysical tendencies, that philosophy's main task is ontological. For our purposes, the most important point is that his definitions make an existential philosophy a contradiction in terms. Philosophy seeks a universal connection between objective and subjective reason in such a way that this connection can be viewed generally and dispassionately, not personally. The Christian theologian, on the other hand, is interested in the Logos not merely as universal, but as "become flesh"; and his relationship to revelation is that of personal commitment. Even when the two disciplines use the same categories, the contents of philosophy are cosmological while the contents of theology are soteriological. But the two converge because no philosopher can really jump out of the concreteness of his existence or permanently detach himself from unconditional concern. Every creative philosopher is implicitly a theologian. On the other hand, the theologian must be capable of some detachment; he must be critical of every particular expression of his ultimate concern; he must take the risk of being driven beyond the boundary line of his Church and his faith. Tillich concludes from all this that while conflict between the two disciplines always reflects some sort of mistake, synthesis between them is impossible. Instead, he incorporates the philosophical element into the "question" side of his system which can be correlated, but not synthesized, with revelation.

Yet if a theologian can incorporate the philosophical element, it is difficult to see why a philosopher cannot incorporate personal concern into his reflection, while remaining a philosopher. Indeed, why should the "pure philosopher" be condemned to the fruitless attempt to hold his personal commitment at arm's length—beyond those transitional and quite legitimate purposes of careful analysis and criticism which the theologian can share with him? How can something incompatible with his creativity (namely, successful avoidance of becoming a theologian) be an essential part of the philosopher's intention? Tillich's distinctions at this point are unfortunate because some of the contemporary attempts to show that metaphysics cannot reach its own fruition except by including an existential element are among the most promising developments in recent philosophy. As Marcel and Jaspers have seen, metaphysics never should have been conceived as a purely speculative and demonstrative discipline. By introducing dramatic categories, imaginative symbols, and historical concreteness into its modes of expression it comes closer to doing justice to the structure of Being than the kind of metaphysics which seeks to exclude human inwardness. As these same writers have also seen, an existentialist metaphysics—partly because it seeks to approach mystery instead of to dispel it—is in a better position to acknowledge the possibility of revelation than is a speculative outlook, though of course it does not necessarily lead to the acceptance of any specific claims to revelation.

Because Tillich makes his own approach to ontology by way of anthropology, and since he has so many other affinities with writers like those just mentioned, he cannot really intend to rule out the possibility of existential philosophy, as his definitions seem to imply.

VII. THE SELF-WORLD CORRELATION

The basic starting point, in Tillich's thought, both for anthropology and for ontology, is man's awareness of the self-world correlation. Man is directly aware of the structures which make cognition possible because he lives in them and acts through them. And if it is true that man incorporates in himself all levels of being, then through self-knowledge he may at the same time reach ontological knowledge. On the other hand, the attempt to regard nature as basic, and to derive an interpretation of man from it, is unsatisfactory. It has to start with objects and processes which man knows indirectly, and although recent naturalism has abandoned reductive mechanism, it cannot overcome the defects which result when selfhood, freedom, and finitude are treated as though they were objects. Science can get along quite well without taking into account the fact that self-relatedness is implied in every experience; but philosophical anthropology cannot. The latter must begin with self-relatedness as logically preceding all questions concerning what may or may not exist. Nevertheless, from Tillich's standpoint this does not involve a radical dualism between man and nature. Individuality in subhuman nature manifests something analogous to "self-centeredness"; and human selfhood includes biological and unconscious aspects which mark man's continuity with nature.

Being a self means that man is both over against the world, as a subject, and in the world, as an object. He is so separated from everything as to be able to look at it and act upon it; he so belongs to the world that he is an episode in the process. But each factor determines the other. It is wrong to assume that the environment wholly explains behavior; for this assumption cannot account for the way in which special characteristics in the surroundings are selectively organized. Moreover, because of self-consciousness man transcends every possible spatiotemporal environment. His "world" cannot be thought of simply as an aggregate containing everything that exists; it is an organized structure, and the organizing reflects the self. In short, the self-world correlation includes not only the environment in which man lives, but the universal norms and ideas by means of which man apprehends and interprets. Every content, psychic as well as bodily, is within the world; otherwise the self would be an empty form. But man is so differentiated from the world that he can look at it as an organized whole; otherwise he would be completely immersed in the flux.

This starting-point avoids the notorious pitfalls involved in trying to generate the world from the *ego*, or the *ego* from the world; it also avoids the dilemma of Cartesian dualism which has to try to unite an empty *res cogitans* with a mechanistically conceived *res extensa*. In so far as it is thought about, everything (including even God) is an object; but in so far as everything involves individual self-relatedness, nothing (not even an atom) is *merely* an object. This is not identity philosophy, however, because its point of departure is a relation instead of an identity, and the ground of the self-world correlation cannot be furnished by reason.

VIII. INDIVIDUALIZATION AND PARTICIPATION

Man, so conceived, is continuous with nature; for individualization characterizes everything that exists. But he is also discontinuous with nature, for in him alone does individualization reach the level of "personality," and participation reach the level of "communion." Furthermore, he alone consciously participates in the rational structure of reality. It is clear from the foregoing that Tillich is not interested in slanting such statements either in an idealistic or in a naturalistic direction. But it is especially important to recognize that he does not regard them as deriving from empirical observation concerning contingent facts. Rather, he conceives of individualization and participation as ontological elements which, in the course of a critical analysis of experience, reveal themselves to be a priori in the sense that experience could not be what it is unless it occurred within them. The reciprocal relationship between "personal" and "communal"—for example, one cannot become fully a self except in relation with other selves—is a structural characteristic of *being*. The polarity between individualization and participation also solves the problem of nominalism and realism. Against the former it affirms that the knower participates in what is knowable, instead of being merely externally related to it; against the latter it refuses to regard individualization as somehow unreal as compared with universals.

IX. VITALITY AND INTENTIONALITY

Another polarity, that of dynamics and form, appears in man as vitality and intentionality. Vitality must here be conceived as connected with potentiality in nature generally. "Potentiality," in this sense, is not an existing something, such as "will" or "the unconscious"; it is rather the *power* of being. By "intentionality," on the other hand, Tillich does not necessarily mean consciously conceived purpose; but he does mean structures that can be grasped as universals. In other words, when vitality becomes human it cannot be thought of as operating by necessity, or chaotically, or without reference to objective structures.

The inclusion of dynamism within the ontological structure of human nature is Tillich's answer to those who eschew all talk about human "nature" because it connotes to them something static. He willingly admits that human nature changes in history, but he insists that one structural characteristic underlies all these changes; namely, "being one who has a history." Man has emerged from animals who had no history (in the strict sense); and he may be followed by beings who have no history; but this simply means that neither animals nor supermen fall within the doctrine of man. Change is just as real as structure; but it is absurd to regard the latter as process, because this would mean that there could be no continuity, within the life of a man, between antecedent and subsequent conditions. Consequently, man can develop indefinitely beyond any given physical and biological situation, transforming both nature and himself through applied science and cultural growth; but he cannot slough off the structure which makes intentionality and historicity possible.

X. FREEDOM AND DESTINY

The foregoing considerations prepare the ground for discussing freedom and destiny. The problem of freedom is often posed in terms of mechanistic determinism versus indeterminism. But Tillich asserts that neither of these theories does justice to the way in which man grasps his own ontological structure. Both of them treat the will as though it were a thing, and then disagree about whether it possesses a certain quality; namely, freedom. So long as the problem is posed in this manner, determinism always wins; by definition, a thing is completely determined. Thus indeterminism, in a blundering attempt to defend man's moral and cognitive capacities, is forced to postulate decision without motivation; for at the level of things a break in the causal nexus can occur only as something uncaused. Needless to say, when the indeterminist holds out for the latter his defense of man's moral and cognitive capacities is not convincing; for he rests his case upon the occurrence of unintelligible accident, which is at the opposite pole from the "responsibility" he is trying to characterize. However, both theories fall into contradiction when they claim to be true, for the grasping of truth presupposes an intelligible decision against the false as a possibility. Mechanistic determinism cannot make room for decision, and indeterminism cannot make room for intelligibility.

Freedom should be approached, therefore, not as the quality of a faculty (the will), but as an element in man's ontological structure. This means that every function which plays a part in constituting man as personal also participates in his freedom. When given segments are naturally or experimentally dissociated from the personal center, they operate automatically; but the determinacy of such segments, viewed in isolation, does not justify regarding the self as a whole as necessitated. It is possible to understand particular mechanisms in the light of the freedom of the self; but the converse is not possible. Since there is no such thing as a motive in abstraction from a person who weighs the motives, it is a tautology to say that the stronger motive always prevails. Only the person accounts for what gives a particular motive its strength. Similarly, the person cannot be equated with a certain aggregate of possibilities, for such an equation leaves out of account the decision which man brings to bear upon possibilities in the course of actualizing some and shutting off others. Hence the self is responsible in so far as its acts are determined, not by something external or by some dissociated segment or function, but by the centered totality of the person's being.

Freedom, as thus defined, goes hand in hand with destiny. The concrete self out of which decisions arise must not be thought of merely as a center of self-consciousness. Decisions issue from a self which has been formed by nature and history; the self includes bodily structure, psychic strivings, moral and spiritual character, communal relations, past experiences (both remembered and forgotten), and the total impact of the environment. Yet having a destiny does not contradict freedom, as "fate" does, because persons can realize their destinies. If man were subject to fate, there would be no point in talking about accepting or rejecting it, inasmuch as the *alternative* would disappear.

The polarity between freedom and destiny distinguishes man from all other levels of existence, yet this distinction arises within continuity. Analogies to freedom and destiny are discoverable even at the inorganic level where we speak of the contrast between spontaneity and natural law; both terms are derived from human experience and then applied to physical events, and both remain indispensable. Empirical science cannot eradicate the former term, because although inductive generalizations can reach very high probability, they can never reach "certainty" in the sense of strict necessity; the latter can be attained only in mathematical formulae and forms of a priori thinking where the propositions involved are not empirical.

XI. FINITUDE

The core of Tillich's doctrine of man is his concept of finite freedom. Having examined his definition of freedom, we must now discuss what he means by finitude. This brings up one of the most difficult aspects of his thought, namely, the problem of nonbeing. He agrees with Heidegger that the logical act of negating presupposes an ontological basis. Man can make particular judgments, noting that something is not real, or does not occur, only because he is already aware of the distinction between being and nonbeing. This means that he views beings in light of the fact that they might not be. He can ask why there is something instead of nothing. He participates in nonbeing as well as in being.

The problem cannot be solved simply by excluding nonbeing. For, as Parmenides' efforts show, this means that not only "nothing," but also the totality of finite existence, is excluded, leaving only static Being. On the other hand, to accord nonbeing some sort of metaphysical status seems equally contradictory; it seems to treat as positive that which is by definition negative. Even if the only power accorded to nonbeing is that of resisting being, an ultimate dualism results if the two principles are regarded as co-eternal. The Christian doctrine of *creatio ex nihilo* attempts to solve the problem by denying that there is a second principle co-eternal with God; but it affirms that there is an element of nonbeing in all finite existence. Tillich denies that when Augustine attributes sin to nonbeing he is following a purely privative theory; rather, Augustine is asserting that although sin has no positive ontological status it nevertheless *actively* resists and perverts being. Indeed, since anything created originates out of nothing, it must return to nothing. This is why any view which regards the Son as a creature (Arianism) had to be rejected by the Church on the ground that a creature cannot bring eternal life. And this is why Christianity rejects the doctrine of natural immortality in favor of the belief that eternal life is given by God alone.

Finitude involves a mixture of being and nonbeing; but if dualism is to be avoided, Tillich suggests, then negativity, which accounts for evil and sin, must somehow be posited in God Himself, that is, God both posits and negates everything finite. He cites several past and present attempts to follow out this line of thought —in Böhme, Schelling, and Berdyaev, for example. And if this essay were primarily concerned with his doctrine of God, it would be necessary to ask whether a dualism which is made internal to God is any less baffling than one which regards evil as external to God. For our purposes, however, it is sufficient to note that man, although finite, looks at his own finitude in a way which transcends it. In grasping his life as a whole as moving toward death, he transcends temporal immediacy. He sees his world in the setting of potential infinity, his participation in the setting of potential universality, his destiny in the setting of potential all-inclusiveness. This power of transcending makes man aware of his own finitude, and at the same time marks him as belonging to Being itself. The latter kinship is shown by the fact that man is never satisfied with any stage of his development; nothing finite can hold him.

XII. ANXIETY

Finitude is the ontological basis of human anxiety. Tillich uses the latter term in this connection, to refer to *Urangst*. As such it must be distinguished, of course, from fear, which is directed toward definite objects and can be overcome by action. It must also be distinguished from neurotic anxiety—which, like *Urangst*, may be independent of any special objects or occasions ("free floating") —but which can be removed psychotherapeutically by the resolution of inner conflicts. Like Kierkegaard and Heidegger, Tillich regards *Urangst* as directed toward "nothingness." Though ineradicable, it can be accepted and used creatively as a part of what it means to be human.

XIII. THE CATEGORIES: TIME, SPACE, CAUSALITY, SUBSTANCE

One of the most illuminating portions of Tillich's system is his analysis of the traditional categories—time, space, causality, and substance—in the light of human finitude. Externally regarded, these categories express the union of being and nonbeing. Internally regarded, they express the union of anxiety and courage. The latter aspect of the interpretation must not be misunderstood as psychological. In accordance with the self-world correlation, the subjective side of the analysis is just as much a piece of ontology as is the objective.

The discussion of each category leads to an antinomy where a decision concerning the meaning involved cannot be derived from an analysis of the category itself. This method has obvious similarities to Kant's, and it leads to a point at which, since metaphysics cannot solve the problem, an existential attitude (positive or negative) is unavoidable.

On the negative side time vanishes by analysis into the present as a geometrical point moving from a nonexistent past to a nonexistent future. On the positive side the temporal process is creative, brings forth novelty and has an irreversible direction. Yet neither side of the analysis is entirely satisfactory. Time cannot be illusory because only if the present is real can past and future be linked together. But neither is it simply creative, inasmuch as it carries all things toward disintegration and obliteration.

To this objective antinomy there corresponds an inward polarity between anxiety and courage. Temporality means, for man, the anxiety of having to die; this hangs over every moment and characterizes the whole of human existence. Yet anxiety of this sort comes from the structure of being and is not due to sin. Since it accompanies finitude, it is actual in "Adam before the Fall" and in the (sinless) Christ. The anxieties due to sin are, in principle, remediable; but as we have already seen, the anxiety of finitude is ineradicable. It is balanced, however, by a courage which affirms temporality; and this power to find meaning in the present is just as ontological as its opposite. Indeed, man is the most courageous of all creatures precisely because he has to come to terms with full-blown anxiety. But our analysis cannot, by itself, tell us what is the foundation for this courage.

Before going on to a discussion of the other categories, it may be well to call attention to a crucial turning point in Tillich's argument. He and Heidegger travel side by side, so far as the main aspects of an anthropological approach to ontology go. Yet when it comes to the relationship between Being and nonbeing, they occupy opposite positions. For Heidegger the ultimate "object" of metaphysics can be characterized as "Being coming from nothing." Tillich, on the other hand, concludes that all finite being, including the negativity which makes it finite, is grounded in Being. The question naturally arises as to how such an issue is to be adjudicated. From Tillich's standpoint only revelation can answer the problem. Yet it is worth asking whether he believes that there are purely philosophical considerations which drive the ontological analysis of human nature toward Christian instead of atheistic conclusions.

The treatment of the other categories follows the lines already laid down in connection with time. Space is interpreted, on the positive side, in terms of the fact that every being strives to maintain a "place" for itself; for man this includes a home, a city, a country, his world. Viewed socially, it also means a vocation, a sphere of influence, a position in one's epoch. These needs are aspects of created goodness and are not intrinsically guilty. But on the negative side it must be observed that no place is definitely one's own; every place must finally be lost, and with it, being itself. This means insecurity which goes hand in hand with finitude, and cannot be eradicated even through faith in God.

The affirmative interpretation of causality points to the power from which things proceed, the power which can produce and maintain realities despite the resistance of nonbeing. The negative interpretation notes, however, that finite things do not possess their own power of coming into being; they are "thrown" into existence; and infinite regress cannot be avoided if God is conceived as *a* being. In other words, the contingency of the world points more directly to the fact that finite existences can lapse into nonbeing than it does to any traditional form of theism. For our purposes the most important point is that human anxiety is here associated with lack of aseity (the self-sufficiency possessed by God alone). We should also note that Tillich's discussion of causality supports the thesis that human existence is not necessitated. If the latter were the case, man would be incapable of anxiety, and he could not ask questions based upon awareness of the fact that he "might not" be. So far as the present category is concerned, the answer to anxiety means a kind of courage which achieves self-reliance despite the inescapable facts of contingency and dependence.

The category of substance, in its connection with human nature, has to do mainly with self-identity; but Tillich is very far from trying to revive a Platonic theory of the soul. The structural factors, he stresses, endure through process, not apart from process. Therefore all change threatens the ground on which one stands, and the radical change from life to death threatens an ultimate loss of self-identity. We cannot solve the problem by trying to attribute permanence to a creative work, a love relationship, and the like. Courage can match anxiety only by being able to affirm the significance of the finite despite the fact that it *can* lose its substance.

XIV. THE CONTEMPORARY RELEVANCE OF TILLICH'S ANALYSIS

Thus all four categories express the union of being (the positive) and nonbeing (the negative) in everything finite. But the ontological analysis cannot answer the question as to how courage is possible in the face of ineradicable anxiety. The answer to this question is furnished by revelation and by the existential decision which enters into faith in God. But quite apart from the theological answer, it can be said that Tillich's analysis throws light upon contemporary unbelief. The cheery forms of secularism turn out to be—to put it quite bluntly—escapist. If their scrutiny of the human situation were more penetrating, the cheeriness would vanish. In the second place, nihilistic forms of secularism either have no answer at all, or an arbitrary one. This leaves a third alternative; namely, those positions which are quite penetrating and realistic in their understanding of the human situation, including anxiety and conflict, but which are able to find grounds for a sober, restrained sort of courage through their acquaintance with man's own potentialities for rational, emotional, and moral growth. Tillich's attitude toward this third alternative, I take it, would be to accept in large measure what it affirms, but to point out that the human potentialities to which it refers cannot be ungrounded. A further scrutiny of this problem of the ground (Being versus nonbeing) would then drive either toward the second alternative or toward something like Tillich's version of the Christian answer. His system as a whole thus addresses a powerful appeal to those thinkers who have come to rest in stoic courage as more honest, more intellectually acceptable, than any form of Christian belief. He incorporates many of their emphases in his own doctrine of man, and then shows that intellectual integrity—instead of compelling one to stop there—will not permit one to stop there.

XV. THE DISRUPTION OF HUMAN EXISTENCE

We have now seen how anxiety is rooted in finitude. The notion that *Urangst* is an aspect of the "good creation" may strike some readers as paradoxical; but the next step is even more so. For the polarity of the ontological elements provides a basis for the possibility, though not the necessity, of an even more serious form of trouble. The anxiety of losing one or another of these polar elements, and hence of losing the balance which makes us essentially what we are, is different from the *Urangst* which accompanies finitude. It is the anxiety of existential disruption—of estrangement from one's "true" self.

For example, in the polarity between individualization and participation, excessive self-centeredness (Kierkegaard says "shutupness") produces the threat of loneliness, while excessive participation produces the threat of complete collectivization. Man oscillates between solitude and submergence in the mass, and either extreme can drive him toward the other. Again, so far as dynamics and form are concerned, every stabilized pattern is a threat to vitality, and vitality can always threaten to lead to chaos.

Likewise the balance between freedom and destiny can be upset by trying to preserve the former by defying the latter, or by trying to fit in with the latter by surrendering the former. Indeed, a free decision can be "right" only if it is taken in unity with a man's destiny, and yet neither his knowledge nor his will can give adequate assurance on the latter score. Many of the compulsive efforts by which men think they are mastering themselves, life and destiny, actualize only a fragment of the individual's true *telos;* they reject important aspects of his creativity and leave him frustrated by large gaps of unlived life. As we have seen, mechanism and indeterminism cannot deal with this problem. No one actually regards a man (who is in any sense normal) as either an automaton in which calculable effects follow from calculable causes, or as a mere locus of contingent happenings. Man is an agent capable of decision, but set in the context of destiny. When the latter comes to be regarded as meaningless fate, one reaction (Sartre's) is to try to make freedom itself the absolute. But the attempt of a finite being to make his freedom absolute turns into an arbitrariness which in fact enslaves him to biological and psychological necessities. When the balance is destroyed, the quest for aseity leads to its opposite.

Because Being is essentially related to nonbeing, disruption is always possible. But how is the transition made from this possibility to an actuality in human life which is universal, and yet neither accidental nor necessary? Tillich's answer is that the transition is mediated by freedom. This transition must not be thought of in temporal terms. What it means is that within *any* historical situation the distinction between essence and existence is already given, and an analysis of it must take into account both man's positive relationship to essence and his estrangement from it. Both factors are at least implicit wherever distinctions between truth and error, good and evil, ideal and actual, are made. Indeed, the presence of both factors is reflected in the ambiguity of the term "essence" itself; for it can mean either (*a*) the "universal" or "nature" in which a thing participates, or (*b*) the normative or "true" nature from which a thing falls short. The first meaning expresses the fact that existence receives its power from essence (its *ousia* makes a thing what it is). The second meaning expresses the fact that existence embodies essence in an imperfect manner. Theories which equate the good with essence alone make existence unaccountable. Theories which equate the good with existence alone fall into an indiscriminate acceptance which abandons norms. Christian theology tries to solve the problem by making a distinction between the "good creation" and the world as it is. So far as man is concerned, this means that he is created good and "spoiled" through his own freedom; but the transition is not temporal. Both the goodness of creation and the universality of sin characterize human history as a whole, and each individual life within it.

XVI. FINITUDE AND SIN

Destructive conflict and tragedy in human life come from sin, not from finitude; yet it is finitude that makes sin possible. This is the point at which the doctrine of Creation and the doctrine of the

Fall join; and this is the point at which one must either accept Tillich's account as doing justice to the mystery of human existence, or reject it as unintelligible. From one standpoint the distinction he draws between finitude and sin seems to be extremely precarious; for the actualization of finite freedom involves differentiation from the creative ground of the divine life, and yet this differentiation at the same time means an existence which is no longer united with essence. Is this not tantamount to saying that the actualization of finite freedom makes sin not merely universal but inevitable? Yet even if the answer to this question must be in the affirmative, it is important to remember that since we are talking about man's freedom and destiny, the category of *necessity* is inapplicable. Sin is inevitable because of what I am, but it is not a fate which operates irrespective of the rôle played by my freedom.

How can God be the ground both of essence and of existence, both of Creation and of the Fall, without being caught in the conflicts these pairs connote? How can God be the eternal process in which separation is posited and is overcome by reunion, without there being any distinction in Him between potentiality and actuality? These questions fall outside our purview, yet the adequacy of his doctrine of man depends on Tillich's answers to them. Even within the confines of this one doctrine, many readers will be baffled by the idea that the actualization of finite freedom is, from one point of view, the *telos* of creation, and from another point of view the ruination of creation. Yet some such way of describing the grandeur and the misery of man seems more faithful to our actual situation than formulae which abide by logical niceties. In terms of the story of creation, Tillich is saying, first, that unless man goes beyond innocence (potentiality) he cannot mature as a responsible person; and secondly, that there is no way of leaving innocence without entering into the sphere of conflicts and of moral distinctions where one becomes sinful and guilty.

The transition from essence to existence covers both collective and individual aspects. If stress were to fall exclusively upon the former, then the Fall would be equivalent to a sort of cosmic fate which disregards individual responsibility. On the other hand, if the individual is thought of as wholly responsible for his becoming guilty, then personal freedom has been artificially lifted out of its context within natural and social forces and within the universality of sin.

XVII. A THEOLOGICAL BASIS FOR DIAGNOSIS

Sin disrupts essential unity between man and God. It is the attempt to center life, power, and meaning in one's own finite self. It is the attempt to reach aseity, absolute self-sufficiency. Man can make this attempt because he is created in the image of God. But he cannot succeed because it involves rejection of his own finitude. Thus it gives rise to unlimited striving and desire for which there is no ceiling, and which lead to endless dissatisfaction. When Tillich introduces the term "concupiscence" at this point, one must remember that he is using it ontologically instead of referring exclusively to sensuality and its psychological concomitants. Nevertheless, many of the disorders treated by contemporary psychotherapy can easily be viewed in the light of this ontological description as a whole. The arbitrary claims, the quest for limitless power, prestige, affection, or independence, and the unrealistic images of what the self really is or ought to be—all these neurotic manifestations are provided for. Tillich's observation that sin destroys the unity between freedom and destiny might be translated into psychological language by saying that in neurosis the individual manifests both grandiosity and compulsiveness. His reactions are arbitrary and automatic simultaneously. He yearns for egocentric omnipotence, and he is enslaved to forces (especially unconscious forces within himself) over which he has no control. Similarly, when the unity of vitality and intentionality is broken, the former becomes lawless desire and the latter becomes a legalistic strait jacket. Where Tillich says that *sin* is simultaneously lawless desire and bondage to the law, Freud speaks of conflict between the *id* and the *superego*.

The negative possibilities we have already noted in connection with the categories also become actual under the conditions of existence. Temporality estranged from eternity becomes sheer transitoriness. Spatial existence estranged from an immovable ground becomes total uprootedness. Causality apart from aseity becomes total necessitation. Contingency apart from lasting substance means total loss of self-identity.

Thus the change introduced by sin can be summarized by saying that although finitude is not essentially evil, under the conditions of existence finitude becomes evil; and the *Urangst* which can be accepted as a part of the good creation turns into guilty anxiety and a horror of death. The legitimate aspects of self-concern become swallowed up in egocentricity. The legitimate aspects of the desire for independence become swallowed up in isolation. The possibilities for error, which are natural to a fallible being, issue in systematic illusions and structured lies, both personal and social. The desire for freedom becomes a demand for absolute autonomy. Legitimate needs turn into arbitrary claims and endless frustrations. The suffering which is part and parcel of life becomes meaningless torture.

Man's inability to overcome the estrangements which characterize sin produces despair. As Kierkegaard saw, despair has two elements: first, self-hatred, including the will to self-annihilation; and secondly, the feeling that man cannot escape from himself, accompanied by the extreme measures he takes to try to escape (such as flight into illness, mental disease, intoxication, accidents).

XVIII. A THEOLOGICAL BASIS FOR THERAPY

At this point Tillich clearly affirms the "bondage of the will (self)" in so far as this means that man cannot, through any rational, mystical, or other expedients, lift himself into a harmony between himself and God. He cannot, because all of his efforts spring from existence and reflect the disruptions which mark the conflict between existence and essence. The universal quest and the universal need of mankind can therefore be specified. They are directed toward a healing of disruption which comes from Essential Being, but is actualized within existence. Tillich's whole doctrine of man reflects a Trinitarian structure, and his doctrine of sin connects specifically with his Christology. When the latter is approached by means of such an analysis of anxiety, sin, neurosis, and despair, it becomes something very different from a pedantic toying with Chalcedonian formulae. Finally, Tillich is not interested in justification by faith because it happens to be Protestant; he is interested in it only in so far as it embodies the truth about how man can reach self-acceptance despite sin.

XIX. SALVATION AND ESCHATOLOGY

It is impossible, however, to follow our theme through those concluding sections which discuss the relationship of human life to the Spirit and the relationship of historical existence to eternal life and the Kingdom of God. This means that we have examined his views of human nature without placing them in the setting of his doctrines of salvation and eschatology. But his chapters on these topics have appeared only in the form of propositions, and will not be available in full detail until the second volume of his *Systematic Theology* is published. In any case, the solutions he offers derive from revelation, and therefore fall outside the scope of this essay. In so far as there is a foundation for these answers within human nature, that is to be discovered in the fact that sin does not totally destroy the image of God (man's capacity for rationality, creativity, and decision). And we have already seen why man cannot supply the answers from within himself, or from nature, or from any combination of the two.

Tillich rejects both double predestination and ordinary views of immortality. By means of his doctrine of participation he arrives at a form of universalism; and the main clue to his view of eternal life and the Kingdom of God is to be found in the fact that man in history can be related to meaning (strictly, the presence of the ground of meaning) which transcends history. His careful distinctions eliminate many false problems and many illusions—both Christian and secular, such as, for example, utopianism—which have arisen in this area. Yet Tillich's main problem is not different from that of the unsophisticated person. How is he able to combine his hope of ultimate fulfillment with an awareness (in his case, especially thoroughgoing) of the fact that history ends, for most individuals, with men so utterly remote from what fulfillment implies? The problem is especially acute for one who rejects the notion of a "second history" beyond this existence. He tries to meet it by his doctrine of *kairos,* and by holding that God is the unconditional fulfillment *intended* in every ambiguous fulfillment in history. There is the further problem of how his universalism can be combined with his concept of freedom, but this is no more difficult in principle than the problem of how sin can be inevitable without being necessitated. If, however, freedom involves the actuality, for some men, of irrevocable spiritual annihilation, then it is difficult to see, at this juncture, how a doctrine of participation can be made to incorporate this fact.

XX. CONCLUDING APPRAISAL

The foregoing pages have brought out some of the strengths and some of the doubtful points which one encounters in Tillich's doctrine of man. One of the strengths which was not sufficiently emphasized, perhaps, is his attempt to conceive of freedom in such a way that it neither (a) externally limits God, nor (b) cuts man off from nature. Anyone familiar with the odd results reached by theologians in their efforts to avoid these two pitfalls will appreciate the massiveness of Tillich's achievement. Yet his own teaching requires (a) some sort of "opposition" within God, and (b) something that often sounds panpsychist in the interpretation of nature.

My final word of criticism would be an unpleasant duty indeed, were it not for the fact that I have repeatedly discussed it with Tillich himself; so it will neither surprise nor dismay him. This criticism has to do with the systematic character of his thinking. I have always been mystified as to how he could be so flexible, concrete, vital, and "close to home" on the one hand, and so schematic, abstract, abstruse, and remote on the other. The struggle between these two tendencies runs throughout his writings, and the schematic aspect is, so far as I am concerned, both an asset and a liability. It is an asset wherever it is used analytically and organizationally, that is, where it is used to clarify concepts and to show their interrelatedness. But it becomes a liability at the point where existential problems, after being high-lighted, are swallowed into an abyss. Somehow Tillich, like God, manages to engulf distinctions without blurring them. He fully realizes (again, no doubt, like God) that such problems are met, in so far as they ever are, by living rather than by constructing systems. But it is a weird experience, which I have undergone many times, to have problems answered with great sensitivity and patience, by being brought into connection with some relevant segment of the system, only to discover later that I do not happen to be the man who carries this system around in his head.

DAVID E. ROBERTS

DEPARTMENT OF PHILOSOPHY OF RELIGION
UNION THEOLOGICAL SEMINARY
NEW YORK CITY

John Herman Randall, Jr.
THE ONTOLOGY OF PAUL TILLICH

7

THE ONTOLOGY OF PAUL TILLICH

I

PAUL TILLICH stands in the classic tradition of Western philosophy, in that long line of thinkers stemming from the Greeks who have been concerned with the problem of being and wisdom. As a theologian, this distinguishes him both from the American liberals whose thought is rooted in the philosophic idealism of the last century, and from the European representatives of a purely kerygmatic theology who will have no conscious traffic with philosophizing at all. Standing, as he likes to put it, at the boundary between theology and philosophy, he has inherited the mantle of both disciplines, and is keenly aware of the long tradition of human thinking which the leaders in both have devoted to the problem of the nature of the world and of man's place in it. To any man with philosophical interests, one of the most stimulating aspects of Tillich's thought is his ability to penetrate beneath the symbolic forms of past philosophy and theology to the problem of human destiny with which they were grappling.

The immediate background of Tillich's philosophy is certain of the more ontological and historical strains of nineteenth century German speculation. The later, post-Böhme philosophy of Schelling, the various mid-century reactions against the panlogism of Hegel, like Feuerbach and the early Marx, Nietzsche and the "philosophy of life," and the more recent existentialism, especially of Heidegger —all these have contributed to his formulation of philosophic issues and problems. In particular they have furnished him with a large part of the philosophic vocabulary with which he talks about the world and about earlier attempts to understand it. To express his own insights, Tillich employs the language of the existential philosophy. Whether this is the best possible language in which to put what he has to say is immaterial. Certainly he has greatly modified and clarified it since coming to this country. But it is obviously a language not too familiar to the vernacular of most American philosophizing, and hardly one with which English-speaking theologians have grown up. This circumstance creates a problem of communication with which it is hoped this volume will be able to deal.

On one occasion Tillich read a brilliant paper to a group of professional philosophers. Among the listeners was G. E. Moore, the distinguished representative of a very different philosophical tradition and language. When it came time for Moore to comment, he said: "Now really, Mr. Tillich, I don't think I have been able to understand a single sentence of your paper. Won't you please try to state one sentence, or even one word, that I can understand?"

Tillich is clearly not a Cambridge analyst. On another occasion a group were discussing that philosophical movement with John Dewey. Dewey remarked: "Well, I have had some pretty hard things to say about German philosophers in my time. But at least they were dealing with the important questions." I do not think any philosophical mind can talk with or read Tillich without being profoundly convinced that he is dealing with the important questions. To be sure, Moore had a point. Like most recent German philosophers, Tillich could profitably cultivate a little more precision of definition. But it was the one systematic philosopher to come out of Cambridge in the last generation, Whitehead, who exclaimed in understandable if not entirely accurate revulsion, "Exactness is a fake!" The precise statement of nothing of consequence is surely specious, and the meaning of human destiny can scarcely be cramped within the bounds of symbolic logic.

I suppose Tillich would say that I have set up a dialectical problem between precision and importance.[1] But I see no reason for not trying to speak as precisely as possible even about important matters, and I am afraid my own doubts begin when in the recent German fashion Tillich is inclined to leave ultimate matters to a final "dialectic." At any rate, it is his epistemology which seems the least adequate part of his thought, and raises the most questions. The one strand of the philosophical tradition which he does not take very seriously, and consequently fails to illuminate, is the empiricism stemming from Locke. This he is inclined to dismiss as the mere

---

[1] Cf. Tillich's analogous statement, *Systematic Theology*, I, 105. Succeeding references, in this essay, to page numbers of quotations from *Systematic Theology* will be given in parentheses after the quotations.

reflection of a transitory bourgeois culture, which for Germany and for him has already disintegrated and passed into limbo. Far be it from me to attempt to defend British empiricism, especially in its present-day decadent form, when it seems to have lost all function. But I should think that "dialectical thinking," if I understand it, might have learned more and absorbed more from it than Tillich apparently has.

It is not my purpose here to attempt anything like a genetic account of the development of Tillich's thought from his early dissertations on Schelling down to his *Systematic Theology*. Rather, I wish to consider his mature philosophy and its core of ontology, primarily from the time he succeeded to Max Scheler's chair of philosophy at Frankfurt in 1929, especially as expressed in the first volume of his superb *Systematic Theology*. His philosophy of history I shall leave in the competent hands of Dr. Adams.

Both as philosopher and as theologian Tillich stands broadly in the great Augustinian tradition, that is, in the central tradition of Christian Platonism. For him the lesson of the *Symposium* has been well learned: the object of knowledge and the object of love are one and the same, and *knowledge* is ultimately a "participation" in true being.[2] This, I take it, is what "existentialism" primarily means for him. Immediately, as with Heidegger, this is a protest against the "bracketing" of questions of existence, and against the exclusive concern with a description of essences that was characteristic of Husserl's phenomenological analysis, the most important philosophical movement in the Germany in which Tillich grew up. But more ultimately, for him the concern with "existence" is a reaffirmation of the Platonic doctrines of *eros* and participation. Historically speaking, this sets him against the Thomism which recognizes a clear boundary between the realm of truths accessible to natural reason and the realm of truths accessible only to faith, and for him renders any natural theology strictly impossible.[3] It sets him against the Aristotle who made science an integral part of wisdom; he finds only the Platonic strain in Aristotle congenial.

It is this fundamental Platonism, fully as much as his natural reaction against nineteenth century optimism, that provokes his hostility to the Ritschlian theology that prevailed in liberal Protestant think-

---

[2] Cf. his suggestive paper on knowledge as participation.

[3] Cf. his paper, "Two Types of Philosophy of Religion," *Union Seminary Quarterly Review* (1946).

ing in Germany down to 1914, with its sharp Kantian dualism between pure and practical reason, and its denial of any theological concern with the former, with questions of existence. It was the Ritschlian liberal theologians, Tillich points out, who in Germany ruined the term "practical" as a means of expressing the importance of human interests and ends in the intellectual life, and forced the quite different vocabulary of "existence" and "existential commitment" upon German philosophical thinking. American thought, moving in a similar direction, and much less constrained to emancipate itself from a Kantian formalism and intellectualism, in Peirce and James was able to build upon the Kantian and post-Kantian "practical reason" to express the same concern with the psychological and cultural matrix of thinking. No one familiar with the long and apparently ineradicable misunderstandings to which this use of the vocabulary of "practice" has exposed Dewey would claim that the term has been a very happy or clarifying one. To be sure, to an American at least, the whole vocabulary of "existence" seems wide open to analogous if not identical misunderstandings. But Tillich, whose concern with the problems of cultural reconstruction has been as intense and as sustained as Dewey's, in his own very different cultural situation and in his own very different philosophical language, has really been working out a philosophy that is certainly comparable to much recent American philosophizing. Perhaps the most fundamental difference is that he came upon the scene at a rather later stage of cultural change—of "the transformation of bourgeois culture," he would say. Hence his thought is to be judged not in comparison with that of Dewey's generation, but with that of men who have proceeded to build upon and modify Dewey's ideas in the light of more recent history.

I am far indeed from suggesting that the American philosophizing of the past generation is a yardstick by which to measure the penetration and insights of Tillich, or of anyone coming out of so different an experience; or of intimating that the enterprise of a philosophical theologian like Tillich is identical with that of a philosopher of political education like John Dewey. Personally, I am inclined to take rather more seriously the fundamental contentions of the classic tradition than do either of these distinguished critics of that type of thinking. I find very congenial Tillich's ultimate concern with the mystery and the power of being, for I too am intensely interested in metaphysics—and I will not, with the unexpected caution of Tillich, water down the time-honored term to a mere "ontology."

One more personal word. I can of course lay no claim to theological competence, and any comments I may inadvertently make on Tillich's theology are strictly amateurish. Having no present "existential commitments" to the Christian revelation, certainly not in any exclusive sense, I believe that even in Tillich's rather generous eyes I could not possibly qualify as a theologian myself. But if, as he likes to assert paradoxically, belief in the existence of God is the worst form of atheism, I am at least free of atheism in that form.

II

Tillich stands in the great tradition of Augustinian philosophy—his relation to the intricacies of Augustinian theology is more complex. This is a way of saying that on certain crucial questions, particularly of epistemology and ontology, his thought differs from that of the equally great tradition of Christian Aristotelianism. For him, it was with Thomas Aquinas that the course of Christian thought went astray. He recognizes no neat line dividing philosophy from theology; the theologian must be a philosopher to formulate his questions, and the philosopher becomes a theologian if he succeeds in answering the ones he asks. In a real sense, for Tillich philosophy is faith seeking understanding—though faith appears now as "existential commitment." For him there can be no natural theology; any argument from the character of the world to the existence of God could never get beyond finite relativities, and God is not a being whose "existence" demands proof. Tillich rests upon a version of the ontological argument—rather, as for all true Augustinians, God (that ultimate in which the symbols of human ideas of God participate) neither needs nor can receive "proof." For that ultimate—Tillich's term is *das Unbedingte*—is a certain quality of the world man encounters, which analysis reveals as "presupposed" in all his encountering. Whereas Augustine's Platonism, however, led him to an intellectual emphasis on the Truth or Logos implied in all knowledge, Tillich has expanded it to the "power of being" implied in all men's varied participations in the world in which they are grasped by an ultimate concern.

Now all this can mean much or little, depending upon how it is elaborated. As Tillich develops it, it becomes a suggestive reinterpretation of the Augustinian metaphysics, fertilized with many of the insights of a century of German thinking. Largely, though not wholly, freed from epistemological entanglements in which classic German idealism mired Christian Platonism, his philosophy is a realistic interpretation of a world in which man can find a meaning for his life. Some of the doubts it leaves in the mind of a sympathetic seeker for wisdom arise from the baggage it carries along from a century of German philosophical engagements. Others are probably inherent in the Christian and Augustinian character of its Platonism, when viewed from the perspective either of an Aristotelian or of a modern empirical approach. But it is not Tillich's central enterprise with which I should want to quarrel: the working-out of a realism with vision and participation—what he used to call a "belief-ful or self-transcending realism."[4] I shall concentrate on the main points, the nature of philosophy, the nature of reason, and the nature of being.

In a brief paper[5] Tillich clarifies the nature of philosophy and its relation to theology:

> Philosophy asks the ultimate question that can be asked, namely, the question as to what being, simply being, means. . . . [It is born from] the philosophical shock, the tremendous impetus of the questions: What is the meaning of being? Why is there being and not not-being? What is the character in which every being participates? . . . Philosophy primarily does not ask about the special character of the beings, the things and events, the ideas and values, the souls and bodies which share being. Philosophy asks what about this being itself. Therefore, all philosophers have developed a "first philosophy," as Aristotle calls it, namely, an interpretation of being. . . . This makes the division between philosophy and theology impossible, for, whatever the relation of God, world, and man may be, it lies in the frame of being; and any interpretation of the meaning and structure of being as being unavoidably such has consequences for the interpretation of God, man, and the world in their interrelations.

Philosophy is thus fundamentally ontology—Tillich regards the traditional term "metaphysics" as too abused and distorted to be longer of any service. The Kantians are wrong in making epistemology the true first philosophy, for as later Neo-Kantians like Nicolai Hartmann have recognized, epistemology demands an ontological basis. The philosophies of "experience" are merely using another word for being itself. Positivists who would restrict philosophy to

---

[4] Cf. *The Protestant Era*, especially Chap. V, "Realism and Faith."
[5] *Ibid.*, Chap. VI, "Philosophy and Theology."

the analysis of the different kinds of being can never succeed with their "No trespassing" signs:

> The meaning of being is man's basic concern, is the really human and philosophical question. . . . Man, as the German philosopher Heidegger says, is that being which asks what being is.

"Now, this is the task of theology: to ask for being as far as it gives us ultimate concern. Theology deals with what concerns us inescapably, ultimately, unconditionally. It deals with it not as far as it *is*, but as far as it is *for us*." Theology is "practical," not in contrast to theoretical, since truth is essential to our ultimate concern, but in that it "must deal with its subject always as far as it concerns us in the very depth of our being." But "practical" is another word ruined by being opposed to "theoretical," especially by the Ritschlians, and therefore Tillich adopts Kierkegaard's term "existential": "existential is what characterizes our real existence in all its concreteness, in all its accidental elements, in its freedom and responsibility, in its failure, and in its separation from its true and essential being."

> Philosophy and theology are divergent as well as convergent. They are convergent as far as both are existential and theoretical at the same time. They are divergent as far as philosophy is basically theoretical and theology is basically existential. . . . Philosophy, although knowing the existential presuppositions of truth, does not abide with them. It turns immediately to the content and tries to grasp it directly. In its systems it abstracts from the existential situations out of which they are born. . . . Philosophy asks on the existential and concrete basis of the medieval church and civilization . . . or of bourgeois or proletarian society or culture. But it asks for truth itself. . . . This is its freedom.

In his *Systematic Theology* Tillich elaborates on his conception of ontology:

> Philosophy is *that cognitive approach to reality in which reality as such is the object*. Reality as such, or reality as a whole, is not the whole of reality; it is the structure which makes reality a whole and therefore a potential object of knowledge. Inquiring into the nature of reality as such means inquiring into those structures, categories, and concepts which are presupposed in the cognitive encounter with every realm of reality (18).

These structures, of course—*pace* the Kantians and the positivists—include structures of values. Now philosophy deals with the structure of being in itself; it undertakes an ontological analysis of that structure. Theology deals with the meaning of being for us. Consequently, the two diverge, first, in their cognitive attitude.

The philosopher tries to maintain a detached objectivity toward being and its structures. He tries to exclude the personal, social, and historical conditions which might distort an objective vision of reality. His passion is the passion for a truth which is open to general approach, subject to general criticism, changeable in accordance with every new insight, open and communicable. In all these respects he feels no different from the scientist, historian, psychologist, etc. (22).

In contrast, the basic attitude of the theologian is commitment to the content he expounds, is "existential." Secondly, the two differ in that the philosopher, like the scientist, is seeking a universal structure, the theologian, a structure manifesting itself in a particular historical event and religious institution. Thirdly, the philosopher deals with the categories of being in relation to the material which is structured by them, while the theologian treats them in relation to the salvation of man.

Actually, of course, the philosopher too is conditioned by his psychological, sociological, and historical situation, and if he be of any significance has his own ultimate concern. His existential situation and his ultimate concern shape his philosophical vision. To the extent that this is true, the philosopher is also by definition a theologian, as all creative philosophers are. He tries to become universal, but he is destined to remain particular.

Two points here require comment. The first is Tillich's definition of the core of philosophy: ontology. He passes easily from "being as such" to "reality as a whole," identifying two very different conceptions. The first is Aristotelian, the second is the object of nineteenth century idealism. The first means those generic traits that can be discriminated in any subject matter; the second means a unified and unifying structure of the universe, "objective reason," what Tillich quite properly calls "the universal *logos.*" The second can be, and traditionally has been, identified with God; the first, though it will be exemplified in religion as in everything else, possesses in itself no religious significance, and is not, as such, of "existential concern." "The structure of being" can hardly mean two such different things. The first is the proper object of an Aristotelian ontological inquiry; the second is the goal of Platonic and Neo-Platonic aspiration, the "Being" that is the Idea of the Good and the One.

Now Tillich clearly means the latter, and he is hence exposed to all the philosophical attacks directed against such a block universe from Peirce and James on. This conception is the core of what is usually called absolute idealism; it is the central target for the objections of all other philosophies. To English-speaking philosophers Tillich would inevitably seem to be offering merely one more variant of philosophical idealism, and to be identifying the whole philosophical enterprise with that historically conditioned existential commitment. Is he not here speaking, in terms of his own distinction, rather as the theologian than as the philosopher? The "structures of being" are the proper goal of a free metaphysical inquiry—an inquiry to which Tillich himself goes on to make significant contributions. But "reality as a whole," or "being-itself," αὐτο τὸ ὄν, seems rather an existential commitment—the proper goal of the theologian, or the philosopher as theologian.

To me this idea seems to have been, in the whole Platonic tradition, one of those great unifying symbols or "myths" by which men bring their encountered world to a focus in terms of their system of meanings and values—of their ultimate concern. It is a symbol by which the world unifies itself. I should say, it is a part of the task of metaphysics or ontology to *understand* such myths and the way they function. It is a part of the task of "practical" philosophy—and I should here include philosophical theology, as well as the philosophy of history—to *use* such myths for the direction of human life, to clarify and to criticize them. This task is obviously of fundamental importance. I suppose it is only natural for a professional theologian to assign it to theology, and for a professional philosopher to include it in the philosophical enterprise. Speaking as a metaphysician, however, it seems to me important to recognize that "reality as a whole" has the ontological status of a myth or symbol rather than that of a descriptive hypothesis. It is, in Tillich's distinction, an existential rather than a theoretical concept.

This brings us to the second point about Tillich's conception of the nature of philosophy. As an Augustinian, he finds it ultimately impossible to set philosophy apart from theology, and his efforts to distinguish their emphases of course in the last analysis break down. The distinction is relative and "existential"—it depends on the specific situation. Now, I have no particular objection to calling all the concern of the philosophical enterprise with "practice" and values really theology, as Tillich does in his broadest extension of that discipline—the sense in which a teacup by Cézanne is a revelation of being and of man's ultimate concern, which makes aesthetics a branch of theology. The difficulty arises not when I discover that as a philosopher I am a theologian, but when I find that to be a good philosopher and answer my questions I must be a Christian theologian. But I am not sure whether for Tillich this is a question of philosophy, of philosophical theology, or of kerygmatic theology.

The root difficulty in all these distinctions seems to lie in the too sharp dualism Tillich accepts between the theoretical and the existential or "practical." It has been one of the major contributions of the broad philosophical movement, of which both existentialism and American instrumentalism are strands, to break down this dualism, which goes back through Kant to Aristotle. The theoretical interest, or "pure reason," it has been abundantly shown, is not something opposed to the practical or existential. Rather, theory and detached objectivity are moments or stages in a broader context or matrix of "practice." Different sciences and disciplines vary in the degree to which they attain universality and detachment; metaphysics, in seeking to embrace all possible situations, can hope to become the most "theoretical" of all—and hence at the same time the most "instrumental" and "existential." Tillich accepts all this, but there seems still a strong remnant of the Kantian dualism left in the way he uses the distinction. This comes out most clearly in his final position on the relation between philosophy and theology, his so-called "method of correlation," in which he finds that philosophy must go to theology for the answers to its own questions. Unless this be a mere matter of terminology, it clearly does not take the "existential" character of theory seriously enough.

III

Just as Tillich develops his conception of philosophy as a preparation for theology, so he analyzes reason in order to lead up to the reality of revelation. He starts by distinguishing two concepts of reason, the "ontological" and the "technical"— Νοῦς or *intellectus*, and διάνοια or *ratio*.

According to the classical philosophical tradition, reason is the structure of the mind which enables the mind to grasp and to transform reality. . . . Classical reason is *logos*, whether it is understood in a more intuitive or in a more critical way. Its cognitive nature is one element in addition to others; it is cognitive and aesthetic, theoretical and practical, detached and passionate, subjective and objective (72).

Technical reason is the capacity for reasoning—it is Aristotle's "deliberative reason," which calculates means to ends.

While reason in the sense of *logos* determines the ends and only in the second place the means, reason in the technical sense determines the means while accepting the ends from "somewhere else. . . ." The consequence is that the ends are provided by nonrational forces, either by positive traditions or by arbitrary decisions serving the will to power (73).

Now this ontological reason—*Vernunft*—is capable both of participating in the universal *logos* of being, and of succumbing to the destructive structures of existence. It is partly liberated from blindness, and partly held in it. In Platonic terms, it can either turn upward to participate in true being, or turn downward to nonbeing. It is itself both subjective and objective: the human *logos* can grasp and shape reality only because reality itself has a *logos* character. To the rational structure of the mind there corresponds an intelligible structure of the world. Subjective reason both "grasps" and "shapes"; the mind receives and reacts:

"Grasping," in this context, has the connotation of penetrating into the depth, into the essential nature of a thing or an event, of understanding and expressing it. "Shaping," in this context, has the connotation of transforming a given material into a Gestalt, a living structure which has the power of being. . . . In every act of reasonable reception an act of shaping is involved, and in every act of reasonable reaction an act of grasping is involved. We transform reality according to the way we see it, and we see reality according to the way we transform it. Grasping and shaping the world are interdependent (76).

Ontological reason has a dimension which Tillich calls its "depth":

The depth of reason is the expression of something that is not reason but which precedes reason and is manifest through it. Reason in both its objective and subjective structures points to something which appears in these structures but which transcends them in power and meaning. . . . It could be called the "substance" which appears in the rational structure, or "being-itself" which is manifest in the logos of being, or the "ground" which is creative in every rational creation, or the "abyss" which cannot be exhausted by any creation or by any totality of them, or the "infinite potentiality of being and meaning" which pours into the rational structures of mind and reality, actualizing and transforming them. All these terms which point to that which "precedes" reason have a metaphorical character. "Preceding" is itself metaphorical. . . .

In the cognitive realm the depth of reason is its quality of pointing to truth-itself, namely, to the infinite power of being and of the ultimately real, through the relative truths in every field of knowledge. In the aesthetic realm the depth of reason is its quality of pointing to "beauty-itself," namely, to an infinite meaning and an ultimate significance, through the creations in every field of aesthetic intuition. In the legal realm, the depth of reason is its quality of pointing to "justice-itself," namely, to an infinite seriousness and an ultimate dignity, through every structure of actualized justice (79).

Reason, in other words, points to something that is one step beyond the intelligible structures it actually finds. This further step is the Source or the One of Neo-Platonism, the Imprinter of the seal, the Original of the copy, of Augustinian thought. For the Platonic tradition this stands one step "above" intellect and Noûs; following Böhme and Schelling, Tillich locates it one step "below," in the "depths." It is the Standard by which finite, human intellectual activity ultimately judges. But though it thus manifests itself in every act of reason, it is hidden there under the conditions of existence, and expresses itself primarily in myth and ritual.

Myth is not primitive science, nor is cult primitive morality. Their content, as well as the attitude of people toward them, discloses elements which transcend science as well as morality—elements of infinity which express ultimate concern (80).

Now actual reason, in being, in human existence, and in life, is finite, self-contradictory, and ambiguous. It is relative, and can grasp only relativities. The classic description of the *docta ignorantia*, the awareness of its own limitations, of such "reason in existence" is to be found in Cusanus and in Kant. Tillich finds three major conflicts within actual reason:

The polarity of structure and depth within reason produces a conflict between autonomous and heteronomous reason under the conditions of existence. Out of this conflict arises the quest for theonomy. The polarity of the static and the dynamic elements of reason produces a conflict between absolutism and relativism of reason under the conditions of existence. This conflict leads to the quest for the concrete-absolute. The polarity of the formal and the emotional elements of reason produces the conflict between formalism and irrationalism of reason under the conditions of existence. Out of this conflict arises the quest for the union of form and mystery. In all three cases reason is driven to the quest for revelation (83).

Reason which affirms and actualizes its structure without regarding its depth is "autonomous." Autonomy means the obedience of the individual to the law of reason, which he finds in himself as a rational being. There has been an endless conflict between this self-sufficient reason and the "heteronomy" which imposes upon a reason a law from outside. But this "outside" is not wholly external; it also represents an element in reason itself—its "depth." "The basis of a genuine heteronomy is the claim to speak in the name of the ground of being and therefore in an unconditional and ultimate way" (84). The conflict is thus tragic, for autonomy and heteronomy are both rooted in "theonomy," and each goes astray when their unity is broken—as in the autonomy of secular bourgeois culture, and in the heteronomy of totalitarianisms.

Theonomy does not mean the acceptance of a divine law imposed on reason by a highest authority; it means autonomous reason united with its own depth . . . and actualized in obedience to its structural laws and in the power of its own inexhaustible ground (85).

"Theonomous reason" is thus for Tillich really a kind of higher autonomy, in the Kantian sense. As for all good Augustinians, this is not so much a statement about the dependence of knowledge upon God as an identification of God with the fullest actualization of the powers of reason—with the Platonic "truth-itself."

The second conflict is between relativism and absolutism. Now reason unites a "static" and a "dynamic" element, its structure and its powers of actualizing itself in life. The static element is expressed in two forms of absolutism, that of tradition, like the Catholics, and that of revolution, like the Communists. The dynamic element appears in two forms of relativism, positivistic and cynical. Positivistic relativism accepts the given situation with its norms, and has no means of rising above it. Tillich here groups philosophical positivism, pragmatism, and recent existentialism, all of which he finds have conservative implications—they all accept the values of the *status quo.* Cynical positivism, the product of disillusionment with utopian absolutism, produces an empty vacuum into which new absolutisms pour. "Criticism," of which Socrates and Kant are representatives, tries to unite the conflicting static and dynamic elements in reason by reducing the static element to pure form without content—as in the categorical imperative. But both the Platonism that came from Socrates and the Idealism that sprang from Kant became pure absolutisms.

In the ancient as well as in the modern world, criticism was unable to overcome the conflict between absolutism and relativism. Only that which is absolute and concrete at the same time can overcome this conflict. Only revelation can do it (89).

The third conflict within reason is between formalism and emotionalism. Technical reason, which flowers in what Tillich calls "controlling knowledge," and culminates in formalized logic, denies that any other method can attain to truth. This intellectualism, which appears in all fields, art, law, society, and so forth, provokes an "irrationalism" which sacrifices the structure of reason entirely. Pure theory strives with a practice unguided by any theory. Neither theory nor practice taken in isolation can solve the problem of their conflict with each other; only revelation can do it.

When Tillich comes to consider the cognitive function of ontological reason, and the nature of human knowledge—"cognitive reason under the conditions of existence"—he emphasizes its basic polar structure. Knowledge he takes, with the Platonic tradition, to be a form of union. "In every act of knowledge the knower and that which is known are united." But knowledge is a union through detachment and separation: in every type of knowledge subject and object are logically distinguished.

The unity of distance and union is the ontological problem of knowledge. It drove Plato to the myth of an original union of the soul with the essences (ideas), of the separation of the soul from the truly real in temporal existence, of the recollection of the essences, and of reunion with them through the different degrees of cognitive elevation. The unity is never completely destroyed; but there is also estrangement. The particular object is strange as such, but it contains essential structures with which the cognitive subject is essentially united, and which it can remember when looking at things (94).

Union and detachment or estrangement are present in all knowledge. But there are two major types, that in which detachment is determining, and that in which union is predominant. The first type, following Max Scheler, Tillich calls "controlling knowledge." This is the product of technical, instrumental reason.

It unites subject and object for the sake of the control of the object by the subject. It transforms the object into a completely conditioned and calculable "thing." It deprives it of any subjective quality (97).

But this is not the way of knowing human nature, or any individual personality. "Without union there is no cognitive approach to man." The type of knowledge where union predominates Tillich calls "receiving knowledge." It always includes the emotional element: no union of subject and object is possible without emotional participation. Knowledge in which there is a balance of union and detachment is "understanding."

Understanding another person or a historical figure, the life of an animal or a religious text, involves an amalgamation of controlling and receiving knowledge, of union and detachment, of participation and analysis (98).

Modern culture has seen a tidal wave of "controlling knowledge," technical reason, which has swamped every cognitive attempt in which "reception" and union are presupposed.

Life, spirit, personality, community, meanings, values, even one's ultimate concern, should be treated in terms of detachment, analysis, calculation, technical use. . . . But man himself has been lost in this enterprise. That which can be known only by participation and union, that which is the object of receiving knowledge, is disregarded. Man actually has become what controlling knowledge considers him to be, a thing among things, a cog in the dominating machine of production and consumption, a dehumanized object of tyranny or a standardized object of public communication (99).

Three main movements have protested: romanticism, the "philosophy of life," and existentialism. They have failed because they had no adequate criterion of truth and falsity. What does "truth" mean for "receiving knowledge"? Positivists would restrict the term either to tautologies or to experimentally confirmed sentences. But this involves a break with the whole classic tradition. Modern philosophy, following Aristotle, has taken "true" as a quality of judgments. Tillich protests by asserting the ancient Platonic and Augustinian position, that the truth of judgments depends on a prior truth in things:

The truth of something is that level of its being the knowledge of which prevents wrong expectations and consequent disappointments. Truth, therefore, is the essence of things as well as the cognitive act in which their essence is grasped. The term "truth" is like the term "reason," subjective-objective. A judgment is true because it grasps and expresses true being (102).

This would have delighted St. Anselm.

Tillich is obviously committed to finding a method of verification for his "receiving knowledge" that is different from that of experimental science.

Every cognitive assumption (hypothesis) must be tested. The safest test is the repeatable experiment. . . . But it is not permissible to make the experimental method of verification the exclusive pattern of all verification. . . . The verifying experiences of a nonexperimental character are truer to life, though less exact and definite. By far the largest part of all cognitive verification is "experiential." In some cases experimental and experiential verification work together. In other cases the experimental element is completely absent (102).
Controlling knowledge is verified by the success of controlling actions. . . . Receiving knowledge is verified by the creative union of two natures, that of knowing, and that of the known. This test, of course, is neither repeatable, precise, nor final at any particular moment. The life-process itself makes the test. Therefore, the test is indefinite and preliminary; there is an element of risk connected with it. Future stages of the same life-process may prove that what seemed to be a bad risk was a good one and *vice versa*. Nevertheless, the risk must be taken, receiving knowledge must be applied, experiential verification must go on continually, whether it is supported by experimental tests or not (102–103).

This suggests that in most of those traits in which the knowledge gained by experimental science has been contrasted unfavorably with knowledge gained by more "certain" methods, "receiving knowledge" is far more "experimental" than "controlling knowledge." It is more tentative, less precise, more subject to reconstruction with further experience. Such knowledge

is verified partly by experimental test, partly by a participation in the individual life with which they deal. If this "knowledge by participation" is called "intuition," the cognitive approach to every individual life-process is intuitive. Intuition in this sense is not irrational, and neither does it bypass a full consciousness of experimentally verified knowledge (103).

Now, neither rationalism nor pragmatism sees the element of participation in knowledge. But the way in which philosophical systems have been accepted, experienced, and verified points to a method of verification beyond rationalism and pragmatism. In terms of controlling knowledge, rational criticism, or pragmatic tests, they have been refuted innumerable times. But they live. Their verification is their efficiency in the life-process of mankind. They prove to be inexhaustible in meaning and creative in power. This method of verification "somehow combines the pragmatic and the rational elements without falling into the fallacies of either pragmatism or rationalism."

Now, the fundamental logical realism of Tillich's—the notion of an "objective" intelligible structure which is grasped by "subjective" human reason—is designedly not in the fashion of much recent nominalistic philosophizing. In this, Tillich is not only in the classic tradition of ontology; he is, I judge, on the side of the angels, and is to be criticized only at those points where he inadvertently allows Kantian epistemology to interfere with it. The difficulties in the working out of such a realism he does not face. They are, I judge, to be met only in a thoroughgoing functional realism; and Tillich remains with a purely structural realism. He defines reason as "the structure of the mind," instead of as "the power of the mind" to operate in the ways it ascertainably does.

That the mind has the power—or, more precisely, is the power—to do what he assigns to "ontological reason," as well as what he calls "technical reason," is undoubtedly true. Tillich himself is inclined to stop short with these facts, rather than to pursue the analysis of what is a much more complex process than he often suggests. Perhaps this is sufficient for his purpose as a theologian. Reason can and does determine ends as well as means, but hardly in the simple sense of the Platonic tradition, of participating in them intuitively— as he himself goes on to illustrate. There are overtones of the Greek Noûs and the idealistic *Vernunft*, as well as of the Christian Logos, that at times obscure what he is really trying to point to.

That mind has and is the power of "depth" no sensitive man would care to deny, nor would he deny that it has a capacity for envisaging more ultimate perfections than it can actually achieve. That the powers of the mind are limited is likewise obvious, and the polarities and tensions Tillich points to are both historically and personally illuminating. The limitations of what he calls an "autonomous reason" that disregards its "depth" have not been exactly overlooked of late; sensitivity to other aspects of experience is certainly needed. The higher autonomy Tillich calls "theonomy": if this be one way of "defining" God, it is surely as good as any other. The polar values both of relativism and of absolutism are equally obvious. That this is a rationally insoluble antinomy, however, is by no means clear. The solution would seem to lie in an objective relativism—a position Tillich does not consider. Even if he is right in contending that "only that which is absolute and concrete at the same time" can solve the antinomy, this would still seem to be a rational answer to a rational question, and not beyond the power of reason, however difficult practically. Finally, the antinomy between formalism and emotionalism seems likewise capable of rational adjustment. In going beyond the traditional "technical" reason to the notion of "intelligence," recent philosophizing has been facing and dealing with precisely this problem.

In other words, the finite and relative character of human reason is clear, as well as that it confronts difficulties and "ambiguities." That any adequate intellectual method, however, faces ultimate self-contradiction Tillich has not established. He contends that only "revelation" can solve these contradictions. Now there is no objection to calling the power of reason to solve its difficulties "revelation," especially if the power be seen as a cooperation with the powers of the world to be understood—if "revelation" be taken as a discovery and not as a mere human invention. That only the Christian "revelation" can solve the problems, however, is another matter again. That particular revelation, philosophically considered, would be one hypothesis among others, and would have to be tested philosophically. "Revelation," that is, would seem to be a symbol for the power of reason to do what revelation notoriously does.

In treating the nature of knowledge, Tillich does not presume to offer a detailed epistemology. His distinctions are important; his language is obviously pointed in the direction of establishing theological "knowledge." But though he has the tradition on his side, there remains a doubt whether greater clarity would not come from calling his "receiving knowledge" by some other name than "knowledge." After all, it is only by a metaphor that knowledge can be called a "union" or "participation." "Love" for the object of knowledge may in many types of knowledge be essential for any real "understanding"; but does that make the love itself knowledge? "Knowing is not like digesting, and we do not devour what we mean," is an aphorism of Santayana's still worth pondering. "Union" with another personality may well be a necessary condition of adequate knowledge of that personality. But union with a text—even a religious text—is hardly necessary to its proper interpretation. Nor have many American students been able to accept the peculiar German view of historical knowledge which leads Tillich to say, "Without a union of the nature of the historian with that of his object, no significant history is possible." In what sense, for instance, does a significant history of capitalism demand "a union between the nature of the historian and the nature of capitalism"? Obviously, only by metaphor.

This may be a mere matter of terminology, and there is, of course, much precedent for identifying forms of immediate experience with "knowledge." Precedent, however, is hardly a philosophical justification. The knowledge of particular situations does involve a very complex gathering together of relevant factors, as well as a narrowly "technical" reason. The classic instance is the process of diagnosis in medicine. But the physician scarcely needs to be "united" with the disease. To strengthen his particular kind of religious "receiving knowledge," Tillich seems to have grouped together quite a variety of types of knowledge that in another connection would demand careful discrimination.

It is obvious that most of our so-called "knowledge" is verified "experientially" rather than "experimentally"—at least in the narrow laboratory sense. But like most idealists criticizing philosophies of "scientific method," Tillich in the end falls back, in language quite worthy of James himself, on a pretty crude pragmatic method of verification—"efficiency in the life-process of mankind." Actually, of course, what he carefully describes as a union of experimental verification with something more, and calls both an "experiential" and an "intuitive" method, is very close to what American pragmatists and instrumentalists have called the "method of intelligence." It is natural for those without scientific interests themselves to conceive "scientific method" very narrowly, to identify it with what Tillich calls "technical reason." But "intelligence" as the best American philosophic thought has conceived it is certainly far more than his technical reason, even if it has still to learn some of the "depth" of his ontological reason. Tillich would really do well to strike up an acquaintance with "intelligence." He might in the end even be willing to participate in it.

IV

Ontology is the core of philosophy, and the ontological question of the nature of being is logically prior to all others. Ontology is possible because there are concepts less universal than "being," but more universal than the concepts that designate a particular realm of beings. Such ontological concepts have been called "principles," "categories," or "ultimate notions." Tillich's analysis of these concepts is the heart of his philosophy.

Such concepts, he holds, are strictly "*a priori*": they are present whenever something is experienced, and determine the nature of experience itself. They constitute its structure, they are its *a priori* "conditions," and hence are "presupposed" in every actual experience. This does not mean that they can be known prior to experience: they are known rather through the critical analysis of actual instances of experience.

This Kantian language hardly seems essential to Tillich's position, or even, indeed, ultimately compatible with it. The structure of experience is discovered *in* experience, by analysis; it is "recognized within the process of experiencing." Why then call it a "presupposition," which suggests that it is brought *to* experience from elsewhere? Why call it a "condition" of experience, "determining" its nature? Can one really combine in this fashion ontology and the Kantian critical philosophy, an epistemological realism with a theory that the knower "determines" the object of knowledge? Taken seriously, such language implies that the "being" to be analyzed is to be found only in the knower, and not, except derivatively, in the known; and this is the essence of an idealistic epistemology.

Tillich has of course broken with Kant on what for him is the fundamental point: this structure of experience may have changed in the past and may change in the future. He takes time seriously. The structure of human nature does indeed change in history. But underlying all such historical change is the structure of a being *which has history:*

This structure is the subject of an ontological and a theological doctrine of man. Historical man is a descendant of beings who had no history, and perhaps there will be beings who are descendants of historical man who have no history. But neither animals nor supermen are the objects of a doctrine of man (167).

Hence the *"a priori"* concepts are after all only relatively a priori, not absolutely static; and thus is the alternative of absolutism and relativism overcome. Tillich attaches his view to the voluntarism of Duns Scotus, which saw an ultimate indeterminacy in the ground of being. The similarity to Peirce, even in the enthusiasm for Scotus, is striking.

Tillich distinguishes four levels of ontological concepts: (1) the basic ontological structure; (2) the "elements" constituting that structure; (3) the characteristics of being which are the conditions of existence, or "existential being"; and (4) the categories of being and knowing. In setting off the "elements," which are polar distinctions that come always in pairs, from the categories, he is most illuminating and clarifying.

The ontological question, "What is being?" presupposes an asking "subject" and an "object" about which the question is asked; it presupposes the subject-object structure of being. This in turn presupposes the self-world structure as the basic articulation of being: being is man encountering the world. This logically and experientially precedes all other structures. Man experiences himself as having a world to which he belongs, and it is from the analysis of this polar relationship between man and the world that the basic ontological structure is derived. Since man is estranged from nature, and is unable to understand it in the way he understands man— he does not know what the behavior of things means to them, as he does know what men's behavior means to men—the principles which constitute the universe must be sought in man himself. Following Heidegger's *Sein und Zeit*, Tillich finds "being there" (*Dasein*)—the place where the structure of being is manifest—given to man within himself. "Man is able to answer the ontological question himself because he experiences directly and immediately the structure of being and its elements" within himself. This does not mean that it is easier to get a knowledge of man "sufficient for our purposes" than a knowledge of nonhuman objects. This is notoriously untrue. It means that man is aware of "the structure that makes cognition possible," the conditions of knowing. Being is revealed, not in objects, but in "the conditions necessary for knowing." "The truth of all ontological concepts is their power of expressing that which makes the subject-object structure possible. They constitute this structure" (169).

The "self" lives in an environment, which consists of those things with which it has an active interrelation. Self and environment or world are correlative concepts. "The self without a world is empty; the world without a self is dead." It is within this polarity that are to be found the derivative polarities of objective and subjective reason, of logical object and subject. Pure objects, "things," are completely conditioned or *bedingt* by the scheme of knowing. But man himself is not a "thing" or object: he is never bound completely to an environment.

He always transcends it by grasping and shaping it according to universal norms and ideas. . . . This is the reason why ontology cannot begin with things and try to derive the structure of reality from them. That which is completely conditioned, which has no selfhood and subjectivity, cannot explain self and subject. . . . It is just as impossible to derive the object from the subject as it is to derive the subject from the object. . . . This trick of deductive idealism is the precise counterpart of the trick of reductive naturalism. . . . The relation is one of polarity. The basic ontological structure cannot be derived. It must be accepted (170, 173–174).

This analysis of "the basic ontological structure," in which Tillich is following Heidegger, assumes without question that the epistemological "subject-object distinction" is absolutely ultimate, not only for knowledge, but for all being: It is not only "prior for us," but also "prior in nature," as Aristotle puts it. The analysis makes no attempt to explore the emergence of that distinction from the larger context of organic and social life, and of their natural conditions. This assumption of itself, coming at the very outset, is likely to prejudice any American philosopher against the whole "existential" enterprise: it smacks so clearly of an antiquated psychology of the knowing process. One of the striking features of Tillich's thought to Americans who have inherited the fruits of the evolutionary preoccupations of the last generation, is the complete absence in his intellectual background of any serious concern for the implications for metaphysics of biological evolution. It may well be that "ontology cannot derive the structure of reality from things," or understand "self and subject" in terms drawn from them alone, leaving man himself out of account. Certainly an adequate metaphysics cannot be formulated by disregarding man and his ways, as illustrations of the powers of being. But God evidently knew how to turn the trick of deriving man from a world innocent of his presence; and there is still more interest in trying to discover how he did it than in denying that it could be done.

There seems to be a basic unclarity in Tillich's thought at this point. At times he follows Heidegger in looking for the structure of being "in man." This is the characteristic method of idealism, as Heidegger has more explicitly recognized since his *Sein und Zeit*. But at other times Tillich, following his own insights rather than another's thought, holds that the structure of being is found *by* man *in* his encounters with the world—that it is not the structure of man, but of man's cooperation with the world, a cooperation of which man is but one pole. This is a quite different ontology, not that of idealism, but of what I should call empirical naturalism, and accept. It would be clarifying to have Tillich decide which position he is really maintaining—idealism, or an experiential and functional realism. *'Raus mit Kant!*

The second level of ontological analysis deals with those "ontological elements" which constitute the basic structure of being. Unlike the categories, these elements are polar: each is meaningful only in relation to its opposite pole. There are three outstanding pairs: individuality and universality or participation, dynamics and form, and freedom and destiny. These distinctions are discovered in the self's experience of the world, and then generalized for all interactions within being.

Individualization is a quality of everything; "it is implied in and constitutive of every self, which means that at least in an analogous way it is implied in and constitutive of every being." The individual self participates in his environment, or in the case of complete individualization, in his world. Man participates in the universe through the rational structure of mind and reality. When individualization reaches the perfect form we call a "person," participation reaches the perfect form we call "communion." The polarity of individualization and participation solves the problem of nominalism and realism. Individuals are real, but they participate in the universal structure, which, however, is not a second reality lying behind empirical reality.

Secondly, being something means having a form. But every form forms something, and this something Tillich calls "dynamics"—a rather unfortunate term. "Dynamics" is the *me on,* the potentiality of being, which is nonbeing in contrast to things that have a form, and the power of being in contrast to pure nonbeing" (179). This element polar to form appears as the *Urgrund* of Böhme, the "will" of Schopenhauer, the "will to power" of Nietzsche, the "unconscious" of Hartmann and Freud, the *élan vital* of Bergson. Each of these concepts points symbolically to what cannot be named literally. "If it could be named properly, it would be a formed being beside others instead of an ontological element in contrast with the element of pure form" (179).

The polarity of dynamics and form appears in man's immediate experience as the polar distinction of "vitality" and "intentionality." Vitality is the power which keeps a living being alive and growing. Intentionality is the actualizing of reason, being related to meaningful structures, living in universals, grasping and shaping reality. The two are the basis of self-transcendence and self-conservation. "Man's creativity breaks through the biological realm to which he belongs and establishes new realms never attainable on a non-human level" (181).

Freedom and destiny form the third ontological polarity. Destiny, and not necessity, is the polar correlate of freedom, for necessity is a category whose contrast is "possibility," not an "element."

Man experiences the structure of the individual as the bearer of freedom within the larger structures to which the individual structure belongs. Destiny points to this situation in which man finds himself, facing the world to which, at the same time, he belongs.

Freedom is experienced as deliberation, decision, and responsibility. Our destiny is that out of which our decisions arise. . . . it is the concreteness of our being which makes all our decisions *our* decisions. . . . Destiny is not a strange power which determines what shall happen to me. It is myself as given, formed by nature, history, and myself. My destiny is the basis of my freedom; my freedom participates in shaping my destiny (185).

Tillich generalizes this polarity in human experience to include every being, though it applies only by analogy to subhuman nature.

It is not clear whether Tillich really maintains that these three polarities alone "constitute the basic ontological structure." One can easily think of a good many more. But without following his discussion in detail, it is impossible to realize the richness of his treatment of the three.

The third level of ontological analysis expresses the power of being to exist, the nature of "existential being," and its difference from "essential being." "This duality is Tillich's form of contrast between the ideal and the actual, between potentiality and actuality, or, as I prefer, between powers and their operation ($\delta\acute{\upsilon}\nu\alpha\mu\epsilon\iota\varsigma$ and $\acute{\epsilon}\nu\acute{\epsilon}\rho\gamma\iota\alpha$).

There is no ontology which can disregard these two aspects, whether they are hypostatized into two realms (Plato), or combined in the polar relation of potentiality and actuality (Aristotle), or contrasted with each other (Schelling II, Kierkegaard, Heidegger), or derived from each other, either existence from essence (Spinoza, Hegel), or essence from existence (Dewey, Sartre).

Freedom as such is not the basis of existence, but rather freedom in unity with finitude. Finite freedom is the turning point from being to existence. Finitude is hence the center of Tillich's analysis, for it is the finitude of existent being which drives men to the question of God.

Historically, the question of what it means to be anything arose from the problem of the meaning of "nonbeing," in Parmenides, and in the *Sophist* of Plato. Plato there determined that "being not" means "being other than." But Tillich, following Heidegger, takes nonbeing much more personally and portentously, as *"das Nichts,"* Nothingness—the body of this death. Man

must be separated from his being in a way which enables him to look at it as something strange and questionable. And such a separation is actual because man participates not only in being but also in nonbeing. . . . It is not by chance that historically the recent rediscovery of the ontological question has been guided by pre-Socratic philosophy and that systematically there has been an overwhelming emphasis on the problem of nonbeing (187).

The Platonists distinguished between the οὐκ ὄν which means "nothing at all," and the μὴ ὄν which meant for them that which does not yet have being but can become being if united with ideas. This Platonic "matter" had a positive power of resisting the ideas. This was what Augustine meant in calling evil "nonbeing"—not nothing at all, but something with no positive ontological standing that yet could resist and pervert being. In Böhme's *Ungrund*, Schelling's "first potency," Hegel's "antithesis," this dialectical negativity was located in God himself. Existentialism has given to nonbeing a still more positive character and power: Heidegger's "annihilating nothingness" threatens man with nonbeing in the form of death, thus giving his life its "existential" character. For Sartre, nonbeing includes the threat of meaninglessness—the destruction of the very structure of being.

Now, being when limited by nonbeing is finitude. Nonbeing is the

"not yet" and the "no more" of being. Everything which participates in the power of being is mixed with nonbeing. It is finite.
Experienced on the human level, finitude is nonbeing as the threat
to being, ultimately the threat of death. It is *Angst*, "anxiety."

Fear as related to a definite object and anxiety as the awareness of finitude
are two radically different concepts. Anxiety is ontological; fear, psychological. Psychotherapy cannot remove ontological anxiety, because it cannot change the structure of finitude. But it can remove compulsory forms
of anxiety and can reduce the frequency and intensity of fears. It can put
anxiety "in its proper place" (191).

Anxiety expresses finitude from "inside." Anxiety is the self-aware-
ness of the finite self as finite.

Every existence is finite, threatened with disruption and self-
destruction. It also participates in what is beyond nonbeing, "being-
itself." It has both "existence" and "essence." Now essence is an
ambiguous term: its meaning oscillates between an empirical and
a valuational sense, between the actual logical nature of the thing,
and its "true" and undistorted nature, that from which being has
"fallen." "Existence" is likewise ambiguous: whatever exists is more
than it is in the state of mere potentiality and less than it could be
in the power of its "essential" nature. Historically, the contrast between "essence" and "existence" has been both the colorless contrast between idea and fact, and the contrast of value between the
ideal and the actual. For Tillich's theology, it is the contrast between
the world as created, and the actual world after the Fall.

The fourth level of ontological concepts consists of the categories. They are "the forms in which the mind grasps and shapes
reality." But they are not mere logical forms, only indirectly related
to reality itself; they are ontological, present in everything. They
are forms of finitude. They are not polar, like the "elements." For
his purposes Tillich emphasizes four main categories: time, space,
causality, and substance.

Time is the central category of finitude. In immediate experience
time unites the anxiety of transitoriness with the courage of a self-
affirming present. The present implies space; time creates the present through its union with space. Not to have space is not to be;
thus in all life striving for space is an ontological necessity. To have
no definite or final space means ultimate insecurity. This anxiety is
balanced by the courage which affirms the present and space.

Causality affirms the power of being by pointing to that which precedes a thing or event as its source. The cause makes its effect real. Causality presupposes that things do not possess their own power of coming into being. They are contingent: as Heidegger says, they have been "thrown" into being. Causality and contingent being are thus the same thing. The anxiety in which man is aware of this situation is anxiety about the lack of necessity of his being. This is the anxiety implied in the awareness of causality as a category of finitude. Courage ignores the causal dependence of everything finite, and accepts contingency.

Substance points to something underlying the flux, something relatively static and self-contained. But it is nothing beyond the accidents in which it expresses itself—it is no "I-know-not-what."

The problem of substance is not avoided by philosophers of function or process, because questions about that which *has* functions or about that which *is* in process cannot be silenced. The replacement of static notions by dynamic ones does not remove the question of that which makes change possible by not (relatively) changing itself (197).

Everything finite is innately "anxious" that its substance will be lost. Courage accepts the threat.

These four categories express the union of being and nonbeing in everything finite. They articulate the courage which accepts the "ontological anxiety" of nonbeing.

It is in this analysis of actuality or "existential being" that existential ontology is most characteristic and most original. It is here also that it is most "existential," in the sense of being most limited by the historical and cultural situation out of which it arose. It is an appropriate philosophic expression of the "age of anxiety," formulating the structure of human experience and of human nature as it has been historically conditioned by the cultural crises of Central and Western Europe since 1914. And since, by its own method, being is to be found in "being as experienced," or "being as encountered"—since the structure of being is the structure of the "self-world polarity"—the way being is encountered at any time by an historically conditioned self is the way being *is*.

This polarity or encountering can be looked at either from "outside"—the side of the world—or from "inside"—the side of the particular type of self.

There is no reason for preferring concepts taken from "outside" to those taken from "inside." According to the self-world structure, both types are equally valid. The self being aware of itself and the self looking at its world (including itself) are equally significant for the description of the ontological structure (192).

Hence Heidegger and Tillich are justified in calling their analysis of the experience of the self in psychological terms, "ontology," and in taking as intentional, for example, what from the "outside" is finitude and from the "inside" anxiety. From his theological perspective Tillich naturally emphasizes the feel of the categories to immediate experience, rather than their function from "outside." The parallel here with the way in which Dewey, for example, describes immediate experience as shot through with values and emotionality, is striking. Indeed, Dewey's familiar "situation" that is objectively "doubtful" is a clear instance of just such existential ontology. Both Dewey and Tillich are open to the same misunderstandings and criticisms—criticisms that are hardly justified for any metaphysics that takes man as an integral part of Nature, or self and world as polar.

The real doubt is not as to whether the self or encounterer is part of the situation, or of being, but as to the character of the self that is made basic to the analysis. *Is* the immediate experience of finitude for the self "anxiety"? Rather, for what kind of self, under what cultural conditions, is this so? I remember Tillich once reporting, after an evening with a Russian, "Wunderbar! Sie hat keine Angst!" Despite the psychiatrists, I think this is still true. "The ontological anxiety of finitude" may well express the way many Continental Europeans feel these days. But in this country I seriously doubt whether for many it can mean more than the latest fashion in theological apologetics.

All existence is finite and determinate—is τόδε τι, as Aristotle puts it. And, as he also pointed out, for illustrative purposes, all men are mortal. But these finite limitations of human life in time and space have rarely provoked emotional disturbance, or "anxiety." It takes a good German Romanticist like Heidegger to get really excited over the natural conditions of human life. One trembles to think of the problems if man were *not* finite! Others have usually felt much more keenly the moral limitations of human nature than the "ontological anxiety" of metaphysical determinateness. In other words, "anxiety" seems to be for Tillich rather a religious symbol and an existential commitment than an ontological concept.

Tillich has no place for any natural theology, nor can metaphysics prove the "existence" of God.

God does not exist. He is being-itself beyond essence and existence. Therefore, to argue that God exists is to deny him (205).

The traditional "arguments" are all invalid: they are neither arguments nor proof. "They are expressions of the *question* of God which is implied in human finitude." God is not *a* being, he is being-itself, or the ground of being. He is the power of being—the power inherent in everything of resisting nonbeing.

Being-itself infinitely transcends every finite being. There is no proportion or gradation between the finite and the infinite. There is an absolute break, an infinite "jump." On the other hand, everything finite participates in being-itself and in its infinity. Otherwise it would not have the power of being. It would be swallowed by nonbeing, or it never would have emerged out of nonbeing (237).

"The statement that God is being-itself is a non-symbolic statement. . . . It means what it says directly and properly" (238). However, nothing else can be said about God as God which is not symbolic. Into Tillich's penetrating analysis of symbols we cannot here go. God is the ground of the ontological structure of being without being subject to this structure himself. He *is* the structure; that is, he has the power of determining the structure of everything that has being.

What remains in doubt here is whether for Tillich "being-itself," the "ground of being," is an ontological, that is, a philosophical concept, or a theological symbol. He seems to identify "the structure of being," which he has analyzed philosophically, with the "ground of being," and both with "the power of being." Now, ontologically speaking, these seem to be three very different concepts, and, surprisingly enough, Tillich never attempts to distinguish or clarify them. The "structure" of being, as he has rationally analyzed it, seems fairly clear. The "power" of being, as the power in everything to resist nonbeing, is likewise clear—though I myself should take the power of being as a polar "element," and treat it in the plural, as the powers to operate in determinate ways. But a structure is hardly in itself a power. Nor is either to be intelligibly identified with a "ground." How does a "ground" differ from a "cause"? Tillich specifically insists that "causality" as applied to the relation between "being-itself" and finite beings is not a category but a symbol. It seems clear that all these notions are actually used by Tillich as symbols, and that they hence do not belong to metaphysics or ontology at all, but to theology.[6] This is especially true of "being-itself," a concept at which ontological analysis can never arrive. Ontology can find only the "being" which is common to all particular and determinate beings. "Being-itself," in any other sense, seems to be a religious myth or symbol. Hence the line which for Tillich is ultimately impossible to draw, between metaphysics and theology, I should draw more narrowly, and find some of the notions he takes as ontological concepts to be religious myths and symbols.

Tillich is not primarily the prophet—the man whose sincerity and stamp of inspiration bring immediate conviction—but rather the philosopher, whose appeal lies in his mastery of reason and rational argument. Paul Tillich seems to me not only the ablest Protestant theologian of the present day, but also by far the most persuasive exponent of the philosophy of existentialism, and, what is more to the point, a real contributor to the present-day revival of metaphysical inquiry. His is a first-rate philosophical mind.

JOHN HERMAN RANDALL, JR.

DEPARTMENT OF PHILOSOPHY
COLUMBIA UNIVERSITY
NEW YORK CITY

[6] Cf. their "metaphorical" character, I, 79.

8

Charles Hartshorne
TILLICH'S DOCTRINE OF GOD

8

TILLICH'S DOCTRINE OF GOD

THE *Systematic Theology* seems destined to have deep and lasting influence. Considering the majestic structure, grandly conceived and patiently executed, the manifestations of intellectual gen-
erosity, and historical knowledge of the religions and philosophies,
this work seems unique and great. One must feel gratitude and veneration toward the author, even if, as in my case, one is not able to
follow him without reservations.

After this warning of my mixed attitude, I shall first attempt to
give a fair and objective, though brief, summary of Tillich's statements about God. I have tried to keep before my own mind the
whole theologico-philosophical setting provided for the doctrine,
even though not all aspects of it are to be discussed here.[1]

God, says our author, is that which unconditionally or ultimately
concerns us. This is offered as an abstract translation of what is implicit in the commandment, "Love the Lord thy God with all thy
heart . . ." Apart from reference to our religious life, we can only
say that deity is "being-itself," or the "power of being whereby it
resists non-being." (Even this we can understand only because of
an element of "ecstatic" or implicitly religious experience in all of
us.) All descriptions of God, other than this, are symbolic, not literal
(146). Professor Tillich often speaks, indeed, almost as though "absolute," "unconditioned," "infinite," "eternal," were synonyms for
"being-itself," and equally literal in application to deity; but he also
insists that being-itself, or God, is "beyond finitude and infinity"
(144), and implies the same with respect to "relative" and "absolute" (cf. 138), "temporal" and "eternal," and even "spatial" and

---

[1] Page references to the *Systematic Theology*, upon which, apart from conversations with Prof. Tillich, my exposition is essentially based, will be given in
parentheses throughout this essay.

"spaceless" (184, 186). Presumably, then, this holds with respect to "conditioned" and "unconditioned"? At any rate, if the finite, relative, conditioned, has being, then "being-itself" would seem somehow to transcend the mere negatives of these concepts.

Among nonliteral or symbolic statements about God, the chief are that He is "living" (149 ff.) and "personal" (151 f.), that He is "the creative and abysmal ground of being," and that He is "Spirit" or "Love" (145). Life is literally "the process in which potential being becomes actual being." But since God "transcends" the distinction between potential and actual, God is "not living in the proper or nonsymbolic sense." God lives in so far as He is the ground of life. " 'He that formed the eye, shall He not see?' " "Ground" is neither cause nor substance, taken literally, but something "underlying" all things in a manner which we can only *symbolize* through causation or substantiality. Literal causes always are also effects, something conditioned (whereas God is unconditioned), while "substance" and "accidents" lack the freedom with respect to each other which Christianity affirms both of God and of creatures. God has self-hood; He is not a mere thing or object; however, "self" implies "separation from and contrast to everything which is not self," whereas God, since He is being-itself, is separate from nothing. He is "the absolute participant" (152), hence He cannot literally be a self. Similarly, He is not that highest order of self which is a person. He is superpersonal, but for us necessarily symbolized as personal.

God is free and yet has a destiny—but this in nonliteral fashion, inasmuch as in God destiny is in "an absolute and unconditional identity" with freedom (151). Not even symbolically does God "exist," since to exist is to be subject to space-time and causality, to be finite, as God is not (110, 143 f.).

Though many of these assertions and denials have a familiar, traditional ring, there seem also to be distinctive features.

To say that God transcends the difference between potentiality and actuality used to mean that He was actuality without potentiality, *actus purus*. Similarly, to say that God is being-itself used to mean that He had no aspect of becoming. And God was held not to be separated from anything only in the sense that he is cause of all and conscious of all. Scarcely even symbolically would the classical theologians, as a rule, allow the substance-accident schema, or potentiality, or becoming, to be used to describe God. But Tillich accepts all of them as symbols. The doctrine of pure actuality is declared to be mistaken, since God is (symbolically speaking) living, and "life is actualization, not actuality" (84, 153). We must, he urges, use both sides of the polarity, potential and actual, or dynamics and form, or self-transcendence and self-preservation, as symbolic of God. Again, "if we say that God is being-itself, this includes both rest and becoming." Finally, it is at least hinted that God is not mere cause or creator, but is also (symbolically) effect or creation. For there is talk of divine "self-creation"; and we are told that the finite creatures are taken up into the divine life, and that what is positive in time is included in that life (165 f., 184 f.). Again, it is said that God and creatures by their freedom mutually "transcend" each other (171). (Is the virtually exact parallel with Whitehead intended?) There is no "divine determinism." All creatures have some spontaneity or freedom. We influence God's direction of the world, though not usually as we desire or expect.

These and numerous other statements make it apparent that Tillich wishes to transcend the old theology of God as Being in the exclusive sense (negative of becoming), or as the "naked absolute" (a phrase which he quotes from Luther), by recognizing, "symbolically" at least, a polarity in deity (or in being-itself) of infinite *and* finite, potential *and* actual, fixed being *and* becoming. I therefore (joyfully) acclaim him as one of the rapidly growing company of "dipolar" theists or "panentheists" to which some of us are proud to belong. But this interpretation is not without its difficulties. It is not merely that Tillich dubs all the dipolar statements as nonliteral. Berdyaev does that too, but when, as in the Russian author, the statements are nearly all there, and form a fairly coherent whole, the addition of "symbolic" seems of problematic value, positive or negative. In Tillich's case there is either somewhat less coherence, or I have not been able to find the key. And to me incoherence "symbolizes" something human rather than something divine. Tillich himself finely and bravely says that the theologian is no more excused from logical consistency than anyone else, legitimate "paradox" being other than logical contradiction. I do not think he means to be less than coherent.

Let us go back to the beginning, the religious concern. This is a total concern. If God is loved with the "whole heart," then nothing else—it seems to follow—can be loved at all, not even our neighbor! The only escape is to say that love of God includes, in the most literal sense, all legitimate love whatsoever. Now Tillich recognizes this. The sacred is not properly an interest alongside secular interests. (That it seems so merely illustrates, for him, the "disrupted" character of our existence.) The religious interest, we might say (our author seems not to have said it), is interest itself, as its object is being or reality (and value) itself. But since it is a religious imperative to be interested in the finite and changeable and conditioned—the neighbor and his welfare—the religious interest must be in a God who embraces the finite, relative, and changeable. Further, since nothing extrinsic to our interest can be recognized, recognition being already an interest, the One who is all that is interesting can only be reality itself. So far I perhaps seem to agree with our theologian. But I ask, is not the unreservedness and inclusiveness of our "concern" one thing, and its "unconditionedness" or "ultimacy"—with the philosophical associations of these terms—another? And just these associations are crucial in some of Tillich's deductions: for example, "what unconditionally concerns us cannot be conditioned" (apparently in *any* philosophical sense), or cannot be "arbitrary," in the sense of involving anything literally "contingent" (156). These implications are not, I suggest, involved in the definitive commandment, Love God with the whole of oneself. "Unreserved" is not the same as "unconditioned" or "without contingency." Surely our actual love of God is literally contingent, and we are powerless to make it otherwise. Had certain conditions been different, God would have concerned me not at all, for I should not have existed. Nor (with suitable alternative conditions) would my concern have included my neighbor's welfare, for he would not have existed. Yet my actual love of God, to which no interest can legitimately be extrinsic, must embrace my actual neighbor. Thus it is conditioned if he is, or if I am, or if anything is, and in the same literal sense. True, there are *aspects* of unconditionedness in the way God concerns me (and in God Himself). (1) There is a common element in all creaturely concern, which is identical through all changes of creatures. (And God, as thus *universally* concerning all alike, is in this aspect simply identical and unconditioned.) This, however, is not the total love commanded of me here and now, but a mere common denominator of all creaturely response to deity, an utmost abstraction. God as involved in this abstraction is indeed God, for "under all conditions" God is Himself, is God; but He is not under all conditions "the Lord thy God" of the commandment addressed to me. For this is God *qua* having created me, who am a contingent, non-necessary reality, and it is God *qua* possessed of the whole truth about me (there might have been no such truth in His possession). This God is then conditioned, as is my love for Him. If it be said that the statement in parenthesis is false, then I can only reply that in that case "conditioned" has no theological meaning which I am capable of grasping, and neither has "unconditioned." (2) To be sure, the conditions, thanks to which God concerns me now as my God, are already actualized, and there can be no *further* conditions for the present response. I cannot legitimately say, "Yes, but . . ." "Yes, unless . . ." "I would if . . ."; nor can I say, "In part Yes and in part No." I simply am to say, "Yes." But this "Yes" means that since I do happen to exist in such and such a world, therefore the God of that world ("my God") is my total valid concern. If, however, what concerns me is only unconditioned in *this* sense, then we may all agree. Yet there is considerable evidence that Tillich does not admit or at least adhere to these distinctions. Does this not confirm the supposition that his formula is misleading? Total, integral, unreserved response seems to be what religion calls for, rather than the philosophical "unconditioned," "ultimate," "absolute," or "infinite." (These are all, no doubt, valid, but of an aspect of God, not of God in His total reality.) "God is what unqualifiedly and totally concerns us" seems a safer definition; but it would not, when properly interpreted, yield some of the deductions referred to.

Let us turn from the religious or "existential" to the philosophical aspects of our problem. Tillich says that God is the answer to the philosophical question. Rightly he holds that theology today must deal with the controversy between the classical philosophies or theologies of being—which treat becoming as an inferior order of reality—and the philosophies or theologies of process, developed largely in modern times (beginning, I should say, with Socinus), which hold that being, so far as other than becoming, is a function, aspect, or constituent of the becoming or process which (Bergson) "is reality itself." Our theologian aims to do justice to both sides in this controversy (154 f.). But—I remark—so did the great modern philosophers of process themselves; certainly Whitehead tried with all his considerable powers to find precisely the adequate, balanced view of the relations between process and fixed being. So did Fechner, Berdyaev, and still others. They were familiar with the doctrine of being. (Berdyaev, for a time, talked in its terms.) The assumption of their failure to achieve balance is not justified by the mere fact that they affirmed (more or less explicitly) the coincidence of process and reality. For "what becomes *and* what does not become," the referent of this entire phrase, does it become—or not? This at least is clear: merely to say that something becomes and something does not, that we must admit "form and dynamics" (in Tillich's phrase), leaves it open what status is assigned to the togetherness of the two. Our author himself says that "being is not in balance with becoming" (154). Just so, but which is it that characterizes their togetherness? (We shall see that the question is not merely terminological.) Process philosophy, in its mature forms, holds that *process includes all the fixed being* that anyone needs or can conceive: (1) past events of process as immortally remembered or objectified (Bergson, Whitehead, and others) in all subsequent process—adequately only in the divine process; (2) the universal structures generic to process as such in the form of abstract constituents of any and all units of process; (3) the emergent structures as less abstract constituents of process subsequent to the emergence.

What is Tillich's reaction to this view? Indeed, has he reacted to it? He does refer to the "process of being"—as though being in its inclusive character were process. But when he says that being comprises movement and rest, process philosophy can only reply: "Movement itself (process, actualization) comprises elements of rest, and this is all the rest we have reason to talk about. Motion is never a mere aspect or constituent of rest, but rest is always a mere aspect or constituent of motion."

Our author, on the one hand, accuses the classical theory of pure actuality with "swallowing" dynamics in pure form; on the other, he implies that philosophies of becoming do the converse. But the point is that, while a total reality cannot be literally "immutable" unless everything in it is immutable, a total process-up-to-now can very well be succeeded by a literally *new* total containing the old, and even something neither new nor old but eternal! Philosophies of being can indeed only "swallow," that is, digest and denature the idea of becoming. (Tillich himself seems to do this in his account (185) of how becoming is, and is not, in the divine "being.") Philosophies of becoming, on the contrary, can perfectly well include—not swallow, destroy—but harmlessly and fully include, fixed being. (Why this is so will be explained shortly.) It follows that God, since He is the inclusive reality, must be *Process-itself as in-*

cluding Being-itself. Process-itself is divine Process, not ordinary process (though including it), just as Being-itself is not ordinary being. Tillich actually suggests that for Whitehead God is perhaps the creative processes of nature. This is as far from Whitehead as it would be from Tillich to suppose that God may be just the various beings in the world. If Being itself is not ordinary being, neither is Process-itself ordinary process. Whitehead doesn't use this language; however, the "consequent nature of God" is a superprocess—*inclusive,* indeed, of ordinary processes, but only as these are its data, its "objective forms." The subjective forms are different not in degree but in principle. "God is not the world, but the valuation of the world." This does not mean that the natural process goes on of itself and that God at most adds His evaluation, or merely originates the process (according to Tillich, the common view in recent times). Through His fresh valuations of each phase of process as it occurs, God is the continuing inspirer of order and stimulus to novelty of each subsequent phase ("special providence for the special occasion"). On the other hand, the divine "flux" contains the absolutely fixed structure and absolutely inexhaustible potentialities of the "primordial nature." This flux is, in sum, the Process which evokes, sustains, and possesses ordinary process, but is essentially different in kind. It may seem to follow that only "symbolically" is it process at all. I prefer "analogically" here. When God is said to be father, king, or lord, everyone sees that this is not literal, but is using "a finite segment of reality" to represent deity. But "process" is no finite segment of anything. (Tillich's term "symbolic" thus is itself used nonliterally.) Process is rather that from which everything is abstracted, or within which everything that is bounded has its limits.

We are told that it is easy to criticize theologically the theory that God has real accidents, taking this idea literally; for it then makes God finite, a polytheistic God, dependent on a fate or accident which is not Himself (154). I am glad that Tillich here brackets me with Berdyaev. But literally is just the way of taking the theory that fails to justify the criticism. For the theory is that the accidental includes the purely necessary, independent, self-sufficient —yes, as we shall see, the absolutely infinite! (This also is negative.) Thus the theory is not that of "a finite God," but of the finite-infinite (relative-absolute, mutable-immutable) God. The theory taken literally and accurately is not polytheistic, but excludes the possibility of rival gods. Nor does it imply a "possible disruption" of deity.

Our author insists that we cannot get rid of "substance," that is, enduring individuality. Now the theory that events are the full actualities includes a positive doctrine as to what is meant by enduring individuality. This is treated as a "defining characteristic," or pervasive quality and order, of a sequence of events or occasions, each objectifying its predecessors. It is held that nothing given in our experiences of self-identity is thereby denied, but rather something additional is asserted, which is that each occasion has, besides the enduring individuality, say, of "John," its own unique, momentary (and subsequently immortal) self or subject pole, more determinate and fully actual than the merely self-identical ego, which is certainly real, but is somewhat abstract. It is thus not "John" who literally says "Yes" today and "No" tomorrow, but two subjects (without names, yet referred to through "John," plus indications of context, or through "I" in the same manner), which subjects are for many important purposes "the same," and really the same. For there is a literally identical individuality structure, but (as follows from the inclusiveness of process) it is the successive occasions which have the common structure, not the common structure which has the occasions. Considering the vast array of ideas Tillich understands and relevantly criticizes or interprets, it is not surprising if he has done less than justice to this one.

In the light of the foregoing analysis, can God be conceived as the substance of the world, that is, its inclusive, enduring individuality, without contradicting the mutual freedom of God and creatures? The answer is that, according to the principles of process and relativity, even ordinary individuals include one another, and yet each has its spontaneity or freedom. The occasions which actualize one individual furnish "data" for those which actualize another. Such data are prehended with a certain passivity, which enables one free or "self-created" occasion to be possessed by another in that deficient manner in which ordinary occasions can possess their objects. The divine prehension or inclusion is the eminent form. This eminence means not the absence of passivity, nor yet symbolic passivity, but perfect passivity, exquisitely and absolutely able to adjust itself to the freedom of the included. Also, whereas ordinary inclusion is qualified inclusion, eminent inclusion is unqualified or absolute, in other words, literal, sheer inclusion of other individuals; but in all cases such inclusion is compatible with freedom. If, however, "substance" is to mean what it did to Aristotle, Thomas, Descartes, Leibniz, Spinoza, or Kant, and the other philosophies of Being (as including Becoming rather than vice versa), then Process philosophy holds that not only does it fail to apply literally to God in relation to the world; it fails to apply literally to anything, for none of these thinkers had a literal, if that means a definite and consistent, meaning for the term "substance." If the meaning is clarified and rendered consistent in the light of the principles of process and relativity, then it will apply most literally to deity, and, with indeterminate qualifications, or as "deficient," to ordinary individuals. Thus where Tillich finds literalness of meaning except in reference to God, I find scarcely a meaning at all, but more or less confused metaphors ("substance," what "stands under"), until clarifications are made which result in unqualified applicability to God alone, convertible into applicability to ordinary things by the highly indefinite qualification "deficient." No doubt the difference between us is partly terminological.

However, the difference is not merely terminological. It would be wrong to suppose that the proposition, "Reality is process as inclusive of fixed being," differs only verbally from Tillich's phrase, "Being includes both motion and rest." For, although I prefer "reality" to "being" for the inclusive term, since *real* contrasts with fictitious or apparent rather than with what becomes, still this, though important, is not the main point, which is rather: whatever the word, the inclusive meaning is not something attached to it once for all. Any wholly fixed sense of "being" or "reality" is necessarily abstracted from the referent of "this present occasion." There is indeed a generic "thisness," realness, or being; but the full this or real is indicated only by context, not by a mere name. "The universe," "reality," "being," "the truth," "God," in their inclusive meanings are demonstrative pronouns, as Whitehead puts it; and he would have agreed with Peirce that it is more appropriate to say, "nouns are pro-demonstratives," than to call "this" and other indicative terms "demonstrative *pro*nouns." Naming is secondary to indicating through context. Each time we refer concretely to "the real," the referent is partly new. God in his fullness is *our* God, *this* divine actuality. He is always the same, but never *merely* the same twice over. (Tillich himself says that there can be no totality of all things; but he does not seem to mean merely that there is a new totality each moment.) "Process" in its most inclusive sense is what now-becomes, including past events and fixed structures as constituent "data" (to human beings, largely hidden or unconscious). Philosophies of being implicitly reduce indication to naming, hence the novel to the fixed. Process philosophy will grant all sorts of fixity; but that in reality or in God which can be named at any time, and once for all, it views as abstract, a common denominator or fixed structure of various becomings, various referents of various uses of "*this* becoming now." To refute doctrines which *deny* fixed structures, yes, eternally fixed and necessary ones, is to talk about something else than systematic process metaphysics—existentialism, for instance, in some of its forms.

The real issue is: Can "time" have an analogical meaning? Can there be two levels of temporality: ordinary, and eminent or divine? Many signs (more or less conceded by Tillich) point to an affirmative answer. We sometimes say the past is no longer actual. But this is a paradox. For we suppose that a description of the past is true or false. Now what is actuality but determinate form (as Tillich himself implies)? The past is not indefinite save for our knowledge. I conclude that it is not inactual, save for our knowledge!

Berdyaev distinguishes "disintegrated" from "integrated" time. One aspect of the distinction is that for integrated time the past is still actual. There is full "memory" of past experiences in all their wealth of vividness and definiteness. Does this mean there is no real change or transition to new presents? Not at all. Time (taken eminently) is "invention or nothing" (Bergson); or more clearly, it is creative synthesis or nothing. Tillich's remark that what is positive in time is in God, implies that creation, as an ever new synthesis embracing all that is not new, is in Him, for this *is* the positive content of time and change! The "data" of each synthesis include whatever is not new. But, whereas the divine counterpart of memory (Tillich allows this, symbolically [185]) has determinate experiences as its data, divine anticipation perhaps does not. For there really are "past inventions"; but are there "future inventions"? Rather, some of us hold, there is the potentiality of further inventing of a more or less determinate kind, with the certainty that *something* definite will be invented. Thus change, as in God, consists in the sheer addition of states without any loss or subtraction, without the lamented temporal "destructiveness" and "separation." The new is always together with what is not new, though the latter was once "separate" from the former—when there was no such thing to be separated from—scarcely a real separation! That every "not yet" is "balanced" in God by an "already" is to me meaningless, unless it merely asserts that God is always "already" Himself, in possession of an unimaginably rich past. That a real "not yet" would be a "divine-demonic power" seems no clearer. There is only God's own power of receptivity to creaturely free acts which *may* be enacted, in response to acts of His own persuasion which also may be enacted. God's power is inexhaustible, hence never exhausted; and the possible creaturely responses to this power cannot be a fixed totality. What is demonic about this?

One sense in which God is indeed our "power of being" now appears. The mere present, as ours, has exceedingly little content, compared to the total wealth of experiences we have had in the past. When we die, that is in a sense a minor change, for nearly all we have actually been is, on the merely human plane, unreal already. We have no abidingness, even temporarily and in our own lifetime, save in God. "Our ultimate concern" for preservation is thus met, not by a merely eternal but by an eternal-temporal God, who *acquires* our experiences as imperishable possessions. Tillich's impressive treatment of immortality is probably not far from this view. Of course, time is "united with eternity," but by including it, not conversely (which, as we have seen, would be contradiction). Also, though our experiences (our only *actual* values) are, in God, indestructible and everlasting, they are not literally eternal, for that would mean ungenerated as well as indestructible. Tillich seems to slur over this distinction. Only God has "eternal life." We have everlasting life. This, to be sure, includes God's eternal life in the radically deficient or nonliteral way in which such "subjects" as we are include their objects, that is, what they are aware of. (We are coming to that.) Our everlastingness, however, is not deficient but literal, for it is due to God's perfect awareness or knowledge of us, not our imperfect awareness of Him.

Tillich, indeed, rejects the idea of "divine knowledge," except as a symbol. Also, he prefers to say that we are related to a spiritual ground or center, because "spirit" is more than mere cognition, since it includes the other psychic functions as well. But it may be suggested that cognition is never "mere," being always an aspect of a whole "experient occasion." Least of all could eminent knowledge be mere cognition rather than spirit. To assert that God knows us is to imply that he values us, enjoys us, and so forth. Are we then to say we are adequately known, but there is none who knows us adequately? Or are we *not* adequately known? I cannot be comforted by the assurance that God does *better* than literally know us. I think there can be nothing better than literal, adequate knowing, which for my theory of knowledge is not separable from adequate loving, that is, valuing another for its own sake. (The knowing in us, like the loving, is always less than unqualified loving of anything.) And my discomfort is not mitigated by encountering here the familiar argument that there must be no condition or finitude characterizing the divine Spirituality. I cannot share this seeming worship, or near-worship, of "infinite" (or "unconditioned") as though it were God, or almost God; even though one is assured that God is *neither* literally "infinite" nor literally "finite." For I think that "finite" is not inferior in any way to "infinite" but has simply a different categorical rôle, and that what is truly less than our God is whatever lacks either (or both) literal infinitude or literal finitude. The one lack characterizes such as we (who, indeed, as will be shown, have both defects); the other characterizes something abstract, the mere power of God considered apart from all accomplishments, his ability to possess worlds, not His possession of any. To worship this abstraction may be a form of subtle idolatry. Advisedly, Berdyaev speaks of "slavery to being," to the mere identity in process. Worship of the divine Process-as-of-now, since that includes but transcends divine fixed Being, is another matter. This Process seems the same as "our God," at once absolutely infinite (in the proper categorical aspect), and also, as a whole, literally finite or relative in the eminent manner (to be more fully explained presently) which excludes even a logical possibility of rivalry by another. This theory (in essence Fechner's, Whitehead's, Berdyaev's, Montague's, as well as mine) is bold, maybe far too bold, yet it might be worth considering on its merits, rather than by criticism of theories only remotely similar. Repeatedly our learned author argues that no such doctrine can be literally applicable because absurd consequences follow from his own (very unliteral) interpretation of it! For example, he denies that divine creating can be either literally necessary or literally contingent (160). It cannot be necessary, for it would then depend "on a necessity above it." But this is not the literal metaphysical meaning of "necessary," which does not, in principle, mean necessitated by, but rather "without possible alternative because common to a range of possibilities." Where, as in the theological usage, the range is unlimited, is possibility-itself;

then no "higher" condition need select between the necessary and any alternative, since here the idea of an alternative is vacuous. If God is Process-itself, possibility-itself coincides with the alternativeness or flexibility of this divine Process—that it is able to occur thus *or* thus. Accordingly, its mere nonoccurrence or cessation is not even a bare possibility, but is mere nonsense. And if, as Tillich himself says (172), God is essentially creative, and of course, as we have just seen, essentially real, this is the same as saying that his not creating is not a possibility, and this is identical with saying that his creating is literally necessary. Yet one may also say, equally literally, that God creates contingently. Tillich refutes this by the argument that, since creating is one with the divine life, it does not just happen to Him. But here too, the distinctions of the "literal" doctrine are missed. God creates some world or other necessarily (not creating was not a possible alternative), but He creates this world contingently (there were alternative world-creating-possibilities). Merely in being Himself, the living God, He creates something. But to create this world is not merely for God to be Himself, and living, but for Him to live in just this relationship and with just this quality of divine "experience" (as good an analogical concept as any, to my mind). God does not contingently "live divinely"; but why must there be only one possible way so to live? I think literal contingency of experiences imposes no limitation on God that is not already granted if one moves unequivocally the least distance away from the "naked absolute," which we agree (I hope) is not identical with God. It cannot "happen to God" to be and to be Himself; but to become "my God"—this, I am sure as I could be of anything theological, does literally happen to Him.

But (Tillich may be thinking) to talk thus is to say that His own creation happens to Him! However, in Tillich's own words, we have freedom, and in that sense "transcend" God. And indeed, if any term is nonliteral, it is "create," as theologians are apt to use it. This usage is not merely nonliteral, it is often not even good symbolism. There is no such thing as "making" a free individual to be or do precisely what it is or does do. For then not "it" but only the maker would "do" what was done. Of course, we should not be free without God's sustaining action; but it is as literally true that God could not have certain experiences without our free acts. If we are free, then we genuinely decide something as to what we are to be; and that means, as to what God is to be. For, since God is the definitive, inclusive reality, not to decide what He is to be, in some degree and quality, is not to decide anything! It seems Tillich must be with us in all this, but his language keeps making concessions to those who are not with us. He allows all sorts of dipolar terms, but denies that they mean what they say, and then arbitrarily (I think) decides to forbid certain terms altogether. Why, for instance, is it not just as easy to formulate the worshipful uniqueness of God in terms of accident or happening as in any other terms? Only to God do all happenings happen, in their full content. What happens to Koreans (even to my wife) "happens" to me only in an infinitely qualified sense. What happens after I am dead will not in the normal sense happen to me at all. But no happenings can escape inclusion in the divine experiences correlative to them. These experiences are literally inessential to God (there could have been other divine experiences instead). To make them essential is the error of pantheism (correctly noted as such by our author). But is the error best avoided by refusing to assert that they are literally *inessential*? The "positivity of inclusiveness" shows that the divine togetherness of qualities with and qualities without alternatives must itself be with alternatives. To say it is not literally with, and not literally without, is to use words in order not to say anything—for all that Tillich shows. It is quite another thing to say that God is neither literally a ruler (that is, a man set over other men) nor yet not a ruler (something at least analogous to such a man). For all sorts of things can be analogous to a human ruler, and there may be an eminent or divine case of this analogy. But how can anything be analogous to "with alternative possibilities"? There are only with and without. True, the Law of Excluded Middle does not apply to everything, but that to which it does not apply is the general, abstract, or possible, as involving alternatives (possible man is neither tall nor not tall, but indeterminate-determinable). Can we then exempt from the law these very disjunctions, with and without alternatives, general or not general, possible or actual, in accordance or not in accordance with the Law of Excluded Middle? I question if we can without pure defiance of logic. And to say that Being-itself is this illogical thing, which yet is literally God, is to forget that there cannot, on that assumption, be a literal meaning for "Being-itself."

Against the argument that our categories refer to the finite only, the reply is easy: Our category of possibility refers directly to the absolutely infinite, since the very meaning of finite (on its negative side) is that some possibility is excluded from actualization. Thus the literal meaning of our conceptual contrast itself "transcends" the merely finite and the merely infinite!

"Transcends" in such usages as the above, or as in "transcends the distinction between potential and actual," seems less symbolic than ambiguous. The quoted phrase might mean, "is not *merely* actual or *merely* potential but (in different aspects) *both*"; then I understand and accept it. It might mean, "is neither actual nor potential but some third something, better than anything literally containing the two." It would literally follow (for me) that actuality and potentiality as such were unreal. For since God is the inclusive, definitive reality, if in Him they are not different, then "in reality" they are not different. Accordingly, the categories must be just as unliteral in application to us as to God! This would be illusionistic monism, not theism. It seems only rhetorically, not logically, that Tillich avoids both the Sankara illusionism and Spinozistic pantheism. I add that even ordinary living, or actualization, in its deficient manner, yet in the legitimate sense, "transcends" mere actuality or mere potentiality, since every actual process is *both* the potentiality of further process and the actualization of potentialities in previous process. The inclusive principle is not something utterly mysterious, to be called being, which is neither in contrast nor not in contrast to becoming, but process itself, with a face of "actuality" (in the literal sense, for there is here no other), viewed in one temporal direction, and of "potentiality," viewed in the other, with an eternal factor of abstract being common to all such potentiality. Each actual synthesis is a "potential" for further syntheses, that is, they can have it as datum in inexhaustibly various ways. (Tillich says something like this [186].) No synthesis, still less any mere "being," nor anything whatever, can have all possible syntheses, all actualized. Tillich says (186) that God can (symbolically speaking) "anticipate any possible future." *If* he means that God can (in advance or eternally) possess the full value that any future would, or will have if or when actual and present, then I think he is simply destroying the meaning of the words employed. Anticipation is not, even in ideal or principle, an advance (still less an eternal) possession of actualities, but preparation for, and means to, their possession. Memory is possession of actualities, and only memory—except in the sense in which present experience possesses present actuality. Of course the future is not "absolutely open," if this means that not even general features are settled, possessed in advance.

Concerning the question of literalness in theological concepts, I wish (with apologies to him) to urge Barth's procedure (when taken to task for treating God in terms of personality). He said, I believe, something like this: We know what personality is because we know God; our understanding of human "personality" is derivative from revelation.[2] Similarly, I suggest, we know what human temporality is because we have (to use Tillich's word) an "ecstatic" sense of divine temporality. The past, *the* past, is not, even for us, simply our past, the mere content, even the possible content, of our memory and reconstruction from monuments and documents. *The* past "as it really was" transcends all human access in every precise aspect. It is the actualized life of God, to which at every moment new additions are made. Or again, what is a "subject" in relation to an object? In principle, it is the awareness of the object just as it is. But then all the quality of the object must be possessed by the subject, and not vice versa. We as subjects are not much like this. We are not literally subjects, that is, literal possessors of objects, but subjects minus something, indeed minus almost everything. We are remote imitations of a subject. Again, what is the finite? That which has definite limits, which is precisely *this,* but not *that.* However, all human perception is more or less indefinite. Only for God could anything be literally finite rather than merely indefinite. It is the divine finitude, God's *definite* perception of just this, not that, when it *might* have been perception of that and not this, that is the definitive, the standard finitude.

On the other hand, God also—and He alone—is literally infinite. For of course the divine in its aspect of potentiality is potentiality itself, coincident with ultimate possibility, the logically conceivable. I am speaking now of the element of "pure" potentiality in God, abstracting from all "real" potentials, that is, those limited to some definite circumstance or moment of process. The notion of "pure potentiality" is free from the difficulties of "pure actuality," since the abstraction implied in "pure" is no difficulty in the former case. Only actuality must be concrete. But the divine pure potentiality is plainly infinite. Omniscience could possess, experience, *anything,* should it occur. To say, "God could have experienced it,"

[2] Karl Barth, *Dogmatics in Outline* (London: Student Christian Movement Press, 1949).

and, "It could have occurred," is one. (By contrast, many possibilities or actualities are such that I could not have experienced them, for instance, your precise feelings in their full vividness.) Thus God's potentiality of possession as such, in its abstract purity, is absolutely without limitation. Any such limitation merely means that we have not carried out the abstraction, that we have not completely negated actual determinations in defining the referent of our thought.

We have seen that the inclusive reality is never negative in comparison with the included. This means, the inclusive reality is not infinite but finite. For finitude is not the mere absence of something, but (as I think Tillich recognizes) the presence of positive differentiation, individuation, variety. If there were nothing positive in "being this," but only the negation "being *not* that," then we should all be monistic mystics and simply depreciate the concrete and particular. Such is far from Tillich's intention. It is the "absolutely infinite" that is essentially negative—in comparison with the finite—and that constitutes *nonbeing* in the dialectical sense spoken of by Tillich and Berdyaev, and which they distinguish from "nothing." It is the pure "power of being" which is only one aspect of God (if language is used clearly), that is, sheer potency, without actuality. This ultimate *power to be* anything at all is strictly infinite. No actual limits exist where there is no actuality at all. It follows that the infinite pure potentiality includes no finite actuality. There is indeed a region of potentiality to which any given actuality relates itself as that which it actualizes (and which it thus includes as its relatum); but the pure potentiality does not conversely include any actualization or any finitude. Tillich says that the power of being is no special being. Then I think we must infer that it includes no special being, for otherwise it would be the special total reality including that special being—whereas there might have been no such special being to include, in which case the total reality must have been a different one. My conclusion is that only a literally finite divine reality can include anything finite, only a literally relative divine reality can include anything relative, and only a literally contingent divine reality can include anything contingent. But a divine reality which, taken as a whole, is relative, finite, and contingent can contain not only all that is finite and relative, but also whatever is nonrelative, nonfinite, noncontingent; for negations applicable to the included need not apply to the including, whereas it is otherwise with affirmations.

Is the abysmal contrast between God and all else denied, as Tillich and so many others fear, in such a doctrine? It seems to me that the contrast is fully preserved, though it is described in a fashion different from the usual one. God is finite, but not simply as we are. The difference, moreover, is an "essential" one, a difference in principle, not merely in degree. Yet it can be literally stated; indeed, just because it is a matter of principle, it can be so stated. I call such a superiority-in-principle "categorical supremacy." Ordinary superiorities can never be quite literally stated, for they involve factual differences which escape full conceptualization. How much better does Tillich know the history of religion than I do? It would be hopeless to try to put this superiority of his into a definition or concept. It is an irreducibly Tillichian superiority. But God's "eminent" superiority in this regard (so far as it is a matter of principle) is easily stated: He has strictly adequate knowledge of man's religious growth; He knows it without qualification, just—knows it. This makes God finite. For man's religious growth might have been otherwise; and this otherwise is known even to God only as possibility, not as actuality. God actually knows as actual only what is actual, and this is in some respects limited and bounded. So his knowledge is in some respects limited. But *this* finitude, besides containing, as we saw above, the absolute infinity of the pure potentiality, infallibly and adequately embraces all actual finitude in a single actuality. No other finitude does anything of the sort, not even that of "the universe"; for this, so far as it can be distinguished from God, is not a single actuality. And, once more, it is not the ordinary cases of finitude that are literally statable. Only omniscience can define your finitude or mine, or even humanity's. (I shall discuss this point presently.) Yet we can define God's *essential* finitude, that which always and inevitably characterizes Him. His inessential finitude, on the contrary, that which happens to characterize Him now, as "our God," is a bottomless mystery into which we have some infinitesimal glimpses, as in saying that He knows "us" and all that we know, and what unimaginable things besides (including for all that I can see, a numerical infinity of past events)! Here indeed we have only symbols. I hope this lessens the distance between our distinguished author and myself. And remember, it is "our God" whom we are to love, not just "God." The "existential situation" we are always to come back to is never twice the same. There are really only situations. They and their God can only be symbolized. But then this is personal piety, not theology. *"The* existential situation" is an abstraction, and its God can be literally described, if the abstraction is carried far enough—"any creature and its God." I hope I am here making legitimate use of the "method of correlation."

Must not "adequate knowledge" be as literal as the concept of "truth," since indeed the two coincide, as Tillich, in his symbolic language, concedes? But how "adequate knowledge of our world" differs from adequate knowledge that would have been if some other world had existed instead of ours—this no man can say with even a remote approach to adequacy or completeness. It is thus the particular and inessential that eludes us, through its unfathomable richness of determinations, not the general and essential. Even the relatively particular, such as "human being," is elusive. The aspect of human finitude that can be literally defined is merely the general negative (applicable to all creatures) of the divine finitude. We can only say that our finitude does not, while the divine does, coincide with the truth. One statement, I submit, is as literal as the other. But suppose we add that "human being" is a "rational" or "conscious" creature. Are there precise boundaries to these concepts? And how does man's rationality differ from that of some more or less superior beings, such as may exist on planet X (Tillich would call these also "human," clearly a somewhat symbolic usage), or from that of slightly subhuman beings? Or when does an infant or embryo become literally a "human individual"? (Ability to use language is no doubt a good criterion, but there are all degrees of such ability.) Thus pure literalness is confined to God in His mere essence, with its negative correlate, "whatever is not God."

Among the signs that something is wrong with the doctrine of nonliteralness is the way in which its sponsors persistently fail to live up to one side of their contention, that talk about God is symbolic in comparison with talk about ordinary matters. Sometimes they speak about man, say, in language which is figurative and vague, often to the edge of meaninglessness; and sometimes they make seemingly literal statements about man which *qua* literal would apply better to God. Thus our author speaks of the human person as "complete," "universal," even "perfect," in its "centeredness" and its "participation" in the world (73–80, 167). But the completeness and universality are, of course, Pickwickian, hedged about with radical but indeterminate qualifications. Man "potentially" participates in all things in that, through abstract universals, he has some faint notions of the whole cosmos. But Tillich shows his awareness of how incomplete this "completeness" is when he says that God is not literally a person since He and only He participates absolutely. I agree. *This* participation is not a matter of degree, but is sheer possession, really "complete" and "universal." But then why not say that only God is literally a person? And there is no opposition between divine "centeredness" and divine possession or participating; for to "possess" here means to include as data in a synthesis with its own unity. That "self implies contrast to everything which is not self" may be accepted, but not that it implies "separation from everything." An inclusive reality contrasts with what it includes, a synthesis with its data; but it is not separated from them.

The dipolar way of contrasting God and all else may be expressed by saying that the relativity of God is itself, in its generic form, absolute. It is complete, adequate possession of all things *on condition only that they exist.* It is *absolute conditionedness*, not mere unconditionedness. Only God reflects adequately, infallibly, all that conditions Him—or that conditions anything else. This does not mean that God is, or is God, only if, or because, there happens to be a world for Him to possess. Divine power is adequate both to insure that there be a world and to possess whatever world there is. But just *what* world there is to possess is no mere question of God's power or freedom, or of His decisions as to its use. There are also *our* decisions—not decided *for* us in detail, even by God, but only *by us,* though of course in response to divine inspiration, which fixes the range of possibilities open to us.

Our philosopher-theologian, indeed, rejects "synergism" as meaning that we cooperate with God on the same plane. But how about our contributing to God, not indeed on the same plane—if that means without categorical difference—but still contributing according to a categorical analogy? As Berdyaev puts it, we by our freedom or creativity "enrich the very divine life itself."[3] We do it freely, that is, God undergoes the result as a sort of fate. Not that any alien power forces Him to be receptive to our determining of Him. Re-

[3] Nicolas Berdyaev, *The Russian Idea* (New York: The Macmillan Company, 1948), p. 243.

ceptiveness to creaturely action is of the essence of His will. But
the detailed action is not divinely chosen; it is accepted. There is
thus real chance, as Berdyaev says, even for God. Why not? There
can still be categorical supremacy. For only God *can* be enriched
to the literal full extent of the values we and all the creatures happen
to offer. We contingently enrich and so contribute to each other;
but this contribution never does anything like justice to what we
have to give. This friend takes this, that friend takes that; only the
divine friend is able to receive all, in its full vividness and exact
quality. But we, not God alone, determine what the contribution
is to be by determining ourselves, our own quality. There still is
"nothing in God that is not by God," if this only means that everything in God presupposes God Himself, at least in His eternal
essence. But it should not mean that the necessity or eternity of the
divine essence imparts its own status to things in God so as to prevent them from being literally generated and contingent. That "there
is nothing in God not affected by his freedom" is indeed clear. To
affect, however, is not fully to determine.

A basic point in common between Tillich and some of the rest
of us dipolarists is that we recognize nothing by which God could
be conditioned or limited other than the free creatures. There is no
eternal stuff or matter which God molds, nor any eternal antagonist
to Him. Divine freedom is unlimited by anything alien, unless the
acts of free creatures are called alien! (They are always responses
to antecedent divine freedom.) Tillich, unlike most theologians of
the past, recognizes that creaturely freedom is not exclusively human
(or angelic), but is, in generic essence, a universal principle of
creaturehood. Only by its own spontaneity or self-determination is
any actuality distinguishable from God. Perhaps our author would
agree to express this by saying that "conditioning" is the social aspect
of freedom. Only because freedom cares about (derives data from)
other freedom is one actuality determined by another. Love is the
key to interaction and causation. Tillich's discussion of the kinds of
love, human and divine, seems superior to Nygren's (188 ff.). Love,
or participation, he seems to agree, is the key to all unity in variety.

From this point of view I am somewhat mystified to be told (78)
that the unity behind the duality of subject-object is an abyss to
reason. Object, as Tillich himself virtually says, is simply whatever
anyone is aware of. This may be another subject. Indeed, I hold

(and there is some support in Tillich for this) that the object is always *either* an abstraction *or* (if concrete) another subject or subjects. To be aware of a subject is to have it as "object"; but this has in principle nothing to do with changing it into an inferior mode of mere "thing," or with rendering it relative to oneself. This is the principle of realism, in its most legitimate meaning. "Being-known" (by a particular subject) is only verbally a relation. It is knowing that relates, and subjects that are relative. (Tillich may hold otherwise; then we do indeed disagree.) So there is no problem as to how God escapes relativity, or reduction to an inferior status, by being known to us, by becoming our "object." This would literally "do" nothing to God, any more than "triangle" changes each time a new pupil studies geometry. It is because we are God's objects, not because He is ours, that His becoming "our God" means relativity and novelty for Him. He knows us; this is what relativizes Him to us! (He knows also our knowing of Him, and in *that* way it too relativizes Him. Knowing or feeling that one is known or felt is a real relation. It is through this principle that we are relative to God's knowing of us.) The persistent illusion that "object" means "*mere* object," mere thing, something less than a spirit, or than Spirit, is due, I suggest, to the fact that our awareness is not categorically literal, but indeterminately deficient and less than categorical. We indeed cannot be fully aware of persons as such, and hence our image of them does reduce their spirituality—not literally, for this image does nothing to them, but it produces an illusion of their reduction. We are not directly aware of other human spirits to any appreciable degree, but rather of changes in our bodies (sense organs and brains) produced by changes in their bodies. This is not at all inherent in the status of being-known, but is merely a character of animal knowing. In principle, knowing is loving, participation in other-life. Absolute, categorical participation is divine; we are capable only of something indeterminately less than sheer participation (most nearly adequate or literal in relation to our own "bodily life" and to our own past through memory). So other-life tends to appear for us as more or less dead, or lacking in intensity and richness, mere "objects" or "things." Still, we do participate, we have the principle; it is no utter mystery. "World" (much discussed by Tillich) as contrasted to self is the inclusive social community as inadequately participated in. God has no world in this sense, only the inclusive community, in its variable life fully participated in or loved. World as such he does not have; the community as such he does have.

How the divine unity is compatible with this is indeed a subtle logical problem which I do not clearly comprehend. But then I cannot understand the unity of the creatures with each other as contemporaries in space (problems of relativity physics, specious presents of different time lengths, and so forth). I suspect that what is profound in the "trinitarian principle" is related to this problem, though perhaps more to the way in which God as Process-itself has identity through eminent time, even though each moment there is a new divine subject-pole of experience. As Tillich well says, the trinitarian principle is not primarily a question of the number three, but is qualitative. We can agree here that God is not bare simplicity; and it would not be hard to concede that the number three has a certain importance, for the idea of synthesis is triadic and process is creative synthesis. But I suspect that infinite number (of subject-poles) should also come in.

The closest Tillich comes, perhaps, to dipolarity is in his doctrine that in God the polarities are present but without "tension" or possible "dissolution" (150, 156). For me this is merely spoiled if it is added that in God the poles are "absolutely identical." The recklessness of this language—which is repeated—is equaled by its lack of coherent meaning. Superiority to tension through infallible power to *harmonize* the poles is one idea; the mere identity of the poles, that is, sheer nonpolarity, is another. To say that polarities are present in God as "overcome" seems mere playing with words.

If "tension" or possibility of dissolution is an inferior relation between the poles, a deficient adjustment of them, then nontension may be an ideal or perfect and infallible relation or adjustment. Does this make it not literally a relation? It seems rather the relation in us that must be qualified, with qualifications that cannot be wholly conceptualized because they vary factually beyond the reach of mere essences. Harmony or sheer adjustment is the definite idea, disharmony is infinitely vague.

In some passages our theologian seems to reason: If God is not merely potential nor merely actual, then He is not literally either. (See, for example, 150.) But "literally containing potentialities" is entirely compatible with "literally containing actualities," and in-

deed every actuality itself contains both actualities and potentialities, and is never "merely" either actual or potential. If we avoid the
non sequitur of inferring "not literally" from "not merely," then
many sayings of Tillich's become intelligible. Thus, that Being-itself
is "neither abstract nor concrete" can legitimately mean only that
it is not exclusively either. For what is in no aspect either is,
I contend, sheer nonentity. God's "self-transcendence never is in
tension with his self-preservation, so that he always remains God"
(151). Yes, since the individual form of deity is the form of Process-
itself, the definitive process; hence no stage of process *could* fail to
express and actualize this form. Thus "tension" is excluded. "God
cannot cease to be God." Certainly not, but it does not follow that
He is now simply what He was before, or what He is eternally.
May we not say that God is always Himself, but that He is never
merely Himself? He is always Himself, but now in "real connection"
(Tillich's phrase) with this world state, and now also (and forever
after) with that world state. No self, indeed, is ever merely itself.
Identity through change is an aspect of life, not the totality. The
totality is always a process-now. The impossibility of disruption
does not mean that God's actuality is always optimal or maximal.
It is optimal only in the sense defined by the divine essence. Always
the divine is "all-knowing," completely adequate in its adjustment
to the creatures, as content of divine experience. But no content
can be maximal, and in that aspect of value which derives from
content, no actuality, as synthesis of data, can be maximal. Nevertheless, none can rival God, for any rival would be a mere element
of content in a synthesis with the unapproachable excellence of
"adequacy" to all content.

It is doubtless best, as Tillich says, not to speak of a "becoming
God" (translating from Scheler's German?), because this suggests
that perhaps God can be born, that there could be something prior
to the divine process, or that God could degenerate or die, that there
could be something subsequent to the divine process—or, as our
author puts it, that God is "subject to a process which . . . is completely open to the future and has the character of absolute accident." However, if ordinary self-identity can be maintained through
some changes, why not an eminent self-identity maintained through
all changes, without possibility of beginning or ending? It would
be so maintained by an appropriate divine process inclusive of, but

not identical with, ordinary processes—in short, by what Tillich calls the divine Life, which on the dipolar view is Process-itself, the definitive process.

Process contains its "power of being," that is, of creating and thereafter preserving ever new process. Ordinary process has this power in an ordinary manner, eminent Process in an eminent, definitive manner. After reading Tillich, I feel more convinced than ever that the contrast between indeterminate power to actualize and determine actuality must be literally, definitively, in God. *Our* actuality may indeed "symbolize" something different from itself in God, eminent actuality. But how the pure concept of actuality and potentiality can symbolize something devoid of difference between the two, I, at least, have not the faintest notion. The concept does not literally mean *your* actuality or potentiality, or *mine*. It does not even mean something localized in space. It means the determinate, in contrast to the determinable; and to the determinate there is no necessity to be part of a larger whole, since definiteness of constituents and of the manner of synthesis of them yields determinateness. (Even the external environment determines only because it is not wholly or with simple literalness external—"fallacy of simple location.")

But whether categorical concepts are literal or not, it is in any case questionable if one should pick and choose among them as Tillich does when, for example, he declares that "not even symbolically" does God exist. Tillich does not intend this as a semantic eccentricity. He argues vigorously for its acceptance. But let us see. To exist *as we exist* of course means to owe our whole reality to accidents, and our continuance to the favor of the environment. So if to exist means "as we exist," then God exists not. But just so, if to live means to live as we do, having been born, destined to die, open to degeneration to any degree, then God lives not. If, on the contrary, to live need not mean "as we do," why must exist mean "as we do"? If anything, it appears more reasonable to suppose "exist" to be free of such restrictions than "live," since superficially it seems that not all that exists lives! I think Tillich and I agree that this is not quite correct ultimately; but does it not show how arbitrary it is to try to make "live" more general or ultimate than "exist"? Of course one can follow Tillich's motives for this attempt. The Thomists did, as he learnedly and subtly points out, get into trouble through identifying essence and existence in God—but why? Because for a philosophy of mere being, either essence or existence of God is just God, in his total actuality. For a philosophy of process, however, existence and actuality are really distinct always, while *individual* essence and existence are, even in ordinary cases, in a certain sense identical, as Tillich himself implies. That a certain man at least has existed is one with his individuality structure, for "never existent men" is a merely intensional concept, not a class of members with fully individual structures. However, the very essence of a man includes in itself contingency, birth, limitedness of time-span. Can we not conceive of an essence which, on the contrary, excludes contingency as to existence (but not contingency as to the total actuality in and by which it now exists), and excludes therefore birth, death, or degeneration? If this is inconceivable, then equally so is a "living" that is similarly eminent and secure.

What exists need not even be finite. To exist is to be actualized in some way appropriate to the essence in question, in *some* actual entities, occasions, or units of process. By this definition "exist" has no necessary finitude except such as inheres in actuality; and, in the eminent case, existence is not itself finite at all. For the alternative possible finite actualities, *any* of which will actualize divinity, vary over the whole of ultimate potentiality, whose absolute infinity is measured by the infinite flexibility, the infinite power to become, of God. How then shall it be established that "actual" or "potential" have at least symbolic rights, and "exist" has none, on the score of finitude? We have repeatedly seen that the infinite is an aspect of the finite, not conversely, as the negative is of the positive, and that God is not simply the nonfinite. Were the Greeks not at least half right in their view that infinity in itself is not richness but emptiness?

Tillich also implies that to "exist" means to be *localized* in space as well as in time. This is arbitrary. To exist or live as we do implies localization. But space (as Tillich in a sense affirms [186]) is as easily viewed in an eminent manner as process. One may do this as follows: To be in space is to have neighbors (that is, those with whom one has intimate dynamic relations). Is not God the neighbor of all things in just this sense that all have intimate dynamic relations with Him? To be impartially neighbor, impartially intimate, with all—is that not to be freed from the limitations of localization? The literal analogical meaning of *neighbor of all* definitely excludes these limitations.

It may be conceded to Tillich that, like every description of the essence of God (but not of His actuality), the divine "existence" is tautology, since the intrinsic status of the divine essence, as that of Process-itself, is all that can be meant by its existing. However, the affirmation of this status, though analytic (as Kant scornfully suggested), is yet significant, since *other* essences *can* be themselves without in the full sense existing, that is, without being the characters of appropriate actualities. All known essences exist in some sense or degree, since if they are in no actuality they cannot be known or conceived. But some essences exist only evanescently or inappropriately, as the essence of a giant exists in a child's thoughts of it. One essence, however, excludes such evanescence or inappropriateness: it can only, and it must, exist in the fullest sense, since it *is* intrinsically the essence of Process-itself, of the moving measure of motion. Here indeed is a distinction which "disappears" or is "overcome" in God, that differentiating two modes of relation between essence and actuality. But note well: this not only does not conflict, it implies that the more basic distinction between essence and actuality—the really ultimate contraries—is fully preserved in God! For that there is but one type of relation between divine essence and actuality, that of "full" existence or "appropriate" embodiment, obviously involves a real difference between the essence and the actuality. Moreover, why is there but *one* relation of actuality to divine essence? Because the divine actualization or process, precisely as such (as divine and as process), is infinitely flexible in its potentialities, so that there is a possible divine actuality for any possible world state, and this in turn means that the difference between fixed essence and variable actuality is incomparably greater in God than in other things, as also follows from the requirement that the variability of actuality in Him must include *all* variations and thus give them their "reality."

In what sense the uniquely essential or tautologous existence of God can be proved through such considerations, I shall not now try to show. I agree with our author that the proof cannot consist in deduction of the divine from something else; rather it is a *reductio ad absurdum* of the denial of God, so that it is God Himself as content of our thought that excludes His own nonexistence, not something else that implies it. And I remark that if a vision of God is the hidden source of all metaphysics (a profound Tillichian doctrine), then we need not suppose that "our categories" are just human affairs: the vision is not simply behind the concepts, it is their essential meaning, apart from mere verbal habits or "operations" conducted unconsciously.

If this be so, the famous nonunivocalness of ultimate conceptions does not necessarily mean that, whereas they are literally true of ordinary things, they are but symbolically true of God. Berdyaev's theory seems to be that it is only the mystic or person with religious intuition as such who understands descriptions of God, hence categories as employed by secular "rationalistic" metaphysics must fail of literal applicability to deity. If, however, we agree also with Tillich that there is no purely nonreligious metaphysics, and that all philosophers are latent mystics, do we not come to the conclusion that metaphysical categories essentially refer, *with whatever meaning they have*, directly to God? And is it not God who, for example, literally "knows," while we guess and have probable evidence or approximately correct beliefs? Is it not of us, rather than of God, that categories must, in Tillich's apparently logic-defying phrase, be "affirmed and negated"? We do know—even more, we do *not* know—ourselves, our neighbors, the world, God, what you will. (Will Tillich admit, I wonder, that I simply know his philosophy? I certainly will not admit that I simply do *not* know it!) Again, is it we who literally "feel with" the feelings of others? Surely our "sympathy" is always qualified, inadequate, partial, infected with illusion to an indeterminable degree. If there be literal sympathy, it is divine only.

Our author says that God symbolically "suffers" with us in our sufferings. But he hedges this about with (to me) unclear reservations. Certainly God does not "suffer" simply as we do; but no more does He rejoice simply as we do. He does not suffer from fear of his own destruction or degradation. Neither does he rejoice to have escaped a threatened evil of this kind. Yet with some greater men, I devoutly believe that God suffers, as he also rejoices, through complete sheer "sympathy" with us in our sorrows and joys. No doubt this is analogical language. But is Tillich's language better when he says, "God is suffering not in his infinity, but as the ground of the finite"? I should suppose that God as absolutely infinite, the ultimate and universal ground, is neither enjoying nor suffering with respect to the world, but is the sheer potentiality of such enjoyment and suffering; while as the particular ground of each moment of process, the eminently finite actuality which includes the previous creaturely actualities—themselves finite in an essentially inferior manner—He shares

alike in their suffering and in their joy, and no invidious distinction between the two is in place. (Perhaps none is intended.) However, we
may agree that there is a sense in which divine joy is ultimate, rather
than divine sorrow. First, God always has as an element of his
spiritual state the enjoyment of the absolute perfection of his fixed
essential nature, the principle of adequate or infinite capacity, which
is common to all concrete, relative, finite states of reality. This principle is Plato's Idea of Good. It is beautiful absolutely, but only in
the way in which an abstract principle or structure can be so. Secondly, satisfaction, not dissatisfaction, is (in spite of Schopenhauer)
the over-all quality of any experience. (When such quality cannot
be achieved, experience lapses into unconsciousness and insensi-
bility.) In God there is eminently and without possibility of failure
such an over-all joy. Nevertheless, He is fully sensitive both to creaturely agony and to creaturely delight. "Sensitivity" has as good
analogical right to be applied to God as "will" or "knowledge," even
though a much more neglected right.

I suspect that Tillich fears the process-God may not be sufficiently
powerful and secure to constitute an adequate providence. But the
divine process can do anything you please, except actualize contradictory possibilities or (this too would be contradictory) nullify
freedom. God has absolute control over our freedom, in whatever
sense freedom *can* be absolutely controlled. Surely Tillich wants
no more than this! (He says some fine things about providence.)
And I think the world's tragedy is not best dealt with theologically
by trying to give the impression that there is an absolute guarantee
that things will come out exactly right, either now or eventually.
Is it not enough that there is always a divine beauty of synthesis
embracing the world's tragedy, a beauty which is lovable with one's
whole heart, which fosters freedom in optimal fashion, and treasures
with infinite care all the value we achieve through this freedom and
love? Perhaps this is really all that Tillich wants to insist upon.

When our author declares that God is not a being (even a highest
being), one wonders as to the scope of the denial. Of course, God
is not simply *a* being, but rather *the* Being, universally relevant to
all beings, and thus universal as much as individual. But I should
argue (though this is highly controversial) that, if one starts with
the idea of universal Being-itself, one will, by analysis, be led to
the notion of an individual being which yet, since it must be universal in scope and relevance, can only be the truly *highest* Being—

not indeed highest merely in fact (that would be a mere god, not God), but highest by necessity, essentially such that no other could rival it. Conversely, starting with the idea of *the* individual being which is highest in this essential manner, one will be led to the notion of universal *Being* (or Process) itself. Thus it seems arbitrary to take sides (perhaps Tillich does not do so) for one of these notions and against the other. Essential superiority to others, such as could not be overcome by anything conceivable, rules out polytheism or idolatry, and coincides with Being-itself (as integral to Process itself)!

I shall give a final example of Tillich's method of arguing for his nonliteral doctrine of the divine Process. If there is no real distinction between possible and actual in God, then there is, he points out, no danger that the realm of essences will constitute a "duplicate reality"; and a serious problem of ontology is solved (163). Certainly, in the night in which all cows are black or all conceivable differences vanish, there are no puzzling patterns of relationship to discern. So much must be granted. But are problems "solved" by dynamiting their terms in this manner? There is a positive solution for this problem, which is to identify determinateness with actuality. (In justice to Tillich, I should concede that even Whitehead's theory of "eternal objects" is not very clear at this point, and that Bergson is, in an opposite way, unsatisfactory. Peirce, in some writings, and Berdyaev, are the best guides here. The problem has indeed been a serious one.) Unactualized essences or possibilities are always more or less general or indeterminate; only existing men have individual natures; and only actual occasions have fully determinate particularized quality. This quality does not duplicate the actuality; it *is* the actuality, considered in its contrast with other things. Yet the actuality remains contingent; for there previously was neither essence nor actuality of that degree and kind of determinateness, and nothing in the previous situation or in eternity implied it. I submit that this is a genuine solution, and that the one we are offered is not.

Many of the foregoing criticisms may be summed up in the following questions:

1. Has Tillich good reason—I find none—for contrasting the literal applicability to God of Being-itself with the merely symbolic applicability of actuality-potentiality, or Process-itself?

2. Has he good reason for contrasting the symbolic applicability

of actualization, or life, with the sheer inapplicability of existence? (Admittedly God does not exist factually, accidentally; but then, too, He does not live because of birth or as subject to death!)

3. Has Tillich good reason for rejecting, or failing to adopt, the principle of process, that the togetherness of what-does-not-become-and-what-becomes itself becomes (generally, the togetherness of the negative and the positive is positive, of the valueless and the valuable is valuable, of the unconscious and conscious is conscious), with the consequence that reality in its inclusive sense coincides with process (as something *indicated,* not merely named; process-now, not just process taken generically) and the further consequence that God, or reality itself, is Process-itself, our God now, more inclusively than He is immutable or eternal Being-itself?

4. Is there good reason for assuming that the "destructiveness" of ordinary "time" (as measured by our deficiencies of retention of achieved qualities of experience) refutes the idea of an eminent or divine time whose past is *the* past in all its determinateness and richness of quality, and whose future is *the* future in all its inexhaustible potencies?

5. Is there good reason for Tillich's usage of "the eternal," "the absolute," "the unconditioned," "the infinite" as quasisynonymous with God (this synonymity being also denied, to be sure) other than this, that while God in His total reality, as indicated in any actual concern, is not eternal, absolute, unconditioned or infinite, He does have what no reality not God could have, an eternal, absolute, unconditioned, infinite aspect unique to Himself? (In other words, what is not God is, in *all that is individual to it,* a product of becoming; God alone, though in his total reality-now a product of becoming, is not so in all that is individual to Him.)

6. Has Tillich good reason—I certainly find none—for using "unconditioned" as translation of "unreserved" or "total" in his description of the religious concern, except with qualifications analogous to those specified in the previous question? (Perhaps he will grant that the traditional philosophical and theological veneration for "absolute" or "unconditioned" is not a good reason.)

7. I should be interested to know whether Tillich finds intelligible the idea of a *literally* finite divine actuality whose finitude is literally unique to God, as essentially beyond the reach of what is not God as is the divine aspect of infinity—a finitude which infallibly embraces every finite actuality, in all its truth, in an eminent actuality as unri-

valled in unity as in richness of content, yet, since possibility (that is, the divine power) is inexhaustible, an actuality not in every dimension and respect infinite, but literally finite in some respects?

8. Is there any way rationally to justify the doctrine of nonliteralness, except by arguments which themselves can be taken literally and as such are cogent? For example, it is clear that we can never put into a concept the wealth of quality of any concrete actuality, least of all the inclusive actuality. This is clear from the literal meanings of "concept" and "actuality." But to state *this* reason for the utter mysteriousness of the divine life (which I grant) is to take the concept of "actuality" literally in application to God. Is it not the case that Tillich's arguments for his more radically symbolic view are themselves at best symbolic, unable to meet logical tests? True, Tillich seems at times to argue from Being-itself, which he says is to be taken literally. But how can it be so taken, when our experience, itself a process, discloses only processes and what can be abstracted therefrom? A "being" which is neither any process nor any datal constituent of process, but something *simpliciter* more inclusive than all process—this *cannot*, it seems, have literal meaning, for nothing of the sort appears in experiencing! Becoming is never given as in anything, unless another becoming! At best, "being" in this sense seems a reference to traditional metaphysics, by faith taken as symbol of what no experience could exhibit. So we return to question three as the most crucial.

It is not my intention to suggest that the importance, the great value, of Tillich's works stands or falls with the answers to these questions. By no means. Whether or not he is always quite as clear and coherent as one could wish, Tillich is always sensitive, profound, comprehensive, honest, learned, and stimulating. Also, in this writing he is very readable. And I wish to end, as I began, with an expression of gratitude for the precious wisdom which I have been privileged to encounter through studying this work and communicating with the man.

CHARLES HARTSHORNE

DEPARTMENT OF PHILOSOPHY
THE UNIVERSITY OF CHICAGO
CHICAGO, ILLINOIS

Further Reflections

I BEGIN with a confession. Reading what I wrote about Tillich nearly thirty years ago raises my opinion of him—and of myself. For I find that Tillich shared more of the ideas I value than I remembered after I largely stopped reading his works.

Tillich was not given to public comparisons of his views with those of contemporaries. But, privately, he would express approval of the thought of others. Why do I recall this point now? Because it is one of many signs of an important cultural change. Theologizing in the twentieth century is profoundly different than it was in earlier centuries. Ideas that in the 15th Century were held, so far as I know, by no one, and in the 16th and 17th Centuries by a few theologians called Socinians, have become increasingly common. In this century, some of the most creative thinkers dealing with religion have accepted them. I refer particularly to the break with the tradition of two thousand years that virtually identified deity with the philosophical absolute, or with being in contrast to becoming, or infinity in contrast to finitude, or independence in contrast to sensitive responsiveness. Tillich's thought helped to move us in this direction.

Since 1952 I have used "the principle of dual transcendence" to name the essence of this cultural transformation. Nothing was more nearly impossible in theology, from Philo or the church fathers to Kant, than the admission of any sort of mutability in God. Now it is the classical veneration of pure immutability and impassibility that is on the defensive. We are in a new world of ideas. Schelling, important to Tillich, was one of the many philosophers who helped to bring about the new climate of opinion. There are many others. Historians of modern philosophy have yet to tell us the full story.

My original essay now seems to me troublesomely long and so closely reasoned as to be difficult to read. Otherwise I have no quarrel with it. I do notice an omission. Where I speak of memory as the way the past persists in the present, I should have said memory *and perception*. I define perception as "impersonal memory," an intuition of the past.

Since the third volume of Tillich's *Systematic Theology* had not yet been published, I was not able to mention the striking passages near the end of that volume suggestive of some doctrines of process theology: "time . . . contributes to Eternal Life in each of its moments," "the symbol 'eschatological pan-entheism,'" "the eternal dimension of what happens in the universe is the Divine Life itself." He makes clear that the creatures are not external to God, but as "essentialized" are taken into the life of God and thus made indestructible. Personally, to Tillich's statements about immortality, I prefer Whitehead's account of "objective immortality" or "everlastingness" in the Consequent Nature of God. I also like Berdyaev's unpretentious and lucid statement, "The creatures enrich the Divine Life itself." But Tillich, in his symbolic, ambiguous, or unclear formulations, rejects the classical concept of a divine perfection so absolute that it can acquire no values from the creatures.

Tillich speaks of "a bold metaphor, absolute memory," but then clouds the picture by insisting that such memory, by completely retaining the past in the present would abolish the distinction between past, present, and future. It would do no such thing. No matter how absolutely I recalled my youth, this would in no way entail that I completely foresaw my future career. Locating past but not future details in present experience is a coherent idea, the idea of cumulative creation. A Y remembering its predecessor X, which did not anticipate Y, is distinguishable from X. It does not by any logical rule follow that Y anticipates Z, the next phase of the cumulatively creative process. Time's arrow need not be abolished even for God. Whiteheadian "prehension," a concept lacking in philosophy before Whitehead, helps here. Berdyaev also seems to me superior to Tillich on the relation of God to time and change.

Admitting value increase in God enables the alleged analogy between God and ourselves—or between God and the creatures generally—to become a real and intelligible analogy. But, Tillich, Barth, Hume, and Whitehead seem to agree that no intelligible analogy obtains between sheer, immutable, wholly independent actuality and our experiencing or living, which is irreducibly a process with a definite, actual past and more or less indefinite, potential future. Such causes are also effects and effects (with respect to the future) also causes.

I repeat, we are in a new world of thought from that of our medieval ancestors. To find an ancient precedent we must, I believe, go all the way back to Plato's World Soul (not his mere demiurge or his Form of Good). Tillich does little with this analogy, but I hold that many scientific, philosophical, and religious changes make it more applicable now than it was in Plato's day, or even in the last century. Plato's Cosmic Soul was not immutable, but "a moving image of eternity." Correcting for an easily demonstrable onesidedness of Greek thought (not wholly escaped by Tillich) with respect to the significance of fixity rather than of creative process, Plato's suggestion gives us a better view than the entire Middle Ages could produce, or than Plato himself could adequately develop.

On the theological side, Tillich is outstanding. He is not merely American or merely Old World, but a synthesis of both.

CHARLES HARTSHORNE

PROFESSOR EMERITUS
UNIVERSITY OF TEXAS
AUSTIN, TEXAS

9

Dorothy M. Emmet
EPISTEMOLOGY AND THE IDEA OF REVELATION

9

EPISTEMOLOGY AND THE IDEA
OF REVELATION

CONTEMPORARY atheism, it has been said, is a problem in semantics. This is, of course, to put "atheism" in its philosophical, and not in its practical and less sophisticated context. But those aware at all of contemporary issues in philosophy must also be aware of the difficulty of justifying as meaningful any way of talking about God. Perhaps a lyrical theology might be possible; perhaps one which is purely pragmatic; perhaps a mystical theology based on the negative way of the rejection of symbols; but not as theology which claims to make positive assertions about what transcends experience. Some may say this is simply a problem which the logical positivists have created for themselves by the arbitrary limitations they have set on what is meaningful. Others of us may think that the positivists' vigorous attempt to raise questions about the conditions under which statements can be significant has brought out something which we have been dimly feeling for some time: that the older veins in philosophical theology, both on Thomist and on Idealist lines, have been pretty well worked out, and that the philosophy of religion will degenerate into being what it has been alleged to be by Dr. Austin Farrer—"a range of topics which seminary teachers have not the time to expound separately"[1]—or else it will be reborn with different methods and a different epistemology.

This is one of the reasons why Paul Tillich's work is important. For he is one of the few living religious thinkers who is moving into a sphere in which theology may once again become philosophically relevant. This is partly because he is prepared to stand,

---

[1] *Finite and Infinite* (Westminster: London, The Dacre Press, 1943), p. vii.

as he himself tells us, on the "boundary" between theology and philosophy, instead of taking up one of the more comfortable positions which can be occupied by those who do not see that there is a frontier, and who settle down securely in the territory on one side or the other. And it is also because he puts the problems of epistemology and the idea of revelation in the center of his thinking.[2] He sees, that is to say, that before making theological assertions we must be prepared to justify the methods by which we make them. Indeed, he says:

> It is more adequate to begin an analysis of existence with the question of being, rather than with the problem of knowledge. Moreover, it is in line with the predominant classical tradition. But there are situations in which the opposite order ought to be followed, namely, when an ontological tradition has become doubtful and the question arises whether the tools used in the creation of this tradition are responsible for its failure. This was the situation of ancient probabilism and scepticism in relation to the struggle between the philosophical schools. It was the situation of Descartes in the face of the disintegrating mediaeval traditions. It was the situation of Hume and Kant with respect to the traditional metaphysics. It is the perennial situation of theology.[3]

We may ask, in view of the illustrations given, whether this is not also the perennial situation in philosophy. Is there a special metaphysical use of reason, and if so, on what criteria does it work? Here I believe that Tillich's main contribution to epistemology lies in what he has seen about the way in which reason can work in *theology*, when he describes the interrelation of the "technical" with the "ecstatic" reason, and the combination of both with a sense for what he calls the "depth of reason." I suspect that what Tillich has seen here might prove more productive in metaphysical philosophy than what he pronounces to be philosophical method proper, which he says should be a phenomenological intuiting of "the structure of reality as such." Perhaps it would be well first of all to raise some of the difficulties I find in his expressed views about the use

[2] It would be impossible to give an adequate exposition of Tillich's subtle and complex views on these problems within the compass of a short discussion; indeed it would probably not be possible to do this much more shortly than Tillich himself has done in the first part of his *Systematic Theology*. In any case this discussion is in no way intended as a substitute for the reading of Tillich's own work. Its aim is rather to promote such reading by indicating where that work seems to be especially of interest, and to seek to elicit Tillich's elucidation by indicating where (to one reader, at least) it presents difficulties.

[3] *Systematic Theology*, I, 29.

of reason in philosophy, and then go on to look at what he has to say about how reason works when it is working creatively in theology.

Tillich's view of philosophy seems to have been formulated under the influence of Husserl's phenomenology, which was the dominant school of philosophical method in Germany a generation ago. He held to this in principle, though from time to time he says things about the practice of philosophers which take him further beyond it than he seems to realise. The term "phenomenology" was used by Husserl to mean an analysis of certain basic types of human consciousness. These are held to be correlated with objective contents, the essences or "structures" of which may be revealed to disinterested reflection. ("Structure" is a word Tillich is continually using, and, like the phenomenologists, I think he gives insufficient explanation of what it means.) These essential "structures" are said to be revealed as contents of experience, but experience contemplated and detached from the particular existence of the knower and of the objects known. Such reflection can then be held to be a pure act of understanding free from belief and from historical entanglement.

Tillich (unlike Husserl) seems to hold that besides such reflection on particular types of experience in order to expose their essential "structure," there should also be a completely general kind of philosophical reflection, which he calls "that cognitive approach to reality in which reality as such is the object."[4] We are told:

> The philosopher looks at the whole of reality to discover within it the structure of reality as a whole. He tries to penetrate into the structures of being by means of the power of his cognitive function and its structures. . . . There is no particular place to look to discover the structure of being; there is no particular place to stand to discover the categories of experience. The place to look is all places; the place to stand is no place at all: it is pure reason.[5]

If the latter part of this quotation just meant that in principle anyone can philosophise, and that in principle anything can provide a starting point for thinking philosophically, most of us would agree. But I think Tillich means considerably more than this. He wants to describe philosophy as a kind of awareness of "reality as a whole," which, elsewhere than in this passage, he distinguishes

[4] *Ibid.*, p. 7.
[5] *Ibid.*, p. 23.

from "the whole of reality," that is, all the realms of empirical detail. In the latter sense obviously no one can look at "the whole of reality." In what sense and by what methods can anyone look at "reality as a whole"; or can there be what Tillich elsewhere, using an older terminology, calls a study of "Being *qua* Being"? At the present stage of thinking in philosophy and theology, I think it is important to look quite specifically at what *philosophers* seem to be doing when they are trying their hardest to do their job. Do they in fact set out to give an account of "Being *qua* Being"? They may say they set out to do so, as Aristotle does in the *Metaphysics*. But in fact Aristotle does not develop this; he develops instead the principles underlying particular kinds of beings studied by particular kinds of enquiry. Or the Scholastics may tell us that the "transcendentals" are predicable of Being *qua* Being; but when pressed, the meaning of these only adds up to telling us that "It is what is." Or we may find with Heidegger that the second, the ontological volume of *Sein und Zeit* never gets written. When Tillich is writing about the actual practice of philosophers, he sees that they cannot separate the question of "Being as such" from the question of "Meaning"—that is to say, the context or situation in which they have an intellectual experience which seems to them to be of particular significance and importance. And rightly; for the notion that there should be a study of Being *qua* Being, out of any context, is likely to lead either to a verbal ontology or to the charge that metaphysics is nonsense.

Tillich in effect sees this. He sees that you cannot separate the question of the "structure" of "Being" from that of its meaning in particular contexts. When he himself tries to talk about "Being" in the second part of his *Systematic Theology*, he speaks of it in terms of the teleological categories we experience in our own lives, and extrapolates from these. He also takes the subject-object relation of knowing as a fair sample which can be used, at least analogically, to describe "the structure of Being as such." But this is to assume that, at least in its fundamental character, the subject-object relation of knowing is not a highly rare and peculiar kind of relation. The problem is to say *what* relations or characteristics we are to select as giving insight into "the structure of Being as such." For no one, in fact, can just sit back and intuit Being as such in a purely general way. One must at least select some type of relation or characteristic as capable of being extrapolated beyond its normal context and as providing an illuminating way of talking about "reality" in a wider sense, and one must try to defend the selection. In other words, the method here is more like what Tillich calls, when he is discussing revelation, "critical phenomenology" than it is like pure phenomenology. That is to say, we have to realize that we are proposing to select some type of experience or situation as providing the kind of categories we are going to try to use in talking about "Being" or "reality," and this selection may well be disputed. Tillich, in effect, as we have seen, does this. But since he thinks that philosophy *ought* to be a detached phenomenological study of Being as such, he solves the dilemma by saying that in fact there is a "theological" element inside every actual philosophy, and we find that it is in virtue of this that it can be interesting and creative. Then the question is surely how we are to recognize and reckon with this element without allowing philosophy to become obscurantist or authoritarian (any more than in fact Tillich thinks that theology should be). We do not want to lose sight of the obligation on philosophers to struggle for objectivity, but it is a *struggle* for objectivity in which they engaged, and not a standpoint that is no particular standpoint which they can occupy, and from which they can detachedly contemplate "Being as such."

What seems to happen is, I think, something like this. When we ask about "reality" we are generally asking whether something is genuine according to the criteria of some particular frame of reference. C. I. Lewis has put this well in his *Mind and the World Order,* and also J. L. Austin in his contribution to the Aristotelian Society, Supplementary Volume XX (pp. 158 ff.). But I think the point is that, while a pragmatist or positivist is content to leave the matter there, a person like Tillich, with a metaphysical or theological concern, is not. For in all these frames of reference we talk about "reality" subject to certain conditions, which define the kind of interest with which we are concerned—economics, history, biology, and so forth. So, granted that there are organisms, or facts about the past, or a currency system, if we want to talk in these contexts we may ask: Did Caesar really cross the Rubicon? Is the pigment spot under this starfish really an eye? Is this bank note really worth £1? The conditions on which these questions are asked are presuppositions which are either taken as axioms, or which raise further questions which cannot be answered in the same terms. So they always leave more to be said, and leave us with a feeling of dissatisfaction. We cannot just accept them as they are "with natural piety," and then, too, I think we are being disturbed by what Tillich calls the sense for the "Unconditioned." That is to say, the thought of something which is not just a matter of one kind of interest contrasted and competing with others, and defining a frame of reference in which we may or may not choose to talk, but something which is always important, always relevant, and which makes a demand on us which would leave no more to be said. Of course we can never formulate this; if we did, our formulation would itself be subject to conditions. (This is why there cannot really be a pure science of "Being as such.") Tillich sees this; it is the nerve of his idea of the "Protestant principle" in the intellectual as well as in the moral sphere, and why he speaks of the need for a kind of epistemological "justification by faith." He says:

> We have characterized the absolute standpoint as a guardian standpoint, as one which is not actually a position, but only a battle, constantly changing with the opponent, against any standpoint that wants to set itself up as unconditioned. But the guardian is at the same time the one who points to the sanctuary which he guards. His existence itself is an indication. The absolute standpoint, that is, the point from which relativism is overcome, is possible only as an indication and defence at the same time. Thus the basic principle of Protestantism, the principle of justification through faith, is applied to the question of truth.[6]

Tillich has given a fuller account of his plea that in the intellectual life there should be a kind of epistemological "justification by faith" in an earlier lecture, *Rechtfertigung und Zweifel*.[7] He is describing an attitude of mind which acknowledges the unconditional claim of truth along with recognizing that no standpoint can be identified with it. This attitude is therefore bound up with radical doubt, including calling in question one's own doubts. That is to say, it is contrasted as an attitude with certain kinds of scepticism, such as some forms of positivism, which do not question radically the principles on which they do their own doubting. Tillich claims that the attitude he is trying to describe gives doubt a religious significance, so that he can speak of the doubter being "justified" religiously, even while he is doubting.

Here we must consider more closely what Tillich says about the nature of *reason*, in particular the "depth of reason" and "the ecstatic

[6] "Kairos and Logos," in *The Interpretation of History*, p. 172.
[7] In *Vorträge der theologischen Konferenz* (Giessen: Töpelmann, 1924).

reason," and finally the correlation of these with the idea of revelation.

First, the depth of reason. What Tillich means by this is indicated by what he says about Kant. Kant's doctrine of the categories is, he says, a doctrine of human finitude.

> By analysing the categorical structure of reason man discovers the finitude in which he is kept. He also discovers that his reason does not accept this bondage and tries to grasp the infinite with the categories of finitude, the really real with the categories of experience, and that he necessarily fails. The only point at which the prison of finitude is open is the realm of moral experience, because in it something unconditional breaks into the whole of temporal and causal conditions. But this point which Kant reaches is nothing more than a point, an unconditional command, a mere awareness of the depth of reason.[8]

No more than Kant can Tillich rest content in the "prison of finitude," because, like Kant, he has the sense for the importance of the "unconditioned." This is not the same as seeking an unconditional quality in what we may hold to be important, because we may have to call in question the final importance of every particular thing on which we set our hearts. It is more like a haunting claim which cannot be identified with that of any *object* whatsoever, and is connected with what Tillich calls "the ground of our being."

Tillich says that he uses the word "ground" because he does not want to use words like "cause" or "substance" which suggest categories of the human mind. The word "ground" "oscillates between cause and substance and transcends both of them." But "ground" is of course a metaphor from the ground or premise from which the conclusion of an argument is drawn. It is perhaps not a very happy metaphor to use, because Tillich does not want to suggest that there is a reason behind Being from which Being is derived. It looks therefore as though the expression "Ground of Being" were tautological. But the point he wants to make comes out in what he says about the "depth of reason":

> The depth of reason is the expression of something that is not reason, but which precedes reason and is manifest through it. Reason in both its objective and its subjective structures points to something which appears in these structures but which transcends them in power and meaning. This is not another field of reason which could progressively be discovered and expressed, but it is that which is expressed through every

[8] *Systematic Theology*, I, 33–34.

rational expression. It could be called the "Substance" which appears in the rational structure, or "Being-Itself" which is manifest in the *logos* of being, or the Ground which is creative in every rational creation, or the Abyss which cannot be exhausted by any creation or by any totality of them, or the infinite potentiality of being and meaning which pours into the rational structures of mind and reality, actualizing and transforming them. All these terms which point to that which "precedes" reason have a metaphorical character. "Preceding" is itself metaphorical. This is necessarily so, because if the terms were used in their proper sense they would belong to reason, they would not precede it.[9]

If this is a way of saying that reality is beyond reason, and inexhaustible even in an infinite number of propositions, this is a point which has often been made. But I think Tillich is trying to say more than this. In speaking of the "depth of reason" he is, I think, saying that every rational expression indicates further meaning and possibilities than it expresses. There is thus a kind of bottomlessness about reason. But there is also a quest for perfection in reason which could only be achieved in an intuitive union with reality. Tillich holds that "essentially" this should be possible; reason and reality should be one. But under the conditions of human knowledge we cannot have this *scientia intuitiva*. "Essentially reason is transparent towards its depths in each of its acts and processes. In existence this transparency is opaque and is replaced by myth and cult."

Besides the "depth of reason" Tillich distinguishes the "technical" and the "ontological" reason. The technical reason is the more familiar and straightforward. It is reason as an instrument, working according to any recognized method of empirical verification, or concerned with the formal perfection of an argument, or with semantic clarification. This kind of reason is the tool which most recent philosophy has been concerned to sharpen. Tillich insists on the importance of the technical reason in philosophy and in theology no less than in science. He has no sympathy with those neo-orthodox theologians who think that they can dispense with the struggle for "semantic rationality" because they claim to be using a Biblical language with no philosophical implications, and that therefore they need not clarify or justify the terms they use. The principle of "semantic rationality," as Tillich says, involves the demand that all connotations of a word should be consciously related

[9] *Ibid.*, p. 32.

to one another and centered in a controlling meaning. This sort of scrutiny would be a function of the technical reason. But Tillich is not prepared, as are some contemporary philosophers, to limit philosophy to the methods of the technical reason. He sees philosophy also as an attempt to grasp reality by means of the "ontological reason." It is here, as will be apparent from what has already been said, that some real difficulties arise. The ontological reason is described as "the structure of the mind which enables it to grasp and shape reality." The same phrase is used to describe "subjective reason," with the addition of the words "on the basis of a corresponding structure of reality," this latter "structure" being also called "objective reason." One would like him to elucidate this further. The conjunction of "grasping" and "shaping" seems to mean that reason must be exercised by a human being who is receptive and active and not just passively aware in his processes of thought. "Grasping" in this context has the connotation of penetrating into the depth, into the essential nature of a thing or event, of "under" standing and expressing it. "Shaping," he says, "in this context has the connotation of transforming a given material into a *'Gestalt,'* a living structure which has the power of being."[10] I must confess that I am completely puzzled by this description of "shaping." "A living structure which has the power of being" in any straightforward sense means an organism. Does Tillich mean to transfer this idea by metaphor to the intellectual children of our minds, our conceptions of reality? Or does he just mean the interrelation of theory and practice, that our theories affect our actions, and that the ways we act affect our theories—"we transform reality according to the way we see it, and we see reality according to the way we transform it"? This is no doubt true, but it is true also of the technical reason. I think the difficulty is that Tillich has what is really an idealist view of the "ontological reason," and that he is combining it with the language of "Being" and "Essence" derived from the Scholastic realist tradition. His main point seems to be that the ontological reason deals with the most general concepts in terms of which we describe anything which we say "is." How do we know that these concepts somehow reflect the structure of the world? I think we can say that our "world," as an interpretation we build up, is hammered out of our experience of the real world in which we live and act; and in so far as this is so, we can suppose it indicates

[10] *Ibid.,* p. 30.

some rapport between our interpretation and certain aspects of the objective world. But I suspect that Tillich's use of the word "structure" leads him to write at times as though any ordered form of expression (music, for instance, is given as an example) was somehow cognitive and reflected a "structure" of reality. But there are very different kinds of expression, and they may be related to reality in very different kinds of ways. Sometimes the distinction may be between different kinds of language and not between different objects of which we are speaking. And some of these kinds of language may not be indicative at all, or may only be indicative in a very indirect way. He says that "it was the mistake of idealistic philosophy that it identified revelation with ontological reason while rejecting the claims of technical reason."[11] I believe that, while he sees this, nevertheless much of what he says about the use of the "ontological reason" in philosophy is dependent on idealistic epistemological assumptions which are insufficiently examined or justified. This can, I think, be seen by looking at what he says about the "autonomy" of the ontological reason.

Reason which affirms and actualizes its structure without regarding its depth is autonomous. . . . Autonomous reason, in affirming itself in its different functions and their structural demands, uses or rejects that which is merely an expression of an individual's situation within him and around him. It resists the danger of being conditioned by the situation of self and world in existence. It considers these conditions as the material which reason has to grasp and to shape according to its structural laws. Therefore autonomous reason tried to keep itself free from ungrasped impressions and unshaped strivings. Its independence is the opposite of wilfulness, it is obedience to its own essential structure, the law of reason which is the law of nature within mind and reality, and which is divine law, rooted in the ground of being itself. This is true of all functions of ontological reason.[12]

In this passage we catch a number of idealist and phenomenological echoes. But if we ask: How do we know that the law of reason is the law of nature within mind and reality, which is also divine law?—and how do we know that we can take this Hegelian view of the coincidence of subjective and objective reason rather than a critical Kantian view or even a metaphysically agnostic view? —then I do not see that Tillich has done more than to say that if we do

[11] *Ibid.*, p. 30.
[12] *Ibid.*, p. 34.

not make these assumptions it will be so much the worse for the *logos* philosophy which he favors, and which he believes has been held by philosophers in the "classical tradition." I suspect that part of the difficulty is an ambiguity in the term "objective reason." Sometimes it is used to mean what Tillich calls the *logos* of being; sometimes it appears to mean something more like the logical structure of organized knowledge, as distinct from "subjective reason," which is the conscious thinking of an individual mind. The "ontological reason" gives us the general logical structure of a "world"; and a "world" to Tillich is not the totality of all that exists, but an organized whole as related to a knowing self, that is, it is an interpretation from a center. So "Reason makes the world a world." But in that case need "the correlation between subjective and objective reason" mean more than that (in Kant's phrase) "reason has insight into that which she herself constructed according to her own plan"? We may find a correlation because we have put it there. What is needed, if we are to avoid this conclusion, is a fuller discussion on how far what Tillich calls the concepts of the ontological reason are *prescriptive* and how far they are *descriptive;* that is to say, how far they are the intellectual apparatus in terms of which we organize our ways of talking about the world, and how far they are descriptive of discoveries about the world (as an objective environment and not only an organized whole of thought); and if they are discoveries how are these discoveries made and tested? This is the central problem of epistemology; and because rather than discuss it he tends to make assertions, appealing to what he calls the "classical tradition from Parmenides to Hegel," I feel Tillich never quite comes to grips with it, though he is continually moving round it. He comes nearest to it when he is speaking of reason as "estranged from its depths" under the conditions of finite existence; that is to say, we cannot always assume a rapport between reason and reality beyond it, especially when we come to the kind of questions generally known as "metaphysical." We might then find that even in philosophy the ontological reason is more dubious, the technical reason more important, and the ecstatic reason less extraneous than he allows.

When Tillich is contrasting philosophy with theology, he says that although the "autonomous" reason rightly struggles against heteronomy (its subjection to any alien authority), it denies the "depth of reason." A reason which was subject to no alien authority, but which, instead of just following its own internal laws, expressed in passionate devotion the nature of reality beyond itself would be not autonomous or heteronomous but "theonomous." We have already raised the questions of why a concern for Being beyond our abstractions should necessarily be a concern for something *holy*. We may ask still more why "the question of the meaning of being as our ultimate concern is the question of *God*,"[13] so that the term "theonomous" becomes appropriate. Why should not the "ground of Being" be something valuationally indifferent, or even, from a human point of view, sinister (as Schopenhauer, for instance, believed that it was)? To consider this adequately we should have to enter fully into what Tillich means by God as Being-itself. It is not for me to try to enter here on this crucial part of his thought. Perhaps, however, I may be allowed to say in passing that, as I interpret it, he seems to be uniting an almost Spinozistic strain, in which God is not *a* being, but the "power of being," almost the *conatus in suo esse perseverandi* within everything that is, with a profound trinitarian interpretation of this, which allows for what is traditionally called "transcendence." Perhaps I may also be allowed to say that, in so far as I can follow what Tillich is saying, he seems to me to be coming nearer to what may be a tenable doctrine of God than any other contemporary attempt I know.

I believe also that by starting from the question, "What do we mean by the Holy?" and not from the question, "Does God exist?" (which he thinks, and almost certainly rightly, is a question *mal posé*), he is able to justify saying that reason in its depth has a "theonomous" character. But why cannot a philosopher recognize this, and why cannot philosophical reason have a "theonomous" character? Tillich holds that the "ontological reason" as he has described it contains at least two unresolved conflicts within itself. There is conflict between the demand for theoretic detachment and the demand for some affective union with the object of knowledge (if you like, the conflict between detachment and interest). I think it is possible to overdo this dilemma by presenting philosophy as in principle *Leidenschaftlos* (free from passion). After all, it is possible to feel deeply and even to be enthusiastic about the struggle to be objective. The second conflict is the more instructive, and whatever it is in the former conflict that puts a real problem for philosophers can, I think, be included in this. This conflict is the

[13] Cf. *Systematic Theology*, Part II, *passim*.

split between the autonomy of reason, its demand for completeness, and the recognition in the depth of reason that "Leagues
beyond those leagues there is more sea"; that whatever we say
about reality is always said in abstractions; and always leaves
more to be said. We discover this, as Tillich says, by a scrutiny
of the actual conditions under which our reason works. This conflict
is never finally soluble under these conditions. And it raises the
question of the selectiveness in our thinking, because of the limitations of the actual situations in and from which we think. When
Tillich says that a philosophy is creative in so far as it is driven
by feeling, and that this conflicts with the call for theoretic detachment, we should here be referring not to the feeling which goes
into an enthusiasm for trying to be objective, or to the feeling that it
is important to try to do this kind of thinking at all, but to more
particular kinds of excitement about particular kinds of experience
as being somehow metaphysically significant. And there is the question of how we justify selecting certain experiences rather than
others, and why we should attach cognitive value to this kind of
metaphysical excitement. This is the question of the relation of
reason to what Tillich calls the "depth of reason" which lies beyond
it; and it can become a question of the competence of any form
of reason other than the technical reason. This is a philosophical
question. By what he calls his *method of correlation,* Tillich holds
that every form of intellectual enquiry puts a question to which
there may be a theological answer, the form of the answer being
dependent on the way the question is asked. The question we have
reached is whether thinking can tell us anything about reality
beyond itself in some more ultimate way than is done in the special
activities of the technical reason, and whether particular experiences
interpreted by particular thinkers may throw light on our "ultimate concern." This is the context within which the idea of revelation becomes relevant. Sometimes in such discussions we are left
with an uneasy feeling that the idea of revelation is produced as a
talisman to solve what would otherwise be a philosophically insoluble problem, and we must ask whether the "method of correlation" means this.

Let us put the question this way: How do we reach the "depth
of reason," seeing that the notion of a detached ontological study of
"Being as Being," without emphasizing any particular kind of experience, is not a method which we can in fact pursue? Tillich holds

that there are certain situations in which people have felt themselves shaken, held, and inspired by a sense of the mystery of existence. He speaks of "ontological shock." But it is unlikely that many people except a few philosophers would put the "burden of the mystery" to themselves just like this, though they might ask: What makes one able to go on living, not just biologically (though this too), but spiritually? For most people this is a question of the context within which some conviction of significance and of possibilities in existence comes home to them. And for some there are certain events or situations in which a sense of significance, charged with "numinous astonishment," is focused. By "numinous astonishment" is meant a feeling of being in the grip of the mystery, yet elated with awe. This kind of experience Tillich calls *ecstasy;* he does not mean a state of emotional excitement (though it may include this), but a state in which reason goes beyond its normal uses. This normal use is described as "the subject-object structure." Presumably the kind of reason which "goes outside this" is some state of immediate awareness in which we are not conscious of a gap between our thought forms and that of which we are aware. Something of this kind of immediacy happens in a low form of sense perception. Tillich is, I think, trying to describe an analogue of this in a spiritual, nonsensory experience. Ecstatic reason is not the destruction of reason, but reason raised to a more creative level, in which the breach between theoretical detachment and affective union is overcome. So he says elsewhere that ecstatic reason in the practical sphere can be called *grace,* and in the theoretical, *inspiration.* However we may describe it, many would, I think, agree that something like what Tillich calls the ecstatic reason is a genuine experience. How much cognitive value has it? Tillich says that the ecstatic reason is the subjective side of a situation in which some event occurs which evokes it, and which can be called a "sign event" (and *in this sense* a miracle). Revelation is the occurrence of this whole situation. By relating revelation to the ecstatic reason, Tillich can speak of it in terms which do not demand a distinction of natural and supernatural. The vehicle of revelation is an experience, but it is an experience which has become charged with a sense of the depth and mystery of existence. "The mystery appears objectively in terms of what traditionally has been called a miracle. It appears subjectively in terms of what has sometimes been called ecstasy." "Miracle" here is not taken to mean a supernatural interference with the course of nature. It is a happening which becomes what Tillich calls a "sign event." The sign events may be historical happenings, happenings in nature, or in the lives of saints, whose "faith and love can become sign events for those who are grasped by their power of creativity." The sign event is in a sense empirical, but the ecstatic reason finds a particular significance in it, because it is linked up somehow with our "ultimate concern." Revelation consists in the whole constellation of sign events as grasped in ecstatic reason, conveying a sense of ultimate concern. The phrase "ultimate concern" indicates not only the mystery of why our existence should be maintained, but also, I take it, some conviction about what is finally important in the character of our existence; in both senses it indicates something without which we could not live. Whether what is thus important for us is also the ground of "everything that is" poses, of course, a vast question. To consider Tillich's answer to it would call for a full discussion of his doctrine of God.

This essay can deal only with general epistemological points, and I cannot enter at its close on Tillich's most interesting views on original and dependent revelations, and on the reasons for which he is prepared to say that the revelation of "the New Being in Jesus as the Christ" is the final revelation, able to be productive of fresh dependent revelations.

There is, however, one more epistemological question on which I may perhaps press Professor Tillich for more elucidation. It may be more important for his idea of revelation, and indeed for epistemology generally, than he at present allows. This is the relation of the empirical (technical) reason to the ecstatic reason and, correspondingly, the status of the empirical aspect of an event which is taken as a "sign event." Tillich insists in various places throughout his works that "knowledge of revelation" is without prejudice to any piece of scientific or historical knowledge, and correspondingly that no outcome of historical criticism of the Gospels is relevant either way to whether or not we find here a locus for revelation. "Knowledge of revelation, although it may be mediated through historical events, does not imply factual assertions, and it is therefore not exposed to critical analysis by historical research."[14] If it is true that the utterances of the ecstatic reason are simply expressions of "numinous astonishment" (more like "Oh, how wonderful!" than like "Caesar crossed the Rubicon"), it is true that they do not entail

[14] *Systematic Theology,* I, 54.

factual assertions. But I cannot help feeling that Tillich is trying to have it both ways. He can speak of the results of historical research as irrelevant to belief in the revelatory event of "the New Being in Jesus as the Christ" because he is tacitly taking for granted the main historical framework. Possibly his view is colored by the peculiar outcome of New Testament criticism. Most contemporary New Testament critics will say that they are unable to establish the exact historical facts about any incident or saying in our Lord's life, and yet they accept the belief that there was an underlying core of historical events. But if historical research could prove (*per impossibile*) that the Crucifixion never took place, this would surely make a difference to what might be said about the revelatory event. Otherwise it seems to me that the concept of the "Christ" becomes simply a *category*, brought in to fill a gap in the view of reason, because of "reason's need for re-integration." But I think Tillich does not really want to say this. The "ecstatic" reason finds numinous astonishment and a kind of creative elation and devotion in contemplating certain events. If the events did not occur, the elation can only be a kind of mystical aspiration. If they did occur, then there is more reason to say that the "ecstatic reason" is not simply an expansive feeling, but is a recognition of possibilities concerning what we believe to be ultimately important, linked with events which really happened. At any rate it should surely be part of a philosophy or theology which is wrestling with the peculiar and elusive Christian conviction about the manifestation of the "Unconditioned" in an actual historic life to take empirical knowledge with complete seriousness. Tillich wants to safeguard the rights of "technical reason" to arrive at empirical knowledge which will be genuinely empirical, without theological dictation. But on the whole he manages to insulate its workings from our "ultimate concern." I believe that we must be prepared to a greater extent than this for the risk of having our treasure in earthen vessels. Tillich's "ontological reason" is, as we have seen, bristling with assumptions. We need not despair of it; but I believe that what we are looking for in the *kairos* of our generation is a way of empirical knowledge which will be (in a broad sense) genuinely scientific, and yet which may from time to time be lighted up by the "ecstatic" reason. It is true that only in supreme instances can we speak of "numinous astonishment," so that the category of "revelation" becomes appropriate. But I think that it may be through exploring the possibilities of the "ecstatic reason" and (this is important) its controls[15] and its relation to empirical reason that we may look for the revival of metaphysics, and certainly for the revival of a serious philosophy of religion. May we hope that some day Tillich will re-examine some of the things he says about *philosophical* epistemology in the light of what he has discovered about how reason actually works in theology? If he were to do so, his "method of correlation" might prove even more fruitful than it has done already.

DOROTHY M. EMMET

DEPARTMENT OF PHILOSOPHY
THE UNIVERSITY OF MANCHESTER
MANCHESTER, ENGLAND

[15] Among these "controls" might be the attempts at careful descriptive analyses of the sort phenomenologists practise. Tillich says (*Systematic Theology*, I, 44) that the method appropriate to theology is not "pure" but "critical" phenomenology, that is to say, we must own that there is a prior problem in the selection of what is to be taken as a typical instance of, e.g., revelation. I have urged that this same qualification applies not only to theology, but to philosophy in so far as we are dealing not only with instances of a generally recognized type, but with the elusive character of inner experiences.

10

Reinhold Niebuhr
BIBLICAL THOUGHT AND ONTOLOGICAL SPECULATION IN TILLICH'S THEOLOGY

BIBLICAL THOUGHT AND ONTOLOGICAL SPECULATION IN TILLICH'S THEOLOGY

E VERY systematic theology engages in more ontological speculations than does Biblical thought. The Bible conceives life as a drama in which human and divine actions create the dramatic whole. There are ontological presuppositions for this drama, but they are not spelled out. The drama is told primarily in terms of the contest of all men and nations with God, and secondarily in terms of a contest between good and evil in history. The Bible is concerned primarily with God's "mighty acts," that is, with those events in history through which and in which the ultimate power which bears history reveals its mystery. This mystery is revealed in specific historical events rather than in the structures of being because the Bible assumes both in man and in God a mystery of will and of personality which is not simply contained in the structures. If, in Tillich's language, God must be apprehended in terms both of ultimacy and of concreteness, the Bible assumes ultimacy and speaks of concreteness.

In the same fashion it assumes certain ontological facts about man. Thus he is a "creature," which is to say that he is involved in, and part of, the temporal-natural process. But he is also made in the "image of God," which means that he is not simply involved in the temporal process but has capacities to transcend it and to ask questions about the character of reality in its totality. A part of the function of a systematic theology is to refute ontological speculations about God and man which falsify or negate the drama about which the Bible speaks; for this drama requires freedom both for

God and for man, and is negated by ontologies which subject either God or man to an ontological necessity. Thus ontological speculations which equate the human self with "mind," as in idealism, or which reduce man to the dimension of an object in nature, as in naturalism, must be refuted from the standpoint of Christian theology. Yet on the positive side theology must show how what is implied about the nature of God, man, and history is related to what may be known about man, history, and reality through all the disciplines of culture.

Paul Tillich's *magnum opus,* his *Systematic Theology,* of which unfortunately only the first volume is available at the time this analysis of his work is attempted, will undoubtedly become a landmark in the history of modern theology for two reasons. First, his ontological speculations are more rigorous and include all of the disciplines of culture more imaginatively than anything which has been done in the realm of philosophy of religion or natural theology in our day or in many decades. Secondly, it distinguishes itself from the natural theology inspired by Hegel and Kant in the past two centuries by a fuller appreciation of the limits of reason in penetrating to the ultimate mystery or in comprehending the mystery of human existence. There is therefore a larger place for the kerygmatic dimension of theology than in all recent theologies which sought to accommodate the Christian Gospel within the limits of ontological speculations. Tillich's method is always to press ontological questions until it is proved that metaphysics points beyond its own speculations to a dimension of reality in which the Biblical assertions and affirmations about God's "mighty act," in short, revelation as apprehended by faith, become relevant and meaningful. This is a prodigious and impressive undertaking which must be compared with the efforts of theology which begin with Origen and run through Augustine and Aquinas. If Karl Barth is the Tertullian of our day, abjuring ontological speculations for fear that they may obscure or blunt the *kerygma* of the Gospel, Tillich is the Origen of our period, seeking to relate the Gospel message to the disciplines of our culture and to the whole history of culture.

It would be both impossible and pretentious to seek to do full justice to this undertaking in all of its dimensions, for there is no one in our generation who so completely masters the stuff, philosophical and theological, with which he is dealing, as Tillich. Even the more modest task of analyzing Tillich's description of the human situation with the purpose of raising questions is really pretentious. Yet I shall dare to ask whether in this field his ontological speculations have not, despite the great precision of his thought, falsified the picture of man as the Bible portrays it, and as we actually experience it.

In Biblical thought man, who is meant to live in fellowship with God and his fellows, becomes a sinner by making himself his own end, by "changing the glory of the incorruptible God into the image of corruptible man." He does this fatefully and not merely in terms of a conscious perversion. The Bible is not Pelagian. The doctrine of "original sin" is not merely contained in the myth of the Fall of Adam. It is a presupposition of all Biblical thinking. But despite this fateful necessity men are held responsible for their sin. "They are," declares St. Paul, "without excuse." Jesus put the paradox succinctly in the phrase, "It must needs be that offenses come; but woe unto that man by whom they come." In modern parlance one could say that though it is inevitable that every ego should also be an egotist, there is no ontological fate in this development. Man is so created that he cannot complete his life within himself. In varying degrees and on various levels he does seek to do so, but never with an easy conscience. He knows in every individual act of self-aggrandizement that he is "without excuse." He is without excuse because the structure of his existence is such that he cannot complete himself within himself but only indeterminately in the life of his fellows and in God. It is this structure of indeterminate freedom, organically related to his contingent and finite existence, which represents the voice of conscience to him when he seeks to complete himself within himself, or uses other life merely as an instrument for his ends. Succinctly, man is "without excuse" because self-seeking violates the structure of his existence. But if the structure of his existence, defined as finite freedom, is inevitably self-seeking, man has every excuse.

When man's uneasy conscience is heightened, it leads to repentance, to a dying to self (that is, the self in its narrow self-centeredness) which has the consequence of the emergence of a new self. This is paradoxically a truer self, because it is not centered in self. The faith by which the self apprehends God as judge and redeemer presupposes repentance even as repentance presupposes faith. Faith in the Bible is not so much the "ecstasy of reason" thinking beyond the limits of reason to touch the divine mystery, as an apprehension of the divine made possible by a destruction of the idolatry of the self, and a destruction of the idolatry of the self by the recognition that the ultimate source and end of life stands against the pretensions of the self.

In this Biblical concept, despite the paradoxical relations between fate and freedom, the emphasis lies upon freedom and responsibility. Original sin, the inclination to make the self its own end, when experienced in specific instances contains conscious elements which leave the self "without excuse" and justify the warning "but woe unto that man by whom offense cometh." In Tillich's thought the emphasis upon the ontological basis of this paradox seems subtly to shift the meaning of the fate, contained in the idea of "original sin," from a historical to an ontological one. With this shift the emphasis falls upon the fatefulness of sin rather than upon our responsibility. Thus what Pascal has called "the mystery without which we remain a mystery to ourselves" is less of a mystery, but also less true to the facts of experience.

Tillich's description of the Fall is close to that of Origen. He does not hesitate to picture it as one aspect of creation. He writes:

In the creative vision of God the individual is present as a whole in his essential being and inner *telos* and at the same time in the infinity of the special moments of his life process. Of course this is said symbolically, since we are unable to have a perception of or even an imagination of that which belongs to the divine life. The mystery of being beyond essence and existence is hidden in the mystery of the creativity of the divine life.

But man's being is not only hidden in the creative ground of the divine life; it also is manifest to itself and to other life within the whole of reality. Man does exist, and his existence is different from his essence. Man and the rest of reality are not only "inside" of the divine life but also "outside" it. Man has left the ground in order to "stand upon" himself, to be actually what he essentially is, in order to be *finite freedom*. This is the point at which the doctrine of the creation and of the fall join. . . . Fully developed creatureliness is fallen creatureliness. The creature has actualized its freedom insofar as it is outside the creative ground of the divine life. . . . "Inside" and "outside" are spatial symbols, but what they say is not spatial. . . . To be outside the divine life means to stand in actualized freedom, in an existence which is no longer united with essence. Seen from the one side this is the end of creation. Seen from the other side this is the beginning of the fall. Freedom and destiny are correlates. The point at which creation and fall coincide is as much a matter of destiny as it is a matter of freedom.[1]

In Tillich's privately circulated *Propositions* he puts the matter in the following words: "The myth of 'the transcendent fall' describes the transition (from essence to existence) as a universal event in ontological terms. The myth of the 'immanent fall' describes the transition as an individual event in psychological terms." There is no myth of "the transcendent fall" in the Bible but only the myth of a historical fall. The idea of a transcendent fall always appears in Christian theology, from Origen on, whenever ontological speculations lead to the conclusion that evil is involved in finiteness as such. It is in the actualization of the potentiality that reality becomes ambiguous, that is, evil as well as good. The sinfulness of man is thus an "ontological fate." It is a fate which he shares with all temporal existence; for all such existence, when it becomes actual, is separated from its "divine ground," which seems to mean undifferentiated existence.

In order to understand this analysis better it may be well to consider the concepts "essential," "innocence," and "existential." Tillich defines "essence" as follows: "Essence as the nature of a thing, or as the quality in which it participates, or as a universal has one character. Essence as that from which a thing has fallen has another character. . . . Why has this ambiguity existed in Philosophy since Plato? The answer lies . . . in the ambiguous character of existence which expresses being and at the same time contradicts it."[2] Thus when Tillich declares that "the structure of man's *essential* nature is the structure of finite freedom,"[3] he is using "essential" in the first sense. Man has a character both of finiteness and of freedom. Incidentally, other finite creatures also have this character. It may be questioned, therefore, whether the uniqueness of human freedom over temporal events is fully established in those definitions in which Tillich deals with the ambiguous character of all existence, though he does define this uniqueness in other contexts. But when he speaks of existence standing in contradiction to essence, "essence" means that from which existence has fallen. It has fallen because it is no longer "inside" the divine ground. "Essence" therefore means not

[1] *Systematic Theology*, I, 255–256.
[2] *Ibid.*, p. 203.
[3] *Ibid.*, p. 199.

the structure of existence, but an undifferentiated unity of being before creation, or transcending the temporal process.

In this sense every existing thing is not merely an imperfect specimen of its essence, but actually stands in partial contradiction to it. Rather it does not stand in contradiction to its own essence, but to "essential" being, to being per se, because it is suspended between being and nonbeing. The word "existential" in this context does not define things actually existing in time, for these things are said to contain both "essential" and "existential" elements in their nature. The "existential element" seems to be their separatedness or, as Tillich says, their "enstrangement" from the divine ground. The "essential" element in them is their not completely dissevered relationship with the divine ground.

If "existential" is thus used to define particularity and discreteness, it is difficult to use it also to define the unique possibility that man has to "contradict" his own nature, as distinguished from the brutes, who simply are what they are, and who are not tempted to center their lives perversely around self, sex, power, glory, and so forth. In short, the Christian doctrine of sin would not seem to be covered by this definition. Tillich does, however, also use the word "existential" to define the Biblical concept of sin. In the one case finite man is subject to sin by reason of his separation from the divine ground. He is subject to a *non posse non peccare,* to the impossibility of not sinning. In the other case man is subject to a *posse peccare,* to a possibility of sinning.

In the first case Tillich declares in his *Propositions,* "Finite freedom, when it becomes actual, disrupts the essential, uncontested, innocent unity between finitude and its infinite ground." Though the word "innocent" has historical connotations, Tillich does not mean to define a historical state, but rather one of potentiality. "Whatever exists," he writes, "that is, stands out of mere potentiality, is more than it is in a state of mere potentiality but less than it could be in the power of its essential nature." Thus "innocency" means a state of potentiality and does not have a historical connotation. He does speak of "innocency" transcending potentiality and actuality; but as he does not define this paradox further, it is difficult to grasp.

In the second use of the words "essential" and "existential," the Biblical idea of sin as a historical fact rather than as ontological fate is emphasized, and the "existential" contradiction of the "essential" is declared to be a "possibility" rather than a necessity. Thus he writes: "Finitude is the possibility of losing one's essential structure and with it one's self. But this is a possibility *and not a necessity.*"[4] In his *Propositions* he declares in a similar vein that "finite freedom implies the possibility of contradicting man's essential nature." Perhaps this seeming contradiction could be explained as follows: All finite existence represents at least a partial contradiction to essential being, since essential being is undifferentiated being. But in addition man has the possibility, not the necessity, of contradicting, not essential being, but his own essential being. I suspect, without being certain, that this is the solution. But this solution is made difficult partly because the same terms are used to express two different dimensions of the problem, and partly because Tillich insists that they are merely the two sides of the same shield. Consider his definitions of "sin," "the Fall," and Adam's innocency.

"Sin," Tillich declares in his *Propositions,* "is the disruption of the essential unity between God and man by man's actualized freedom. Sin is 'Suende,' 'Sonderung,' separation." Up to this point sin is an ontological fate, that is, the fate of all particular existences in time. But he goes on to say, "Sin is fundamentally 'unbelief' which includes theoretical denial and practical disobedience." This second definition makes sin a historic corruption, as in the Bible.

Tillich thinks of these two facets as two dimensions of sin, but the ontological outweighs the historical. There is no Augustinian warning: "We should not in our sins and vices accuse the nature of the flesh to the injury of the Creator. For in its own kind and degree the flesh (i.e., finite existence) is good. But to desert the creator and to live according to the created good, that is not good."[5]

How clearly the ontological overpowers the historical is seen in Tillich's refusal to regard the myth of "Adam's innocency" before the fall as a historical symbol. He declares:

Early theologians attributed to Adam as representative of man's essential nature all perfections otherwise reserved for Christ or to man in his eschatological fulfillment. Such a description makes the fall quite unintelligible. Therefore recent theology attributes to Adam a kind of dreaming innocence, a stage of infancy before contest and decision. This interpretation makes the fall understandable and its occurrence *unavoidable.* The

[4] *Ibid.,* p. 201.
[5] *De Civitate Dei,* XIV, v.

goodness of man's created nature is that he is given the possibility and necessity of actualizing himself and of becoming independent by his actualization, in spite of the estrangement unavoidably connected with it. Therefore it is inadequate to ask questions concerning Adam's actual state before the fall, for example whether he was mortal or immortal, or whether he was in a state of righteousness. The verb "was" presupposes actualization in time. But this is exactly what can not be asserted of a state which transcends potentiality and actuality. This is true even if we use psychological symbols and speak of a state of dreaming innocence, or if we use a theological symbol and speak of the state of being hidden in the ground of the divine life.[6]

Adam's "created goodness" is spoken of; but this seems to be a goodness before creation, before actualization in time. It seems to be a state of potentiality rather than actuality, though it is said to "transcend potentiality and actuality." Whatever difficulty those of us have who use the symbols of innocency and perfection in history, they seem to me no greater than the difficulty in this symbolism which presupposes a state which is neither potential being nor actualized being in time. If it is thought of as a state of God's design for creation, it would have to be a design of discrete "essences" of human individuality, which are not yet "created," but which are anticipating creation. Yet even then they would not really be good because they would be designed to be separated beings, finally to be estranged from the divine ground.

In contrast to this symbolism, which rests upon the presupposition that particular existence is partially evil by reason of being "separated," I think there is much to be said for the idea of using the concepts both of "innocency" and of "perfection" as Christian theology has usually done. Tillich's definition of innocency as "a stage of infancy before contest and decision" is really meaningful only in historical terms. What could "infancy" mean without historical connotations? In actual history we have the symbols both of the child ("Except ye be as little children") and of the primitive community in which freedom is not yet fully actualized, and in which life is therefore in harmony with life in a way in which it should be ultimately under conditions of a fully developed freedom. It is important to recognize the historical fact (upon which rest Stoic conceptions of the Golden Age, the Marxist idea of a period in which man has not yet been alienated from his social essence,

6 *Systematic Theology,* I, 260.

and every man's nostalgia about childhood) that in both the individual and collective life of mankind there is a historical period in which there is a considerable harmony of life with life or harmony of life within itself. Increasing freedom disturbs this harmony. But it also creates the possibility of wider harmonies and larger communities. Therefore the "perfection of Adam" is alternately or somewhat illogically defined in Christian orthodoxy as both innocency and the perfect love of Christ. Obviously it is absurd to attribute the perfect love of Christ to Adam before the fall. But this absurdity arises from the fact that Christian thought seeks to do justice to "essential" man as a historic creature. The "essential" is partly defined in terms of the primordial and partly in terms of the ultimate possibility. The ultimate possibility for the human self is that it realize its "true" self, that is, its "essential" self, by "losing" itself. Thus the "perfection before the fall" is the higher possibility of self-realization through self-giving which exists before every act in which the self actually resolves its problem by seeking itself more narrowly than it should.

Tillich challenges "those theologians who are not willing to interpret the creation story and the story of the fall as reports about two actual events" to "draw the consequence and posit the mystery where it belongs—in the unity of freedom and destiny in the ground of being." That may not be the only possibility. For one thing it makes one story out of the two stories, and there is significance in the fact that there are two stories, the one symbolizing the beginning of history and the other, the corruption of freedom in history. It is important that the two stories be separated. The separation points, on the one hand, to an actual historical state in which there is not so much separation, but the unity of life with life, showing that the character of man, even as separated and particular existence, contains possibilities of relating himself harmoniously with other life. On the other hand, it symbolizes the fact that every act of estrangement, of isolation, or of imperialism is a "fall" from a more ideal possibility of relating life with life in terms of love.

Such a formulation makes history more real, for it does not set it in contrast to some symbolic period before creation when all particular things were not yet separated existences. Rather it sets every historical act, achievement, and event in contrast to the primordial and the eschatological, that is, to innocency and perfection. Thus every historic decision, which must be either for the self or for God and the other, has a historic urgency and reality which it cannot have if its fate of self-seeking is identified with its fate of being a self.

This alternative does, of course, involve an affirmation about temporal and historical reality, which seems to be absurd from the ontological standpoint, namely, the affirmation about the "goodness" of creation, despite the inevitable tensions, conflicts, and frictions between particular existences in the temporal scene. That is exactly what Biblical faith does assert. It could be claimed, therefore, that it does not really come to terms with the problem of "natural evil" as distinguished from the historic evil of sin. Biblical thought implies this evil in the "curse upon the ground" in the myth of the fall, which Tillich uses to cover his whole concept of the ambiguity of all existence. It is also suggested in the hope of a transfigured nature in Biblical eschatology. But on the whole the Bible is not greatly concerned with the problem of natural evil. It is concerned with the drama of human history, and in that drama with the rebellion of man against God, and God's overcoming of that rebellion by his power and his love. The affirmation that creation is good leaves the problem of the "evil" of the inevitable frictions between particular existences unsolved. But if an effort is made to solve it ontologically, we end with the difficult conclusion that temporal existence is really evil. It is good only when it is potential and not actual. Thus the line is breached between what has always separated Christianity's attitude toward time and history from the ontological speculations of Western classical thought and Oriental mysticism.

If these conclusions corresponded to the facts, we would not have to be concerned. We could merely say that it is necessary to augment Biblical thought with the ontology of Plato or Plotinus or of the Orient.

But the conclusions may not correspond to the facts. The facts in this case are what we experience in our historic existence. We experience ourselves as creatures with indeterminate possibilities of good and evil, possibilities of seeking our life at the expense of other life, and of finding our life by losing it; and these possibilities and perils always confront us as persons and wills within a particular historical context, quite above the level of ontological fate.

In many ways Tillich does justice to this dimension of the historical, particularly by his final definition of the "essential" in eschatological terms, that is, in terms of the "New Being" in Christ. If one were to deal with Tillich's thought adequately, one would have to have a full view of his Christology in the second volume of his great work. On the basis of what he has thus far written, it is obvious that the strongest Biblical elements appear in this realm of his thought. But even here the thought remains strongly colored by the original ontological speculation. Thus in very excellent analyses of the meaning of the *agape* of Christ, love as forgiveness (so strongly emphasized in Scripture) seems to be lacking, even as there is little of the Christian doctrine of atonement. "The Kingdom of God," he declares, "as the ultimate fulfilment is the universal perfection of all qualities of being in the new being beyond essence and existence." This covers the last but not the first phrase of the final words of the creed: "I believe . . . in The Forgiveness of sins: The Resurrection of the body: and The Life everlasting." Forgiveness of sins deals with the divine annulment of the contradictions between the human and the divine will, above the level of the contradiction between the finiteness of man and the eternal ground of his existence.

The drama of life is not identical with the stage of time and eternity upon which it is played. There is fate, as well as freedom, in this drama; but this fate is constructed of acts, events, relationships, and juxtapositions which can be grasped only poetically, because they are not determined by ontological structure. It may be that selves, wills, the sins of selves, and the grace of the love by which selves are saved from sin—that all these realities can be stated only in dramatic-poetic form. This Tillich himself does again and again. But the drama is determined ontologically in his thought, and the "end of history" is defined "as the reunion of the separated elements of existence within the totality of the new Being." Thus in the end, as in the beginning, it is "separation" which is wrong with life, and "reunion" is the culmination. Tillich attempts to bring all that has been wrought in history into this "reunion" so that the drama of history will not be annulled. That is why his thought is so much richer than anything attempted in a similar vein.

Tillich's greatness lies in his exploration of the boundary between metaphysics and theology. The difficult task of "walking the tightrope" is not negotiated without the peril of losing one's balance and falling over on one side or the other. If Barth refuses to approach the vicinity of the fence because he doesn't trust his balance, Tillich performs upon it with the greatest virtuosity, but not without an occasional fall. The fall may be noticed by some humble pedestrians who lack every gift to perform the task themselves.

REINHOLD NIEBUHR

DEPARTMENT OF CHRISTIAN ETHICS
UNION THEOLOGICAL SEMINARY
NEW YORK CITY

11

A. T. Mollegen
CHRISTOLOGY AND BIBLICAL
CRITICISM IN TILLICH

11

CHRISTOLOGY AND BIBLICAL CRITICISM
IN TILLICH

THE three major words in the title of this essay describe the genius of Tillich's theological system and express the point of view from which he speaks and writes about everything. Tillich is Biblical, Christocentric, and critical.

Tillich's theology, while it is "apologetic," that is, it seeks relevant and suasive ways to relate itself to all human knowledge and experience, is wholly and finally determined by the revelation of God recorded in the Bible.

Again, his theology is radically Christocentric. He always speaks about art, science, philosophy, history, and religion with the purpose of understanding and disclosing their relation to Christ.

And finally, Tillich is critical in every sense of that word. This critical element stems directly from the prophetic aspects of the Bible and from his Christology. Christ who gives and fulfills the criteria of final revelation is "completely transparent to the mystery he reveals."[1] "Jesus is the religious and theological object as the Christ and only as the Christ. And he is the Christ as the one who sacrifices what is merely 'Jesus' in him. The decisive trait in his picture is the continuous self-surrender of Jesus who is Jesus to Jesus who is the Christ."[2] The criteria of final revelation, therefore, are contained within the statement: "A revelation is final if it has the power of negating itself without losing itself."[3] It is out of the basic principle of his theology that Tillich writes, "My Christology and Dogmatics were determined by the interpretation of the cross of

[1] *Systematic Theology,* I, 133.
[2] *Ibid.,* p. 134.
[3] *Ibid.,* p. 133.

Christ as the event of history, in which divine judgment over the world became concrete and manifest."[4]

The acceptance of the divine criticism of everything not divine is "the Protestant principle" which has given Protestantism the courage to open itself to every kind of criticism. It turns upon itself, its sacred history, and its holy document, the criticism of the historian, the psychologist, the sociologist, the physicist, and the philosopher. Historical criticism of the Bible, therefore, is merely one aspect of the critical character of Tillich's theology which opens everything to critical interplay with everything else. At one and the same time every human experience, every existing reality, every science and art is given its autonomy in regard to everything which would despoil it, and also receives its relationship to God who criticizes, supports, and seeks to transform all things.

Because this Biblical, Christocentric, and critical character of Tillich's theology is not yet generally understood, he seems neo-orthodox to the liberal theologian, liberal to the neo-orthodox, modernist to the fundamentalist, indiscriminately Biblical to the modernist, historicist to the idealistic philosopher, and idealistic to the historicist.

Even D. M. Baillie, who is not far from Tillich's own Christological position, can see him as a Hegelian who is "without any interest in the question as to whether what the dogma says is true about an actual historical Jesus," and who believes that "the Absolute cannot pour its fullness into any one historical moment."[5] Since Tillich holds neither of these positions which are widely attributed to him, and since his Christology is central and determinative for all of his work, it is necessary to be clear about this side of his thought.

I. THE BIBLICAL HISTORICAL CHRIST AND THE HISTORICAL CRITICAL JESUS

Perhaps Tillich's position in respect to "an actual historical Jesus" can be interpreted without too great a loss with five simple statements. First, the Incarnation happened. Put bluntly, the Incarnational events were photographable. A sound-recording cinematograph could have captured the physical actions and words of a human individual who is the Christ. "The Incarnation is an historical

[4] *The Interpretation of History*, p. 32.
[5] D. M. Baillie, *God Was in Christ* (New York: Charles Scribner's Sons, 1948), pp. 78–79.

event, and occurs only once in time and space."[6] No one, however, had a purely historiographical interest in this man. No saving of uninterpreted facts about him took place. In this sense he is unknown. Tillich writes:

> The event is unknown in any photographic sense, but the religious picture resulting from it has proved to be the power of transforming existence. This is our primary requirement; and in saying this, I may express the hope that one false view is excluded by everything I have tried to say: namely, the mistake of supposing that the picture of the New Being in Jesus as the Christ is the creation of existential thought or experience. If this were the case, it would be as distorted, tragic and sinful as existence itself, and would not be able to overcome existence. *The religious picture of the New Being in Jesus is a result of a new being: it represents the victory over existence which has taken place, and thus created the picture."*[7]

This is the "historical" aspect of "the Biblical historical Christ."

Secondly, this man was received as Christ, and the New Testament portrays him as Jesus who is the Christ, the Son of God, the Logos. Tillich calls the New Testament portrait "the Biblical picture of Jesus as the Christ." It is the result of the revelation of God which came, and could only come, in the context of Jewish prophetic and apocalyptic expectation of the Messiah on the one hand and of receiving faith on the other hand. There is no revelation, except the primordial one, without preparation, and there is no revelation without reception by someone. Revelation always comes, and the final revelation came, in a history of revelation. Without such a history revelation would come as "a strange body which has no relation whatsoever to human existence and history. Therefore it cannot be assimilated by man's spiritual life. It either destroys this life or is thrown out by it."[8] Final revelation cannot be leveled to a history of revelation nor can "the history of revelation" be leveled to a history of religion; but neither can final revelation be a destructive supernaturalism which eliminates the history of revelation. Tillich stands in contrast to, but in some agreement with, both the *Religionsgeschichte* school, which was popular on the Continent before World War I, and Barthianism.

The New Testament portrait, the Biblical historical Christ, is all

---

[6] "A Reinterpretation of the Doctrine of the Incarnation," in the *Church Quarterly Review*, Vol. 147, No. 294, January-March, 1949.

[7] *Ibid.* Italics mine.

[8] *Systematic Theology*, I, 138.

we have. Data were saved about the man only because he was received as the Christ. Nothing can be known with certainty, therefore, about this man apart from the faith portrait. One point here should claim our attention as a qualification of this statement. Tillich would have no reason to deny that data might have been saved about Jesus received as Elijah, the forerunner of Christ, and that these data might have been caught up in the reception of Jesus as the Christ in such a document as Q. Such hypotheses are matters for historical criticism to inquire into and test by its own criteria and methodology. Indeed, in the great sermon *He Who Is the Christ,* Tillich says that Peter's Confession at Caesarea Philippi was that of a preparatory faith which had to be negated by the Crucifixion and transformed by the Resurrection as well as affirmed. "To the Crucified alone can we say: 'Thou art the Christ.' "[9] The real point is that all we have now is the New Testament portrait. This Biblical historical Christ is normative for Tillich. The quest of the historical Jesus which Schweitzer so brilliantly described in his book of the same name, and to which he added a revolutionary chapter, can neither replace nor support the Biblical portrait in as much as faith and theology are concerned. Conservative criticism cannot give us a purely factual Jesus which guarantees the photographic details of the Biblical historical Christ's life, nor can theological liberalism by critical methods reconstruct a "historical Jesus" who becomes a new canonical scripture supplanting the New Testament portrait, nor can radical criticism destroy the human flesh and blood existence of "the Biblical Christ." Tillich can say, therefore, that the Johannine literature is correct in affirming that in the Incarnation, "The logos becomes history, a visible and touchable individuality, in a unique moment of time."[10] And he can also say, "The photographic picture (not the photographable object) has never existed, either for Jesus himself or his apostles. The original picture, which existed from the beginning, was of a numinous and interpreted character, and it was this which proved to have the power to conquer existence."[11]

---

[9] *The Shaking of the Foundations,* p. 148. Tillich's sermons are the best introduction to his thought. They speak directly both to the sophisticated and to the unsophisticated mind.

[10] *The Protestant Era,* p. 30.

[11] "A Reinterpretation of the Doctrine of the Incarnation," in the *Church Quarterly Review,* Vol. 147, No. 294, January-March, 1949. Parenthesis mine. Available in the United States only in a mimeographed copy of the original manuscript.

Thirdly, Tillich maintains that historical criticism's quest for the historical Jesus, like all historical inquiry, can achieve at best only a high degree of probability. Religious certainty cannot rest on a probability the degree of which changes with more inquiry. "While the historicity of the divine revelation is a matter of the immediate certainty of faith, the historicity of the Biblical reports is a matter of grades of probability reached by historical research."[12] It is obvious that there are two kinds of "historicity" here. Tillich distinguishes them clearly: " 'Historical,' for the Biblical view of things, is the continuous process of the divine self-revelation in a series of events, combined with the interpretations of these revelatory events. It is in this sense that we must speak of 'historical revelation,' namely, of revelation through historical events. 'Historical,' for the scientific view of things, are those events which are verified, within the limits of every historical verification, by special methods of research."[13] In this latter sense "the historical Jesus" is an artifact composed of historians' judgments upon facts verifiable with only degrees of probability. This "historical Jesus" can neither support nor shake religious certainty.

Two things should be said at this stage of interpreting Tillich. He does not maintain that historical criticism is of no value, but only that it is not of ultimate value. Again he is not saying that such works as Goguel's *Life of Jesus* or the thirteenth century Franciscan *Meditations on the Life of Jesus Christ* might not become the portrait which informs the religious certainty. But this would be true only to the degree to which these very different pictures participate in and mediate the New Testament picture which is normative for them both. Nothing about any life of Christ can support with historical probability the Biblical historical Christ.

Fourthly, the "historicity" of the revelation portrayed in the New Testament as "Jesus who is the Christ" means not only that a human individuality existed, but that he was such as supports the Biblical picture. In theological discussion Tillich speaks of "an analogy of pictures" by which the photographable figure who is the Christ and the Biblical Jesus Christ are related. Perhaps a single illustration will suffice to show what he means. The Gospel "pictures" of the Baptism of Jesus will serve as our material. The Fourth Gospel has a picture analogous to the Synoptic picture of the Bap-

[12] *The Bible and Systematic Theology,* an unpublished manuscript.
[13] *Ibid.*

tism.[14] The latter portrays the action of John the Baptist baptizing Jesus in water. From the Johannine story, however, this action is only an inferable possibility with no high degree of probability. It is doubtful if such a Baptism would occur to the reader if the Fourth Gospel were his only source. Furthermore, this picture interprets the descent of the Spirit as a divine sign, divinely prearranged with John the Baptist, by which he knows Jesus as "he who baptizes with the Holy Spirit," "the Son of God," and "the Lamb of God, who takes away the sin of the world."[15] St. John's Gospel portrays John the Baptist as knowing before Jesus' ministry begins all that Christians know only after the coming of the Spirit.[16]

Anyone who reads the Synoptic accounts and the Johannine account can see the analogy. John the Baptist is the forerunner of Jesus, the Christ, who will baptize with the Holy Spirit. This is profoundly true for Christians. It is the Christian truth about John the Baptist and his relation to our Lord. But in the Johannine account this Christian meaning of John the Baptist slips into the consciousness and speeches of the Baptist and, together with the Spirit as sign, becomes a sensuously perceivable phenomenon while the act of baptizing with water slips out of the picture altogether. The Johannine portrait is true in relation to the Synoptic portrait's meaning, but it not only loses some but also changes some of the photographic details. Tillich suggests that this analogous character relates not only the New Testament pictures to each other, but also these pictures to the original events. Baldly put, if there existed an absolutely accurate motion-picture film with color and sound effects of the words and acts of the Incarnate One, this picture would support the Biblical pictures as to their Christian meaning. The figure that would be known through the film is unknown to us photographically, psychologically, and biographically. But he is known to us by faith as the New Testament Jesus the Christ, and this is all that we need for salvation.

Fifthly and finally, the certainty given by faith, which includes the photographable event character of the Incarnation, belongs to the Christian in an experience with two aspects. He participates in them "partly as a member of the Church which is the actual con-

---

[14] The Synoptic narratives vary among themselves, of course, but this fact can be ignored for our purposes here.

[15] John 1:24–34. Cf. Mark 1:1–11.

[16] John 20:19–23. This is an Easter Sunday event which seems to be the Johannine equivalent of Pentecost in Acts. See John 14:25, 16:14.

tinuation of the history of revelation, and partly as an individual who is grasped by the revealing event and becomes 'contemporaneous' with it. *The participation* of the believer gives him certainty about the 'event,' as witnessed by the Bible, but not about the biographical and psychological facts which made the event possible."[17] As St. Paul says, "in Christ" means at one and the same time incorporation into the Body of Christ, the fellowship of the Holy Spirit, the *ecclesia,* and "to be hid with Christ in God." St. Paul's Christ is Jesus who was born of a woman under the law, crucified, declared Son of God by the resurrection, and who now sits at the right hand of God and is present in his Body the Church and in the new selfhood of each believer. Tillich describes all of this by saying that the New Being appears in Jesus as the Christ and grasps us with a transforming power both as individuals and as the Church which, by definition, is the continuing place of reception of Jesus as the Christ. Certainty of the Biblical historical Christ comes only in this way, and that certainty is independent of the historical critical Jesus.

A popularizer of Tillich may risk a simple analogy. One knows that one's wife loves one by direct participation in her love, not by detached empirical observation of her acts and words and by reflection which infers that she probably loves one because her verifiable acts seem to indicate that she loves. At the end of a day one may have participated in a wife's love without having recorded, even in one's memory, all of the dishes cooked and served, the exact words said, and the gestures made. The absence of such historiographical details, or their rearrangement, dramatization, or factual inaccuracy in a fallible memory, does not affect the reality of the love, the existence of the wife, or the factuality of the original words and acts through which the love was proffered and received. For Tillich the history of revelation which centers in Christ is certain in divine meaning and power and in the factuality of its appearance, but not certain in historiographical accuracy.

It should be clear, therefore, that Tillich's theology does not destroy but sustains the incentive to carry on historical investigation. Indeed, for modern theology it is an imperative which saves theology from intellectual dishonesty. It is not only true that the believer should never depend upon the Biblical critic, even himself as a critic, in regard to the factual basis of faith, but it is also true that the scientific historian should never depend upon the believer, even

[17] *The Bible and Systematic Theology.* See note 12.

himself as a believer, in regard to verifying factuality. When faith predetermines the result of scientific investigation, it destroys the integrity of the investigator and his science, and perverts the conception of divine revelation. For divine revelation does not give what may be discovered nor does discovery give what is received by revelation. "The Gospels," wrote St. Augustine to some of his fellow Christians, "do not tell us that our Lord said, 'I will send you the Holy Ghost to teach you the course of the sun and the moon'; we should endeavor to become Christians and not astronomers."[18]

For Tillich historical criticism assists the theologian in three ways. It shows that mythical, legendary, and symbolical elements have been materialized in the Biblical records, and thus emancipates the mind from having to receive them as sensuously perceivable phenomena. The Bible can be "demythologized," eliminating the false offense of every kind of fundamentalism and permitting the Gospel to confront men with only its true offense. Again, historical inquiry shows how the Biblical authors developed the implications of their participation in revelation, and thus encourages the theologian to attempt this in his own time. And still again, critical investigation shows how Biblical writers used and transformed the categories and symbols of contemporary religion and culture. The theologian as critic sees the power of the New Being over all religion and culture, as well as its relatedness to all human experience, so that he attempts self-consciously what was done naïvely.

It is this latter task which Tillich is attempting so rigorously and with such success. He defends the critical method, honestly faces the human side of revelation, and rejects a "monophysite" theory of revelation. He risks a decision about the degree to which the symbolic, mythical, and legendary elements of the Bible may be used and which elements are usable. And he seeks to write theology with a self-conscious discernment of the message (kerygma) as it correlates with the human situation of the age. Each new historical period has its own relation to God on the basis of the final revelation, so that each period and cultural situation has its own special and unique capability of receiving continuing revelation.

II. THE NEW BEING

The New Being appears in the Incarnation, communicates itself to men by the Atonement, and indwells and transforms the receiv-

[18] *De Genesi ad litteram,* Lib. I, Cap. xix.

ing community. Christ is not Christ except in the history of revelation and as the center of the dialectical movement from the Jewish folk to the Christian community. The theologian inevitably, then, speaks of all Christian doctrines at once, even as he is forced by necessity to focus upon one doctrine at a time. The Christocentric character of Tillich's thought is so radical that an exposition of his Christology is almost impossible without also developing his whole system.

He begins his Christological thinking with "the man from heaven" in I Corinthians 15. The New Testament does not affirm that God becomes man, as Tillich writes in "The Reinterpretation of the Doctrine of the Incarnation," "but that a divine being, either the heavenly man, or the pre-existent Christ, or the divine Logos appears in the shape of a physical man or a man in the flesh. The statement is not that God becomes man, but that a divine being with human characteristics, the spiritual or heavenly man, or a moral being who chooses self-humiliation, or the creative Reason and Word, appears in time and space and is subject to the law of the flesh and of sin, namely, human existence." Demythologized, this means that "the Incarnation is the paradox of essential Godmanhood manifesting itself within and under the conditions of human existence which contradicts original Godmanhood."

Two things are said here. Christ is essential manhood in existence. Essential manhood is Godmanhood. This is an interpretation of the Biblical portrait of Jesus Christ in terms which derive from Western philosophy and are transformed by understanding them in relation to the New Being. Classical Greek theology and classical German philosophy attempted to express the Incarnation in terms of the relation of the infinite to the finite. The two-nature Christology of the Councils, modern idealism and positivism, and their combinations, did not realize that the central problem of theology, and therefore of Christology, is that existence is less than, and at enmity with, essence.

The Biblical picture of Christ has "two outstanding characteristics: his maintenance of unity with God and his sacrifice of everything he could have gained for himself from this unity."[19] The first characteristic is, in Tillich's language, the identity of essential manhood and Godmanhood. The second gives the criterion for all revelation and is the self-identifying mark of final revelation, namely,

[19] *Systematic Theology*, I, 135.

that "it has the power of negating itself without losing itself."[20] Christ possesses himself completely so that he can surrender himself completely, and he possesses himself completely because he surrenders himself completely. "For this reason the Father loves me, because I lay down my life, that I may take it again. No one takes it from me, but I lay it down of my own accord. I have power to lay it down, and I have power to take it again; this charge I have received from my Father."[21]

This final revelation gives the point of view from which everything is understood so that the whole history of philosophy can be grasped and reshaped in relation to Christ. Man is seen in terms of Christ, and all of reality is grasped through a radically anthropological analysis. Subhuman nature participates analogically in the basic ontological structure which is that of the relation of the self and the world. This self is related to the world by the affinity of its reason to the reasonable structure of the world and separated from itself and its world by the finite freedom by which it transcends itself and its world. This structure includes polarities between individuality and universality,[22] dynamics[23] and form, freedom and destiny.[24]

The basic ontological structure of the self in communion with the world is distorted in the actualization of finite freedom. The beginning of the fall and the end of creation are simultaneous. The fall coincides with creation but is neither identical with nor necessarily resultant from it. Mythically the fall is a possibility which God risked, foresaw as actuality but did not decree. The disruption of the basic ontological structure means that the polarities of existence are related not only by dialectical interdependence but by contradiction. Individuality and universality, dynamics and form, freedom and destiny struggle against each other. Essential being is what should be, the world as the divine creation. Existential being is the fallen world deriving from and yet contradicting its essential being. Existential being is being distorted by its threat of nonbeing.

The Biblical picture of Christ is that of a personal life who creates

[20] *Ibid.*, p. 133.

[21] John 10:17 ff., R.S.V. This is a word which is parallel to the Incarnational Hymn in Philippians 2:5–11. Cf. also Mark 8:34–38.

[22] The self is "centered" so that it is an individual but it participates in all universal structures so that it has a world.

[23] Dynamics is nonbeing ($\mu\dot{\eta}$ $\delta\nu$) in contrast to formed being, and it is the power of being in contrast to nothing ($o\check{\upsilon}\kappa$ $\delta\nu$).

[24] Freedom and destiny have analogues on the subhuman levels, spontaneity and law.

a community which in principle is universal. His vital powers are not self-destructive or weakened but heightened, and his form (humanity) is dynamically carried beyond ordinary expression without distortion. His freedom serves only his destiny so that he has perfect freedom. He is the New Being transcending existential being because it is the actualization of essential being. And he is the New Being transcending essential being because the New Being exists. The New Being manifests itself against, and overcomes nonbeing.

All of Christ's words and deeds and sufferings manifest the New Being. In Synoptic portrayal he is the eschatological (Son of Man) Messiah who comes in the power of the Kingdom of God. His words are signs of the Kingdom, his exorcisms and healings are sign-wonders of the Kingdom's power, his sufferings and death are the Kingdom's victory over the autonomous powers who can slay him but cannot beguile him into autonomous reaction against, or into subjection to, themselves. The New Being in Christ, therefore, fulfills every partial and broken appearance of essential being in prophets, thaumaturges, saints, and martyrs. They are all preparatory and expectant revelations which point to him.

The Biblical Christ is the divine life received by perfect human faith which knows doubt but no despair, by courage which is anxious about death but not in terror, by finite freedom which does not exalt its finitude, by desire which desires only the Kingdom of God for the world and the world for the Kingdom. This is man in unity with God. But the Biblical Christ is also unable to do other than this. He is not unable with the necessity of mechanical or rational structures but by divine predestination. He is essential God-manhood present in, but transcending, existence. He is tempted but sins neither by unfaith, nor by *hybris*, nor by concupiscence. He is perfectly obedient to God in his vocation of Messiah.

The portrait, therefore, focuses in two representative pictures, the Crucified and the Risen Christ. Every part of the New Testament portrait expresses these two aspects of Christ. The Cross exposes the full enmity of existence to essential being and the undefeatable presence of the New Being in existence. The Resurrection shows the New Being as the victorious power over the self-destructiveness of existence. The Risen Christ is Lord of all powers, visible and invisible. The angels cannot separate the faithful from the love of

God in Christ Jesus and themselves become possibilities for salvation.

The Crucifixion-Resurrection event is the breaking through into human consciousness and existence of the New Being in Christ. The divine life maintains community with all human life, and through human life with all existence by taking upon itself the fact and the consequences of existential separation (sin and tragedy). The divine love suffers with, but not instead of, those who receive that love. It suffers for, but not instead of, those who resist it. The divine love, rejected, rejects the rejection and is seen as wrath by the rejector. The wrath of God is therefore the surgical knife of the love of God. The demand of essential being is no longer demand or judgment when it is given as the New Being. God gives what he commands and commands what he gives (Augustine).

The communication of the New Being in Christ to others is the saving work of Christ who "at-ones" God and man and, through man, unites God and the whole creation. It is Pentecost, Justification, New Being, Regeneration, Sanctification, according to which aspect is emphasized.

III. THE NEW BEING AND THE WORD OF GOD

This, in brief, is Tillich's Christology. It will be set forth in detailed elaboration in his second volume. The critical question which it raises can be asked in terms of his doctrine of "the Word of God." It is a question addressed to the center of the whole system.

Tillich rejects both Barth and Brunner, who tend to reduce the Logos to Divine speaking and the image of God in man to communion with God. For Tillich the Logos is not merely the spoken Word; and the image of God in man is his rational structure, his logos. The human logos is the structure of freedom implying potential infinity. Man can transcend every static structure of himself and his world. It is man's "nature" to transcend his "nature." The divine Logos and the human logos are related by analogy so that revelation can occur without destroying man or creating superman.

The classical Logos doctrine, begun in the New Testament most explicitly with the Fourth Gospel and the First Epistle of St. John, is not "intellectualistic," nor is Greek philosophy at its best.[25] It is

[25] Tillich says that Ritschl and Harnack misunderstood Greek philosophy, for which metaphysical knowledge was existential union with reality.

the "Logos of life," creative power as well as shaping structure. The Logos "is first of all the principle of the divine self-manifestation in the ground of being itself."[26]

"In the beginning was the Word and the Word was with God, and the Word was God."[27] The infinite mysterious depth of God supports and sends forth forms graspable by human reason. The Word also is the creative power of the divine freedom bringing free selves into actuality and implanting spontaneity as well as law in the creation. Again, the Logos is God revealing himself in the history of revelation and, finally, as Jesus Christ, "the Word become flesh" (man). From this meaning of the Word comes the affirmation that the Bible is the Word of God. This can mean only that Scripture records the preparatory and the final revelation, and participates in that revelation. The Bible cradles Christ (Luther). Lastly, the Word is the revelatory reality in the Church's speaking and acting.

All of these meanings have a common element. The Word is " 'God manifest'—manifest in himself, in creation, in the history of revelation, in the final revelation, in the Bible, in the words of the church and her members. 'God manifest'—the mystery of the divine abyss expressing itself through the divine Logos—this is the meaning of the symbol, the 'Word of God.' "[28] These six meanings break into two groups. The first one has to do with the Word in God, the others with the Word embodied in existence. These point to the final revelation, the Logos as a personal life in history, Jesus Christ—or participate in it. Jesus as the Christ points to himself, that is, Jesus as Jesus points to his Christness in God. "Are you the Christ, the Son of the Blessed?" asked the high priest at Jesus' trial. And Jesus replies with a statement in substance identical with that with which he met Peter's, "You are the Christ"; "I am; and you will see the Son of Man sitting at the right hand of Power, and coming with the clouds of heaven."[29]

The question which is raised—at least for an Anglican clergyman—is: What is the relation between the Word of God manifest in himself and the Word of God which is equated with essential Godmanhood? Tillich says, in his work cited on the incarnation, that the equation "between essential being and essential Godmanhood

[26] *Systematic Theology*, I, 157.
[27] John 1:1.
[28] *Systematic Theology*, I, 159.
[29] Mark 14:61–62; cf. Mark 8:29–33.

. . . simply indicates that divine self-objectification and essential manhood belong together, because man is essentially the divine image, and anthropomorphism contains an indestructible element of truth." If the divine Logos is only actualized in the creation and completely in Jesus Christ, then this conception seems to be in contradiction with Tillich's many statements that "in God as God there is no distinction between potentiality and actuality." However symbolic may be the statement that God is beyond potentiality and actuality, it means that both are analogies of a living unity in God. This seems to be the point of view from which Tillich can speak of an analogical relation between the Divine Logos and the human logos. "Man is the image of God because in him the ontological elements are complete and united on a creaturely basis, just as they are complete and united in God as the creative ground. Man is the image of God because his *logos* is analogous to the divine *logos,* so that the divine *logos* can appear as man without destroying the humanity of man."[30]

If the divine Logos is essential being in relation to the Creation and nothing else, then God "actualizes" himself only in the Creation and perfectly only in Jesus Christ. But if in a symbolic sense the Logos, Godmanhood, the Son of God, the Son of Man, is actualized in God, then his appearance as man with an analogous *logos,* an actualized essential manhood, must be by a union of Logos and logos, not by identity of the two. It does not seem to me that Tillich has escaped the problem which classical theology sought to answer by affirming the hypostatic union of the two natures. That affirmation meant that God became man in the sense that manhood was taken into the Son by the conception of Jesus by the Holy Spirit, and that this union is indissoluble and eternal. It certainly did not mean either the metamorphosis of the Son into a man or the kenosis of the Son by which the Son is wholly limited by his manhood.

Perhaps all of this is entirely due to a misunderstanding of Tillich with which most ordinary readers will have some sympathy.

The general tenor of Tillich's theology seems to me to stand within the classical dogmas. He does not deny that God became man. His assertion that the New Testament myth of the Incarnation is not that "God becomes man, but that a divine being with human characteristics . . . appears in time and space" is not made in order to move in an Arian direction or finally to deny that God becomes

[30] *Ibid.,* p. 259.

man in Christ. It is made as the beginning of an argument which says that the real problem does not lie in the Greek presupposition that man because of his finite character cannot be united with Deity. The real wonder of the Incarnation lies in the overcoming of the contradiction between essential manhood and existential manhood. The problem of man answered by the Incarnation is sin and tragedy, not finiteness and the natural necessity of death. "The *sting* of death is sin," said St. Paul. It is *human* death, that is, *existential* (sinful) death which is the wage of sin, not biological death. Man cannot die a merely natural death, he is not a merely biological creature. He must die in self-exaltation, rebelling against death or destroying himself—which are two forms of self-centered affirmation of self. Or he must die in faith, entrusting himself to God. "Father, into thy hands I commit my spirit."[31]

The paradox—that which comes against the opinion of existential man—is that the fully perceived contradiction between essential being and existential being has been overcome, and the overcoming may be participated in. The appearance of the New Being above essence and existence is a historical event which overcomes existence by transforming it. The Creation is being saved.

Tillich seeks at one and the same time to prevent any segment of the Creation from making itself God and to shut out no segment or aspect of the Creation from being saved. He wars against everything that usurps the place of God and everything that mutilates man and the subhuman orders, and he sees that these things are the same thing. He stands against all idolatry, in the power of the Protestant principle. God is God, and there is none beside him. But he also stands against Barthian supernaturalism because it violates the logos of the creation. Again, he stands against all naturalism because it does not take the disruption of creation seriously enough or finds creation ultimately meaningless. The central concern of Tillich seems to me to be expressed in a single passage:

God as being-itself transcends nonbeing absolutely. On the other hand, God as creative life includes the finite and, with it, nonbeing, although nonbeing is eternally conquered and the finite is eternally reunited within the infinity of the divine life. Therefore it is meaningful to speak of a participation of the divine life in the negativities of creaturely life. This is the ultimate answer to the question of theodicy. The certainty of God's directing creativity (Providence) is based on the certainty of God as the

[31] Luke 23:46.

ground of being and meaning. The confidence of every creature, its courage to be, is rooted in faith in God as its creative ground.[32]

This is Tillich's *Canticle to the Sun*, his eighth chapter of the Epistle to the Romans. It is Biblical, but it rests only in the New Being in Christ. All affirmations of Creation are made by participating in Salvation.

A. T. MOLLEGEN

DEPARTMENT OF NEW TESTAMENT
THE PROTESTANT EPISCOPAL THEOLOGICAL SEMINARY
ALEXANDRIA, VIRGINIA

[32] *Systematic Theology*, I, 270.

12

Nels F. S. Ferre
TILLICH'S VIEW OF THE CHURCH

TILLICH'S VIEW OF THE CHURCH

INTRODUCTION

PAUL TILLICH is a front-line theologian. He stands at the forefront of profundity. Our question concerning him, let us immediately say, is to what extent he expounds a Christian position. Our own responsibility in this book is his doctrine of the church, but this cannot be understood apart from the total content of his thinking. At the very beginning we must therefore stress the fact that the ontological content of Tillich is alone decisive for the appraisal of the Christian nature of his doctrine of the church. Any mainly phenomenological critique would consequently be misdirected.

In method Tillich combines the rational and the existential, as one surely must who in the content of his thought combines being and abyss, or meaning and mystery. For such thinking "the choice of symbols" becomes "decisive for truth and error."[1] Yet, even so, not the symbols which are available in the ontic realm, but the reality intended by those symbols, "the theological ontology"[2] of his thinking, is determinative for his doctrine of the church.

The church, which he considers always to have been "his home,"[3] and which certainly plays a leading role in his thinking throughout, finds him also a stranger. Tillich lives and thinks on the borderline where the story of the church, in its deepest sense, is the story of history, and where he nevertheless can also be said to be more concerned with "the religious bases and implications of the whole cultural process."[4] At times he seems to bind all existence to the

[1] H. G. Wood, *The Kingdom of God and History* (Chicago: Willett, Clark & Company, 1938), p. 121.
[2] Paul Tillich, *The Interpretation of History*, p. 270. See also *Systematic Theology*, I, 238–240.
[3] *The Interpretation of History*, p. 41.
[4] Paul Tillich, *The Protestant Era*, p. 273.

dynamic meaning and fulfillment of the church; then again he seems almost entirely to dissolve any high and cohesive doctrine of the church. How is this possible?

I. THE CHURCH AND THE ULTIMATE

A. "The ultimate is the transcendent meaning of history."[5] God is "the ultimate meaningfulness . . . which surpasses all that is conceivable."[6] This meaning is unconditional and inexhaustible,[7] neither beside nor above any meaning. The church can, therefore, at best represent, but can never *be* the Kingdom, for "the Kingdom of God is a symbolic expression of the ultimate fulfillment in which the contrast between essence and existence is overcome universally and completely."[8] The Kingdom of God is theologically the counterpart to "the ultimate meaning of history" as "the suprahistorical unification and purification of historic meanings. It is never static essence, but a dynamic conception, overarching the 'battlefield of the divine and the demonic,' "[9] designating "the necessity that the ultimate meaning of existence is never given," "acquiring reality only in the overcoming of meaninglessness and the distortion of meaning."[10]

As far as the question of ontology goes, there is ultimately no personal God nor ultimately any eternal destiny of persisting personalities as such. God, in fact, is not the dominatingly ultimate category in Tillich, but such categories as being and abyss, the unconditioned or unconditional, and the Kingdom.[11] There is no supernatural being before and above all beings, as their creator, judge, and redeemer, but there is rather "only the Ground of Being."

[5] *The Interpretation of History,* p. 274.
[6] *Ibid.,* p. 222.
[7] *Ibid.,* p. 223. Nor is God beside or above any *being.*
[8] Paul Tillich, *Propositions,* Part V, p. 14. Cf. Wood, *op. cit.,* p. 116. Prof. Ferré, even more than Professors Niebuhr, Adams, and Daubney, very properly found it necessary to refer a number of times to these *Propositions.* Parts III, IV, and V constitute the material which, when fully developed by Professor Tillich, will become Vol. II of his *Systematic Theology.* They are mimeographed for the private use of his students. All the essayists were furnished copies of this material to assist them in the preparation of this work.—The Editors.
[9] Wood, *op. cit.,* p. 117.
[10] *Ibid.,* p. 118.
[11] Cf. *The Protestant Era,* p. 119. Cf. also: God is "being-itself," and this is the only legitimate "nonsymbolic" statement about god, in *Systematic Theology,* pp. 238 ff. "Personal God" does not mean that God is a person; it means that He is the ontological ground of personality, and therefore not less than personal *in this sense* (*ibid.,* p. 245). Tillich insists that God is not "a self."

To be unconditionally seems to mean to possess pure unity of meaning, and to exist eternally seems to mean to participate in being in this sense of unconditional meaning and being itself. That God, or the ultimate form of life in any sense, is not unconscious or impersonal does not mean that it is personal or conscious, but rather that such categories are transcended within the unification and purification of meaning and self-being as such. Ontic symbols, though they suggest a Christian kind of reality, do not imply the structural content of historic Christian affirmation.

B. The church represents the Kingdom, and Christ is its foundation, for he is "the concrete point at which something absolute appears in history and provides it with meaning and purpose."[12] This center must be absolute "or it is no center at all."[13] Christ is explicitly the center of the church and implicitly of all history. He is "the ultimate criterion for challenging and changing" all actual powers.[14] He is, nevertheless, as far as structural content goes, also the ultimate foundation as the appearance in history of "a superhistorical unconditioned meaning."[15] Christ is the *kairos* or New Being which appears as the fullness of time,[16] thereby dividing the historical process into a period of preparation and a period of reception, though these categories also involve overlapping manifestations of each other. Yet not only does he thus exactly divide the whole history of the church by being its center in history, but he is also the criterion which determines the content of all suprahistorical symbols, for organically related to him are the suprahistorical categories of the fall of man, or the suprahistorical beginning of history; and the reign of Christ within the church, or the suprahistorical end of history.[17] Christ is the New Being "in which the contrast between essential and existential being is overcome," and as such constituting the center of history;[18] he is also the New Being as the end of history, whereby existence is transformed beyond both essential and existential being.[19] This New Being is universal love, incarnate in history, represented in history, and fulfilled beyond history by the

[12] *The Interpretation of History*, p. 243.
[13] *Ibid.*, p. 251.
[14] *Ibid.*, p. 263.
[15] *Ibid.*, p. 261.
[16] *Propositions*, Part V, p. 18.
[17] *Ibid.*, p. 18.
[18] *Ibid.*, p. 17.
[19] *Ibid.*, p. 28.

universal spiritual community of the church as universal agape, including the fulfillment of nature.

The problematic aspect of this thinking is not the content of the symbols involved, nor its vigorously Christian structure as far as language goes; it is not *the accuracy of Tillich's phenomenological analysis as a whole,* but to what extent the appearance of the New Being is phenomenological clarification and consequent historic power, or is actually an ontological objectification within history from an eminently suprahistorical realm, in the transcendent rather than in the merely transcendental sense. Tillich, to be sure, uses both the words "transcendent" and "transcendental," but his consistent stress on (1) there being no Being above or besides other beings, (2) his doctrine of eternity as the unification and purification of meaning, (3) his declaration that, regardless of historic, explanatory power, love is finally indefinable, and (4) his total stress on symbolism in relation to being and the abyss makes questionable any genuine Christian doctrine of incarnation. This is certainly true in the classic Christian sense of (1) a supernaturally transcendent realm of being, (2) a genuine creation from beyond this cosmic realm, and (3) a goal-centered historical process with personal destinies beyond physical death, into which the incarnation came as its center of meaning, judgment, and salvation. Upon the ontological significance of Tillich's doctrine of the Kingdom and of the New Being in Christ, in any case, hangs the deeper and fuller meaning of his doctrine of the church.

C. The church is related to the ultimate as representing the Kingdom through its acceptance of Christ as the New Being, whether in preparation or in fulfillment. In the perspective of the ultimate, the church, then, relates itself to history as its bearer.[20] The deepest meaning of history is salvation, and the content of salvation is the church as the spiritual community in the New Being. The church is the declaratory center of all implicit meanings, which anticipatorily and fragmentarily are organically related to its being, not, to be sure, in the sense of any approximation through process to the reality of this meaning itself, but as the constant center of all meaning which is the Kingdom. This means that the church is "from above" in this symbolic sense, that it originates in the divine inbreaking and not in human growth, and that it is a corporate entity, primarily related to the ultimate as such, so that no individual

20 Wood, *op. cit.,* p. 122.

participates "in the Kingdom of God except by participating in the historical manifestation of the Kingdom of God."[21] The relation of the church to history, in the ultimate perspective, can be said to be such that history can be understood only in terms of the meaning of history, which is the church with Christ as its center.[22] The church in this sense "has the key to the meaning of history."[23]

We must always remember that for Tillich history is "the outstanding category of interpreting reality,"[24] and that "history is essentially the 'history of salvation'" wherein "true being, or the ultimate good," "realizes itself through a dynamic process of self-realization within and above temporal existence."[25] Though the world is ontologically good, it is mythologically a battlefield, within which the New Being has appeared and appears, history thus being saved through history, beyond mere cyclic change, because the Lord of time controls and acts in history.[26] From the ultimate perspective, then, the church must be viewed in relation to the Kingdom as the sum and unity of meanings beyond history, but also in relation to Christ as the New Being in history, without which Christ cannot even exist any more than the church without Christ.[27] Christ is then the decisive appearance of the truth and power of the ultimate, and the church is the bearer of this truth and power as the only interpreter of them in their original and plenary meaning, through daring faith in the unique and nonrecurring *kairos*, the Christ, while history as a whole is the total story of salvation as the continuum in which the church lives,[28] for which it works and witnesses, and from which the church is continually gathered as the elect.[29] The church, then, to summarize, represents the Kingdom because it expresses the Christ both in the original explicit meaning and within and through all implicit meanings of history as a whole.

The ultimate being always beyond our ken, the church also merely representing but never embodying the Kingdom, Tillich's "Protestant principle" is easy to understand. The finite can never be frozen as

[21] *Propositions*, Part V, p. 27.
[22] *The Interpretation of History*, p. 249.
[23] *Propositions*, Part V, p. 19.
[24] *The Protestant Era*, p. 26.
[25] *Ibid.*, p. 27.
[26] *Ibid.*, p. 27.
[27] *Propositions*, Part IV, p. 22.
[28] *Ibid.*, Part V, p. 11.
[29] *The Protestant Era*, p. 31.

the content of infinite revelation. The infinite proceeds sovereignly to judge every form of authority in actual history as human and relative. Not the historic Jesus as such, not the Bible as such, not the church as such, not creed as such, not Reformation theology as such —all these are subject to judgment by the eternal and contemporary Christ. His cross symbolizes the human boundary situation[30] which is inescapably part of the relation between the ultimate and the immediate, between the Kingdom and the church.

II. THE CHURCH IN RELATION TO ITSELF

In relation to the ultimate the church can be analyzed with respect to the Kingdom, Christ, and history. In relation to itself the church can be viewed from the perspective of its faith, its field, and its functions.

A. Few theologians are freer from stifling dogmas than Tillich. His thinking illustrates the freedom wherewith Christ has set us free. Theologically this can be put as faith in the adequacy of the Holy Spirit to lead us into all, and therefore into new, truths. Philosophically this can be expressed in terms of Tillich's vital and comprehensive category of the *logos,* which alone gives right content to *kairos.* "The Logos is the eternal criterion of the Kairos,"[31] or it can be considered in terms of his readiness to use the category of creativity. Tillich, furthermore, illustrates this principle in terms of his own continuous and profound creativity. Whatever he touches shines with personal insight and illuminating newness. Naturally his doctrine of the Protestant principle has delivered him from all scribism. He is free from the burden of the past whether in institution, creed, or book. And this freedom he has along with such a strong stress on tradition and on the past in experience that he calls the past central to all human consciousness.[32] Faith for him is, nevertheless, never reduced to seeing, but soars with and beyond seeing into the fuller light of creative newness. Notice, for instance, his stress on creativity, which he ranks alongside word and sacrament: "The spiritual foundation of the church in all generations is the New Being in Jesus as the Christ, actualized by the creative power of the divine

---

[30] *Ibid.,* p. 200.
[31] *Propositions,* Part V, p. 19.
[32] *The Interpretation of History,* p. 256.

Spirit, through the means of his *creativity*, word and sacrament."[33]

The strength of this stress, however, is that creativity is not sporadic subjectivity, but structured in Jesus as the Christ, and in the word and sacrament. These are decisive directives or permanent patterns for the being and the faith of the church, as Christian, in any organic and systematic sense. The foundation and the steady strands throughout history do not confine creativity, but direct and gather it into the unity represented by the Kingdom as the symbol beyond all closed community of the earthly church. Creativity thus never contradicts the true essence of word and sacrament, but complements and fulfills their relative historic meanings and enactments.[34]

The word is the main instrument in the foundation of the church.[35] When the divine Spirit works through the human word, this becomes the "word of God." The content of this word must always be the New Being in Jesus as the Christ,[36] for by being eternally the Word of God he determines beforehand all that can become the word of God. What makes the word, then, the word of God is, on the one side, this content of the New Being, but on the other, the reality of the witnessing presence of the Spirit to a real recipient. Only when the word is received within a personal confrontation, from the Spirit into the spirit, so to speak, has the word become consummated as the word of God. The Bible may be this word, obviously, but the Bible can never exhaust the source[37] for it or exclude the common word of the commonplace situation from becoming afresh the living Word of God[38] when the content is the meaning of Christ and the form is the persuasive activity of the Spirit authentically received by man.[39] The Word become flesh is ever the criterion of the Christian content, and the Spirit becoming flesh is ever the criterion of the Christian form of the word of God.[40]

The faith of the church thus is constituted by the Spirit and the word, but also by the sacrament. Tillich has a profound yet free understanding of sacramentalism. Together with the Spirit and the

[33] *Propositions*, Part IV, p. 22. Italics mine.
[34] *The Protestant Era*, p. xxi; note especially the concept, "Gestalt of Grace."
[35] Introduction, *Systematic Theology* I, pp. 51–52.
[36] *Ibid.*, pp. 50 ff.
[37] *Ibid.*, pp. 34 ff.
[38] *The Protestant Era*, pp. 177 and 202.
[39] Cf. *Ibid.*, p. 211.
[40] *Propositions*, Part IV, p. 23.

word, it helps to found the church on Jesus as the Christ. He avoids both intellectualistic antisacramentarianism and magical sacramentalism by holding a realistic conception of the sacraments[41] based upon a realistic interpretation of nature.[42] Water, bread, and wine, for instance, are not arbitrarily connected with saving efficacy through divine command, nor are they accidentally connected with their Christian function, but symbolize and convey the total interrelation between the spiritual reality, the meaning of the word, and the organic relatedness of nature and history to spirit and meaning. Meaning and natural power are thus combined. The church, through such symbolic use in the realistic sense and manner, lays hold both on the conscious and on the subconscious through word and sacrament, through act and interpretation; the Spirit working through sensuous objects uses "irreplaceable"[43] means. A defensive and restrictive use of sacramentalism is arbitrary, since the sacraments minister organically to main events in the lives of persons, at times, and in the life of the church, at times. Such freedom of mind and spirit combined with the natural urgency of the life of the church *within nature and history* is exceptional. One could only have wished, at this point, that his understanding of the total concern and organic relationship between persons and the church and between nature-history-meaning transmission and the organic necessity of historic-systematic appropriateness had been even more integrated.[44]

B. With relation to itself we have now looked at the faith of the church. We must now look at its field in the same respect. The church is the community of faith and love, both visible and invisible, both manifest and latent, being holy, universal, and undivided with regard to its foundation, the New Being in Christ. All the functions of the church with respect to its own inner life and with respect to the world at large, too numerous even to enumerate intelligently within this chapter,[45] stem from the basic nature of the church as "the community of faith" and as "the community of love," receiving and actualizing the New Being.

---

[41] *The Protestant Era*, p. 98.
[42] *Ibid.*, pp. 99 ff.
[43] *Propositions*, Part IV, p. 24.
[44] Cf. especially *ibid.*, Part IV, pp. 23 ff.
[45] *Ibid.*, Part IV, pp. 29 ff.

The cornerstone of the foundation of faith is that Jesus is the Christ. Whether or not this is accepted as the eternal and completely central core of the Christian community determines all principles of inclusion and exclusion, whether for individual membership or for the correctness and adequacy of its teachings.[46] This core also decides whether or not a community actualizes the New Being in love. True love levels all spiritual inequality and all such social and political inequalities which would thwart such spiritual inclusiveness, or equality with respect to our ultimate concern. It also serves as the decisive principle of discipline within the church.[47] The church is also "always and everywhere theological and sociological, at the same time";[48] it is a concrete embodiment in history of ultimate meaning, among its own finite fractions and distorted fragments. As such it is both invisible, or open to faith alone, and visible, or open to empirical investigations.[49]

The church is holy because of its holy foundation: the new being in Christ. Similarly, it is also universal and unified. These attributes are authentic in spite of actual sinfulness, or "existential separation," and actual division, whether in terms of existential particularity or of confessional divergence. Paradoxically, the existentially unholy church is holy because of its regeneration and justification by the New Being in Christ, and every particular church as Christian is universal by its very foundational essence; and beyond all confessional divisions lies the unmovable unity of the foundation of the church in which it necessarily participates as long as it remains the church.[50] This paradoxical nature of the church negates all "realistic" interpretations of it which maintain a permanent contradiction between its meaning and reality, and also all "idealistic" interpretations of it which affirm any "permanent approximation of its reality and meaning."[51]

This affirmation by Tillich reinforces the view that his analysis is mostly a phenomenological description of experience rather than an ontological expectation, for if the latter were true, his entire scheme of eschatology in the last part of his systematic theology is intelli-

[46] *Ibid.*, p. 25.
[47] *Ibid.*, pp. 25–26.
[48] *Ibid.*, p. 26.
[49] *Ibid.*, Part IV, pp. 26–27.
[50] *Ibid.*, pp. 27–29.
[51] *Ibid.*, p. 27.

gible on the assumption, and only on the assumption, of the "permanent approximation of the reality and meaning of the Church."

C. The last aspect of the church in relation to itself is its functions. As has been said, no full mention can be made of these. In the main, however, they are the function of constitution, the function of expansion, the function of construction, and the function of transformation related, respectively, to the spiritual foundation of the church, its historical existence, its own life, and the outside world. Tillich has here an unusual depth in combining immediately and organically the inner expression of the nature of the church and the functions which it serves. Both the arbitrary and the accidental are thus avoided,[52] for "the systematic doctrine of the Church is the immediate basis of all practical theology."[53]

III. THE CHURCH AND THE WORLD

Having looked at the church in relation to the ultimate and to itself, the main topic remaining is the relation of the church to the world. The three facets of our thinking on this topic are the relation of the church to humanism and secularism, its relation to other religions openly avowed, and its relation to social problems.

A. Tillich has a profound and comprehensive understanding of the first relationship because of his understanding both of church and of culture as responses to the ultimate. "Church and society are one in their essential nature; for the substance of culture is religion and the form of religion is culture."[54] Man's total activity must be viewed in the light of his ultimate questions and concerns. How very true this is, and to what extent, for that matter, the Christian world view underlies much of modern humanism and secularism, Tillich has demonstrated in two razor-sharp articles: "Nichtkirchliche Religionen" and "Kirche und humanistische Gesellschaft," wherein he illustrates that "nicht der Gegensatz von Kirche und Humanismus, sondern das dialektische Verhältnis von Kirche und christlichen Humanismus ist das eigentliche Problem,"[55] particularly as far as

[52] *Ibid.*, Part IV, p. 29.
[53] *Ibid.*, p. 22.
[54] *The Interpretation of History*, p. 235. Cf. *The Protestant Era*, p. xvii: "The central proposition of my philosophy of religion . . . Religion is the substance of culture, culture is the expression of religion."
[55] *Kirche und humanistiche Gesellschaft* (lecture given at the Berneuchen Work Conference in Patzig, Oct. 5, 1930), p. 6.

the Occident is concerned. All life relates its deepest questions to the unconditional and is thus religious, whether of church or of culture.

The real problem here is, of course, that since Tillich (with an unflagging zeal) repudiates the supernatural, from his early German writings on, naturally the distinctive difference between the church and "secular" humanism disappears. Existentially, to be sure, if God be transcendent or supernatural as well as transcendental, all experience does relate itself ultimately to Him, but in that case does it not make a decisive difference whether there is conscious faith in the supernatural or not, in contrast to all secularism and humanism? Though all religion may be thus existential as a depth relation and depth response inescapably, does not the church in nature and reality differ more deeply from general culture than in the way in which form is related to content in the response of our collective ultimate concern?

What doctrine of the church is, in truth, left if the *kairos* is put in universal terms,[56] if no identification with the unconditional is made in history,[57] if the Christian symbols and confession are incidental,[58] if autonomous forms within secular culture can become the bearers of ultimate meaning,[59] if, indeed, the Protestant principle can itself be a basis of renewal over against even the Christian church?[60] This is, indeed, what was meant when in the introduction we stated that *at times* Tillich's doctrine of the church seems to evaporate into a general theory of religion as a response to the unconditional. When he claims that the world can be the conscience of the church as well as the church the conscience of the world,[61] would it not also be better to say that the true church is at times more fully present outside *formal organization* than within formal ecclesiastical structures? In this case the primary definition of the church in terms of its foundation would be consistently observed.

B. Not only is there organic relation between the church and

---

[56] *The Protestant Era*, p. 36.
[57] *Ibid.*, p. 205.
[58] *Ibid.*, p. 205.
[59] *Ibid.*, p. 221.
[60] *Ibid.*, p. 233.
[61] ". . . the Church is the perpetual guilty conscience of society, and society the perpetual guilty conscience of the church."—*The Interpretation of History*, p. 227.

secularism and humanism, but also between the Christian church and explicit religions. The main structural relationship between both the implicit and explicit religions and the church are the categories called the "latent" and the "manifest" church. The latter is the actuality of the New Being manifest in history, while "the church as prepared by history is latent in history."[62] Both phases of the church are always present in history, at least in all periods, but before the coming of Jesus as the Christ the church could be manifest only by anticipation, whereas afterward it could be "manifest also by reception."[63] "The latent church is an indefinite historical group which within paganism, Judaism or humanism actualizes the New Being, while the manifest church is a definite historical group in which the New Being is actualized directly and manifestly."[64]

The latent church is "always under the quest" to become manifest, while the manifest church is always subject to criticism, both positively and negatively, from the latent church. Thus the Christian Church is latently present in all religions as a proportion: in paganism mostly indirectly; in Judaism more directly. This claim to truth for the latent church, it must be pointed out, cuts athwart all absolutistic pretensions on the part of any and all ecclesiasticisms, without robbing the church of its primary claim to actualize the New Being in Christ. This, then, is the organic depth and comprehensiveness of the church as man's total relationships and response to the ultimate; his total community of ultimate concern, on the one hand, and the incisiveness of the church, on the other hand, of its life as the community of faith and love in the New Being in Christ.

If this New Being were only understood as having the content of the personal God of *agape,* and if the involvements of this existential ultimate were then explored and accepted before, above, and beyond earthly history, the profound Christian doctrine of the church would begin to come into its own! The meaning and reality of the whole doctrine of the church depends upon the definitional availability and the ontological acceptance of the personal love of God and of personal immortality, without which we are left with the emptiness of verbal analysis and affirmation, for without these there are no adequate empirical justifications or explanations on the part

---

[62] *Propositions,* Part IV, p. 27.
[63] *Ibid.*
[64] *Ibid.*

of the Christian faith. Within such fuller meaning and reality of the faith, however, the organic relatedness of the church and other religions, professed as such or not, takes on proper proportions of inclusion and exclusion.

In this context we need also to consider Tillich's stand on missionary activity. This is nothing less than the actualization of the church universal, and inheres in the very appearance of the New Being in Christ. Missions are "the only and continuous confirmation of Christ as the center of history—the victorious struggle of the Kingdom of God in history."[65] Missions are the inevitable expression of the Gospel as the ultimate meaning of history and refer completely to pagans, secularists, and Jews. Not to be completely concerned with missions is to deny the essence of the Christian faith.[66]

C. Something must also be said with regard to Tillich's view of the relation of the church to social problems. The church is responsible for the outside world and, to be true to its own nature, it must accept "the function of transformation."[67] The only standard for this transformation is the unique, nonrecurring *kairos*, or the Christ. The church stands ever between its transcendent meaning and its cultural task. The transcendent meaning is fixed in the absolute revelation, but the cultural task depends upon the specific character of its epoch of history. To each age there is a special *kairos*, a special pattern of relevance between the unique, nonrecurring *kairos* and specific cultural tasks. But since each *kairos* combines its tasks distinctively according to its own nature, there can be no one-to-one rational method of application, but the relevance of Christ to culture must always be understood by means of "daring faith."[68] The transforming function is carried out by means of indirection, or by the "silent" effect of the church in simply living and working as a formative influence within the world as a whole, by direct attack upon the evils and ambiguities of the world and, again, by the indirect raising up of individuals of prophetic stature and practical wisdom who will work within both perspectives, thus actualizing within the world as a whole the vision and the power of the church.[69] Deeper than political structures as such lies, moreover, "the exis-

---

[65] *Ibid.*, Part V, p. 23.
[66] *Ibid.*
[67] *Ibid.*, Part IV, p. 35.
[68] Wood, *op. cit.*, p. 124.
[69] *Propositions*, Part IV, pp. 35–36.

tential foundation of politics and the ethical side of the law."[70] The main impact of the Christian Gospel on social and political conditions is, therefore, through the pulls and pressure of Christian culture, where the Church as a political body may or may not be a direct participant or recipient. There is thus a degree of real mutual autonomy as well as organic interactions of church and the socio-political components of civilization.

No one can read Tillich long, furthermore, without realizing how strongly he feels about religious socialism as one aspect of this present pattern of relevance, though by this is meant not any one political form of organization, but the total criticism from the religious perspective of the demonic nature of autonomous capitalism and the working for an emergence of some new social order without its peculiar ambiguities and contradictions. He also considers nationalism and totalitarianism to be demonic parts of this pattern of relevance for Christian social action in our own day. Tillich's view of the relationship between the church and social action is, without misuse of the word, a profound combination of the ultimate and the immediate, of the rational relevance of sustained criticism in the light of Christian truth, and the demand for continual openness to historic newness and the consequent necessity of ever recurring existential decisions.[71]

APPRAISAL

To say that any adequate appraisal of Tillich's work is exceedingly difficult is a decided understatement. Without the slightest doubt he ranks at the top, with few peers, as far as his combination of depth and comprehensiveness goes. This chapter cannot, in fact, more than point to an outline of the outline of Tillich's own work on the subject. Even to indicate the development of his thought for between thirty to forty years is completely out of the question, except to say that there is a remarkable consistency of basic insights and relations, and for that matter even of several categories, yes, even of words like "manifest" and "latent." However widespread or deep-plowing is his thought, moreover, it always exhibits organic connectedness. The more Tillich is read, the more imposing becomes

[70] *Ibid.*, p. 36.
[71] *The Interpretation of History,* pp. 179–241.

the grandeur of the total structure and of the interrelation among the parts.

As a whole, too, his theological perspective operates with authentic Christian categories, both with relation to the ultimate and with relation to cosmic process. The interrelation between these two realms, again, is characterized by profundity, dynamic flexibility, sure-eyed explication of the implications of major presuppositions or of plenary perspectives. The illumination of the eternal verities never precludes careful following through both of depth and of detail, making the Christian method and mood—in so far as the system is genuinely Christian, at least—dominate the whole and every part.

Almost unparalleled, too, is his natural intertwining of the theoretical perspective with the existential. Here is no reliance on rational coherence to hide the essential freedom which characterizes all history and historic knowledge; nor is there here any dissolving existentialism which undercuts rational explanation, whether of ultimates, like metaphysics and theology, or of process-centered disciplines, like the philosophy of religion or jurisprudence. There is full stress placed both on the systematic nature of theology and on the pragmatic nature of "practical" theology. Both are organically interrelated without being in any way curtailed or absorbed by the other.

We have given our phenomenological critique together with the description, reserving for the main critique the basic ontological issue. If Tillich can be counted ontologically as thoroughly within the Christian perspective, he must be ranked as one of our greatest Christian thinkers. Unfortunately, there are grave doubts on this point, which he is now, however, free to clear up in his own reply. Does he actually operate within the transcendental perspective, rather than within the transcendent? His refusal to accept the great, immemorial Christian perspective of supernaturalism at least seems to convince us of this, whatever his use of occasional words may be. Is God *in fact,* the Creator of process, *and in this sense,* above, before, and behind it? Is He personal Spirit in the sense of a separate consciousness and an eternal being, beyond all created beings, and therefore other than and beside all else, however different in kind? Is supernaturalism, *defined in this sense,* to be taken as normative, including secondarily all truth of naturalism, or are both to be transcended in terms of some formal realm of meaning, or in terms of some relation of being and the abyss to which we can refer finally only in terms of myth and symbol? Tillich's latest formulations in his *Systematic Theology* unfortunately show no indications of his accepting the classical Christian presuppositions. The Christian doctrine of the church, however, stands or falls with its ontology.

Secondly, is history real in the sense of one great event of consummation toward which it moves, or is it a continual interaction between being and meaning, in the way in which meaning becomes continually actualized in history? Is it in this latter sense that all theological interpretation must be historical in nature, or in the sense of an end of process in terms of personal immortality in the form of the persistence of separate consciousness, no matter under what new form within the next world or worlds? Does his stress on "participation" rather than on merger mean the active, conscious, personal participation of the saints beyond the grave, or does it mean some participation in meaning or in being which has self-identity in some way, but not in the full sense of personal persistence and fellowship? Without such full meaning of history, individually and collectively, there can be no full doctrine of the Christian church, either with regard to the communion of saints or to the import of last things.

Thirdly, not only are the questions of ontology and of history crucial for Tillich's doctrine of the church, but also his doctrine of the New Being in Christ. His current full-powered insistence on the identification of the Christ with Jesus is curious in one who for so long a time refused to anchor the eternal at any point in history as such. The love of God in Christ is certainly ontologically true regardless of specific historic findings about the human Jesus, but for the purposes of this chapter this is a secondary problem. Certainly the historic faith lives on a vital identification of Jesus with the Christ. What really matters, however, is whether or not the revelation in Christ is dominantly definable or not. At present it seems not to be, as ultimate, according to Tillich's thought; in which case we are left with mystery rather than with revelation, and have thus fallen far short of the Christian claim to truth. If Christ is not accepted as conclusive light on the very nature of the ultimate, a life that is definable light, the church quite naturally cannot *be* the Kingdom present through Christ and the Holy Spirit—present, to be sure, amidst human frailty and sin—but can at best only *represent* the Kingdom. The truth of an event differs, to be sure, from the truth of a principle, but however existential, if revelation is real, such truth must be *dominantly definable, not mystery.* The church, to be Christian, must be a fellowship of revelation, however mysterious in quality and depth.

Fourthly, though Tillich has of late developed a far fuller doctrine of the Holy Spirit, his theology still seems to fall short on the score of the Holy Spirit's being the determinative or constitutive nature of the church as well as His being the power and personal reality of radical progression in the saint, both through birth and through growth. There is as yet not present in Tillich the full assurance and understanding of the New Testament doctrine of sanctification, whether as a church doctrine, "holy and without blemish," or of the member saints, "filled with all the fullness of God." The question is not one of regulative meaning, but rather one of constitutive and expressive being and power both in the church and in the saint. The radical nature of the Christian church and of the Christian saint within history, as life and light, as truth and power, seems not adequately present in Tillich's theology. The Christian nature of the church, to a great extent, is determined by the doctrine of the Holy Spirit. Very little is made of personal conversion and remaking as matters of human experience and categories in terms of which the Christian, as a member of the church, differs from the world. Nor is the church a distinctive enough kind of community with genuine nonconformity to the ways of "the world" and redemptive transcendence over it.

What really matters then, as far as Tillich's doctrine of the church goes, is not questions of a minor analytical nature, but decisively the import of Tillich's philosophy: his ontology, his doctrine of myth and symbol, his understanding of history and of life everlasting. Of importance also is the question whether the revelation is definitely definable and can be used as a basis for all theological implications and involvements. Similarly basic is the question as to the sanctifying power and presence in the church of the Holy Spirit in a radical, personal sense, creating in and through history a new church as well as authentic saints. Of climactic Christian importance is the main question whether or not God is the supernatural creator, ruler, and redeemer, who saves and fashions the church as an eternal fellowship, not merely in the sense of some eschatological aspect of experience or participation in "being-itself," but of personal persistence within the objective reality of life everlasting. Within such presuppositions alone, this writer feels certain, can we have an adequate Christian doctrine of the church.

NELS F. S. FERRÉ

SCHOOL OF RELIGION
VANDERBILT UNIVERSITY
NASHVILLE, TENNESSEE

R. H. Daubney
SOME STRUCTURAL CONCEPTS IN TILLICH'S THOUGHT AND THE PATTERN OF THE LITURGY

13

SOME STRUCTURAL CONCEPTS IN TILLICH'S THOUGHT AND THE PATTERN OF THE LITURGY

I. INTRODUCTION

PAUL TILLICH has defined his allegiance to the Lutheran tradition in terms of "birth, education, religious experience, and theological reflection"; and he confesses that the "substance of my religion is and remains Lutheran."[1] The writer of this essay might well adopt the same terms to define his allegiance to the Anglican tradition; but he would add that questions of church order and denominational difference, considered in themselves, have never appeared to him to be of primary theological importance. He has been more deeply concerned with the religious interpretation of human existence in its state of contradiction; and in this respect he would acknowledge an initial affinity with Tillich's thought, and pay tribute to the profound stimulus which he has received from it. This affinity, however, has entailed elements of attraction and repulsion: it has compelled him time and again to inquire how far Tillich's insights find a counterpart in his own tradition, and to consider the significance of divergences where they occur.

The purpose of this essay is strictly limited in its scope, and may be indicated as follows. The concept of structure plays a significant role in Tillich's work,[2] and there are a number of specific concepts in it which are themselves most appropriately described as structural. It is proposed to examine two of these concepts as a prelude to the exposition of a structural concept which plays an equally significant rôle in Anglicanism. There may appear to be a lack of proportion

[1] Paul Tillich, *The Interpretation of History*, p. 54.
[2] See the essay by George F. Thomas, "The Method and Structure of Tillich's Theology," in this volume.

between these two parts of the essay; and this should not be interpreted either as minimising the value of Tillich's contribution, or as exaggerating the importance of the Anglican interpretation of the matter in hand. The last section of the essay is, in fact, intended to serve a twofold purpose. It is, on the one hand, a constructive attempt to show that one of Tillich's essential ideas finds a counterpart in Anglicanism; while, on the other hand, there is an implicit criticism running through it which shows that two other factors in his thought have not received the structural interpretation which they require.

The demonic is the first structural concept to be analysed in the light of a symbol of human existence and the problem of Protestantism. The structural and inescapable character of evil, which receives mythical and symbolic expression in the concept of the demonic, can only be overcome, Tillich declares, by a divine structure of reality which he calls the "Gestalt of Grace." It is this which provides the second concept for analysis; and the Anglican interpretation of the pattern of the liturgy is then suggested as its counterpart. The description of the pattern pays particular attention to the peculiar understanding of temporal existence in liturgical action; and this in turn provides an appropriate context for reference to Tillich's doctrine of the *kairos*. It attempts to show that the *kairos* is, in fact, a structural concept, and that its liturgical expression overcomes the disintegrated character of cosmic and historical time which are subject to demonic perversion. The pattern of the liturgy is also an embodiment of the sacramental principle in relation to nature and history, as well as in relation to the New Being as community. Its true character is revealed only when it is understood as an economy or *Gestalt* of the sacraments; and the neglect of this fundamental feature detracts seriously from Tillich's otherwise most illuminating discussion of sacramentalism and his salutary insistence upon the necessity for its recovery in contemporary Protestantism.

"The boundary line between philosophy and theology is the centre of my thought and work,"[3] Tillich maintains, while at the same time his systematic exposition of philosophical theology is declared to be implicitly rather than explicitly Biblical.[4] To those who have known it hitherto only in terms of the admittedly frag-

---

[3] *The Protestant Era*, p. 83.
[4] Preface, *Systematic Theology*, I, 1.

mentary character of his earlier writings,[5] it has appeared that he held somewhat loosely to the Biblical presuppositions of the Christian faith. It was clear, however, that the demonic and the *kairos* were deliberate revivals of neglected Biblical and, in particular, New Testament concepts;[6] while his reinterpretation of the central Christological reality as the appearance of the New Being in the picture of Jesus as the Christ was perceived to rest upon the Pauline doctrine of the new creation,[7] which placed a renewed and necessary emphasis upon the cosmic significance of redemption.[8] Such an oblique approach to the Biblical material may be justified, to some extent, on the ground that it represents an unknown world and a strange language to man in the modern age, whose mythology has been formed by cultural, political, and economic factors which have been severed from their roots in the Hebrew-Christian interpretation of existence. Moreover, Tillich's perpetual concern with the apologetic task of theology required that the original Biblical message should be reinterpreted by the church in terms of the boundary situation.[9]

Tillich has now defined more precisely the rôle and significance of the Biblical element in his thought in the Introduction to his *Systematic Theology*. The Bible is the original document which bears witness to the preparation for and the reception of the revelatory event which the Christian message proclaims; while at the same time it embodies the beginning of the creative interpretation of that message which is perpetuated in the tradition.[10] It is, therefore, employed as a source, as a medium, and as a norm in systematic theology. This position may be indicated briefly by two

[5] "A Reinterpretation of the Doctrine of the Incarnation," the *Church Quarterly Review* (London), Vol. 147, No. 294, January-March, 1949, p. 148. Cf. *The Interpretation of History*, p. 72.

[6] Paul Tillich, *The Kingdom of God and History* (English ed., p. 119), and *The Protestant Era*, pp. 27–28.

[7] Cf. "A Reinterpretation of the Doctrine of the Incarnation," p. 146, and *Systematic Theology*, I, p. 21.

[8] Cf. "The Relation of Religion and Health: Historical Considerations and Theoretical Questions," *Review of Religion*, Vol. 10, No. 4, May, 1946, and "Redemption in Cosmic and Social History," *Journal of Religious Thought*, Vol. 3, No. 1, Winter, 1946.

[9] *The Interpretation of History*, pp. 46–47; *The Shaking of the Foundations*, pp. 153–154; "A Reinterpretation of the Doctrine of the Incarnation," p. 148.

[10] *Systematic Theology*, I, 14. Cf. "The Problem of Theological Method," *Journal of Religion*, Vol. 27, No. 1, January, 1947.

quotations without trespassing too far from the matter in hand. "Systematic theology," Tillich observes, "requires a Biblical theology which is both historical and critical without any restrictions; and which is, at the same time, devotional and interpretative, taking account of the fact that it deals with matters of ultimate concern."[11] Again, he says: "the Bible can be described as normative for systematic theology only because the norm itself (namely, the New Being in Jesus as the Christ) is derived from the Bible. But it is derived from it in an encounter of the church with the Biblical message. The norm, derived from the Bible, is at the same time the criterion for the use of the Bible in systematic theology"[12] within the theological circle.

The implicit and underlying Biblical character of Tillich's work has been noted because this fact warrants its serious and cordial attention from Anglican theologians. Anglicanism is, indeed, an enigmatic and perplexing phenomenon, to its internal adherents as well as to its external observers. The present writer would make no claim to being an official interpreter; but he believes that it is true to say that Anglicanism has, in its own way, always regarded Scripture as a source, as a medium, and as a norm, and that the revival of Biblical theology is one of the most significant factors in its life today. It is, in many respects, still in a tentative and experimental stage, and this makes it difficult to define its tendencies or results with any precision. Nevertheless, it is possible to indicate two factors which are present in it. The first is the investigation of the relation between the two Testaments in the attempt to apprehend the unity of Biblical revelation.[13] It has been pursued along many lines; but in essence it is concerned with the character of the transition between expectation and fulfilment[14] which, according to Tillich, constitutes the unique *kairos,* and which has already had important repercussions on the Biblical interpretation of history. The second factor is the renewed understanding of the use of the Bible in the liturgy, which is leading to a deeper perception of the nature of the church, both as it is revealed in Scripture and as it is expressed in

[11] *Systematic Theology,* I, 15.

[12] *Systematic Theology,* I, 21.

[13] See L. S. Thornton, *Revelation and the Modern World* (London: A. & C. Black, 1950).

[14] See A. G. Hebert, *The Throne of David* (London: Faber & Faber, Ltd., 1941).

the common act of worship.[15] This, in turn, is but one aspect of another significant feature in contemporary Anglicanism which is usually described as the Liturgical Movement. It is in the light of these two elements in his own tradition, the Biblical and the liturgical, that the present writer wishes to make some modest contribution to the discussion of Tillich's theology.

II. SOME STRUCTURAL CONCEPTS IN TILLICH'S THOUGHT

The appropriate context for the discussion of the demonic and the *Gestalt* of grace in their character as structural concepts is provided by Tillich in the following passage: "There are two lines by which the meaning of human existence can be symbolized: the vertical and the horizontal, the first one pointing to the eternal meaning as such, the second to the temporal realization of the eternal meaning. Every religion necessarily has both directions, although different religions overemphasize the one or the other. The mystical element, which belongs to all religion, is symbolized by the vertical line; the active element, which also belongs to all religion, is symbolized by the horizontal line."[16] He explains further that "the human soul cannot maintain itself without the vertical line, the knowledge of an eternal meaning, however this may be expressed in mythological or theological terms"; while "the horizontal line becomes empty and distorted if it is not united continuously with the vertical line."[17]

It is important to notice, however, that this symbolic representation of the religious view of human existence is, in certain respects, both ambiguous and incomplete. On the one hand, it should be made clear that the vertical line denotes the whole hierarchy of finite being. It descends below the horizontal to symbolize the roots of human existence in the natural order, the realm of mysterious depth which provides the material foundations of economic and cultural life; and therefore it is endowed with a sacramental as well as with a mystical potentiality which enables the human mind to climb the ladder of being towards the realm of eternal meaning which lies beyond the finite order. On the other hand, the horizontal line symbolizes more appropriately man's relations to his fellows, the

[15] See A. G. Hebert, *The Authority of the Old Testament* (London: Faber & Faber, Ltd., 1947).

[16] *The Protestant Era*, p. 186. Cf. "Vertical and Horizontal Thinking," *American Scholar*, Vol. 15, No. 1, Winter, 1946, and V. A. Demant, *Theology of Society* (London: Faber & Faber, Ltd., 1947), p. 229.

[17] *The Protestant Era*, p. 187.

beings which possess the same specific nature and therefore occupy the same status in the scale, articulated in the widening circles of community. It follows, therefore, that the picture must be completed by a third line cutting through the point of intersection to denote the direction of history. Each dimension of existence is the realm of a peculiar dynamism which is rooted in the tension between potentiality and actuality in the different levels of finite being.[18] Natural and social organisms develop towards their appropriate forms, and the reality of this development is the source of the temporal character of existence, cyclic in the realm of nature, both cyclic and linear in the realm of society and history.[19]

The relation of man to the different dimensions of existence is at once objective and subjective, external and internal. It is a relation of transcendence and immanence which can only be interpreted adequately as an analogue of the transcendence and immanence of the Unconditional[20] to finite existence as a whole. The reality of human transcendence and immanence is the ground of man's manipulation of natural resources, which may be expressed in two ways; namely, the magical and the technical, or the mystical and the sacramental.[21] The first way, however, simply offers a spurious mode of transcendence, and is, in fact, its virtual denial, so that existence is enclosed in its own finitude. The second way permits the genuine expression of transcendence, and opens the different realms of finite existence to the Unconditional without severing man's roots from their immanence in those realms.[22] The reality of human transcendence and immanence in respect of the different dimensions of existence is the metaphysical ground for the creation of new forms, involving the modification or destruction of existing forms which emerge spontaneously in the finite order. At this point we are introduced to the picture of the demonic.

A. The demonic. Professor Tillich has expounded his conception

---

[18] Cf. *Systematic Theology*, I, 82–86.

[19] Cf. the distinctions between cosmic, historical, and existential time in Tillich and Berdyaev. *The Interpretation of History*, pp. 243 ff., and N. A. Berdyaev, *Slavery and Freedom* (New York: Charles Scribner's Sons, 1944), pp. 255 ff.

[20] I have simply borrowed Tillich's term without further comment. See G. Marcel, *The Mystery of Being* (London, 1950), pp. 39 ff., on the question of transcendence and immanence.

[21] See Tillich's discussion of various types of realism in *The Protestant Era*, Chap. V; and cf. Chap. VII.

[22] Cf. Tillich's concept of theonomy, *The Protestant Era*, pp. xvi *passim*.

of the demonic in an essay included in *The Interpretation of History,* and I do not propose either to summarise or to criticise this essay as such.[23] He takes his point of departure from the study of art, and of primitive art in particular, which has played a significant rôle in his intellectual development,[24] and he observes that in this realm the demonic is manifested characteristically as resting upon "the tension between form-creation and form-destruction"[25] in the inexhaustible nature of existence. He explains further that "form of being and inexhaustibility of being belong together. Their unity in the depth of essential nature is the divine, their separation in existence, the relatively independent eruption of the 'abyss' in things, is the demonic."[26] It is clear that the human personality and the various types of human community are the most significant and interdependent foci of this tension between the creation and destruction of form. Thus he argues that "the demonic comes to fulfilment in personality, and personality is the most prominent object of demonic destruction, for personality is the bearer of form in its totality and unconditioned character. Therefore, the contradiction of it, the cleavage of personality, is the highest and most destructive contradiction. Therewith the demonic is disclosed in a new stratum: the personality, the being which has power over itself, is grasped by another power and is thereby divided."[27] Moreover, the corollary of this cleavage is "the personality standing in social connection": the social structure, articulated through personal relationships, becomes itself an object of demonic destruction. "Thus we have here not a question of the cleavage of the personality by the powers of its own psychical depth, but the breaking of personality by the superindividual social structure."[28]

I have noted these salient passages because they delineate the actuality of the demonic which is at the same time the actuality of man's fallen state: the state of original sin which is the contradiction of his essential nature under the conditions of existence.[29] They provide a somewhat abstract commentary on the universalized Pauline

[23] *The Interpretation of History*, pp. 77 ff.
[24] *Ibid.*, pp. 49 ff.; *The Religious Situation*, pp. 53 ff.; *The Christian Answer,* (English ed.), pp. 29 ff.
[25] *The Interpretation of History*, p. 80.
[26] *Ibid.*, p. 84.
[27] *Ibid.*, p. 86.
[28] *Ibid.*, p. 92.
[29] *Ibid.*, pp. 93 ff.

experience described in the epistle to the Romans;[30] while the implications of this experience are further illuminated by the Beelzebub controversy recorded in the Synoptic gospels,[31] where the internal cleavage in communities belonging to the natural order, conceived in the widening circles of family, locality, and state, is interpreted as a discrepancy between their essential power to exist; namely, their form, and the element which is destructive of form and therefore of existence itself.

It would be fascinating to pursue this analysis further, and to examine some of the sociological manifestations of the demonic as they involve the mutual relations of personality and community.[32] It is necessary, however, to turn to a consideration of the metaphysical mystery which lies behind the reality of the demonic; namely, the question of the relation between essence and existence, of the form of being and the possibly of its distortion. It is the familiar theme of the distinction between finite freedom and original sin. Tillich introduces a preliminary discussion of the subject in the first section of the second part of the *Systematic Theology*, where he notes some of the different meanings which have been ascribed to the terms "essence" and "existence." He concludes that "Christianity has emphasized the split between the created goodness of things and their distorted existence";[33] and then remarks that "a complete discussion of the relation of essence to existence is identical with the entire theological system. The distinction between essence and existence, which religiously speaking is the distinction between the created and the actual world, is the back-bone of the whole body of theological thought. It must be elaborated in every part of the theological system."[34] The most important development of the discussion is, in fact, made in the first section of the third part, which is at present available only in the form of propositions. It is possible, therefore, that some of the ambiguities may be clarified in the final text.

The initial ambiguity seems to lie in Tillich's attempt to combine the traditional meaning of the term "existence" with the more spe-

---

[30] Romans 7:15–23.

[31] Mark 3:22–26; Matthew 12:24–26; Luke 11:15–18.

[32] *The Interpretation of History*, pp. 115 ff.; *The Kingdom of God and History* (English ed.), pp. 132 ff.

[33] *Systematic Theology*, I, 109.

[34] *Ibid.*, p. 109.

cialised sense that it has acquired in contemporary existential philosophy. In the former case existence must denote the act of circumscribing a specific essence,[35] although in this respect Tillich tends to attach undue weight to the Platonic element and consequently to the primacy of essence in the Thomist doctrine. In the latter case the emphasis is laid upon the virtual obliteration of essence in the act of existing, and issues in a confusion of the primary and secondary acts of being, as we shall see in a moment. The uneasy alliance between these two usages allows Tillich to speak of the "transition"[36] from essence to existence as the doctrine of the fall; of the structure of existence as the doctrine of sin; and of the self-destruction of existence as the doctrine of evil.[37] He is not altogether faithful to this position, however, in describing life as the actuality of being in which essential and existential elements are combined.[38]

It cannot be denied that the existential philosophy has performed a valuable service in making us more deeply aware of the elements of ambiguity, anxiety, and tragedy in human existence. But in doing so it has tended to assume that human existence is a reality of an entirely different character from the existence of any other level of finite being. It is perfectly clear that there are significant differences, just as it is equally clear that there are necessary similarities. The concept of existence, however, cannot be limited to the human situation alone without an intolerable strain upon language. It follows, therefore, that if the question of the likeness-in-distinction between the different levels of created existence is to be handled in any intelligible manner, it can only be by some form of the doctrine of analogy which can combine the analogy of attribution with the analogy of proper proportionality.[39]

The fundamental weakness of Tillich's discussion of the doctrine of creation lies in the fact that he ignores the question of analogy completely. The conclusion of this discussion is, therefore, the equa-

[35] See the later works of E. Gilson, *e.g.*, *God and Philosophy* (New Haven: Yale University Press, 1941), p. 64.

[36] One cannot help feeling that this is an unsatisfactory term to use in this connection.

[37] Paul Tillich, *Propositions*, Part III, Sec. 1, A, B, and C.

[38] *Ibid.*, Vol. II, Part IV, Sec. 1.

[39] See E. L. Mascall, *Existence and Analogy* (New York: Longmans, Green & Co., 1949). Tillich remarks in one of his essays that he accepts the traditional doctrine of analogy, although he is not prepared to employ it as a basis for rational construction. Cf., "Symbol and Knowledge," *Journal of Liberal Religion*, Vol. II, No. 4, Spring, 1941. p. 203.

tion of finitude and evil: "the end of creation is the beginning of the fall."[40] To be a creature means to be rooted in the divine ground where essential nature is intact; but the fulfilment of the creation is the actualization of finite freedom which involves "a separation from the creative ground through a break between existence and essence."[41] If the creature is separated from the creative ground, however, it must presumably mean that its existence is annihilated; and it is difficult to see how Tillich reconciles this with the sustaining and directing creativity of God.[42] The second weakness of his discussion lies in the fact that he ignores the distinction between the primary and the secondary acts of created being: the act of existing, which is given to it in creation; and the act of operation peculiar to it, which derives from its essential nature circumscribed by the act of existing.[43] It follows from this that he is forced to interpret the question of original sin almost entirely in terms of the vertical dynamism of human existence, which derives largely from Kierkegaard;[44] and this is emphasized to such an extent that it virtually precludes any interpretation of it in terms of the horizontal dynamism (although it must be admitted that an undue concentration upon this aspect has been a serious limitation in traditional Christian thought on the subject). The upshot of the matter seems to be, nevertheless, that the equation of finitude and sinfulness is a disguised form of monism which is just as dangerous as the various forms of dualism which it seeks to overcome.

Tillich's inquiry into the character of the demonic is genuinely illuminating. It performs a valuable service in emphasizing the structural character of evil as it is woven into the texture of human institutions, creating a realm of power which unaided human virtue is unable to overcome. But at the same time the writer believes that the metaphysical presuppositions upon which the concept is elaborated are ambiguous and unsatisfactory. They are unable to provide an adequate interpretation of the twofold mystery of original sin which is the source of the demonic destruction of existence: that it is the transgression of man's ontological status which involves the distortion of his ontological structure. The element of illusion in this mystery is the fact that the status has been transgressed in terms of

[40] *Systematic Theology*, I, 164.
[41] *Ibid.*, p. 164.
[42] *Ibid.*, pp. 170 ff., and 172 ff.
[43] See Aquinas, *De Ente et Essentia*, cap. iv; *Summa Contra Gentiles*, ii. 52.
[44] Especially *The Concept of Dread* and *The Sickness unto Death*.

temptation to go beyond the possible limits of transcendence for finite freedom, so that the status itself which defines the essential nature of existing within it has not been changed in reality, although it has been distorted in the attempt.

B. *The* Gestalt *of Grace.* At this point we must turn to the conception of the *Gestalt* of Grace which stands in correlation to the conception of the demonic. Tillich has not elaborated the full implications of the *Gestalt* of Grace in a separate essay, however, and therefore it is necessary to piece together his view of the matter from various incidental allusions. In the essay on the demonic, to which we have already referred, he observes that "the possessed state and the state of grace correspond; the states of being demoniacally and divinely overcome, inspired, broken through, are correlatives."[45] And in another passage he maintains that "if evil has demonic or structural character limiting individual freedom, its conquest can come only by the opposite, the divine structure, that is, by what we have called a structure or 'Gestalt' of Grace."[46]

It is important to notice that we have here a significant example of the theological method of correlation which is one of the guiding principles upon which Tillich's work is articulated. This method

makes an analysis of the human situation out of which the existential questions arise, and it demonstrates that the symbols used in the Christian message are the answers to these questions. . . . These answers are contained in the revelatory events on which Christianity is based, and they are taken by systematic theology from the sources, through the medium, under the norm. Their content cannot be derived from the questions, that is, from an analysis of human existence. . . . There is a mutual dependence between question and answer. In respect of content the Christian answers are dependent on the revelatory events in which they appear; in respect of form they are dependent on the structure of the questions which they answer.[47]

We are therefore justified in considering the demonic and the *Gestalt* of Grace in close relation with each other.

It is also important to notice the peculiar urgency with which the correlation of these two structural concepts is raised in Protestantism. The universal validity of the Protestant principle judges the

[45] *The Interpretation of History*, p. 87.
[46] *The Protestant Era*, p. xx.
[47] *Systematic Theology*, I, 26–27.

pretension of every finite reality toward absoluteness in which the forms achieved by a perverted human creativity manifest their demonic character. But at the same time it has been the historical fate of Protestantism to be confronted with the dilemma of finding a form in which its universal protest can be expressed effectively.[48] Thus it is in his discussion of "The Formative Power of Protestantism"[49] that Tillich relies largely upon his conception of the *Gestalt* of Grace for a way out of this dilemma. "We raise the question," he says, "as to how formative power and protest against form can live together in a church, how form and protest against form can create a new, overarching form."[50]

In the elucidation of this question he claims that "the *Gestalt* embraces itself and the protest against itself; it comprises form and the negation of form."[51] The attempt to guard the Unconditional against the tendency toward the usurpation of its character on the part of finite realities implies that these realities must actually participate in the Unconditional itself; so that "the participating in the infinite, in the unconditional, in a trans-human authority, means living in the reality of grace . . . in a '*Gestalt* of Grace,' in a sacred structure of reality."[52] For Protestantism this structure of sacred reality is created by the Word and the Spirit. The utterance of the divine Word is both transcendent and immanent. It is the manifestation of Jesus in the totality of his being, "to which his deeds and his sufferings belong, and not his words alone," and which "creates faith as the formative power of a personal life and of a community."[53] But at the same time, "being moved by the Spirit is the *prius* of faith," and "to be moved by the Spirit or to be grasped by the unconditional means to be drawn into the reality and the life of a *Gestalt* of Grace."[54]

Now there is one point in theological discourse at which the correlation between the demonic and the *Gestalt* of Grace is brought to a focus with peculiar clarity; namely, the question of the sacramental order. Tillich recognises that sacramentalism is one of the

[48] Cf. *The Religious Situation*, p. 154.
[49] *The Protestant Era*, Chap. XIV.
[50] *Ibid.*, p. 206.
[51] *Ibid.*
[52] *Ibid.*, p. 209.
[53] *Ibid.*, p. 210.
[54] *Ibid.*, p. 211.

most significant ways in the history of religion in which the demonic is overcome.[55] It is also admitted that Protestantism has lost its hold on sacramental reality to a very great extent, and has suffered from a tendency which Tillich himself betrays; namely, to atomise the sacramental economy, so that its interpretation is concentrated too sharply upon some particular aspect. At the same time it must also be admitted that Catholicism has tended to place undue reliance upon its security in the sacramental economy, so that the mutual questioning of each other upon this point should prove fruitful.

The common weakness of both Catholic and Protestant sacramental doctrine, however, lies very largely in their failure to provide an adequate account of grace in ontological terms. The economy of the sacraments is, in fact, the realm in which both the divine and human creativity are interwoven upon all levels and in all areas of existence in order to give expression to the integrity and wholeness of essential nature. The original creation and the new creation are equally manifestations of the divine graciousness; and the creative response of man to this reality in terms of his transcendence and immanence in existence is the creation of a theonomous structure or pattern which is the sacramental order. Such an order is intended to be both the archetype and reflection of the essential order of human existence in its communal, cultural, political, and economic articulation. The creative response of man, however, is frustrated by the distortion of human nature and existence through original sin; and it becomes possible, therefore, only through the manifestation of the New Being in whom the contradictions of existence are overcome. Tillich appears to have a deep intuition of this truth in his discussion of sacramentalism[56] in which he argues cogently for an interpretation of the two sacraments of Baptism and the Eucharist in relation to nature, history, and the New Being in Christ. He does not, however, draw out the implications of his analysis for the total dimensions of human existence; and it is possible that he would be reluctant to identify the sacramental economy with the *Gestalt* of Grace.

In the concluding section of this essay, therefore, we shall presuppose Tillich's discussion of sacramentalism; and we shall attempt to show that he is mistaken when he says that "in the Catholic view the finite form (of the sacrament) is transmuted into a divine

[55] *The Interpretation of History*, pp. 105–106.
[56] *The Protestant Era*, Chap. VII.

form, . . . the material of the sacrament is as such filled with grace."[57] Such a notion has, in fact, played a very limited role in Catholicism, which, in its more genuine form in the Biblical and patristic tradition, is much more profoundly concerned with the historical and eschatological interpretation of the sacramental structure. It is therefore in the attempt to bring this aspect into the greater prominence which it deserves that Tillich's doctrine of the *kairos*—which endows temporal existence in its totality with a structural character and therefore overcomes the tendencies to disintegration which accumulate within it through the conflict between the creation and destruction of form—should be assessed.

III. THE PATTERN OF THE LITURGY*

The administration of the sacraments in the church is enshrined in a ritual pattern of words and symbolic actions which express their meaning and perpetuate their effect in such a way that the members of the church continually participate in the reality of their transformed existence in the New Creation. The rationale of each sacrament is embodied to some extent in its ritual structure; and the complex of these structures constitutes a liturgical pattern for the life of the church as a whole. It is a pattern which expresses the true nature of the church as the New Creation in each of its local manifestations; and thereby it expresses the redeemed nature of man, the transformation of the conditions of his existence in nature, society, and history as embodying an anticipation of his eternal destiny. To speak of such an intangible reality as a pattern, however, is to admit at once that it cannot be described with any degree of precision or completeness. A pattern is a reality which must be apprehended intuitively, entered into and lived through both consciously and unconsciously, if its true character is to be perceived and its formative power is to be experienced.[58] Neverthless, some kind of description must be attempted, because the pattern of the liturgy is both the archetype and the context of redeemed human

[57] *Ibid.*, p. 211.

[58] "We might say that a Gestalt of grace is a possible object of 'imaginative intuition.' The transcendent meaning of a finite reality is not an abstract concept but a matter of imaginative perception."—*The Protestant Era*, p. 212.

* This valuable section on the pattern of the liturgy is really an interpretation of the ideas implied in Professor Tillich's doctrine of the *Gestalt* of Grace in his essay on "Nature and Sacrament" (*The Protestant Era*, Chap. VII), and in his discussion of the sacraments in the *Propositions*. For this reason the Editors have deemed it fitting to include it.

existence as it is understood by the Christian faith. If, therefore, we resort to pictorial representation in such a description, it must be done with the proviso that in the last resort it is quite inadequate.

The liturgical pattern of the church's life in the world and in history may be conceived in terms of four concentric circles with an ellipse at the centre. Three circles lie close together at the circumference of the pattern, and denote the structure of the liturgical year, which is composed of the cycle of the events of the life of Christ from the Nativity to the descent of the Paraclete, the cycle of the events of the life of the Blessed Virgin from the Annunciation to the Assumption, and the cycle of the saints.[59] The fourth circle lies nearer to the centre of the pattern, and represents the daily cycle of the divine office, composed on the twofold principle of reflecting the rise and the decline of light throughout the course of the natural day, and of commemorating the phases of the passion of the Redeemer. The two foci of the ellipse at the centre of the pattern represent the sacraments of Baptism and the Eucharist, each of which incorporates the relation of human transcendence and immanence towards the total dimensions of human existence which we depicted in symbolic form on an earlier page.[60] The sacrament of Baptism is concerned with the organic structure of the church, in which the historic community sanctions and assumes responsibility for the admission of new members. It is set forth in the sacramental realm as a new birth and as a cleansing from sin by the passage through the redeeming act of Christ's death and resurrection to union with him in his Mystical Body:[61] in the ontological order it actually constitutes a death to sin and a new birth to righteousness in which the powers of the soul are hierarchised; while in the historical order it constitutes a transition from the present evil age to the life of the age to come which has been established in Christ.[62] The sacrament of the Eucharist is concerned with the organic life of the church, in which the historic community performs the *anamnesis* of the redeeming act in such a way that its effects are made operative with living power in the present,[63] and

[59] The second and third cycles derive their significance from their relation to the first.

[60] See Introduction to this essay. The Editors.

[61] See John 3 and Romans 6.

[62] I Corinthians 10:11.

[63] On the meaning of *anamnesis*, see G. Dix, ed. *Treatise on the Apostolic Tradition of Hippolytus* (London: Macmillan, 1937), pp. 73–75.

at the same moment sets forth its eschatological hope for the future consummation of all things in Christ.[64] Past, present, and future, the disintegrated phases of cosmic and historical time, are thus integrated and made whole in the existential moment of its celebration. Finally, the whole pattern is completed and woven together, and is given articulation, movement, and rhythm by the propers of the liturgy which interrelate the seasons of the year with the office and the mass.

The pattern sets forth Christianity as an historical and sacramental religion. It is concerned with the fact that the New Being has entered into the processes of nature and the dynamics of history. From one point of view the redeeming act is superimposed upon every phase of the natural process and is recapitulated in every historical event; while from the other point of view every level of natural reality and every historical decision is incorporated into the redeeming act itself.

A. The Year and the Office. The significance of the liturgical year and the divine office corresponds to the incorporation of the wider and the narrower aspects of cosmic time into the redeeming act. Cosmic time is symbolized by the circle, and points to the disintegrated character of temporal existence through the spontaneous creation and corruption of form, marked by the four phases of birth and growth, decay and death. There is, therefore, both a correspondence and a contrast between the natural and the liturgical cycles. The latter is divided into two phases, focused in the festivals of the Incarnation and the Resurrection, each of which is preceded and followed by a period of preparation and continuation in the time of their celebration. The Incarnation and the Resurrection constitute the unique *kairos* of the Gospel, which is itself temporarily extended and composed of the specific *kairoi* of the life of Christ.

Thus the first phase of the natural year embodies a movement towards the appearance of new life, just as the first phase of the liturgical year culminates in the appearance of the New Being. In the former, however, the new life is the product of natural processes, while in the latter the New Being enters nature and history from beyond. The second phase of the natural year embodies a movement towards the disintegration of life, just as the second phase of the liturgical year embodies the permanence of a new existence. It points to the fact that the cyclic character of temporal

[64] I Corinthians 11:26.

existence is broken open. It is no longer enclosed in its own finitude, but open to the eternal and the unconditional. It is the function of the *kairos,* moreover, to endow temporal existence with a structural character, and thereby to overcome its tendency to disintegration. Thus Tillich explains that the *kairos* "designates the fulfillment of the period of expectation or preparation, and the beginning of the period of reception or fragmentary actualization";[65] and he goes on to say that "if the New Testament idea of the *kairos* is applied within a definite period, it expresses the conviction that that which has appeared once for all in 'the fulness of time' has reappeared in a special way as the centre of a particular historical period. The unique, non-recurring *kairos* remains the standard for all the particular forms in which it reappears."[66] Moreover, as he remarks in another essay, "there is, in the doctrine of the *kairos,* not only the horizontal dialectic of the historical process but also the vertical dialectic operating between the unconditional and the conditioned."[67]

If, however, the appearance of the Christ in "the fulness of time" provides a valid ground for the interpretation of history in terms of the *kairos,* and we believe it does, it must also provide an equally authentic ground for the interpretation of temporal existence. Just as the appearance of the Christ in the unique *kairos* creates the centre of history, from which the fundamental division between the period of expectation and the period of reception derives its character, and finds a recapitulation in other historical periods in the manner suggested by the consciousness of religious socialism;[68] so also the same reality is recapitulated[69] in the liturgical structure of temporal existence. The church, as the heir of the old Israel, lives in the creative attitude of preparation and expectation, during the seasons of Advent and Lent, for the manifestation of the New Being in the festivals of the Incarnation and the Resurrection;[70] just as in the recitation of the morning office it lives in the same attitude

[65] *The Kingdom of God and History* (English ed.), p. 119.

[66] *Ibid.,* p. 123.

[67] *The Protestant Era,* p. 48.

[68] See the essay by E. Heimann, "Tillich's Doctrine of Religious Socialism," in this volume.

[69] I have borrowed this term from Irenaeus, with the implications it carries in his thought.

[70] On festival and *kairos,* see G. van der Leeuw, *Religion in Essence and Manifestation* (London: Macmillan, 1938), Chaps. 55, 56; and cf. S. Bulgakov, *The Orthodox Church* (London: Morehouse, 1935), p. 150.

towards the sacramental manifestation of the New Being in the Eucharist, both of which derive their significance from their relation to the unique *kairos*. In the same way the Church, as the reconstituted Israel, lives in the reception of the New Being during the seasons of Epiphany and Trinity, and in the recitation of the evening office. Thus expectation and reception are perpetually recreated in the liturgy as the wider and narrower aspects of cyclic time are broken open in the manifestation and representation of the New Being: the historical and eschatological reference of temporal existence predominates; and this is reinforced by the temporal reference of Baptism and the Eucharist.

B. *The Focus of Initiation.* Baptism by immersion was the normal practice of the primitive church. It was followed immediately by the anointing with oil and the laying-on of the bishop's hands, and was accompanied by the renunciation of the world and the confession of faith by the candidate. The threefold symbolism of this complex action indicates immediately the significance which was attached to it. The natural element of water is the symbol of cleansing from the defilement of sin, and as such bears a certain analogy to Jewish ceremonial purifications. The natural element of oil is the symbol of anointing by the Holy Spirit, and as such bears witness to Israel's hope of the new covenant after the Spirit;[71] at the same time it expresses a twofold historical reference for the Christian sacrament in that it makes the recipient partaker of the mystery of Pentecost and seals him unto the day of redemption,[72] when history shall be brought to its consummation. We shall find a precisely parallel reference in the case of the Eucharist. The sacramental use of water and oil imply, moreover, that token elements of the natural creation are being taken up into the representation of the redemptive act in which the new member of the church is being made to share, signifying that the whole creation which had been made subject to bondage and corruption through the sin of man is equally being redeemed in man's redemption.[73] We shall find again that this aspect has a precise counterpart in the offertory at the Eucharist.

The ritual of immersion contains two symbolic aspects: on the one hand, it expresses the mystical death and burial of the old man as he is plunged beneath the water, and the correlative mystical resur-

71 Jeremiah 31:31 ff.
72 Ephesians 1:13; 4:30.
73 Romans 8:19 ff.

rection of the new man recreated in the Christ, since the pattern of the whole action reproduces the death and resurrection of Jesus as the central moment of his redeeming work, and thus incorporates the new member into him; on the other hand, it expresses this birth of the Christian by water and the Holy Spirit in such a way that his entry into the church is understood as an entry into the supernatural order, since it confers upon him the status of divine sonship by adoption and grace, and makes him partaker of the outpouring of the Spirit upon the sons of God at Pentecost according to Joel's prophecy.[74] The different elements of this total symbolism inevitably interpenetrate and react upon one another in such a way that they cannot be separated in actual fact, so that the description of the one implies a reference to the others also. In the same way the ritual of anointing with oil and the laying-on of hands contains two symbolic features: the first signifies the anointing with the Holy Spirit, and is already involved in what has been said about the new birth; while the second denotes the divine blessing which confers fruitfulness upon the new creature, and is already implicit in his resurrection in Christ.

It may be perceived, therefore, that the ritual of initiation relates the Christian to the three Persons of the Trinity, and in establishing this relation transforms him in the centre of his being and in terms of his existence in nature, society, and history. It is, in effect, the recreation of the form of man through his participation in the form of the New Being as community; and within this form it embraces a twofold relation to history which overcomes its disintegrated character by making him contemporary with its centre and its end.

C. *The Focus of Consummation.* It is impossible, within the limits of this essay, to discuss the structure of the Eucharist with the fulness which it requires. It must suffice to draw attention to three aspects of its action which refer directly to the realms of nature, community, and history as the dimensions of human existence which are infected by demonic distortion and which must be overcome by the *Gestalt* of Grace. The discussion must presuppose an understanding of the historical development of the rite itself, and of the theological and mystical themes concerning man's nature and spiritual pilgrimage to which it gives expression.

a) The Eucharist, in the strict sense, begins with the offertory

[74] Joel 2:28 ff.

which, in the primitive church, was one of the most impressive features of the whole action. Every member of the congregation made his or her offering in kind, and from these the material of the sacrament was chosen.[75] The action expresses man's fundamental dependence upon the resources of the natural world, and is a token of the labour which he has expended upon it in the sustenance of his life. Thereby it symbolises not only the interior self-oblation of the individual, but also the total corporate offering of the church, which is to be made in and through the unique mediatorial work of the Christ.

The offertory is not merely the prelude to the consecration, but is equally the condition both of consecration and of communion, since he who did not make an oblation was not normally permitted to communicate.[76] Just as the offering of the Christ at the Last Supper looks forward to the consummation of his sacrifice in the cross and the resurrection, so the offering of the gifts in the Eucharist[77] looks forward to their consecration and distribution in communion in such a way that all phases of the action are inseparably united. The Eucharist has, in fact, two *foci*, as Hebert observes: "the consecration unites each mass with the one sacrifice, the sacrifice which God made once for all; and the communion unites with that sacrifice the ever renewed self-oblation of the church."[78] Thus the action of the liturgy is not merely a dialogue in its structure which involves all the orders of the church in its celebration; it is also a dialogue between time and eternity as the action moves between these two realms at the Preface, which unites the offertory with the consecration and the communion.

b) The celebration of the Eucharist is the *common* action of the Christian community, and we must now turn to this aspect of the matter. The reality of community in the natural order, which is presupposed by the community of the church, must be understood in the dimension of breadth as well as in the dimension of depth. Community in the natural order is symbolized by a series of con-

---

[75] There is the story of a Roman lady in the days of Gregory the Great who smiled to herself as she communicated, and explained to the pope afterwards that she had recognized a piece of the loaf which she had baked herself.

[76] See Cyprian, *Epistles* 16, 14.

[77] "The hallowing of the gifts" is the phrase of Irenaeus. See *Against Heresies*, IV., xviii, 5, and cf. Augustine, *De Civitate Dei*, ix, 6.

[78] A. G. Hebert, "The Idea of Oblation in the Early Liturgies," *Theology*, Vol. 23, No. 134, pp. 78–79.

centric circles, since the fact of communication between the members, and their participation in the rituals which embody the meaning of their common life, grows weaker as the area of locality extends. The community of the church, however, overcomes this centrifugal tendency to disintegration because the mystery of catholicity expresses the essential nature of the church in every local manifestation of it through the celebration of the Eucharist. It represents, therefore, not only the integration of every local community itself in Christ, but equally the integration of community as such in the transformation of existence.

This aspect is carefully described by Thornton in the following words:

> The *koinonia* is a focus of new relationships between God and man in Christ. It is not simply a new type of human fellowship. Its distinctive character is wholly derived from the fact that it is a fellowship, not only of man with man, but also of man with God. It is an expression of the fact that God has tabernacled amongst men in a new way inaugurated by the Incarnation. Secondly, in this new focus of relationships there has taken place and is taking place a transformation of one particular relationship, namely, that which connects the inward life with its outward manifestations, the inner spirit with its outward organs and embodiments.[79]

It implies, therefore, that the reality of community must also be symbolized in the dimension of depth in the scale of being in such a way that the extent to which every community spreads requires for its integration a coordination at every point with the depth of existence. The theological expression of this integration is provided by the doctrines of the Incarnation and the Holy Spirit in relation to the sacramental economy. The eternal Trinity of Persons is the archetype of the integration of community, in which the Word eternally possesses the fulness of deity in the circumcession of the divine Love. In the Incarnation the Second Person of the Trinity tabernacles within the forms of human community and becomes the focus of their integration; while in this same act human nature, and the forms of community belonging to it, are incorporated into the divine life thus extended to them. In the sacrament the Incarnate Word tabernacles within the lowest level of the natural creation, which man in his common mediatorial work has offered to God in acknowledgment of his responsibility and dependence. It is

[79] L. S. Thornton, *The Common Life in the Body of Christ* (London: Dacre, 1942), pp. 16 ff.

the Holy Spirit who effects the hallowing of the creation, represented by the offered gifts, just as he brings into existence the distinctive type of social reality which is the church, and which thereby participates in his life-giving and sanctifying power.

c) The integration of community in the Eucharist is bound up with the transformation of historical existence, and this also is given concrete expression in the eucharistic action. In the celebration of the sacrament the historic community looks back to the past, to the moment in history in which its existence is reconstituted as the people of God; while at the same moment it looks forward to the future, and the consummation of its mission, thus holding together the disintegration of these two temporal directions. In considering this aspect of the meaning of the Eucharist, however, it is necessary to remember that it cannot simply be identified with the Last Supper; and in actual fact the Pauline narrative of the institution is careful to indicate the historical perspectives of both of them.[80]

The action of "the Lord Jesus in the night in which he was betrayed" looks forward to the consummation which shall be achieved in the passion and the resurrection, while in the Synoptic versions it looks beyond this to the heavenly banquet in the kingdom of God.[81] In the same way the fragment of Pauline interpretation of the Eucharist explains its significance as the proclamation of the Lord's death until he shall come again in the Last Judgment at the end of history.[82] The eschatological reference of the Supper and the Eucharist are, therefore, parallel to one another, but they are not identical. Similarly, they are both endowed with a retrospective reference, which is explicit in all the New Testament accounts, which are again parallel but not identical. In the Synoptic versions the Supper is clearly set within the context and atmosphere of the Passover Festival as the memorial of the great redemptive act of Israel's deliverance from Egypt. The dominical words over the supper are set against the double background of the old covenant on Sinai and Jeremiah's prophecy of the new covenant after the Spirit. The saying concludes with a prescription for the celebration of the Eucharist, so that this act is to be regarded not merely as a subjective remembrance of Christ in his passion, but as an anamnesis of the redeeming work in its totality. Finally, it

---

[80] I Corinthians 11:23–26.
[81] Mark 14:25; Matthew 26:29; Luke 22:18.
[82] I Corinthians 11:26.

is clear that the Supper is incorporated as an integral element in the whole series of events which constitutes the unique eschatological crisis at the centre of history. It follows, therefore, that in the celebration of the Eucharist the church is made to stand within the same crisis, as contemporary with it while still subject to the temporal conditions of historical existence. It is this mysterious reconstitution of history ever again at its centre in the eucharistic life of the church which prompts Paul to describe it as the community in which the ends of the ages overlap.[83]

It is immediately apparent, in indicating the temporal perspectives of the Eucharist, that we have been introduced into a microcosm of the Christian understanding of historical existence. Time prior to the unique *kairos* is the time of preparation and expectation, as it was in the mystery of the Old Israel's life and mission which the church inherits and reinterprets. Time present is the *kairos* itself, as it is eternally in the person and work of the incarnate Word, which has been manifested historically and extended to mankind in his body. Time future is the time of anticipation, as it is in the mystery of the church's life, which embodies the transformation of human existence and the foretaste of man's destiny. But the significant feature about all these temporal directions is that, while they provide the framework of human experience and the schema of history, they are also subject to, and vehicles of, human sinfulness, which has introduced disorder into the created world and subjected temporal existence to disintegration. It follows, therefore, that the meaning of the Eucharist for the redemption of history lies in the fact that it unites all these disintegrated directions of time within the moment of its celebration. Time is thereby reconstituted with the centre of history which is eternally its origin and its judge. It is the redemption of history because it incorporates historical existence within its action.

The interpretation of the pattern of the liturgy which has been sketched briefly in the preceding pages provides a structure of sacred reality in which the total dimensions of human existence may participate. It is precisely as a pattern that it overcomes the destructive tendencies in existence, and therefore answers to the requirements of a *Gestalt* of Grace, because it is concerned with the reformation of man and his activities according to his new crea-

---

[83] I Corinthians 10:11. See L. S. Thornton, *The Common Life in the Body of Christ,* pp. 333–334.

tion in the Christ. It is fair to add that a great deal of specific liturgical evidence might have been brought forward to exemplify the richness and articulation of the pattern, drawn, for example, from the rites for the blessing of the font on the vigils of Easter and Pentecost and from the rituals for exorcism, which are particularly concerned with the overcoming of the demonic perversion of existence. But this would have entailed a much more elaborate treatment than space permitted; and it was our primary intention to exhibit the structural character of the pattern as a whole. When all is said and done, however,

it is not so important to produce new liturgies as it is to penetrate into the depths of what happens day by day, in labor and industry, in marriage and friendship, in social relations and recreation, in meditation and tranquillity, in the unconscious and the conscious life. To elevate all this into the light of the eternal is the great task of cultus, and not to reshape a tradition traditionally. . . . Protestant formative power is at work wherever reality is transformed into an active expression of a Gestalt of Grace.[84]

ROBERT H. DAUBNEY

THE THEOLOGICAL COLLEGE
ELY, CAMBRIDGESHIRE, ENGLAND

[84] *The Protestant Era*, p. 219. Cf. G. Dix, *The Shape of the Liturgy* (London, 1943), p. 333.

14

James Luther Adams
TILLICH'S INTERPRETATION
OF HISTORY

14

TILLICH'S INTERPRETATION OF HISTORY

THE interpretation of history is no merely academic or optional concern. In "Kairos," one of his earlier essays on history (1922), Tillich asserts it to be his intention to "present a summons to a consciousness of history, a demand for a consciousness of the present and for action in the present in the spirit of *kairos*." In partial explanation of the term *kairos* he says that "if a special moment of time is good for the fulfilment of something, this moment is its *kairos*." The present moment, or period, is a propitious one for interpreting, or reinterpreting, history. Ours is a period in which previously attractive and seemingly viable interpretations have broken down. What men have done in the name of philosophy of history has undone them. Our philosophies of history have been less powerful than the fate of history. Man lives or dies of his philosophy of history. He cannot escape history, and this means he cannot escape interpreting history. Communism, fascism, national socialism, capitalism, socialism, and even the transcendentalism that turns its eyes from history, have all been born out of, and have lived on, a theory of history. These rival theories of history today have thrown large sections of the planet into violent, carrion struggle. The interpretation of history, then, is not a luxury. It is the most pressing problem of our period, for it is the question as to whether there is a power through which our conflicts can be overcome.

In face of the great expanse and complexity of Tillich's treatment of the problems of the interpretation of history, I propose to pursue as the leitmotiv of his work his dialectical method, and also in some measure to present this method in its relation to other types of historical dialectic. To record what I have grasped will be to confess what I have missed or misunderstood. For the most part my questions will be reserved for the end of the chapter.

330

I. THE KEY TO THE INTERPRETATION OF HISTORY

History is never understood by the philosopher standing outside history. "The meaning of history," Tillich writes, "can be discovered only in meaningful historical activity. The key to history is historical action, not a point above history; historical activity is active participation in the life of a historical group. The meaning of history manifests itself in the self-understanding of a historical group." The key, namely, historical action, is found by some in the life of a nation, by others in a class group, by still others in a group that aims to transcend both nation and class. In our society we can scarcely escape belonging to several groups, but if we have a key to the interpretation of history some one group will be decisive. Tillich asserts, therefore, that the quest for an interpretation is identical with the quest for the group in which the meaning of history is manifest.

What is a group? Human groups have a "we-consciousness," and they have the power to exist as a group and to bear a definite system of values. This "we-consciousness" involves also the conception of "others," with the consequence that there is a dialectical unity and separation between, and even within, groups. In the development of this "we-consciousness" group migration has often played an important role; frequently it is through migration that a decisively new "we-consciousness" is formed. In so far as a group has the power to act with a united will, it possesses something like political organization. In a group that maintains itself and grows, there will emerge a consciousness of a special historical vocation. This sense of vocation is related to the memory of events, places, and figures of peculiar significance for the origin, the continuance, and the destiny of the group (George Washington, George Fox, the Battle of Hastings, Jesus, the Buddha, Mount Sinai). These events and figures are viewed as turning points in the past of the group, and they become associated with "myths" of origin and destiny. The historical consciousness of a group therefore exhibits a qualitative sense of time: the symbolically powerful events in the development of the "we-consciousness" and its vocation are center points in relation to which ("before and after") the meaning of the group life is defined. The key, then, to the interpretation of history is participation in a group that has a center in which the meaning of history becomes manifest. The decisive group from which Tillich speaks as a member is that group—the Christian church—for which the center is Jesus as the Christ, the power of the New Being. In this group the "we-consciousness" finds its focus of crystallization not in a doctrine or in a series of empirical events, but in an ontological ground that supports and transforms the historical process.

Membership and active participation in even this group, however, does not guarantee meaningful, relevant historical action. The church, as an historical entity, like any other group, can become caught in, and even bound to, merely divisive forces or to stagnant backwashes in the stream of history, and it can thereby betray the system of values and the New Being to which it claims devotion. Without the spirit of prophecy the church loses a vital relation to its center. One can sometimes find more of the spirit of prophecy in utterance against the church than in the witness of the church itself. This is possible because the spirit of prophecy cannot be "contained." It bloweth where it listeth.

For the interpretation of history a prophetic Protestantism, for one thing, must recognize that there are nonreligious realms to which God is related as much as to the specially religious realms —God, and not "religion," is sovereign. For another thing, it must recognize the broken, ambiguous character of its relation to these nonreligious realms. On the one hand, it may betray its own message; and on the other, a nonreligious manifestation in a hidden way may itself express the prophetic demand of that message. The Protestant must possess a dialectical attitude.

Tillich's dialectical interpretation of history aspires to present the basis for a Protestant philosophy of history—something which, in Tillich's view, has not been available. Such a philosophy of history must discover the point from which prophetic and rational, concrete and timely criticism may be proclaimed—a criticism to be directed at the special religious spheres as well as at the "nonreligious." This is the Archimedean point which his dialectic of affirmation and negation seeks.

II. THE MEANING OF DIALECTIC

Although it has been employed in a variety of ways since ancient times, the term "dialectic" is probably most familiar today in the Hegelian and Marxist analysis of identity and contrast, issuing in the positing of a threefold process of thesis, antithesis, and synthesis. Generally, and also by Tillich, the term has been applied to four different areas of discourse: the logical, the ontological, the historical, and the religious. For Tillich, each level involves all the others; and identity and contrast prevail in each. In the logic of inquiry, dialectic, for Tillich, denotes affirmation and negation leading to the discovery of truth, though not necessarily to synthesis. On the ontological level dialectic involves the discernment of the identities and contrasts in existence, and the awareness of a synthesis lying beyond the existential order. On the historical level it refers to the dynamic processes wherein through unity and separation the configurations of social existence drive beyond themselves to new identity and contrast, in ever recurring creative syntheses and disruptions. In the religious dimension dialectic denotes the identities and contrasts both within man and between man and the infinite, the ground and abyss of his existence.

The existential character of Tillich's dialectic and its implications for the interpretation of history can be brought into sharp relief if we compare and contrast it with the dialectic of the "mature" Hegel and with that of his existential critics, Schelling, Kierkegaard, and Marx. Although Tillich finds some basis for agreement with all of these figures, we shall find that in his fundamental presuppositions with respect to dialectic he stands nearer to Schelling than to any other one named above.

The Hegelian dialectic is a dialectic of *spirit*. In its "one total act" spirit posits itself in opposition to itself and at the same time reconciles in itself this contradiction. Estrangement and reconciliation are bound together in this synthesis. In this separation and unity the synthesis of subject and object is taken as the clue to all experience. The dialectic of spirit is the activity of the universal spirit achieving self-consciousness in human knowing and doing.

Applying this conception of dialectic to the interpretation of the temporal successions of history, Hegel asserted that affirmation and negation proceed by the stages of thesis, antithesis, and synthesis which mark the epochal course of progress in history, and also the processes of thought moving toward complete self-consciousness. In this fashion Hegel interpreted all world history as a coming from and returning to God. In history this process is the realization of freedom. If the striving for freedom is the inner nature of spirit, the means are the passions of men and the external occurrences of history. But even though freedom is the goal, Hegel thought the universal movement toward synthesis to be a law of necessity; for him it almost, if not quite, reached completion in his own system and time. Its presupposition was that essence *is* existence.

The criticisms of this Hegelian dialectic have been legion, and under the impact of various schools of existentialism they have become familiar to many, more familiar, indeed, than Hegel himself. Kierkegaard exposed the *hubris* of Hegel's presumptuous claim to have got the universe into his iron cup of synthesis. In actuality, he said, Hegel ties everything into a hard knot of logical and historical necessity, and thus eliminates the existential integrity and freedom of the individual in his anxious, personal decision; at the same time he suppresses the dialectical No by trying to conceal the qualitative distance between the infinite and the finite, and between essence and existence.[1] Karl Marx, demanding the application of dialectic to social existence, held that Hegel transcendentalized reality and thus reckoned without his host, the forces of production that determine consciousness; that he erred in imagining that the dialectic of history would come to a stop with *his* synthesis; that Hegelianism conceals the antitheses in mankind—the alienation of man from man and from himself and of class from class—and issues in a spuriously dialectical contemplation and protection of this alienation rather than in a demand for the overcoming of it; in short, that Hegel's dialectic teaches us that the world is as it ought to be. Accordingly, Marx seized upon the dynamic, revolutionary element of Hegelian dialectic and used it to combat the conservative, bourgeois element; the affirmation of Hegel, he insisted, must be negated by a new thrust of the dialectic which will achieve synthesis in the classless society. The presupposition of these criticisms is that essence *is not* existence, at least not yet.

Tillich agrees with most of the criticisms made by the existentialists Kierkegaard and Marx, if not with all of the implications they drew from them. Particularly important for his interpretation of history is his agreement with Marx's demand for the unity between theory and practice—an axiom of existential thinking. Marx is right also, he thinks, in emphasizing material production as the foundation of the whole historical process, though he points out that the Marxists have distorted this into a mechanistic materialism.

Tillich's first criticism of Hegel, like Kierkegaard's, is that his

[1] The influence of Schelling upon Kierkegaard's dialectic has been largely neglected, though Kierkegaard is by no means silent about the impact upon him of this first of the existentialist philosophers.

hubris consists in the false assumption that his method can encompass the whole of reality. But he asserts that "the dialectical method must be accepted as a method of describing the movements of life and history in their inner tensions, contrasts, and contradictions and in their trend toward more embracing unities."[2] Kierkegaard is at fault in restricting dialectic to the relation between the individual and God; he showed little interest in history as the unfolding of group life.

Tillich's second criticism is that Hegelian dialectic is not genuinely dialectical: it dissolves the contradictions in existence by making them come to a halt in synthesis. "In the last moment essence triumphs over existence, completion over infinity, and the static over the dynamic. . . . The circle is closed."[3] To use a Hegelian expression, the estrangement between essence and existence is not "serious." For Tillich, the contradictions are never resolved in history. Synthesis is always accompanied by diastasis. To assert the complete resolution of contradictions in history is antidialectical. History is a "challenge to every conceivable synthesis." Nothing can be unbrokenly realized in history. Progress always brings new problems and tensions. Each gain in one respect is accompanied by loss in another.

Tillich's third criticism is that Hegel was wrong in making the dialectic into a law of all-embracing necessity. For both Hegel and Marx the dialectic turns out to be a dialectic of "things."[4] It fails to reckon with the unpredictability of human freedom and of the accidents of events and leadership. Reality is shot through with dynamism. History has within it always the possibility of the new. Destiny expresses itself in this dynamism. In both Hegelian and Marxist dialectic the freedom of the individual is of little moment. Hegel and Marx are right, however, in asserting that freedom and destiny belong together; but they join them undialectically, Hegel by resorting to his theory of the "cunning of the Idea" (presuming a preestablished harmony of idea and history), and Marx by looking toward the completed synthesis in the classless society when "history" is to begin.

For Tillich, freedom and destiny remain in tension so long as they both shall live. To Hegel and Marx he replies that ultimate synthesis

---

[2] *The Protestant Era*, p. 259.
[3] *The Interpretation of History*, p. 166.
[4] Paul Tillich, *Die sozialistische Entscheidung*, p. 150.

occurs only beyond history. Yet their search for meaning through reconciliation testifies to their consciousness of standing in a cleft world, even if they did not recognize the depth of the cleavages. Moreover, their optimism regarding the possibility of complete reconciliation in history, even though it was unjustified, must be seen as an expression of their hidden Christian belief that the tragic character of existence does not belong to the essential nature of things. The estrangement is from an original unity. But as "theologians" Hegel and Marx offered undialectical answers to the question concerning the overcoming of alienation.

Tillich, like Schelling, holds that the meaning of history is found in the process whereby the divine, through the instrument of human freedom, overcomes estrangement through love. This process cannot be described by a rationalistic dialectic; it requires a historical dialectic, an existential dialectic. Unlike Hegel's this dialectic recognizes the real, historical estrangement of man from his original unity. This existential dialectic, then, is the dialectic of identity and of real contrast between man and the infinite polar power, the ground and abyss of being. These conceptions are presupposed in Tillich's dialectical interpretation of history, the realm of the unique and the universal, the rational and the irrational, the *kairos*, the logos, the divine and the demonic, the realm of decision and of "being decided."

We can now summarize and restate the meaning of dialectic for Tillich. His dialectic is more than "a conversation of 'yes' and 'no' " in any ordinary sense. It is "the art of determining the relation of ideas to one another and to existence. . . . Dialectic grasps truth only when the ideas themselves are dialectical. Thus from an art of discovering relationships, dialectic becomes an expression for a certain kind of actual relationship."[5] What is the relationship? It is expressed in Tillich's conception of "living on the boundary," at the point where one recognizes limitations and receives something from beyond. "Everything must be defined by its limits, a fact to which the very word 'definition' refers," writes Tillich. "Whoever is so related to a thing that he does not see its limits . . . cannot know it."[6] To see the limits of existence is to see beyond existence to its essential ground. Dialectic should penetrate to the depth, "the *ousia*, the 'essence' of things, that which gives them the power of being. . . .

---

[5] *The Interpretation of History*, p. 165.
[6] *Religiöse Verwirklichung* (Berlin: Furche-Verlag, 1929), p. 11.

This is their truth, the 'really real.' "[7] No idea can be appropriate so long as it is self-enclosed, for in actuality all realities and ideas stand in a relation of identity and contrast. Self-sufficient finitude, even in concepts, is unecstatic finitude. The concepts should point to the inexhaustible ground in all beings—called by Nicolas of Cusa the "coincidence of opposites." This means that the dialectic of identity and contrast expresses an "actual relationship" that is paradoxical: between essence and existence there is *essential* unity, but everything in historical existence (including knowledge) is ambiguous in that it is estranged from the power of being. Here we have the dialectic between the created goodness of things, their estrangement (or distorted existence), and their possibility of reconciliation. Here we have also the "standpoint" from which prophetic and rational criticism may issue.

It is doubtful whether or no Tillich's dialectic may properly be called a method of *inquiry*, apart from the fact that it aims at consistency and may be systematically applied. It is not a method for the discovery of truth in the sense of "a metaphysical-deductive or of an empirical-inductive approach" projecting and testing hypotheses. Indeed, Tillich asserts that, like every method, it *presupposes* an ultimate concern, "an *a priori* of experience and evaluation." Thus it would appear that he does not start with a method of investigation, trying to *find* something he does not have; his dialectic is rather a principle for showing the implications of what he already *has*. As a theologian he studies other disciplines in order to clarify his concepts and to gain a better intellectual grasp of them, or in order to discover anew and make clear the relevance to the human situation of what he *has*. (This is the method of correlation.) The "original" or "basic decision" is not rooted in "formal evidence" or "material probability" but rather in a "third element."[8] The decision occurs in "a transcendental stratum of knowledge" that "corresponds to the transcendental stratum of being."[9] Tillich, therefore, asserts that, regardless of any claim to do otherwise, all theologies proceed on the basis of an a priori "original decision," "an immediate experience of something ultimate in value and being, of which one can become intuitively aware. . . . The theological concepts both of idealists and of naturalists are rooted in a 'mystical a priori,' an

---

[7] *Systematic Theology*, I, 101.
[8] *The Interpretation of History*, p. 143.
[9] *Ibid.*, p. 158.

awareness of something that transcends the cleavage between subject and object." The Christian theologian "adds to 'the mystical *a priori*' the criterion of the Christian message."[10] Its verification, he says, is the "efficacy in the life-process," and the process of verification is itself a process within "the theological circle."[11]

III. THE FRAMEWORK FOR THE INTERPRETATION OF HISTORY

If Tillich's dialectical principle presupposes the Christian view of "the one total act" of estrangement and reconciliation, his basic concepts give expression to motifs central in the Protestant-Christian interpretation of time and history. His conception of history is oriented to the Old Testament prophetic view that history is always under crisis and judgment and at the same time has an aim toward which it is moving; that the struggle between good and evil forces is the main content of history as it moves towards its "end"; and that this struggle occurs not only in the individual soul, but also through social groups and institutions. With the New Testament transformation of this eschatological thinking, history finds a center at which its meaning becomes visible and where the divine, reconciling, healing power gives definitive expression to the overcoming of estrangement. The Pauline-Protestant doctrine of justification by faith points to the experience that at the very depth of the doubts and contradictions of existence there appears the decision (and the "being decided") whereby the New Being in Christ invades and overcomes the estrangement both of thought and of existence; it expresses also the Biblical insight that the total dialectical process will be completed only beyond history. The doctrine of the kingdom of God, like the doctrine of justification, affirms that, in face of the demonic forces of history, the divine invading power has already broken into history and promises a fulfillment to come. This reconciliation of estrangement comes not through the human contrivance of law or asceticism: man does not control the Kingdom, it is God's Kingdom; man prepares for it through repentance and the fruits meet for repentance.[12]

[10] *Systematic Theology*, I, 9.

[11] *Ibid.*, pp. 102–105.

[12] Tillich's emphasis on the doctrine of justification should not be interpreted as a warrant for identifying him with what is called the Neo-Reformation School. His dynamic protesting interpretation of history shows much closer affinity to the sectarian prophetic impulses expressed in the Left Wing of the Reformation, despite the fact that in many instances their eschatologies were Utopian. Actually, Tillich's partially positive estimate of Utopianism, as we shall see, provided the impulse for him to recover the concept of "the *kairos*."

Tillich, it will be recalled, says that "dialectic grasps truth only when the ideas themselves are dialectical." The application of this principle is to be observed not only in the concepts he employs for describing the structure and interpreting the meaning of history, but even in the concept of "interpretation" itself. This dialectical conception of "interpretation" becomes evident in the answer to the question, What is history?

Hegel was probably not the first to point out that the word "history" unites "the objective with the subjective side; it comprehends no less what has *happened* than the *narration* of what has happened." For Tillich, history as *remembered events* is a realm in which subjectivity and objectivity merge and belong together. History as remembered is history interpreted; it is a cultural creation that is an expression of human freedom, an expression of "risking" decision. Interpretation is the creative "ecstatic" union of the interpreter and the interpreted in a "third" beyond them. The historian must combine the "distance" of objective analysis (separation) with the empathy (or union) of understanding. In interpretation there is a reception and a creation of meaning. The dialectical character of interpretation appears also in the assertion that "the subjective-objective character of history implies that the interpretation of history determines history and is determined by history, at the same time."[13] This dialectic is given a strongly practical turn by Tillich's declaration that the interpretation of history must be undertaken on the basis of action in history and toward the end of action if it is to be an effective expression of the historical consciousness. Decision goes deeper than thought; it is a participation in being. Only by this depth-path of decision do we become aware of what S. Alexander calls "the historicity of things."

The decisive category of historical existence is time. Like Schelling, Troeltsch, and Bergson, Tillich defines historical time in terms of a contrast between space and time, between nature and history. Here again he approaches the problem of definition by means of dialectic; he stresses the contrast between space, the static, and time, the dynamic and creative dimension, between space, the realm of quantitative time, and history, the realm of qualitative time. In the inorganic realm of nature, physical time prevails, the quantitative time of pure motion; in the organic realm biological time prevails, the time of genesis and decay. "Natural" time is bound to space (the

13 *Propositions*, Part V, C, I, p. 3.

animal, for example, is bound to its spatial environment). Its symbol
is the circle. Although nature displays some elements of spontaneous
creativity, its events in the main repeat themselves according to a
law of necessity. In human personality and history, existence
achieves a certain power over itself; it breaks through the circle of
repetition in space, freeing itself from the immediate course, and
from the unselfrelatedness, of nature. Man as a social creature is not
bound to his spatial environment, as is the animal: he is able to remember long stretches of the past; in terms of meaning he can interpret the past in relation to the present; he can posit something new
for the future.

Because of this orientation of freedom to meaning, time can pre-
dominate over space; quality can overtake quantity. Thus history
gains an independent character, though its permanent basis is in
nature. Accordingly, historical time is to be measured primarily in
terms of qualitative meaning. Its symbol is the arrow, for time is
now directed; it forges ahead and makes for a point. It is ecstatic toward the future. Moreover, each "moment" in the process is different.
Historical events or *Gestalten* do not repeat themselves; they are
unique, original, unrepeatable. They are always driving forward toward the new—impelled by destiny and freedom, and oriented to a
system of values. Thus they unite individuality with universality.

On the basis of these distinctions between space and time, nature
and history, Tillich elaborates a classification of the major interpretations of history. Presupposed in the classification is the view that
the basic difference between interpretations is to be determined by
answering the question as to whether or not a given interpretation
holds that *in history* we are confronted with that which unconditionally concerns us, a universally operating process bearing independent meaning. If the answer is affirmative, then we have a historical interpretation; if it is negative, we have a nonhistorical
interpretation and a denial of universal history. The nonhistorical
interpretations do not take time seriously. They interpret it through
nature; they spatialize it.

Both in the historical and in the nonhistorical interpretations of
history the rhythms of time appear as epochs. Nonhistorical interpretations of history tend to devise theories of periodization on the
basis of genesis and decay (for example, Plato, Stoicism, Nietzsche,
Spengler). In historical interpretations the rhythm of genesis and

decay is superseded by the rhythm of periods (Parsism, Judaism, the Joachites, Anabaptism, modern doctrines of progress, Marxism). In directed time periods never repeat themselves. Each period has its own unique qualities, and each is dialectically related to the others. Each period is interpreted as having its center of pregnant meaning. A number of centers, however, may be oriented to the center of centers, the New Being. The several centers bear a derivative relation to the center. The impulse in history varies in different periods through the predominance of one or other element (economic, political, religious). The quality of a period depends upon the special concrete difficulty out of which a central question arises to dominate the age.

IV.   CENTRAL CONCEPTS

At the outset we referred to Tillich's intention to issue "a summons to a consciousness of history." His definition of a consciousness of history is: "to be penetrated by the forces and tensions of the historical process and to be grasped by the creative significance of the present moment." We must now examine the concepts by which he brings to a focus the meaningful possibilities and threats in historical existence—the concepts that indicate what it means "to be grasped by the creative significance of the present moment."

For Tillich, two forces in our time have been peculiarly inimical to the achievement of an awareness of the creative significance of the present: regressive conservatism and progressive liberalism. Both of these forces resist radical criticism and transformation: regressive conservatism resists change in the name of return to the past; progressive liberalism resists it in the name of gradualism. Neither regression nor progress possesses a forward-moving dynamic. The most effective challenge to both of these views has appeared in socialism. But, as we have observed, Marxism, with all its prophetic criticism of the *status quo,* exempted itself from radical criticism; it has ignored the existential dialectic and it has therefore issued in Utopianism. The outcome of Utopianism is always disillusionment. Indeed, the slowing-down of progressive liberalism was itself the consequence of a disillusionment following upon its previously revolutionary Utopianism. It would appear that truly prophetic power, in its awareness of the creative significance of the present moment, always confronts the temptation of Utopianism. Yet without the dynamic element in Utopianism, time loses its directedness and succumbs to spatialization. Utopianism offers both promise and threat.

Tillich's conception of the "*kairos*" was born out of an attempt to come to terms with Utopianism—to capture its sense of promise and at the same time to offer warning against its dangers. The term, which means "the fullness of time," "qualitatively fulfilled time," is drawn from the New Testament, and it connotes all that is distinctive in the Christian conception of time; namely, that time may be invaded by eternity, that it has a direction, that it has a center and therefore a periodization based upon qualitative differences, and yet that in time itself man may never achieve the fullness of the eternal.

From this characterization one can observe that Tillich has generalized the concept which appears in the New Testament when St. Paul attaches it to the coming of Jesus Christ "in the fullness of time." Tillich calls this Pauline usage the unique and universal sense of *kairos*. But "kairotic" moments appear at every turning point in history in which the eternal judges and transforms the temporal; for these moments the term *kairos* is used in its general sense. It may be used also to refer to the fulfilling moment of a particular situation; this is the *kairos* in its special sense.

In accord with his existential dialectic, Tillich stresses the uniqueness of each moment in history. Every historical situation approaches us as destiny that offers only a limited number of possibilities and that demands decision in freedom. The decision involves risk. The renunciation of security is possible for the Protestant. "The fundamental Protestant attitude," Tillich says, "is to stand in nature, taking upon oneself the inevitable reality; not to flee from it, either into the world of ideal forms or into the related world of super-nature, but to make decisions in concrete reality."[14] The decision is not made by an absolute subject standing above history, it is a decision made in history where creation must emerge from conflict and ambiguity.

But although decision must be relevant to the moment, it must unite individuality and universality if it is to be meaningful. Otherwise, decision can only be an expression of the arbitrary. The decision must not ignore that it is made in a world that has interconnections and in a world in which meaning can be achieved only through intelligible structures. The relation between *kairos* and

[14] *The Interpretation of History*, p. 134.

Logos is not one of disjunction; it is dialectical; *kairos* points to the limits set for the realization of *Logos* in a particular historical situation and yet it opens up a new, unique way for the realization of *Logos*. In the light of these ideas we must understand the significance of the concept of the Kingdom of God. Indeed, only those who know the tragic meaning of history can understand what the symbol of the Kingdom of God means.

"Progressive" liberalism, with its middle-class, moralistic tendency to conceal the ambiguities of existence, looks for an infinite approximation to fulfillment in history. It is true that there may be progress in technical control, in political unification, and in the humanization of relationships among men; but there is no progress in cultural creations (in the arts, for example) or in the morality of mankind. Meaningful cultural creations and relevant morality must always be won anew. Moreover, achievement in the moral sphere always gives occasion for new problems and new distortions. Special forces inimical to meaning may be removed in special moments, but not the antidivine structure of our existence nor our involvement in non-being. Creative courage is always accompanied by anxiety.

Orthodox supernaturalism, on the other hand, offers a more realistic interpretation of the ambiguities of historical existence; at least, it does so in so far as it stresses the impossibility of completely overcoming estrangement or alienation in history. But it wrongly looks for complete fulfillment in a supranature or suprahistory unconnected with history. This dualism can only issue in a nonhistorical interpretation of history. Time is created in the ground of the divine life, and eternity is therefore essentially related to it as the transcendent unity of the dissected moments of existential time.

The symbol of the Kingdom of God connects history with its fulfillment. The Kingdom of God does not belong entirely to another world, it appears in the continuous struggle against the antidivine in history, in a continuous transformation of the forms of existence into forms anticipating or receiving the New Being; for history is the history of salvation. The ground and fulfillment of meaning have found decisive focus in the unique *kairos* of the Christ as the center of history, and they may become ambiguously manifest in a special *kairos* which is the juncture of decision and destiny belonging to a particular historical situation. The symbol therefore expresses the relationship of the unconditioned meaning of existence to actual existence. The Church, which is more than the Christian churches, is the community of those who live in the light of this unconditioned meaning, and its norm is the unique *kairos*.

But because every actualization of meaning is only fragmentary, the symbol of the Kingdom of God points beyond the struggles and transformations of history to a fulfillment in a dimension that transcends history. The fulfillment is always "at hand," but its complete achievement of unity and purity of meaning is suprahistorical, for this unity and purity cannot be expressed merely in terms of time and history. Every attempt to express the fulfillment in terms of time will "spatialize" the ultimate meaning, making it a segment of the totality of meanings or a "space" that is a history after history, a time after time. The ultimate fulfillment is the transformation of existence into the New Being beyond essential and existential being. In this fulfillment antidivine structures and nonbeing itself are overcome, indeed they are excluded from Being. The disrupted unity is restored in the totality and purity and unity of the New Creation, a unity of man with nature, of man with man, of group with group. In short, the symbol of the Kingdom dialectically points not only to the "end" of history which is present in every historical moment and in history as a whole, but also to the ultimate synthesis and fulfillment of everything meaningful that has been estranged and fragmented in history. The synthesis which Hegel and Marx posited within the becoming of history is thus by Tillich projected beyond history. For him, dialectical identities and contrasts of history are gathered up, purified, and unified in a suprahistorical synthesis which lies beyond historical existence, beyond potentiality and actuality, beyond subject and object.

Whatever one may think of Tillich's interpretation of history as a whole or of this or that detail, one must grant that the interpretation is the most elaborate and substantial one that has been worked out in the history of Protestant philosophical theology. Not only in its own intrinsic structure and through its highly original shaping of concepts, but also in the motifs that it has drawn from the wide range of Biblical and Western thought and experience, it is for a long time to come destined to serve as a stimulus and a point of reference for Protestant agreement and disagreement.

I want to close with a list of questions, in addition to those raised in the previous exposition:

1. If God is beyond essence and existence, how can he be related to history?

2. If the "theological circle" is based on a mystical intuition, how can a verification take place except through empirical analysis?

3. If the ultimate religious decision is a matter of faith, how can historical relativism be overcome?

4. If dialectic means "being driven beyond itself," is synthesis the end of dialectics or not?

5. If Christian faith is related to the historical Jesus, why should historical investigations "neither comfort nor worry theologians"?

6. If theonomy includes a special social organization, is not the voluntary association of decisive importance?

7. If the fulfillment of history transcends history, how can one know about it?

8. If the Kingdom of God consists of the "unity, totality, and purity" of meaning beyond history, how can history influence the Kingdom of God and even God himself?

JAMES LUTHER ADAMS

DEPARTMENT OF ETHICS AND SOCIETY
THE MEADVILLE THEOLOGICAL SCHOOL
THE UNIVERSITY OF CHICAGO
CHICAGO, ILLINOIS

Further Reflections

PAUL TILLICH forged his philosophy of history in the teeth of the crucial events of his time and in the light of earlier writings on the philosophy of history. Among those philosophers important to him was Ernst Troeltsch (1865–1923). Tillich often spoke of him as "my great teacher," and said that his writings are a presupposition for all subsequent consideration in the philosophy of history. It is instructive, therefore, to see Tillich's work in this area in relation to Troeltsch's conception of the philosophy of history.

Important for Tillich was Troeltsch's view (set forth at length in the *magnum opus* of his later years, *Historismus und seine Probleme* [1922]) that very few writers present what may be properly called a philosophy of *history*. Beginning with antiquity and through Augustine and the medieval and early modern writers, the philosophy of history was not grounded in a study of history itself;

rather, it imposed on history a framework extraneous to it. Augustine is typical in deriving from scripture his conception of history and also his articulation of the periods of history. Kantianism, to take a modern example, represents a rationalistic system incapable of becoming the basis of a genuine philosophy of history. It was preoccupied with "genuinely valid, unchangeable, timeless ideals," formally distant from the specificities of history.

Hegel's philosophy of history illustrated his logical dialectic that found its culmination in his own system, the final manifestation of the Absolute. The phenomena of history were pressed into the *apriori* grooves of logical process. It is said that Hegel was reproached by one of his critics for the discrepancy between his system and historical facts; Hegel retorted, "So much the worse for facts." The orientation, moreover, was to the past, offering no way into the future. Positivism for its part surrendered any fundamental concern for values and issued an anarchy of values in nominalistic, ethical relativism. Troeltsch's criticism of positivism, however, goes beyond his belief that the philosophy of history should be based on a direct study of historical data. For both Troeltsch and Tillich, philosophy of history should be derived from examining human social existence and not from some idealistic framework. Here they reflect the social realism demanded by Marx.

Tillich's intention, accordingly, was to discern patterns in the characteristic concerns of the individual and collective actors in different periods of history. On the basis of these realities, Troeltsch and Tillich aimed to retain the historic interest in periodization. The selection and description of these realities by the philosopher of history represent a creative or constructive task. They require discussion and criticism at the hands of the historians, for the patterns come from revisable sociological and cultural analysis and synthesis.

For Troeltsch, however, this concern for analysis—what he called the achievement of "a formal logic of history"—did not constitute the crucial, constructive task of presenting "a material philosophy of history." A material philosophy of history does not remain contemplative; it aims to confront the conflicts, frustrations and crises of the present and, interpreting the signs of the times, to offer guidance for the present in its lunge towards the future. In this respect, the philosophy of history relates the past to the present and to the possibilities of the future, moving toward decision and action.

In Troeltsch's view, the modern proponent of a material philosophy of history recognizes the time-conditioned character of the values in the cultural matrix of past and present, and yet must claim and defend the validity of the value preferences proposed. Here, then, the task involves grappling with fundamental philosophical and theological problems concerned with meaning in past and present. This confrontation is mandatory in the present moment of "a crisis in the values of European civilization," mandatory if one faces constructively the "problem of damming and controlling the historical stream of life." More than detached, objective analysis is required. The demand is for what Troeltsch called "a contemporary cultural synthesis" and his point of departure was in what he called "Europeanism" (we would call it "the West").

In general, we may say that the "basic pillars" out of which and beyond which a new cultural synthesis could emerge were, in his view, the ancient Hebraic tradition, classical Greek, the Hellenistic-Roman period, and the Occidental Middle Ages. Troeltsch did not live to work out his material philosophy of history, nor did he consider seriously the problems posed by the developing relations between West and East.

In Troeltsch's essay, "The Ancient Church" (1917), he explains his concept of *synthesis.* "One could look upon this as a syncretism of a period of exhaustion. . . . But it is actually not syncretism but a vast . . . synthesis. . . . It is the dark womb of a coming world. . . . Everything here is fruit of the past and seed of the future. . . . The modern world has inherited a dynamism, depth, and antithetical character unknown to Antiquity but constituting the essence of the modern world, which will endure as long as the modern world itself endures" (*Gesammelte Schriften,* IV, 95).

Troeltsch then delineates the dialectic of *contrasting* ingredients leading to this cultural synthesis in the ancient church and concludes by stressing the need for "action, risk, decision," and by warning against "taking refuge in contemplation, analysis, origins. . . . What counts today is to know what is needed and to shape the future accordingly. But that requires a new delineation of what is essential in the Christian ideal for us today, and a new ordering of its relationship to the cultural heritage of Antiquity. . . . This may be a difficult undertaking, with unforeseeable consequences. But it must be done."

Tillich discussed Troeltsch's concept of "cultural synthesis" in his lengthy review[1] (1924) of Troeltsch's *Historismus und seine Probleme* (1922). He stressed Troeltsch's concern to overcome the ethical relativism of "bad historicism," and laments his failure, in his treatment of Europeanism conditioned by time and place, to develop a metaphysics of history whereby he might have overcome the relativism. Tillich was not satisfied with Troeltsch's willingness to accept a limited relativism in his view that truth must remain polymorphous—differing truths standing alongside each other. Yet, he agrees with Troeltsch when he states that the "synthesis of autonomous cultural and societal creativity with religious traditions into a 'theonomous' unity is the social-ethical goal in an absolute sense." An ethical-prophetic attitude is "the attitude toward whose portals Troeltsch has led us, and which is the deepest meaning of his work" (page 114). For Troeltsch and Tillich, the concept of *theonomy* represents a transcending synthesis of autonomy and heteronomy in their ultimately religious rootage. This triad of dialectic and synthesis is the integrating concept of Tillich's theology of culture, using terms that had appeared in Troeltsch's writings. Troeltsch coined the term "autotheonomy" in order to indicate that theonomy does not abrogate autonomy, and Tillich accepted this view.

A year before this 1924 review, Tillich (just at the time of Troeltsch's death) published his *System der Wissenschaften* (1923), an elaborate analysis and classification of all the "sciences," including metaphysics and theology.[2] Here, as in his previously published dissertations on Schelling, Tillich finds the embracing synthesis in metaphysics and theology. In his subsequent writings the concept of synthesis continues to appear in connection with the concept of the dialectic of Yes and No. We must take into account especially the books published after Tillich's death [*Perspectives on 19th and 20th Century Protestant Thought* (1967), *My Search for Absolutes* (1967), *A History of Christian Thought* (1968)].

Tillich often has been characterized as a mediating theologian;

---

[1] The review appears in English translation in *Journal of the Scientific Study of Religion*, I (1961), pp. 100–114.

[2] This work has been translated into English by Paul Wiebe, *The System of the Sciences* (Lewisburg, PA: Bucknell University Press, 1981. In his Preface, Tillich expressed thanks to Troeltsch for "the influence his work has had upon the spiritual foundations of this book," and he dedicated the volume to him.

he saw himself as living and thinking "on the boundary" between opposing perspectives. The concept of synthesis, however, and not that of mediation, best describes the central thrust of his philosophy, theology, and philosophy of history; that is, he intends to go beyond mediation or interpenetration. A characteristic statement appears in his "Autobiographical Reflections" in the present volume. Referring to "the basic spiritual conflict" between the religious and the humanistic traditions, he says that this tension brought about his effort "to overcome the conflict constructively."

The latter way, the way of synthesis, was my own way. It follows the classical German philosophers from Kant to Hegel, and remained a driving force in all my theological work. It has found its final form in my *Systematic Theology*.

Tillich held that nineteenth-century German theology made its "great contribution" by virtue of its urgent need to find "creative synthesis" as the path to truth. Wherever significant, divergent elements are not brought into dialogue, the opposing perspectives only "run beside each other, without touching each other."

The concepts of dialogue and synthesis may be traced to Greek philosophy. Tillich identifies four areas of discourse for dialectic and synthesis—the logical, the ontological, the historical, and the religious. The logical form is familiar enough. The historical is to be seen in Augustine's writings. Like Clement, he was a promoter of synthesis, "a philosopher in whom the great synthesis between the Old Testament idea of Yahweh and the Parmenidean idea of being was achieved. More than anyone else in the history of the Church Augustine was responsible for the communion of Jerusalem and Athens." Or again, "the Swiss Reformation is the synthesis of the Reformation and humanism."

In the religious dimension, Tillich employs conceptions such as finite and infinite, the divine and the demonic, kairos and logos and the Eternal, and autonomy, heteronomy and theonomy. Initially these conceptions were spelled out vividly in Tillich's Kairos Circle of religious socialists who confronted the crisis of capitalism after World War I. In this context, God was seen as a sovereign over and through the culture as well as over and through the church. According to what Tillich calls the Protestant principle, "the sacred sphere is not nearer to the Ultimate than the secular sphere."

The Lutheran churches in Germany emphasized the vertical dimension in relation to the Eternal and neglected the horizontal, social-structural dimension. The religious socialists viewed certain prophetic secular movements as struggling more effectively against the demonic forces in nationalism and capitalism than the churches. In short, God could work through the atheists and the secular critics of "religion" and the churches. Here the religious socialists were saying Yes and No to both the churches and the secular socialists. They looked for a "cultural synthesis" beyond both of them, a synthesis of the sort asked for by Troeltsch. Tillich later came to view the outlook of the religious socialists of that time as utopian. The reactionaries won out, and within a decade the Nazis took over. In any event, it was in the struggle against demonic powers in history, powers both secular and ecclesiastical, that the main lineaments of Tillich's philosophy of history were given conceptual shape.

In the ontological dimension, Tillich sets forth a metaphysics of history that rests upon a metaphysics of being. Here he develops perspectives drawn especially from Schelling's existential, anti-Hegelian dialectic (leading to an open and not a closed synthesis), and explicates the "polarities" (contrasts) that pervade the *Systematic Theology*. The foundation with its contrasts is seen in Luther's distinction between the wrath and the love of God; in Boehme's triad of ground and abyss and mysticism's God beyond God; and in Schelling's triadic formula of being, nonbeing, and supra-being (*Uebersein*); and in the concepts of creation, estrangement and reconciliation (re-affirmation). *Agape* in the historical, ontological and religious dimensions re-unites the separated (an idea Tillich adapted from the young Hegel).

These various dimensions of dialectic are brought together in Tillich's Christology and his conception of the New Being. He recognizes the predicament of human beings in their finitude and estrangement, a predicament requiring the transforming of estranged individuation through participation in the universal. Both individuation and human participation are transcended and united in the New Being, an ontological reality. Tillich sees this process as manifest in Jesus' action and teaching. In subjecting himself to the cross, Jesus "crucified the particular in himself for the sake of the universal." He recognized authentic love in the action of the despised Samaritan. He even called for the love of the enemy. In his view, the saying "Be ye perfect as your Father in heaven is perfect" has been rightly translated "Be ye all-inclusive as your Father in heaven is all-inclusive." This inclusiveness, looking ever to newness of life, is the paradigmatic synthesis.

Schelling speaks of God as "the Great Synthesizer" in history; we may say that Tillich's constructive philosophy "to overcome the conflicts constructively" aims to be a venture and risk in pursuing an *imitatio dei*. Tillich sees history as a drama of dialectic and synthesis. Augustine, a quondam professor of classical literature, saw a universal paradigm in the idea that drama requires opposing actors. Accordingly, this paradigm appears in his depiction of the dramatic struggle between Two Cities. In this respect and in many others, Tillich is an Augustinian philosopher of history. Perhaps he was even more aware than Augustine of idolatry and especially of a possible veering away from relevance to the "historical stream of life," an irrelevance that brings failure or even demonic destruction.

In the last decades of his life, an awareness of the breakdown of previous syntheses repeatedly engages Tillich's attention. Although Hegel and Schleiermacher produced what he calls "the great synthesis," by 1840 both of these ventures broke down completely in the face of "extreme naturalism and materialism." Ritschl and his followers made a new attempt that failed at the turn of the century, partly because of a Kantian, moralistic and rationalistic overemphasis on ethics to the neglect of metaphysics and because of a sharp separation of the ethical personality from nature. It also broke down because of a rejection of mysticism and the synthesis of the ancient church. The end came with World War I which brought about the collapse of idealism and the end of the era. In the wake of the War, Karl Barth insisted on the diastasis against any synthesis of Christianity and the modern mind. Tillich rejected Barth's view of radical diastasis, considering it to be non-dialectical. "Synthesis," he wrote, "can never be avoided, because man is always man, and at the same time under God. He can never be under God in such a way that he ceases to be human."

But now comes a surprise. In the fifties Tillich apparently abandons the Troeltschian plea for a "contemporary cultural synthesis," for he writes that

In order to find a new way beyond the former ways of synthesis, I used the method of correlation. I try to show that the Christian message is the answer to all the problems involved in self-criticizing humanism; today we call this existentialism; it is a self-analyzing humanism. This is neither synthesis nor diastasis, neither identification nor separation, it is correlation. And I believe the whole story of Christian thought points in this direction.[3]

Note here the contrast with the earlier commitment to "the way of synthesis." Correlation apparently does not look towards impending synthesis; it aims instead to provide guidelines for Christianity in face of culture. The "sacred void" of "complete disruption and meaninglessness" in which we live requires a more radical stance than the search for synthesis. It is significant that in the third volume of the *Systematic Theology* (published one year before Tillich's death), one finds an abundant discussion of dialectic but little about synthesis. To be sure, he always insists (against Hegel and Marx) that "ultimate synthesis occurs beyond history." Meanwhile, Christians and the churches must adjust themselves to waiting constructively and critically for a new theonomy in the future. This, he held, is not a baseless hope, for a theonomous culture has appeared in earlier times.

Tillich's sense was that of a creative waiting, a preparation for the new—for grace. Especially instructive is the careful way in which he deals with ethical issues, both personal and institutional. As in previous writings, he sets forth (but more elaborately than before) a doctrine of ethical natural law, an unpopular idea (especially among the Barthians) except in Roman Catholic circles. In expounding a conception of natural law, Tillich took up a theme particularly associated with the writings of Troeltsch, who had made abundantly clear the varieties of natural-law doctrine acclaimed in the history of Christianity since the second century. In a famous essay, Troeltsch had predicted the collapse of German culture as a likely consequence of its abandonment of natural-law presuppositions in favor of naturalism, ethical relativism, and historical jurisprudence bound to the national spirit. With the rise of Nazism, a new interest was exhibited for a time in natural-law doctrine.

For Tillich, natural law is ontologically rooted in "our true and essential being [of divine provenance] that confronts us in the moral command" and "over against our state of existential estrangement." He exposes meticulously the ambiguities of the human situation (subjective and objective) and the ambiguities of application in *Systematic Theology III* and *My Search for Absolutes*. The latter

---

[3] *A History of Christian Thought*, p. 293.

volume, published two years after Tillich's death, presents lectures he delivered at the Law School of the University of Chicago. Before this time, Chancellor Robert Hutchins had promoted a vigorous discussion of the metaphysically-grounded Thomistic conception of natural law.[4] One regrets that Tillich does not here explicitly discuss Thomistic doctrine, and that he does not treat the issues raised by those democratic theorists who prefer Precedent to natural-law doctrine. He does, however, present a dynamic view analogous to what has appeared in Catholic circles (for example, under the influence of Blondel).

Tillich makes a careful distinction between the problems of personal and institutional ethics. Here, without mentioning his name, he takes issue with Otto von Gierke's view of the personality of the group, asserting that such a theory is in danger of opening the way for dictatorship. Fundamental for Tillich is the derived dignity of the Person. "We do not belong to ourselves but to that from which we come and to which we return—the eternal ground of everything that is. This is the ultimate reason for the sacredness of the person . . ." (*My Search for Absolutes*, p. 96). Here we encounter part of the ground for Tillich's criticism of capitalism with its "technological reason" that produces the homogenized person of consumerism and of emptied meaning. This technological reason also brought us to the secularism with its "organized injustice," to callous exploitation of nature and to the crisis in face of dwindling resources and nuclear warfare. And what, he asks, will be the outcome in our new, unavoidably interdependent world? We recall Tillich's earlier discussions of the present "world situation," though we should remember that for him the philosophy of history aims to give us an understanding of ourselves and our present predicament in the light of the past that has brought us to where we are.

A related topic that engaged Tillich's attention in the last period of his life, especially the period following upon his visit to Japan, was the relations between the world religions. Here again, synthesis is not the watchword, though dialogue is to be promoted.

In this dialogue, the Christian will recognize that the religions of

---

[4] For an elaborate account of this and similar discussions see Edward A. Purcell, Jr., *The Crisis of Democratic Theory: Scientific Naturalism and the Problem of Values*. Lexington, Kentucky: The University Press of Kentucky, 1975. The author does not mention Tillich's lectures which contain subtleties and dimensions not taken into account in this book.

East and West confront quasi-religions, covert religions that promote an empty secularism or are demonic forces such as Communism and Fascism. Christianity presents "a long line of Christian universalism affirming revelatory experiences in non-Christian religions, a line starting in the prophets and Jesus, carried on by the Church Fathers, interrupted for centuries . . . , and taken up again in the Renaissance and Enlightenment."

The Bampton Lectures at Columbia University (1961) present a lucid and rich discussion of the present situation and its possibilities, including high points in the history of Christianity's disposition to recognize fundamental values in other religions and also a willingness to accept criticism "from the outside."

In terms of polarities and not of antitheses Tillich gives an account of his own dialogue, especially in Japan, with Buddhists. The dialogue reveals radical contrasts but also affinities between Christianity and Buddhism—contrasts in the conception of history and the human self, and certain affinities in mysticism as an experience of the immediate presence of the transcendent, a possible guard against stagnation and also against secularism. A principal difference is the emphasis on the vertical dimension to the detriment of the horizontal, Buddhism showing little or no concern for social transformation. Tillich, by centering attention on Zen Buddhism, overlooks the socialism today in certain types of Buddhism. He also overlooks the participation of Buddhists and representatives of other religions of the East in the growing organization, World Conference of Religion and Peace. He points out, however, that possibilities of cross-fertilization between West and East are seen in Japan as the question is being raised regarding the philosophical foundations for a viable democracy. In any event, he does not, on the religious level, urge any effort in the direction of synthesis. Yet, recognition of certain affinities should be kept alive, and in every respect dialogue must continue. From conversations with Tillich, I add that he fully recognized that the world situation in our nuclear age will make a search for common cause inevitable.

Yet, Tillich recognized that a philosophy of history centered in the idea of synthesis is impeded at the present juncture. In important respects, then, he would seem to be pressed to the position taken over half a century ago by Troeltsch; that is, to encourage dialogue and cross-fertilization, but also to remain in a pluralism that permits the high religions to stand alongside each other. But he goes beyond Troeltsch and relativism. The religions may not only stand alongside each other claiming polymorphous truth, but in the name of all-inclusiveness may complement each other.

To be sure, embracing, severe crisis can change the ethos and temper of all dialogue. As Tillich warns, the major threat then is likely to resort to "religious" escape or to severely authoritarian "synthesis." In any event, in face of the human predicament, correlation will continue to be the vocation of the Christian philosopher of history who possesses at the same time the expectation and willingness "to learn from the outside."

JAMES LUTHER ADAMS

PROFESSOR EMERITUS
HARVARD DIVINITY SCHOOL
CAMBRIDGE, MASSACHUSETTS

15

Eduard Heimann
TILLICH'S DOCTRINE OF
RELIGIOUS SOCIALISM

15

TILLICH'S DOCTRINE OF RELIGIOUS SOCIALISM

IN three versions of his autobiography, written for different occasions at different times, Tillich has emphasized the central importance in his development which he himself attributes to his
doctrine of religious socialism. Since his autobiography is obviously
not meant to be of anecdotal interest but to describe in personal form
a development representative of his generation, he implicitly claims
central importance for religious socialism in the theonomous system
which his theology is designed to build. At the same time, it probably is his doctrine of religious socialism which, more than any other
chapter of his system, has drawn upon him—not only for political
but for theological reasons—the suspicion of Hegelianism or Gnos-
ticism. What, then, is religious socialism for Tillich?[1]

I

The religious dignity of the secular struggle for social justice and
peace has found powerful expression in Tillich's doctrine of the
kairos. Alarmed by the irrelevance of contemporary ecclesiastical
preaching in a tragic world—the substitution of otherworldly comfort
for the doctrine of universal redemption; the reduction to idealism
and moralism of the call for regeneration, both personal and social;
the faulty individualism and rationalism in psychology and sociology
which know nothing of the objective nature of sin—the doctrine of
the *kairos* was conceived to restore the struggle for justice to its place
in piety without either dragging God down from heaven or raising
man to heaven. Even more than the name of religious socialism itself,

[1] Emil Brunner's critical observations (*The Divine Imperative,* in a number
of notes) seem to me to be well taken, especially those which are directed
against my own attempts in the framework of Tillich's thinking. Brunner's discussion naturally deals only with publications prior to the appearance of his
book in 1932.

which had already been much used before Tillich by Blumhardt, Kutter, and Ragaz, the doctrine of the *kairos* was an assault both on the otherworldliness and individualism of ecclesiastical piety and on the this-worldly complacency and utopianism of the socialist movement. That is, the doctrine is, in the first place, a protest against the pernicious separation of the two which had long been accepted by both sides. The problem is that of the possibility or impossibility of Christian ethics, if this is to include all relations between men rather than a selected group of personal relations.

More specifically, the doctrine of the *kairos* can be understood as a generalization of Tillich's personal experience, upon returning from the First World War, in recognizing participation in the struggle for justice and peace and against a repetition of the catastrophe as his supreme Christian duty, true to the line of thought and action laid down by the great prophets of the Old Testament. If the time was ripe in 1918, so also was it ripe at many other turning points of history, all of them characterized by "the invasion of the temporal by the Eternal," the call to the conditional "to surrender to the unconditional," the moment where "the Eternal judges and transforms the temporal."[2] In other words, these turning points of history reflect the one great *kairos*, in which "the eternal has broken into the temporal," and which, according to Tillich's elaborate doctrine, is the center of history in the sense that it sheds the light of meaningfulness on the whole of history and all its parts, while history without this center would be nothing but an empty, meaningless, irrelevant sequence of facts, as it had appeared to the classical philosophers. It is in this sense that Tillich wants the secondary *kairoi* to be understood: "we must conceive of the *kairos* in universal terms."[3]

Being essential in Tillich's thinking, the doctrine of the *kairos* is closely linked to the other phases of his understanding of history. We mention three of them, whose examination cannot be included in our discussion. First, there is the doctrine of the religious nature of culture, the incarnation of faith in culture, as it were—a good Protestant idea, denying the separate sphere of the sacred because, even if put above the profane, the sacred would in a way be compared and juxtaposed with the profane; whereas it is the sacred which is the life in the profane, for nothing can live outside the sacred power of its origin. Thus Tillich arrives at the brilliant and far-reaching for-

---

[2] "Kairos" (1922), reprinted in *The Protestant Era*, pp. 42, 45, 47.
[3] *Ibid.*, p. 36.

mulation, which no doubt will be among the pillars of his reputation in the future, that culture is the form of the sacred and the sacred the content of culture. We mention this doctrine only as the framework in which the doctrine of religious socialism must be understood, and which makes the paradoxical combination of the two words in the name of "religious socialism" only a special case.

In the second place, the influential doctrine of the demonic needs to be mentioned in the same context, that is, the doctrine of the corruption of the creative impulse in life, in which, nevertheless, the original creative power survives and manifests itself; nothing that lives powerfully can have a different source of its continued vitality, and nothing thus alive can escape demonization. The category of the demonic thus covers the widest field and gives expression to the deep ambiguity of all things human. It is the insight into the demonic structure of every creative impulse which guards religious socialism against the utopianism of secular socialist movements and theories. The secondary *kairoi* always remain in history, they do not reach beyond history.

In the third place, the doctrine of the dialectical movement of heteronomy, autonomy, and theonomy is relevant for an understanding of religious socialism. More specifically, religious socialism is associated with the reaction against an empty and demonized autonomy in a new turn to theonomy, which, far from subjecting autonomy to a new heteronomy, drives the superficial autonomy to its own real depth and meaning which are corroded by its own critical proclivities: "*kairos* is the coming of a new theonomy on the soil of a secularized and emptied autonomous culture."[4] The bourgeois era, the autonomous reaction to late medieval heteronomy, gives way to the new theonomy of socialism.

This is not all that we are taught about the secondary *kairoi*. To this "special sense" of the term *kairos* is added a "general sense" "for the philosopher of history"; namely, "every turning point in history in which the eternal judges and transforms the temporal."[5] This naturally includes those turning points in which theonomy, after hardening into heteronomy, is judged and transformed by the rise of autonomy, which is "not necessarily a turning away from the unconditional," being "the obedient acceptance of the unconditional character of the form, the *logos*, the universal reason in world and

[4] *Ibid.*, p. 47.
[5] *Ibid.*

mind," the acceptance "of the norms of truth and justice, of order and beauty, of personality and community." A number of examples, very different in individual complexion, are produced to illustrate this principle of the "general *kairos*," where "the eternal breaks into the temporal, shaping and transforming it and creating a crisis in the depth of human existence." But religious socialism does not only come under this heading of general *kairos* but under that of special *kairos,* the emergence of new theonomy.

The adjective "religious," in the name of religious socialism, must not be understood, of course, as designed to pull the teeth of socialism and make it respectable. On the contrary, Tillich has always been emphatic on the religious dignity of the proletarian class struggle such as it is. The "vices of the oppressed" (Ferdinand Lassalle), real as they are, can logically and morally be blamed only on the oppressors. The rejection of bourgeois idealism implies that proletarian materialism, the historical protest against bourgeois idealism, is at least parallel to Christian criticism. Materialism rediscovers —and overstresses—the truth neglected and snobbishly despised by idealism, that the human situation cannot be understood apart from its material basis. Collective historical structures dominate the individual mind and shape or thwart its "ideals." Alienation from the center of meaning and of personal life reaches its climax and truly symbolic expression in the proletarian situation, which is the dialectical mirror of bourgeois idealism, making it possible and revealing its insincerity. The deeper the degradation of proletarian man, the more Christian love demands that we identify ourselves with him.[6] If proletarian socialism is defiantly autonomous, this is no reason to reject it; religious socialism drives it to its own theonomous depth.

Religious socialism after the First World War seemed to be that judgment on, and transformation of, the temporal "which created a crisis in the depth of human existence." Whatever the conceptual framework, it is essential to see the doctrine as a reflection in theory of the experience lived through not only by Tillich himself, but by many of his generation in Germany at that time, all of them inspired and transported by the feeling that this was the crisis that could end only in new creation: Germany defeated, humiliated, punished for her saber-rattling overbearingness, shaken and purged and thereby enabled to bring to the world religious socialism, which the vic-

---

[6] See particularly "The Proletarian Situation," published as a brochure in Germany in 1931, now reprinted as Chap. XI of *The Protestant Era.*

torious nations, being all of them members of a disintegrating bourgeois world, needed no less that the defeated, but could not achieve
precisely because of their victory. The spiritual imperialism of the
defeated people, the exuberance of the call to the *kairos,* the sense
of the grace that had come in the form of defeat, to break the old
and pave the way for the new—this is the historical background of
the doctrine.

II

All too soon it became clear that there was no *kairos.* German national leadership in universal religious socialism became national
socialism, and to climax the travesty its theologians—the theologians
of the "German Christians"—borrowed the terminology of the *kairos.*
Ideas, of course, are as little immune to abuse and misquotation as
any other good thing in this ambiguous life. But the question which
here arises, and would arise even without this flagrant abuse, is
whether and to what extent the idea of the *kairos* has been formulated by its author in such a way as to preclude the abuse as much
as humanly possible.

The most specific question here is that of the criterion by which
Tillich himself bars national socialist theology from legitimate use
of his doctrine. He has done that in a brilliant article, "The Totalitarian State and the Claims of the Church," in *Social Research*
(1934). The criterion is found in the "myth." Tillich defines as religious and finding expression in a myth a world view which has the
inherent power of encompassing man's entire being and driving him
on to unconditional self-surrender. Myth is defined as "a real but
conditional force which has been elevated to the rank of absolute
sanctity"; in other passages Tillich used the word "unconditional"
instead of its synonym "absolute." The German nation is "a real but
conditional force" which claims absolute sanctity for its presentation
in the myth of the "mysterious sovereign"; likewise the Marxist
"myth of social justice" and the myths of other totalitarian systems.
The clash with the absolute sanctity of the object of Christian worship is inevitable.

Now the distinction between "myth" and the worship of absolute
sanctity is only a special form of the ultimate and decisive distinction. Religious socialism, as will further be shown below, is distinguished from Marxism in rejecting the Marxist utopia, the claim of
the Marxist myth to absolute sanctity. It would follow that the doc-

trine of the *kairos* is applicable to national socialism if the claim to absolute sanctity of the myth of "the mysterious sovereign," which is "the nation in essence," is given up. That Tillich did not and never could offer this way out is due to the supreme criterion developed in his "Kairos and Logos" (first published in German as early as 1926, reprinted in *The Interpretation of History*). Without the universality and rationality of the *logos* criterion, the dynamic of the *kairos* might be interpreted in a fascist way, as movement for the sake of movement, particularist and irrational; just as without the criterion of the *kairos* the eternity of the *logos*, of the pure form, might be empty. *Kairos*, then, is the form-creating process itself; but as such it stands under the criterion of the *logos*, of justice and truth, before which fascism does not qualify—nay, which fascism explicitly repudiates. If the secondary *kairos* refers to the unique primary *kairos*, from which it is "derived," the *logos* character of the "appearance of the Christ in history" controls and defines the secondary *kairos* and excludes the antirational.

This difficulty clearly solved, there are enough difficulties that remain. They all center in the concept of the secondary *kairos*. The only argument by which this idea is introduced by Tillich is that "we must conceive of the *kairos* in universal terms." Why "must" "we" do this? Once we have done it, we may have foregone the possibility of discerning the primary *kairos*, which Tillich characterizes as unique, from all the derived and secondary *kairoi*. In terms of a mode of reasoning frequently used by Tillich, the uniqueness of the unique *kairos* is destroyed by the existence of secondary *kairoi*; even subordination is a way of juxtaposition. To deny or destroy the absolute distance is Tillich's purpose, but then he gets dangerously close to a vulgar liberal theology, which too easily claims divine inspiration for any human effort.

The definition of these secondary *kairoi*, with its emphasis on self-surrender or on the shaking of existence, seems to add to the diffusion of the meaning. "What happened in the unique *kairos*, the appearance of Jesus as the Christ, that is, as the center of history, may happen in derived form again and again, thus creating minor centers of importance" is perhaps the most puzzling of these statements.[7] Religious quality, furthermore, is claimed for socialism, because religion means life out of the roots of being. This description can be understood in the light of the characterization of bourgeois society as "*in*

[7] *The Protestant Era*, p. xix.

sich ruhende Endlichkeit"; it then means the break-through to the deeper and deepest layer of life. If religion were Christian by definition—a question not to be decided here—the problem would be solved. But this is extremely doubtful in view of the doctrine of the demonic. The deliberate use of the word "religious" to the exclusion of the word "Christian" in all these repeated definitions reinforces the liberalizing tendency and the ensuing vulnerability of the doctrine.

The problem is not only one of principle—which would always imply far-reaching practical consequences, of course—but of immediate practical importance. The brilliant formula according to which socialism is religious in essence although antireligious in conscious intention is a great help in fighting ecclesiastical legalism and phariseeism, but it leaves us with the question of whether atheism is really as good as faith. There are two logical possibilities. Perhaps we are to distinguish an essentially religious atheism from an essentially unreligious one, and subsume modern socialism under the first so as to define religious socialism as the attempt to make the religious essence of atheist socialism explicit; this seems to be the meaning of the doctrine. But can there be anything essentially unreligious? Can man live without believing anything at all? Is not man to be defined as the religious animal? And is not then the real distinction to be made between the different religions in which men believe? Concretely, is not Marxism, however profoundly religious, an antireligion? We shall discuss this question in the next section.

I have tried to distinguish in the following way: "The human soul is so constructed as to require a religion, a doctrine about the meaning and center of life. To provide such a center of meaning is the psychological, subjective function of religion." This function, in other words, is common to all religions and found in all men except complete cynics, if there are such. But "religion reflects, in the imperfect way accessible to the limited mind of man, the structure of the universe and man's place in it. This is religion in the objective sense of the word."[8] The structure of the world and man's place in it are interpreted differently by different religions. Not all of them can be true, or be approximations to the truth. This is what makes it impossible to speak of religion in general, except as a psychological func-

---

[8] Eduard Heimann, *Freedom and Order* (New York: Charles Scribner's Sons, 1947), p. 264. The quotation two sentences above is from the same work, p. 263.—ED.

tion; it is necessary to distinguish between religion and pseudore-ligion.

Tillich, of course, is too discerning to ignore that there are differ-ences in religious dignity between the various "turning-points in his-tory," but he does not introduce any differentation into the doctrine of the *kairos,* as can be seen from the bold and paradoxical conclu-sion to which he is led in his polemic against Karl Barth's concept of crisis.[9] "The appearance of the new is the concrete crisis of the old, the historical judgment against it. The new creation may be worse than the old one which is brought into crisis by it. But in the special historical moment it is *en kairo,* while the old creation is not." If the criticism of Barth is to the effect that his aloofness preaches judg-ment without creation, the critic now seems to bestow the dignity of the creative *kairos* on any and every turning-point in history. But it is difficult to see how this can be done if *kairos* is defined as "the appearance of Jesus as the Christ, that is as the center of history," and the minor *kairoi* as repetitions of this event "in derived form"— whatever that may mean. In other words, where is the *logos* criterion?

The power of origin, of course, is transmoral; and the category of demonization stands ready to explain how that which is *en kairo* can be worse than that which it conquers. The demonic is creative—its power and fascination is in its creativity. But is then *kairos* only an-other name for creation? Was it not to be the name of a new turn to theonomy? And if that which is *en kairo* is worse than the old, what is the Christian answer to its challenge? Is one to support it because it is *en kairo* or to oppose it because it perverts the *kairos* demoni-cally? Tillich himself chose the latter position when the expected socialist revolution assumed the communist form; so the argument from the wave of the future does not suffice to him. And it would not be a way out to argue that what was *en kairo* was not communism but religious socialism; religious socialism did not acquire enough historical power to qualify for the *kairos.* From Tillich's personal decision rather than from his writings an important qualification of his doctrine seems to follow.

Without this qualification there is "a remnant of speculative phil-osophy, of unChristian optimism in the doctrine." It then says that "the new principle, because it is new, must have a creative lease on life before degenerating sooner or later. But human corruption is such that the new creative force may, and does, enter history in com-

[9] "Kairos," in *The Protestant Era,* p. 38.

plete perversion at the very outset."[10] This would reduce the doctrine of the *kairos* to a doctrine of historical power without any special religious distinction beyond the general proposition that everything that there is is God's, and that it asserts itself with the power of its origin.

III

Tillich's religious socialism is inspired by the historical consciousness of the crisis in which bourgeois individualism disintegrates and cries for some kind of socialism, of community restored and justice established, to save the life of society and the soul of man. That socialism is *en kairo* in this sense can be doubted today even less than it could thirty years ago, when Tillich first proclaimed the doctrine. What must remain in doubt is whether socialism, after the terrible bloodletting of its struggle with communism, can have enough power to overcome both communism and individualism. That socialism represents a different and higher principle and stands outside the fateful dialectic of the two has been explained elsewhere.

Tillich has never written anything more beautiful, richer in ideas, more full of life, and more radiant of goodness than the two meditations, German and English, of his *Principles of Religious Socialism.*[11] His vision of the socialist theonomy is immaculate. What is objectionable is his understanding of Marxism and its relationship to religious socialism. The trouble is not in any principle of his thinking, but simply in a faulty appraisal of the facts of the Marxist doctrine. He rightly sees the barrier between religious socialism and Marxism in the latter's utopianism, but wrongly assumes that Marxism can logically be dissociated from it; he does not see that the conflict is not between the utopianism of Marxism, that is, the Marxist vision of the future, and the realism of religious socialism, but between the two doctrines of man. Tillich's error is in associating Marxist utopianism with its doctrine of revolution rather than with its doctrine of man, which, in an atheist system, occupies the place of theology.

In the article of 1934, Tillich has this to say on Soviet Russia. "The motivating force . . . is not the state but the individual and the full development of his collectivistic activities. . . . The totalitarian char-

[10] Quoted from an article of mine in *Christianity and Society,* Fall, 1940, p. 17.

[11] It is most regrettable that these writings have not been republished for a larger audience than the original one, and have been overlooked in the list of Tillich's writings as compiled by his faithful students.

acter of the Soviet state, therefore, is to be understood . . . as the education of an entire continent in communistic enlightment. Every step forward in this educational process means essentially a strengthening of the critical anti-authoritarian and anti-totalitarian forces among the people."[12] The word "critical," which is in the strategic position in this passage, is used by Tillich as almost synonymous with the word "creative," and he believes that the Marxist goal is the creative person. This tallies with his repeated contention that what reacts to capitalism in socialism is the power of origin,[13] that it is the man in the proletarian worker who reacts to the proletarian situation.[14] That is, it tallies with Tillich's own doctrine of man as a creative creature constantly threatened by demonization and thereby prevented from ever establishing the Kingdom of Heaven on earth. That is why Tillich can say in many passages that Marxist utopianism must be rejected, but that Marxism must be retained in its purified form.[15] From this position Tillich is led to the conclusion, again expressed on many occasions, that it is only through "a kind of miracle"[16] that the transition from the present to the utopian future of mankind as envisaged by Marx can be understood, that this transition is "a jump which can in no way be made intelligible from the given reality,"[17] and that hence, the elimination of this accidental element, however painful to atheist psychology, is possible and necessary to restore the scientific purity and religious profundity of Marxism as an essential element in religious socialism.

This, to the present writer, is a very serious misreading of the main scientific message of Marx. All his economic analyses are directed toward the goal of proving that the decline and beginning catastrophe of capitalism is, by the same token, the ascendancy of socialism, in the sense of making socialism the logically necessary effect of that cause. According to Tillich, it is the dehumanization of the proletarian existence under capitalism and the discrediting of capitalism even by its own technical malfunctioning in the economic crisis which become intolerable, and which make socialism a humanly

---

[12] Op. cit., p. 413.

[13] Die sozialistische Entscheidung (Potsdam: Protte, 1933), p. 123.

[14] Ibid., p. 124.

[15] "Marxism and Religious Socialism," The Protestant Era, p. 257; "Kairos," ibid., pp. 37–42; Die sozialistische Entscheidung, pp. 92–126; "Marx and the Prophetic Tradition," Radical Religion (1935), p. 28.

[16] "Marxism and Religious Socialism," The Protestant Era, p. 256.

[17] Die sozialistische Entscheidung, pp. 92, 161.

necessary reaction. According to Marx, it is the institutional transformation of industrial life by capitalism which makes a homogeneous industrial proletarian society its logical result. How it is that
this logically necessary result should become historically real, according to Marx, is a further and even more fundamental question,
to which we shall address ourselves a little later.

It is remarkable that Marx, in a system which makes economic life
the "substructure" of society, should designate the communist revolution exclusively as a "social revolution," that is, a revolution in the
superstructure, never as an economic revolution. This is the key to
the understanding of Marxism. "Ultimately" the economic requirements determine the social structure, at least in the sense that in
case of incompatibility it will be the changing requirements of economic life which would assert themselves. While economic progress
was originally achieved piecemeal, that is, in private properties, each
proprietor experimentally perfecting his own property as he deemed
fittest on the basis of available and growing knowledge, private property finally hits upon large-scale industry and makes this its climactic
achievement and the cause of its undoing. For industry, starting
with the collectivization and degradation of manual labor and
thus revealing private property as the organization of social injustice, finally requires wholesale unification, as it becomes obvious
that piecemeal operation by unconnected decisions misses the increasingly precarious task of interlocking. If the proper method of
short-run integration in the still decentralized earlier industries was
the market, centralized large industries and their expansion can be
balanced and integrated only by unified planning on the basis of unified ownership. Planning, however, is nothing new or revolutionary;
the growth of large enterprise in capitalism is tantamount to the
growth of the principle of planning, which unites and unifies hun-
dreds and thousands of separate activities under one management
and needs only elongation and completion in the transition from
separate privately owned large-scale enterprises to the unified collectively owned industrial system. This is what the early Marxist
literature called the "ripening of conditions" for socialism.

The corresponding "ripening of men" is again the achievement of
capitalist transformation. The workers are collectivized both in their
work and in their private existence; they learn that there is no longer
any such thing, if there ever was, as a private existence, that man is
a member in a big collectivity, and nothing else. Being deprived of

private property, they are freed from that narrowness of mind and distortion of perspective that goes with such a spurious piecemeal stake in what is essentially one huge machinery, which can prosper or go down only as a whole. On the piecemeal basis of private properties the bourgeois had been needed to develop rational methods of production because feudal lords in their prerational existence and prerogatives were incapable of doing this; likewise now the proletarians are needed to unify industrial life in that all-inclusive collective rationality which is its ultimate destination, because the bourgeois mind, shaped by private property, cannot transcend the preliminary industrial state of piecemeal rationality. Only proletarian man is fully rational man.

Among the things which this argument presupposes are not only the superior rationality and productivity of the larger unit of production, but also—just as essential, although much less known—the simplification by technological mechanization of the higher functions both in production and in administration. It is not just an accidental utopian whim but an essential argument if Marx and Lenin predict the leveling of the pyramid of functions, which would enable workers to take turns in various jobs in production and government. Far from meaning only a remedy against monotony in work, this is the guarantee of social and political equality through equality of functions. The state, sociologically speaking, is the bureaucracy; what Marx and Lenin suggest is that no training for higher functions will set one special group of functionaries apart; the "withering away of the state" means the withering away of the special ruling caste of bureaucrats.

Given the premises, all this is logical, and it makes the transition from capitalism to socialism a progress in logic rather than "a kind of miracle." The system of production will be unified by the socially homogeneous people who run it and know that there is no salvation outside this rational unification; there can be no doubt that this will come to pass, because the workers in this act achieve their self-realization, the realization of what may aptly be called their historical nature. That which is logical must happen because man is rational and the workers are the fullest, most highly developed embodiment of reason. This is Marx's doctrine of man, which underpins all of his economic and sociological theories: man is rational and materialistic, that is, the vessel of economic reason, which from the beginnings of primitive undeveloped and unscientific collectivity leads through individualization and alienation to the dialectical achievement of unified, collective rationality. Because man's potential nature is at last actualized in the communist society, therefore the state, the instrument of coercive integration in the period of alienation, loses its function. This, far from being a utopian adornment of a new theonomy, is the test and climax of Marx's anti-Christian doctrine of man, which denies the glory and misery of man's essential freedom.

Tillich mercilessly derides the idea of "a universal mechanism of calculable processes,"[18] and insists that it has nothing to do with the original meaning of dialectic. He is right on both counts, but he is wrong in believing that there can be a "combination of Christianity and dialectical materialism";[19] he is wrong in believing that the Marxian dialectic preserves the original creative meaning of dialectic. Tillich ignores that the end of the dialectic is much more essential in Marx than in Hegel, and that it witnesses to the degradation of the noblest instrument of thought to a mere means for the final establishment of "a universal mechanism of calculable processes." For, according to Marx, man potentially is and dialectically becomes such a mechanism, which on the one hand cannot sin because on the other it can no longer create.

IV

After thirty years of disappointment, Tillich drew the conclusion[20] that this time of ours is no *kairos;* that religious socialism, while right in the long run, is not applicable to the foreseeable future; that this is the period of living in a vacuum, which should be accepted and endured without attempts at premature solutions, and deepened into a "sacred void" of waiting. This is a truly prophetic position:[21] Tillich believes in the coming of the morning, but he does not say that it shall be we who shall emerge into it. The logic and honesty of this acceptance of defeat are unmistakable; whatever romantic enthusiasm may have crept into the original doctrine of the secondary *kairos,* its counterpart in the doctrine of the sacred void cannot be blamed for a lack of Christian sobriety. The only question one may raise is whether, thus waiting for the distant and unknown *kairos* and guarding ourselves against premature solutions, we may not pos-

[18] "Marxism and Religious Socialism," *The Protestant Era,* pp. 257–258.
[19] "The Attack of Dialectical Materialism on Christianity," *The Student World* (Geneva: World Student Christian Association, 1938).
[20] "Beyond Religious Socialism," *The Christian Century,* June 15, 1949.
[21] *Isaiah* 21:11–12.

sibly miss minor assignments of a makeshift nature, which, however uninspiring and preliminary in themselves, could be the earnest and symbol of the coming light in the midst of darkness.

EDUARD HEIMANN

THE GRADUATE FACULTY OF POLITICAL AND SOCIAL SCIENCE
THE NEW SCHOOL FOR SOCIAL RESEARCH
NEW YORK CITY

III

REPLY TO
INTERPRETATION AND CRITICISM
BY PAUL TILLICH

ANSWER

THE preceding essays may be divided into two main types: those in which description prevails over criticism and those in which criticism prevails over description. Of course, description and criticism are present in all of them, for the one is not possible without the other. Nevertheless, the division is important. While the more descriptive papers are useful in introducing the reader to my thought, the more critical essays give the "subject" an opportunity to explain his ideas and to answer the charges brought against him; all this enables the reader to participate in living dialectics—a possibility which fortunately is provided by the special character of this series of books.

The criticisms I have to answer are so varied and valuable that I intend, in spite of the limit of allotted space, to deal with all the main points which have been made. In many cases several contributors have dealt with the same problem, so that my answer refers to them jointly. In order to simplify my answer, I am reducing the many points made to seven main problems which will be discussed in turn.

I. SYSTEM

Some questions, asked from two points of view, concern the formal character of my thought. Certain of the philosophical critics (Randall, Hartshorne, Emmet) are concerned about a lack of precision in definitions or a lack of consistency in assertions. Mr. Randall speaks of a dialectical tension between importance and precision. On the other hand, one theological critic (Roberts) expresses a feeling, voiced by many theologians, that there is a conflict between the existential and the systematic character of every theology, including

374

my own, and that the systematic form threatens to choke the living quality of my thinking. I can only answer with the words I often voice to my students: "Those of you who are most opposed to the system show least patience if they discover inconsistencies in my thought. The way to organize a group of ideas consistently is to put them into systematic form." But there is a real danger felt by those who are uneasy about the system; namely, that its form becomes self-sufficient and determines the content. Should this occur, the truth is molded till it fits the system. This is almost unavoidable in a deductive system, and there are deductive elements in every system. As a corrective against this danger I have begun each of the five parts with an existential analysis of the questions to which the theological concepts are supposed to furnish the answer. I do not doubt that in spite of this method there are passages in my systematic writings in which it is difficult to find the existential roots.

To the opposite criticism, that precision and consistency are sometimes lacking, I have already called attention in the autobiographical chapter to the way in which much of my work has been produced; namely, by way of speeches and essays on special occasions and with different scopes. An explanation, however, is not an excuse, and where precision and consistency are wanting it is a mistake and not an intention. I once said to a Logical Positivist that I would like him to attend my lectures and to raise his finger if something is said that lacks rationality. He answered that he could not accept this task because he would have to raise his finger during the whole lecture. He meant that the material being discussed was not subject to strict canons of logic. I do not believe that this is so, and I do not believe that there is a necessary conflict between the importance of a subject and the possibility of stating it in precise terms. One must, however, distinguish between two kinds of consistency and precision, the definitional and the configurational. There are notions which resist definition and whose meaning can only be shown by their configuration with other notions. The basic ontological concepts fall in this category. The philosophical task with respect to them is not to define them but to illuminate them by showing how they appear in different constellations. This way of "showing" may be precise or lacking in precision, consistent or inconsistent. But the criterion is not the definitional precision and consistency. Miss Emmet, for instance, questions me about the definition of the term "structure." I don't believe that this question can be answered. It is only possible to show the configurations in which the concept appears, and to do this consistently. Perhaps this is not always the case in my frequent use of the word. Mr. Hartshorne points to the distinction between unreserved and unconditional, and my failure to make the distinction. But if in our relation to God no reservation is permitted, does this not presuppose that the surrender is unconditional? For many years I have avoided the term "absolute" with reference to God. "Unconditional" means that the realm of finitude is transcended, "absolute" excludes finitude from a static infinite, a position which I, like Mr. Hartshorne, reject. In such cases precision is not the problem, but conceptual implications.

II. EPISTEMOLOGY

Many contributors ask me about my epistemology, some of them with misgivings about the lack of a developed doctrine of knowledge. Again I answer, first, with a biographical comment: I come from "the age of epistemology," and from a country in which, since the rise of neo-Kantianism, the doctrine of knowledge had completely obscured the question of being. In reaction to this state of affairs I have followed those who made it clear that every epistemology has ontological assumptions, whether hidden or open. And I decided that it is better to have an open, critical, and constructive ontology than a surreptitious one. That in spite of this attitude I did not mean to neglect epistemology is proved by the First Part of my *Systematic Theology*, which contains under the title "Reason and Revelation" my theological epistemology. But more important than these general considerations are the critical questions about special problems of knowing. From the theological side (Thomas) I have been asked whether experience cannot be called a source of systematic theology. I called it a "medium" in order to prevent the individual theologian from looking at his religious experiences and making them directly a basis of his theological thought. If, however, the experience of the theologian is taken as a part of the ecstatic revelatory participation of the Church in the New Being, his experience becomes indirectly a source of systematic theology like that of every Christian who actively and therefore experientially participates in receiving revelation. The distinction between the medium and source of theology has the purpose of preventing the theologian from copying his own experience in his theological system. This answer implies an answer to another theological question concerning my epistemology, namely, the question "whether the revelation is dominantly definable" (Ferré). I first refer to what I said before about definition and configuration. In this sense, no definition of the contents of revelation is possible. But the question aims at something more. It tries to find out whether the Christian revelation can be expressed in definite statements in a series of sharply formulated dogmatic propositions. This, of course, I have to deny even more emphatically. The concept of "receiving revelation" (which is derived from the doctrine of the Spirit in the fourth gospel), my insistence on the correlative and existential character of revelation, the idea of a participation of every new generation in the final revelation: all this forces me to say that the revelation is *not* definitely definable, although the one pole of the revelatory correlation—namely, Jesus as the Christ—is final, definite, and beyond change. But we don't have this pole apart from the correlation and its openness.

From the philosophical side two main questions have been asked, the one about the nature of cognitive participation (Randall), the other about the meaning of objective reason (Emmet). The first question points to a problem which has come only recently into the foreground of my thinking. Therefore I want to confine myself to the following remarks. I believe that in every cognitive relation an element of participation is involved. But it is less obvious in controlling knowledge than in what I have called uniting or receiving knowledge. The latter certainly embraces the knowledge of other personalities as well as their cultural expressions and historical actions. Participating in them, for instance, in a text, is realizing in one's self the meanings communicated, whether in agreement or disagreement. The same is true of the cognition of personalities or historical events. The way of participation shapes the character of the knowledge itself, and is not only an external precondition of it. I gladly accept the pragmatic term "method of intelligence," if it means what the word indicates, "reading between," not from the outside, but in terms of participating and understanding. And I agree with Mr. Hartshorne when he says that in some, however limited way, we participate in everything real, that there are no objects in an absolute sense. The epistemological questions asked by Miss Emmet are due to the semantic difficulty connected with the term "reason." Today reason is usually identified with the cognitive faculty of reason. I extend the meaning of "reason" in two steps. First, I call subjective reason all meaningful functions of the human mind, for example, the ethical and aesthetic as well as the cognitive, not because ethics and aesthetics have also a cognitive element (which they certainly have), but because they create meaningful expressions of the ground of being. The term "shaping" in correlation to "receiving" points to what is usually called "practical" in the sense of Kant's "practical reason." The terms "receiving" and "shaping" are less worn out and nearer to the biological relation of man to his environment than "theoretical" and "practical" are. But beyond this another step has been made which induces me to speak of ontological reason in the sense of *logos*. It is the step from mind to reality, from subjective to objective reason. The relation between them is the basic epistemological problem. But instead of taking sides, I describe four different types: the idealistic, the realistic, the dualistic, and the monistic. Theological considerations do not demand a decision between them, and do not favor any one decision. Theology only presupposes that meaning is rooted in reality itself, and that the world can be recognized because its structures and laws have the essential character of being intelligible. It presupposes, moreover, that the world can be shaped according to the demands of practical and aesthetic reason, because the really real is at the same time the foundation of value. This presupposition underlies all types of solution of the epistemological problem. Even the materialist must explain the possibility that such a thing as a thought, for example, the materialistic theory, can occur in a being called man. No materialistic or, for that matter, idealistic reduction can argue away the correlation between subjective and objective reason, between the functions of the mind and the structure of reality, because every argument is based on the assumption that through the argument a character of the real is grasped. With respect to the terminology, I want to add that the terms "essence" and "existence" are no private property of existentialism, but that they come from the idealistic tradition, although they are used against idealism by the existentialists.

III. SYMBOL

The center of my theological doctrine of knowledge is the concept of symbol, and it is natural that for many years this part of my thought has been under question. An early criticism by Professor Urban of Yale forced me to acknowledge that in order to speak of symbolic knowledge one must delimit the symbolic realm by an unsymbolic statement. I was grateful for this criticism, and under its impact I became suspicious of any attempts to make the concept of symbol all-embracing and therefore meaningless. The unsymbolic statement which implies the necessity of religious symbolism is that God is being itself, and as such beyond the subject-object structure of everything that is.

The most interesting criticism of this point is made by Mr. Hartshorne, who insists in different places on the nonsymbolic meaning of the essential assertions about God. There are some aspects of his profound treatment of this problem, discussion of which would require a large part of this whole volume. I must restrict myself to a methodological remark about statements like these: "Why not say that only God is literally a person?" or that "metaphysical categories essentially refer, with whatever meaning they have, directly to God?" The core of the argument is that what in man is incomplete, indefinite, distorted, is in God complete, truly finite and infinite, perfect. Therefore concepts like person, as well as the other ontological concepts, are derived from their total actualization in God and applied to man. The argument in the doctrine of *analogia entis* is here turned around. I would not deny that since God is being itself, the essential structure of being must be rooted in him, and that the categories have their perfect actualization in him. But just this perfect actualization is their negation as polar or qualitatively distinct categories. In this sense the classical doctrine that the divine attributes are identical in God is correct. Moreover, if this is correct, the symbolic character of every attribute is a necessary consequence. The *via eminentiae*, which is used consistently by Mr. Hartshorne, needs as its balance the *via negationis*, and the unity of both is the *via symbolica*. If one says that God has personality in an eminent, namely, an absolutely perfect sense, one must add that this very assertion implies the negation of personality in God in the sense of "being a person." Both statements together affirm the symbolic character of the attribute "personal" for God. May I add here something which I repeat again and again in my classes. He who says "only a symbol" has completely misunderstood the meaning of symbol; he confuses symbol with sign, and ignores that a genuine symbol participates in the reality of that which it symbolizes.

Mr. Randall seems to agree with the basic tenets of my doctrine of symbols, but he wants to include in symbolism the statement which I call the only nonsymbolic one, namely, that God is being-itself. Being-itself, according to Randall, is a mythological and not a metaphysical concept. Metaphysics has to deal with the structure of being; the latter should not be identified with being-itself. The theologian, even if he happens to be a philosopher, can talk symbolically of being-itself, or being as a whole, or the power of being, or the ground of being. These concepts symbolize different sides of what concerns us ultimately, but they are not philosophical concepts. In answering this argument, I must first concede that the structure of being, although it is rooted in being-as-such, is certainly not identical with it, and should perhaps have been more sharply distinguished from it. Secondly, I agree that "ground" and "power" of being are symbolic notions, in so far as they use elements of being (power, cause) in order to circumscribe being-itself. Thirdly, I accept the criticism that "being as a whole" is an ambiguous phrase, used only as the opposite of "the whole of being." It actually means for me no more than "being-itself." But is "being-itself" symbolic, and therefore theological and not philosophical? I do not think so, because I believe that every philosophy has an implicit or explicit answer to the question: What does the word "is" mean? Even the anti-idealistic philosophers, who fight against the "block universe" of the Platonic-Neoplatonic tradition, have the notion of another, for instance, a dynamic-pluralistic universe. But it is "a universe." They say something about the character of being which logically precedes all statements about that which participates in being. Up to this point philosophy must go, and always does go. If, however, this being-itself becomes a matter of ultimate concern, or, as Randall says, of "aspiration," words like "ground" or "power" of being appear which express both the theoretical and the existential relation of the mind to being-itself. This is the point (to which I often refer) in which I see the basic identity as well as the basic divergence of the philosopher and the theologian. There is no ontological statement about any element in the structure of being which has not the same dual character. An outstanding example in my *Systematic Theology* is the treatment of the categories both as structural elements of being and as expressions of creaturely finitude. This, however, leads from the problem of symbolism to the larger question of the relation between philosophy and theology.

IV. PHILOSOPHY AND THEOLOGY

Most of my critics ask some questions about the relation of philosophy and theology. The preceding answers anticipate parts of any answer to the central problem. But more must be said about this. Miss Emmet suggests that in order to know what philosophy is one should look at what the philosophers are doing. But under the title of "philosophy" they may do things which other philosophers would call theological or something else. Mr. Thomas speaks of a relative, not an absolute difference between philosophy and theology. But the question is whether there is a real or essential difference which can be described.

There are many motives in my thought which point to a basic identity of theology and philosophy. Primary among these is the doctrine of the mutual immanence of religion and culture. I could say that in a perfect theonomy the philosophical analysis of the structure of being-in-itself would be united with a theological expression of the meaning of being for us. The idea of theonomy requires such an eschatological vision. Because the *"eschaton,"* moreover, according to my teaching, is real not only in terms of the future, but also in terms of the present, the eschatological unity of theology and philosophy must also have a present actuality, however fragmentarily. This unity must, as Mr. Thomas argues, be present in the way the method of correlation develops the existential question, to which revelation is the answer. It must, as the same author emphasizes, be present in a philosopher who has discovered in the event of Christ the entrance to the universal *logos*. It must, as Miss Emmet requires, make possible a philosophical doctrine of God. It accounts, moreover, for the fact that she stresses the view that philosophy does not deal so much with being-as-such, as with the meaning of being in a concrete situation. It must, as Mr. Roberts desires, support a Christian, or at least religious existentialism. The mutual immanence of theology and philosophy, though never perfect, is a partially fulfilled eschatology. It is, in my own terminology, a state of theonomy. I am greatly indebted to all those mentioned, because they strengthen my hand in the discussion with those who are suspicious of any kind of philosophical theology or theological philosophy. But all this cannot prevent us from establishing a qualitative difference between philosophy and theology—a difference which must be stated sharply and clearly. In spite of the theonomous union between religion and culture, these two do not lie on the same level. Religion is the depth-dimension of culture, and theology points to this dimension not only in philosophy, but also in art and politics (which makes neither of them a theological discipline, as Mr. Randall supposes). Unity does not exclude definitory distinction. And this distinction between the two becomes important even if the unity is real only in a fragmentary way.

This answer is also valid in relation to the scientific elements in theology to which Mr. Horton points. Here, again, I would agree that the complete union between science (in the larger sense of the word) and theology is implied in the *eschaton,* but that the actual unity is partial and fragmentary. A world of conflicts would have been avoided if theology had been prevented from interfering with science on the scientific level, and if science had been prevented from interfering with theology on the theological level. Only after the difference of the dimensions has been acknowledged can a union of science and theology take place—a union in which the religious dimension, the dimension of "depth" shines through the dimension of methodological cognition. It is also a union in which the symbols of transparent depth open the eyes for cognitive problems and their methodological treatment. In view of this essential interdependence between theology and science, I have taken, for example, historical research, sociological analysis, and therapeutic psychology more seriously than traditional theology usually has.

I am asked whether philosophy does not have arguments of its own which solve the antinomies of existential reason without the "Christian hypothesis" (Randall), and whether philosophy has not arguments of its own against atheism (Roberts). To both questions I answer in the affirmative, in so far as philosophy is theonomous, using "ecstatic" and not calculating reason. Kant's moral argument for the existence of God, for instance, is, as a series of conclusions, as weak as the theoretical arguments he has destroyed. As an exhibition, however, of the point at which something unconditional (the moral imperative) breaks into the context of the conditioned, it is a piece of theonomous philosophy. In the same way the antinomies of existential reason can be solved by ecstatic reason, that is, in revelation. The "Beloved Community" described by Royce is not an abstract conceptualized ideal in which the conflicting elements of human existence are logically balanced; it is a reality in which existential conflicts are fragmentarily overcome by love. This reality is the New Being, socially embodied, that is, the Christian Church. Christianity can be called a hypothesis (Randall) only in the large sense that the Christian faith includes an element of risk, and that it is subject to the continuous test of the power to overcome existential estrangement—including the estrangement between philosophy and theology. But it is not a hypothesis in the sense of a scientific theory which can be tested by detached experiments.

From the theological side Mr. Niebuhr has made some critical remarks about the relation of theology and philosophy. He correctly states that faith in the Bible is not primarily "ecstasy of reason" but an apprehension and recognition of the divine as the ultimate source and end of life, "made possible by the destruction of the idolatry of the self." But I never intended to define faith by "ecstasy of reason." I have described faith (and shall describe it more fully in connection with the doctrine of the Spirit) as the state of being grasped by the ground and abyss of being and meaning. Niebuhr uses the words "apprehension and recognition," which belong to the cognitive function of reason. If they function in the ordinary way in the act of faith, faith on its cognitive side is an act of reason, made possible by an ethical act of self-negation. But this is not Mr. Niebuhr's opinion, because repentance and self-negation are only possible by faith. The cognitive side in faith is an element within a larger whole, and it is neither an act of ordinary reason nor a surrender of reason; it is "apprehension," but it is reason in self-transcendence or ecstatic reason. In another place Mr. Niebuhr tries to protect the realm of acts, selves, wills, and the like—in short, the personal-historical realm—against ontological analysis, and to restrict their expression to the dramatic-poetic form. If this were so, life and thought would be separated in such a way that theology should abdicate. Again, Mr. Niebuhr can not mean this. He is afraid that the analysis of ontological structures determines the drama of history in a deterministic fashion, thus depriving it of freedom, chance, and responsibility. But ontological analysis is just as open for the element of freedom as it is for that of destiny, for the characteristics of personality and history as well as for those of life and nature, for the meaning of symbols and images as well as for that of concepts and ideas. If, in full agreement with Mr. Niebuhr,

I define man as "finite freedom," is it preposterous to ask for the meaning of these two words, for their standing within the whole of being, for their ontological character? And if it is justified, one should not point to the danger of ontology as such, but to special mistakes of a special ontology.

V. GOD

The discussion about philosophy and theology comes down to concrete problems in the criticisms of my doctrines of God and of man. Mr. Hartshorne gives most of his space to a confrontation of his and my doctrines of God. It would be very tempting for me to answer his questions as fully as he has elaborated them. Because this is impossible, and because at the conclusion of his paper he summarizes by means of eight points, I shall try to comment on these as briefly as possible. The first two points deal with the question of the symbolic and the literal meaning of concepts applied to God. They are partly answered in the discussion of symbolism. I wish to add here, however, something that at the same time answers Mr. Hartshorne's third question about process-itself as a better characterization of God than being-itself. I am not convinced by any of the criticisms of my use of the phrase *esse ipsum* as the first (certainly not the last) assertion about God, that it can be omitted or replaced by anything else. Being as the negation of possible non-being is the basic cognitive position, which precedes in logical dignity every characterization of being. I am not disinclined to accept the process-character of being-itself. On the contrary, the idea of a living God seems to me to contradict the Aristotelian-Thomistic doctrine of God as pure actuality. But before this can be said, being *qua* being must have been posited. If I assert that potentiality as well as actuality is in God, I add that these are not separated in God as in finite beings. If this is true, the two terms are not used in the sense in which they are created through experience and reflection, but they are used analogically or symbolically. The same is true of essence and existence. Mr. Hartshorne agrees that God does not exist factually. But as long as a discussion goes on about the existence or nonexistence of God, his factual existence is affirmed or denied. In this sense I call the assertion of the existence of God blasphemous. If existence in God is thought of as united with his essence, I could apply this concept to the divine life. I should do so, however, analogically or symbolically. To the fourth question I can only answer by pointing to my development of the concept of eternity as the dynamic unity of the temporal modes and moments which are separated in empirical time. Since I speak of the positing and the negating of the finite within the process of the divine life, I must also include the positing—and negating—of time as a category of finitude. But the negating side in both cases makes the positing side symbolic. I really do not know what past and future are in the ground of being. I only know that they are rooted in it. The next three questions deal with the concepts of the unconditioned, absolute, infinite, and the like, in their application to God, and with the possibility of speaking of a "finitude" which is literally "unique to God." Actually, I do not use the phrases, "the absolute," or "the infinite," or "the unconditioned" for God, except in some early writings. But I do speak of "unconditional" or "ultimate" or "infinite concern," thus making those concepts "existential" in the very beginning. To say "unreserved" for "unconditional," as Mr. Hartshorne recommends, is no help. But Mr. Hartshorne's resistance against the term "unconditional" follows from his doctrine that creaturely contingency conditions God in some respect and makes him literally finite in relation to it. My resistance against this doctrine (not against the positing of the finite in God) is rooted in the overwhelming impression of the divine majesty as witnessed by classical religion. This makes any structural dependence of God on something contingent impossible for me to accept. The justified religious interest in Mr. Hartshorne's concept of the divine finitude is much better safeguarded by Luther's symbolic statement that the intolerable "naked absolute" makes himself small for us in Christ. In such a formula God's unconditional freedom is safeguarded in spite of his participation in finitude. In spite of these differences, I feel a close affinity to the philosophy of religion represented by Mr. Hartshorne, perhaps because of common intellectual antecedents, for example, Bergson, Schelling, and Böhme.

The positing of the nonbeing, and therefore of the finite in the process of the divine life, is not as baffling as a doctrine which posits evil as an ontological reality outside God (Roberts). First of all, finitude is not evil, but the potentiality of evil. Secondly, if the finite is an element in the divine life, the divine freedom, his aseity is preserved, which is not the case in an ontological dualism, for example, between God and a resisting matter. The mystery of life, which precedes every thought, is not removed by any of the solutions, but the one is more compatible with other motives of religious thought than is the other. Miss Emmet calls the "ground of being" an unhappy metaphor because she understands ground in the sense of reason or cause. If this were meant, "ground of being" would be tautology, as she suggests; for there is no other cause or reason of being than being-itself. But "ground of being" means the creative source of everything that has being. And if this is the meaning of the phrase, sinister connotations in the sense of Schopenhauer are excluded. They are included, however, as a possibility in the metaphor "abyss of being," the depth in which everything finite disappears. Religiously speaking, this is God as "burning fire."

To Mr. Thomas's request to think of God as *a* being, not alongside but above the other beings, I answer that logically the "above" is one direction of the "alongside," except it means that which is the ground and abyss of all beings. Then, however, it is hard to call it *a* being. Certainly in the I-Thou relationship of man and *his* God, God becomes *a* being, *a* person, *a* "thou" for us. But all this is on the ground of his character as being-itself—an insight which is important for the meaning of prayer and meditation.

A fundamental difference seems to exist between Mr. Ferré and myself about the supranaturalistic interpretation of Christianity. Mr. Ferré is aware that I have fought supranaturalism from my early writings on, not in order to support naturalism but because I tried to overcome the alternative between naturalism and supranaturalism. I still hold emphatically to this position which could be called self-transcending or ecstatic naturalism. Mr. Ferré is afraid that this attitude makes my idea of God transcendental instead of transcendent, that it prevents a genuine doctrine of incarnation, that it implies the negation of personal immortality, that it evaporates the independent character of the Church, that it denies a realistic eschatology. He is right if "transcendent" means the establishment of a "world" behind the world, if "incarnation" means the descent of a divine being from a heavenly place and its metamorphosis into a human being, if "immortality" is understood as the continuation of temporal existence after death, if the latent church within cultures and religions is denied, if a dramatic end-catastrophe some time in the future is affirmed. All this is a supranaturalism against which my theology stands. But I believe that this kind of thought is a rationalization of the Biblical symbols into an objectifying description of physical-supraphysical processes. I believe that not those who understand the mythical character of these concepts but those who take them literally are the rationalists of our time. This is the reason I must continue my fight against any supranaturalistic theology.

VI. MAN

Mr. Randall asks a very illuminating methodological question about man as the entering door to ontology. He asks whether it is man in isolation or man in encounter with whom we start. I definitely mean the second, as my foundation of the basic ontological polarity, the self-world correlation, shows. In the light of such questions I cannot suppress some regret that world history combined with physical limitations have prevented me from developing a "philosophy of encounter" whose rudimentary elaboration was presented in a Frankfurt lecture course. Yet it is not adequate to call such a method naturalistic, as Mr. Randall wishes. He also asks why I do not discuss the biological ascendancy of man, a question which requires two answers. The first is negative, pointing to the fact that, while dealing with ontological structures, I nowhere refer in my system to results of empirical research. The second answer is positive, expounding the continuous references to subhuman nature in the section on the polarities of being. I could also mention the fourth part of my system, "Life and the Spirit," where a biological side of the life process has been dealt with more fully.

But the main criticism of my doctrine of man comes from the theological side and is summed up in the reproach that I identify finitude and evil. This surprises me not only when it is stated without restriction, as by Mr. Daubney, but also when it is asserted more cautiously and as a matter of implication, as by Mr. Roberts and Mr. Niebuhr. My surprise is based on the fact that not only is my whole system constructed in view of the distinction between essential being (discussed in the section on "Being and God") and disrupted existence (discussed in the section on "Existence and the Christ"), but that several passages express my intention sharply and directly. Yet there are two things which make the criticism understandable. First of all, it is my assertion that the fulfillment of creation and the beginning of the fall are, though logically different, ontologically the same. Perhaps I should have said "actualization" instead of "fulfillment." "Fulfillment" seems to connote that an unfinished creation has been finished in an evil way. This, of course, is not my idea. The fall is the work of finite freedom, but it happened universally in everything finite, and therefore unavoidably (a word used by Mr. Niebuhr for the same purpose). The universality and consequently the unavoidability of the fall is not derived from "ontological speculation," but from a realistic observation of man, his heart, and his history. We find the observation in the Bible as well as in Augustine, Luther, Calvin, Barth, and Niebuhr. We find it outside the Biblical literature in Greek tragedy and in modern existentialism and in many other places. Perhaps Mr. Niebuhr will say: "So it is, but don't try to explain it ontologically; it is a mystery and can be explained only in the dramatic-paradoxical form of the doctrine of original sin. Even the symbols of a transcendent fall are not helpful, nor are they Biblical." To this I have to say that neither in Genesis, nor in Job, nor in the prophets, is the Bible without indications that cosmic powers, the serpent, the beast of the chaos, Satan, demonic-angelic figures, the irrational forces of nature are partly responsible for the human predicament. Further, I think that theology should take seriously the fact that some of the greatest philosophers (Plato, Origen, Kant, Schelling), in spite of their belief in the power of reason, have been driven to the myth of the transcendent fall. It is not "speculation" (today a disparaging word) but their impression of the radical and universal nature of evil which drove them to conceive of a myth in which both human freedom and the tragic nature of existence are asserted —though not explained—in terms of structural necessity. Theology should take this especially seriously if it dismisses a literal interpretation of the Genesis story. And theology should not be afraid of losing by such ideas its dramatic concreteness and its moral power. If words like "universal sinfulness" have any meaning, they point to something in finite freedom which makes the fall unavoidable, though something for which we are responsible at the same time. The "supralapsarian" Calvinists were not afraid of asserting that God had foreordered Adam's fall. This means that if God creates, he creates that which will turn against him. This is dramatic language, but it demands a theological interpretation which itself is not dramatic but ontological. The second reason for the theological criticism of my doctrine of man is a certain ambiguity in the use of the term "separation." Separation can mean individualization; in this sense it is an element in the structure of being, and is rooted in the divine life: it is one condition of love—the other being reunion. Separation as individualization is good, it is the presupposition of all actual goodness. But separation is also used for the estrangement and the conflict between God and man, between man and man, and even within man. Taken in this sense, separation is sin and reunion is salvation. Separation from God in an ontological sense is annihilation, as Mr. Daubney correctly states. I intend to use the term "separation" in the first sense and to use for separation in the second sense the term "estrangement." I hope that the discussion has made it clear (except to a complete Pelagian) that I do not identify finitude and evil, explicitly or implicitly.

Another point about my doctrine of man is raised by Mr. Ferré. He rightly says that he does not find in my theology a doctrine of sanctification and sainthood. I cannot help agreeing with him in this respect. A doctrine of "the Christian" as the counterpart to the doctrine of "the Church" is not presented by me, not even in the *Propositions*. This cannot be excused by my Lutheran, anti-Pietistic background, nor by external difficulties, nor by the need I feel to relate such a doctrine to the basic insights of depth-psychology. In a theology whose normative idea is the New Being, the individual as well as the social embodiment of the New Being must be discussed, and I intend to do so in the section entitled "Life and the Spirit" of the second volume of my *Systematic Theology*.

At this point I want to add a few remarks about the position of ethics in my thinking. Mr. Thomas questions the wisdom of considering ethics as an element of the theological system instead of giving it independent standing. But all his arguments are arguments of expediency. Essentially, my thesis is that Christian ethics is a description of man in his created goodness, his disrupted existence, and his participation in the New Being—all this from the point of view of his action toward other beings, himself, and the ground and aim of his being. If this is done, concrete application of it to the ever changing problems of ethical existence are as much needed as concrete applications of the apologetic principles to the ever changing apologetic scene. In this work theological ethics and theological apologetics receive an independent function. But the elaboration of the principles is implicit in the theological system.

Mr. Daubney and Mr. Siegfried are under the impression that the horizontal line of ethics is neglected for the sake of the vertical. I certainly follow the line of Augustine and the Reformation: that unbelief, namely, estrangement from God, is the root of sin. But my whole social ethics, as expressed chiefly in my writings on religious socialism, emphasizes the horizontal line in terms of the Kingdom of God, fighting *in* history, or "the religious obligation" in balance with the "religious reservation." The problem of Protestant action (in spite of the critical guardianship of the Protestant principle) to which Mr. Siegfried refers lies in the background of almost every section of my book *The Protestant Era.* He is, however, right when he states that my critique of an extreme Protestant-Humanist personalism has caused me to neglect a positive analysis and valuation of personality. In the section on the New Being as personality in the second volume of my *Systematic Theology* I intend to deal fully with this question. (See my answer to Mr. Ferré.)

VII. HISTORY

The last questions lead into the realm of problems which I want to discuss under the heading of "history." The central idea of my interpretation of history is that of the *kairos.* Its difficulties are discussed by Mr. Siegfried, who, however, believes that the doctrines of the New Being and of love essentially solve the problem, while Mr. Heimann thinks that these difficulties have rightly induced me to give up the whole doctrine. To this I must answer as follows: First, the *kairos*-doctrine was conceived in a situation in which it was necessary to find a way between socialist utopianism and Lutheran transcendentalism. The "present moment" had to be interpreted as the bearer of a demand and a promise, both breaking from eternity into time. And the "present moment" was taken as the concrete moment in history, in which we, in a special period, in a special country, experienced promise and demand. I believe that this is just the way in which the prophets in Israel and the prophetic minds in the Church, and sometimes outside the Church, experienced their special historical vocation. That is what we did in the years after the First World War, and this experience was expressed in the symbol of the *kairos.* Like those who interpret "the signs of the time," we always were both confirmed and refuted. We were refuted with respect to the immediate actuality of the social and spiritual transformation we envisaged, we were confirmed with respect to the basic criticisms of the old and the basic demands for the new period. When, after the Second World War, I spoke of a "void" which we should experience as "a sacred void" by taking it patiently upon ourselves, this also was an interpretation of the present moment in the light of the eternal; it also was a proclamation of a *kairos*. Only this *kairos* was not a *kairos* calling for transforming action, but for waiting in a vacuum. It is, of course, easier to avoid every remnant of utopianism and every risk of being disavowed in one's interpretation of the present moment by giving up the idea of the concrete *kairos*, by seeing the relation of the eternal to the temporal as an ever equal crisis, with the so-called dialectical theology, or by accepting *one kairos* only, the appearance of Christ as the center of history, in agreement with supranaturalistic Lutheranism. I myself am convinced that the prophetic spirit will not leave the churches and mankind forever, and that the venturing judgment of a concrete historical moment, in spite of its unavoidable errors, will prove more creative than an ecclesiastical conservatism which clings tenaciously to the past. Of course, the past in terms of the central *kairos* and the *logos* made manifest in it is the criterion of every *kairos* in our personal as well as in our historical existence. But the universal criterion cannot replace the daring interpretation of the present moment.

Mr. Heimann criticizes the religious-socialist attempt to combine Christianity and Marxism. Marx exegesis has in common with the exegesis of the Bible or that of the American constitution the fact that it is open to many contradictory interpretations. It is impossible to go into the question in this place. In my autobiography I have indicated what I myself, and I think most of us, have gotten out of Marx, especially his early writings. For the fact that the dialectical materialism of Marx was later distorted into a metaphysical materialism he is certainly not without some responsibility, although it is not *his* doctrine. His revolutionary appeal to the workers, his moral aggression against the bourgeoise, the prophetic wrath at the self-estrangement of man prove that he knew that institutional changes not only determine, but also are determined by, human actions. And this is genuine dialectics, as it appears in all moments when the message that "the time is ripe" and that "the moment is at hand" has produced moral decisions and political activities of a most passionate and creative character. Consciousness of historical and personal predestination often has enhanced moral activity more than the emphasis on undetermined freedom. In any case, it is not possible to put Marx on the deterministic side and Christianity on the indeterministic.

The question of whether there is an atheistic culture, asked by

Mr. Heimann, is difficult to answer without giving a complete philosophy of religion. My first answer would be No; because no human mind is entirely without an ultimate concern and some practical and theoretical expressions of it, and religion means "being ultimately concerned." There is, however, as he rightly implies, a difference between a culture which is theonomous, determined by direct and intentional expressions of an ultimate concern, and a culture which oscillates between an empty autonomy and a suppressive heteronomy. It was the vision of a new theonomy which brought us to religious socialism and the idea of the *kairos*.

The eight questions asked by Mr. Adams will, as he himself indicates, be given only brief answers.

1. To his question, "If God is beyond essence and existence, how can he be related to history?" I reply that the phrase "beyond essence and existence" does not mean *without* it. It does mean not being determined by it in the way in which finite beings are determined. (See also my answer to Mr. Hartshorne.)

2. To his question, "If the 'theological circle' is based on a mystical intuition, how can a verification take place except through empirical analysis?" I answer in terms of another question. If the basic theological decision (which is a matter of destiny and freedom together) is to become an object of empirical verification, in which kind of decision is the method of empirical verification rooted—especially if it unavoidably includes value judgments?

3. To his question concerning historical relativism, I answer that it belongs to man's existential finitude that he cannot escape historical relativism theoretically. He can only take the risk and the danger of a decision for that which is for him the absolute in history; that is what I term the "center of history."

4. To the question as to whether or not synthesis is the end of dialectics, I reply that in space and time no synthesis is final. Every fragmentary theonomy carries in itself the tension between a fragmentary autonomy and heteronomy, thus driving beyond itself.

5. My only comment to his fifth question concerning the historical Jesus is to refer to the five points in Mr. Mollegen's article.

6. Mr. Adams also asks, "If theonomy includes a special social organization, is not the voluntary association of decisive importance?" Yes, I agree that it is, but I believe that I, more clearly than Mr. Adams and some of my Quaker friends, see the tragic necessity of centralization in later industrial society.

7. When he asks how one can know about the fulfillment of history which transcends history, I answer: In the same way in which one can know about God, through his presence as the ground and goal of being in everything that has being, and through the possibility of an encounter with him as the power of fulfillment in everything that is.

8. Mr. Adams writes, "If the kingdom of God consists in the 'unity, totality, and purity' of meaning beyond history, how can history influence the Kingdom of God and even God himself?" I reply that the sentence that nothing is in the *eschaton* that is not in history gives history an influence on the character of the Kingdom of God which contradicts radically the static idea of the Kingdom of God in supranaturalism and neo-orthodoxy. Even the symbol of the "suffering god" is accepted, though with restrictions, in my systematic theology!

The universal *kairos* is the appearance of Jesus as the Christ in the "center of history." Therefore, it is understandable that the problem of the historical Jesus has been raised from several sides (Siegfried, Emmet, Ferré, Mollegen). An answer to this question would completely trespass the frame of this chapter, but an answer by myself has been made unnecessary by the contribution of Mr. Mollegen, who has presented a clear exposition of the topic of the historical Jesus. This subject is dealt with by him under five headings to which the reader is referred, and this explication by Mr. Mollegen has, I confess, a clarity which I have myself found it very difficult to achieve.

Mr. Ferré has presented my doctrine of the Church without special criticism, but he has asked about the whole of my system, including the doctrine of the Church, the question of its supranaturalistic character. To this I have already made answer. There is, however, one formulation, to which I must take exception: Mr. Ferré says that the Church "*is*" the Kingdom of God. This is not even Augustinian (and far less is it Reformation) theology. The Church represents the Kingdom in history, but the Kingdom transcends the Church not only in terms of an unambiguous perfection, but also in terms of an all-embracing universality. When Church and Kingdom are identified, Roman Catholic aspirations are not far away. Mr. Daubney suggests and elaborates a "sacramental economy" as a necessary complement to my doctrine of the Church. It is a kind of temptation for me to follow him in this task, but I am afraid I cannot follow him as a systematic theologian. I still believe what I said in my *Propositions* about the Church: the concrete organization of the sacramental symbols is a matter of tradition and a problem of determining their adequacy to the present situation. It cannot be derived systematically from the nature of the New Being in Jesus as the Christ.

Not all questions that have been posed by my critics are discussed in my Reply. Some are answered implicitly, some fuller answers must be postponed for further writing, not only to the second volume of the *Systematic Theology* but also to the Terry Lectures on *The Courage to Be*. The criticisms I have received in this book are extremely valuable and helpful as I continue my work. This is true whether the criticisms are presented as direct questions or are presented as implicit in the way in which my thought is interpreted. I can only conclude, therefore, with an expression of deep gratitude to every contributor.

PAUL TILLICH

UNION THEOLOGICAL SEMINARY
NEW YORK CITY

IV

BIBLIOGRAPHY OF THE
PUBLICATIONS OF PAUL TILLICH*

Tillich's collected works are published in fourteen volumes under the title *Gesammelte Werke* (Stuttgart: Evangelisches Verlagswerk, 1959–1975). To date, there are five supplementary volumes to the collected works, 1971–1980.

1909

Über die Einsamkeit. Handwritten manuscript. (XIII: 64–68.)

1910

Die religionsgeschichtliche Konstruktion in Schellings positiver Philosophie, ihre Voraussetzungen und Prinzipien. Breslau: Fleischmann, 1910. English translation (ET)—Lewisburg, Pa.: Bucknell University Press, 1974.

1912

Mystik und Schuldbewusstsein in Schellings philosophischer Entwicklung. Beiträge zur Förderung christlicher Theologie, XVI, No. I. Gütersloh: Bertelsmann, 1912. ET—Lewisburg, Pa.: Bucknell University Press, 1974. (I: 13–108.)
"Selbstanzeiger." *Kant-Studien* 17 (1912): 306–307.

---

* This bibliography was prepared by Jack Mouw under the supervision of Robert P. Scharlemann. Except for book reviews, it includes every known publication, listed according to first appearance. For those works also published in the *Gesammelte Werke*, volume and page numbers are printed in parentheses after the entry in this Bibliography. The most complete bibliography, including a list of Tillich's unpublished materials, is to be found in *G.W.*, vol. 14.

1913

Kirchliche Apologetik. Handwritten manuscript. (XIII: 34–63.)

1914/15

Bericht über die Tätigkeit als Feldgeistlicher an den Herrn Feldpropst des IV. Armeekorps. Handwritten manuscript. (XIII: 71–79.)

1915

Der Begriff des Übernatürlichen, sein dialektischer Charakter und das Prinzip der Identität, dargestellt an der supranaturalistischen Theologie vor Schleiermacher. Königsberg: Madrasch, 1915.

1919

Der Sozialismus als Kirchenfrage. Leitsätze von Paul Tillich und Carl Richard Wegener. Berlin: Gracht, 1919. (XIII: 80–82.)

"Über die Idee einer Theologie del Kultur." In *Religionsphilosophie der Kultur.* Berlin: Reuther & Reichard, 1919. (IX: 13–31.) ET—In *What is Religion?* Edited by James L. Adams. New York: Harper & Row, 1969.

"Christentum und Sozialismus." *Das neue Deutschland* VIII, 6 (Dec. 15, 1919): 106–110. (II: 21–28.)

"Revolution und Kirche." *Das neue Deutschland* VIII (July, 1919): 394–397.

1920

"Die Jugend und die Religion." In *Die freideutsche Jugendbewegung.* Ursprung und Zukunft. Edited by Adolf Grabowsky and Walter Koch. Gotha: F.A. Perthes, 1920.

"Masse und Persönlichkeit." In *Die Verhandlungen des 27. und 28. Evangelisch-Sozialen Kongresses.* Edited by W. Schneemelcher. Göttingen: Vandenhoeck & Ruprecht, 1920. (II: 36–56.)

1921

"Masse und Religion." *Blätter für Religiösen Sozialismus* II (1921): 1–3, 5–7, 9–12. (II: 70–90.)

"Die Theologie als Wissenschaft." *Vossische Zeitung* 512 (Oct. 30, 1921): 2–3.

"Religiöser Stil und religiöser Stoff in der bildenden Kunst." *Das neue Deutschland* X (1921): 151–158. (IX: 312–323.)

1922

Masse und Geist. Studien zur Philosophie der Masse. Berlin, Frankfurt: Verlag der Arbeitsgemeinschaft, 1922. (II: 35–90.)

"Albrecht Ritschl. Zu seinem hundertsten Geburtstag." *Theologische Blätter* I, 3 (March, 1922): 49–54. (XII: 151–158.)

"Anthroposophie und Theologie. Das theologische Ergebnis des Berliner anthroposophischen Hochschulkursus." *Theologische Blätter* I, 4 (April, 1922): 86–88.

"Religiöse Krisis." *Vivos voco* II, 11 (April-May, 1922): 616–621. (XIII: 86–91.)

"Kairos." *Die Tat* XIV, 5 (August, 1922): 330–350. (VI: 9–28.) ET— In *The Protestant Era*, edited by James L. Adams. Chicago: The University of Chicago Press, 1948.

"Die Überwindung des Religionsbegriffs in der Religionsphilosophie." *Kant-Studien* 27 (1922): 446–469. (I: 367–388.) ET—In *What is Religion?* Edited by James L. Adams. New York: Harper and Row, 1969.

"Gotteslästerung." *Vossische Zeitung* 485 (1922): 1–2. (XIII: 140–142.)

"Renaissance und Reformation. Zur Einführung in die Bibliothek Warburg." *Theologische Blätter* I, 12 (December, 1922): 265–267. (XIII: 137–140.)

"Zur Klärung der religiösen Grundhaltung." *Blätter für Religiösen Sozialismus* III, 12 (December, 1922): 46–48.

1923

Das System der Wissenschaften nach Gegenständen und Methoden. Ein Entwurf. Göttingen: Vandenhoeck & Ruprecht, 1923. ET—Lewisburg, Pa.: Bucknell University Press, 1981. (I: 111–293.)

"Die Kategorie des 'Heiligen' bei Rudolf Otto." *Theologische Blätter* II, 1 (January, 1923): 11–12. (XII: 184–186.)

"Ernst Troeltsch." *Vossische Zeitung* 58 (February 3, 1923): 2–3. (XII: 175–178.)

"Grundlinien des religiösen Sozialismus. Ein systematischer Entwurf." *Blätter für Religiösen Sozialismus* IV, 8–10 (1923): 1–24. (II: 91–119.) ET—In *Political Expectation*, edited by James L. Adams. New York: Harper and Row, 1971.

"Kritisches und positives Paradox. Eine Auseinandersetzung mit Karl Barth und Friedrich Gogarten." *Theologische Blätter* II, 11 (November,

1923): 263–269. (VII: 216–225.) ET–In *The Beginnings of Dialectical Theology*, edited by James M. Robinson. Richmond, VA.: John Knox Press, 1968.

"Antwort." *Theologische Blätter* II, 12 (December, 1923): 296–299. (VII: 240–243.) ET–In *The Beginnings of Dialectical Theology*, edited by James M. Robinson. Richmond, VA.: John Knox Press, 1968.

1924

Kirche und Kultur. Tübingen: J.C.B. Mohr, 1924. (IX: 32–46.) ET–In *The Interpretation of History.* New York: Scribner, 1936.

"Rechtfertigung und Zweifel." In *Vorträge der theologischen Konferenz zu Giessen.* Giessen: Töpelmann, 1924. (VIII: 85–100.)

"Erwiderung." *Wingolfs-Blätter* 53, 2 (February 21, 1924): 27.

"Christentum, Sozialismus und Nationalismus." *Wingolfs-Blätter* 53 (1924): 78–80. (XIII: 161–166.)

"Jugendbewegung lnd Religion." *Werkland* IV, 1 (April, 1924): 61–64. (XIII: 130–133.)

"Antwort." *Blätter für Religiösen Sozialismus* V, 5/6 (1924): 18–22.

"Die religiöse und philosophische Weiterbildung des Sozialismus." *Blätter für Religiösen Sozialismus* V, 5/6 (1924): 26–30. (II: 121–131.)

"Ernst Troeltsch. Versuch einer geistesgeschichtlichen Würdigung." *Kant-Studien* XXIX, 3/4 (1924): 351–358. (XII: 166–174.)

Christologie und Geschichtsdeutung. Die Furche. Vol. XIV, 1924.

1925

"Religionsphilosophie." In *Lehrbuch der Philosophie*, edited by Max Dessoir. Vol. II: *Die Philosophie in ihren Einzelgebieten.* Berlin: Ullstein, 1925. (I: 297–364.) ET–In *What is Religion?* Edited by James L. Adams. New York: Harper and Row, 1969.

"Die Staatslehre Augustins nach *De civitate Dei.*" *Theologische Blätter* IV, 4 (April, 1925): 77–86. (XII: 81–96.)

"Denker der Zeit: Der Religionsphilosoph Rudolf Otto." *Vossische Zeitung* 308 (July 2, 1925). (XII: 179–183.)

1926

Die religiöse Lage der Gegenwart. Berlin: Ullstein, 1926. (X: 9–93.) ET–*The Religious Situation.* New York: Henry Holt, 1932.

Das Dämonische. Ein Beitrag zur Sinndeutung der Geschichte. Tübingen: J.C.B. Mohr, 1926. (VI: 42–71.) ET–In *The Interpretation of History.* New York: Scribner, 1936.

"Kairos: Ideen zur Geisteslage der Gegenwart." In *Kairos: Zur Geisteslage und Geisteswendung*, edited by Paul Tillich. Darmstadt: Otto Reichl, 1926. (VI: 29–41.)

"Kairos und Logos: Eine Untersuchung zur Metaphysik der Erkenntnis." In *Kairos: Zur Geisteslage und Geisteswendung*, edited by Paul Tillich. Darmstadt: Otto Reichl, 1926. (IV: 43–76.) ET—In *The Interpretation of History*. New York: Scribner, 1936.

"Die geistige Welt im Jahre 1926." In *Reichls Bücherbuch*, XVII. Darmstadt: Otto Reichl, 1926. (X: 94–99.)

Das Berneuchener Buch. Vom Anspruch des Evangeliums auf die Kirchen der Reformation. Edited by the Berneuchener Konferenz. Hamburg: Hanseatische Verlagsanstalt, 1926. (Tillich collaborated in this work.)

"Denker der Zeit: Karl Barth." *Vossische Zeitung* 32 (January 20, 1926). (XII: 187–193.)

"Der Begriff des "Dämonischen und seine Bedeutung für die systematische Theologie." *Theologische Blätter* V, 2 (February, 1926): 32–35. (VIII: 285–291.)

"Zum Problem der evangelischen Sozialethik." *Blätter für Religiösen Sozialismus* VII (July-August, 1926): 73–87.

Die Geisteslage der Gegenwart: Rückblick und Ausblick. Typescript. (X: 108–120.)

Beitrag zu einem Prospekt der Tanzgruppe Gertrud Steinweg. Dresden: 1926. (XIII: 134–137.)

Der Glaube an den Sinn. Typescript. (XIII: 105–109.)

1927

"Predigt zum Semesterschluss vor der Theologenschaft der Universität Marburg." *Neuwerk* VIII, 11 (February, 1927): 469–472. (XIII: 181–184.)

"Die Überwindung des Persönlichkeitsideals." *Logos* XVI, 1 (March, 1927): 68–85. (III: 83–100.) ET—In *The Protestant Era*, edited by James L. Adams. Chicago: University of Chicago Press, 1948.

"Ostern." *Hannoverscher Kurier* 79, 179 (April 17, 1927): 1. (XIII: 109–112.)

"Gläubiger Realismus." *Theologenrundbrief für den Bund deutscher Jugendvereine e. V.* II (1927): 3–13. (IV: 77–87.)

"Logos und Mythos der Technik." *Logos* XVI, 3 (November, 1927): 356–365. (IX: 297–306.)

"Die Idee der Offenbarung." *Zeitschrift für Theologie und Kirche* VIII, 6 (1927): 403–412. (VIII: 31–39.)

"Eschatologie und Geschichte." *Die Christliche Welt* 41, 22 (November 17, 1927): 1034–1042. (VI: 72–82.) ET—In *The Interpretation of History.* New York: Scribner, 1936.

"Diskussionsbeitrag." *An die Freunde* (Korrespondenzblatt der Freunde der Christlichen Welt) 88 (1927): 1012–1013.

1928

"Der soziale Pfarrer." Diskussionsrede. In *Die Verhandlungen des 35. Evangelisch-Sozialen Kongresses in Dresden am 29.–31. Mai 1928,* edited by Johannes Herz. Göttingen: Vandenhoeck & Ruprecht, 1928.

"Das religiöse Symbol." *Blätter für deutsche Philosophie* I, 4 (January, 1928): 277–291. (V: 196–212.) ET—In *Religious Experience and Truth,* edited by Sidney Hook. New York: New York University Press, 1961, pp. 301–321.

"Das Christentum und die Moderne." *Schule und Wissenschaft* II, 4 (1928): 121–131, 170–177. (XIII: 113–130.)

"Die technische Stadt als Symbol." *Dresdner Neueste Nachrichten* 115 (May 17, 1928): 5. (IX: 307–311.)

"Über gläubigen Realismus." *Theologische Blätter* VII, 5 (May, 1928): 109–118. (IV: 88–106.) ET—In *The Protestant Era,* edited by James L. Adams. Chicago: University of Chicago Press, 1948.

"Die Bedeutung der Gesellschaftslage für das Geistesleben." *Philosophie und Leben* IV, 6 (June, 1928): 153–158. (II: 133–138.)

"Das Christentum und die moderne Gesellschaft." *Student World* XXI, 3 (July, 1928): 282–290. (X: 100–107.) ET—In *Political Expectation,* edited by James L. Adams. New York: Harper and Row, 1971.

"Zum 'theologischen Nachwort zu den Davoser internationalen Hochschulkursen.'" (Reply to G. Kuhlmann.) *Theologische Blätter* VII, 7 (July, 1928): 176–177.

"Der Geistige und der Sport." *Vossische Zeitung* 608 (December 25, 1928): 2.

1929

"Der Protestantismus als kritisches und gestaltendes Prinzip." In *Protestantismus als Kritik und Gestaltung,* edited by Paul Tillich. Darmstadt: Reichl, 1929. (VII: 29–53.) ET—In *Political Expectation,* edited by James L. Adams. New York: Harper and Row, 1971.

"Diskussionsbeitrag." In *Sozialismus aus dem Glauben.* Zürich, Leipzig: Rotapfel, 1929.

"Nichtkirchliche Religionen." In *Volk und Reich der Deutschen,* edited by Bernhard Harms. Vol. 1. Berlin: Hobbing, 1929. (V: 13–31.)

Religiöse Verwirklichung. Collected essays. Berlin: Furche, 1929.

"Religiöse Verantwortung." *Berliner Tageblatt* LVIII, 1 (January 1, 1929): 2.

"Gegenwart und Religion." *Neuwerk* XI, 1 (April, 1929): 2–11.

"Philosophie und Schicksal." *Kant-Studien* XXXIV, 3/4 (1929): 300–311. (IV: 23–35.) ET–In *The Protestant Era*, edited by James L. Adams. Chicago: University of Chicago Press, 1948.

1930

"Mythus und Mythologie: I. Begrifflich und religionspsychologisch." In *Die Religion in Geschichte und Gegenwart*, edited by Hermann Gunkel and Leopold Zscharnack. Vol. 4. Second edition. Tübingen: J.C.B. Mohr, 1930. (V: 187–195.) ET–In *Twentieth Century Theology in Making*. Vol. 2, New York: Harper and Row, 1970.

"Offenbarung: Religionsphilosophisch." *Ibid.* (VIII: 40–46.) ET–In *Twentieth Century Theology in Making*. Vol. 2, edited by Jaroslav Pelikan. New York: Harper and Row, 1970.

"Philosophie: Begriff und Wesen." *Ibid.* (IV: 15–22.) ET–In *Twentieth Century Theology in Making*. Vol. 2, edited by Jaroslav Pelikan. New York: Harper and Row, 1970.

"Philosophie und Religion, grundsätzlich." *Ibid.* (V: 101–109.) ET–In *Twentieth Century Theology in Making*. Vol. 2, edited by Jaroslav Pelikan. New York: Harper and Row, 1970.

"Sozialismus." *Neue Blätter für den Sozialismus* I, 1 (January, 1930): 1–12. (II: 139–150.)

"Religiöser Sozialismus." *Neue Blätter für den Sozialismus* I, 9 (1930): 396–403. (II: 151–158.) ET–In *Political Expectations*, edited by James L. Adams. New York: Harper and Row, 1971.

"Neue Formen christlicher Verwirklichung. Eine Betrachtung über Sinn und Grenzen evangelischer Katholizität." *Reclams Universum* XLVII, 10 (December 4, 1930): 194–195. (XIII: 92–94.)

"Kult und Form." *Die Form* V, 23/24 (December 15, 1930): 578–583. (IX: 324–327.)

Adolf von Harnack. Handwritten manuscript. (XII: 159–165.)

Natur und Geist im Protestantismus. Typescript. (XIII: 95–102.)

1931

Protestantisches Prinzip und proletarische Situation. Bonn: Cohen, 1931. (VII: 84–104.) ET–In *The Protestant Era*, edited by James L. Adams. Chicago: University of Chicago Press, 1948.

"Religiöser Sozialismus." In *Die Religion in Geschichte und Gegenwart*, edited by Hermann Gunkel and Leopold Zscharnack. Second edition. Tübingen: Mohr, 1931. Vol. 5. (II: 159–174.)

"Theonomie." *Ibid.*

"Wissenschaft." *Ibid.* (IV: 36–39.)

"Das Wasser." In *Das Gottesjahr 1932*, edited by Wilhelm Stählin. Kassel: Bärenreiter, 1931. (XIII: 102–104.) ET–In *Paul Tillich's Philosophy of Culture, Science, and Religion*, by James L. Adams. New York: Harper and Row, 1965.

"Mensch und Staat." A weekly column in *Der Staat seid Ihr. Zeitschrift für deutsche Politik.* (XIII: 167–177.)

"Goethe und die Idee der Klassik." *Bühnen-Blätter* 17 (1931/32): 193–207. (XII: 112–124.)

"Das Problem der Macht. Versuch einer philosophischen Grundlegung." *Neue Blätter für den Sozialismus* II, 4 (April, 1931): 157–170. (II: 193–208.) ET–In *The Interpretation of History.* New York: Scribner, 1936.

"Kirche und humanistische Gesellschaft." *Neuwerk* XIII, 1 (April-May, 1931): 4–18. (IX: 47–61.)

"Zum Problem des evangelischen Religionsunterrichts." *Zeitschrift für den evangelischen Religionsunterricht an höheren Lehranstalten* XLII, 6 (1931): 289–291. (IX: 233–235.)

"Zum Fall Eckert." *Neue Blätter für den Sozialismus* II, 8 (August, 1931): 408–409. (XIII: 166–167.)

"Die Doppelgestalt der Kirche." (Reply to criticisms of "Kirche und humanistische Gesellschaft.") *Neuwerk* XIII, 4 (October-November, 1931): 239–243. (IX: 77–81.)

"Gibt es noch eine Universität?" (Fachhochschulen und Universität.) *Frankfurter Zeitung* LXXVI, 869–871 (November 22, 1931): 11. (XIII: 144–149.)

1932

Hegel und Goethe. Zwei Gedenkreden. Tübingen: Mohr. 1932. (XII: 112–150.)

"Zehn Thesen." In *Die Kirche und das Dritte Reich.* Fragen und Forderungen deutscher Theologen. Edited by Leopold Klotz. Gotha: Klotz, 1932. (XIII: 177–179.)

"Der Sozialismus und die Geistige Lage der Gegenwart." *Neue Blätter für den Sozialismus* III, 1 (January, 1932): 14–16.

"Protestantismus und politische Romantik." *Neue Blätter für den Sozialismus* III, 8 (August, 1932): 413–422. (II: 209–218.)

"Beitrag zu einem Symposium: Haus Gottes." Stimmen über den Kultbau der Zukunft. *Eckart* 8 (1932): 418–419.

"Selbstanzeige." *Neue Blätter für den Sozialismus* 3 (1932): 667–668.

Christentum als Ideologie. Typescript. (XIII: 179–181.)

Freiheit der Wissenschaft. Typescript. Probably 1932. (XIII: 150–153.)

1933

Die sozialistische Entscheidung. Potsdam: Protte, 1933. (II: 219–365.) ET—In *The Interpretation of History.* New York: Scribner, 1936.

"Das Wohnen, der Raum und die Zeit." *Die Form* VIII, 1 (January, 1933): 11–12. (IX: 328–332.)

"The Religious Situation in Germany Today." *Religion in Life* III, 2 (Spring, 1934): 163–173. (XIII: 227–238.)

"Die Theologie des Kairos und die gegenwärtige geistige Lage. Offener Brief an Emanuel Hirsch." *Theologische Blätter* XIII, 11 (November, 1934): 305–328.

"The Totalitarian State and the Claims of the Church." *Social Research* I, 4 (November, 1934): 405–433. (X: 121–145.)

1935

"What is Wrong with the 'Dialectic' Theology?" *Journal of Religion* XV, 2 (April, 1935): 127–145. (VII: 247–262.)

"Um was es geht. Antwort an Emanuel Hirsch." *Theologische Blätter* XIV, 5 (May, 1935): 117–120.

"Marx and the Prophetic Tradition." *Radical Religion* I, 4 (Autumn, 1935): 21–29. (VI: 97–108.)

"Natural and Revealed Religion." *Christendom* I, 1 (Autumn, 1935): 159–170. (VIII: 47–58.)

1936

The Interpretation of History. New York: Scribner, 1936.

"The Social Functions of the Churches in Europe and America." *Social Research* III, 1 (February, 1936): 90–104. (III: 107–119.)

"Christianity and Emigration." *The Presbyterian Tribune* LII, 3 (October 29, 1936): 13, 16. (XIII: 187–191.)

"An Historical Diagnosis: Impressions of an European Trip." *Radical Religion* II, 1 (Winter, 1936): 11–17. (XIII: 238–248.)

1937

"Brief an die Redaktion." *Aufbau/Reconstruction* III, 3 (February 1, 1937): 6.

"The End of the Protestant Era." *Student World* XXX, 1 (First Quarter, 1937): 49–57. (VII: 151–158.)

"Statement of Principles." *Radical Religion* III, 1 (1937): 30–32.

"The Church and the Economic Order." Geneva: Research Department, Universal Christian Council for Life and Work, 1937.

"The Church and Communism." *Religion in Life* VI, 3 (Summer, 1937): 347–357. (X: 146–158.)

"Mind and Migration." *Social Research* IV, 3 (September, 1937): 295–305. Reprinted as "Migrations Breed New Cultures." *Protestant Digest* III, 2 (February, 1940): 10–19. (XIII: 191–200.)

"Protestantism in the Present World-Situation." *American Journal of Sociology* XLIII, 2 (September, 1937): 236–248. (VII: 159–170.)

1938

"The Kingdom of God and History." In *The Kingdom of God and History*. New York: Willett, Clark, 1938.

"The Meaning of Our Present Historical Existence." In *The Hazen Conferences on Student Guidance and Counseling*. Haddam, Conn.: Edward W. Hazen Foundation, Inc., 1938.

"The Significance of the Historical Jesus for the Christian Faith." *Monday Forum Talks* (Union Theological Seminary, New York.) 5 (February 28, 1938): 1, 4–5, 6.

"The Attack of Dialectical Materialism on Christianity." *Student World* (Geneva) XXXI, 2 (Second Quarter, 1938): 115–125. (III: 120–128.)

"Nicholas Berdyaev." *Religion in Life* VII, 3 (Summer, 1938): 407–415. (XII: 289–299.)

"The Gospel and the State." *Crozer Quarterly* (Chester, Pa.) XV, 4 (October, 1938): 251–261. (IX: 193–204.)

"German-Americans Take Stand for Democracy Against Nazis." *Deutsches Volksecho/German People's Echo* (New York) II, 48 (November 26, 1938): 1–2. Revised and expanded as "The Meaning of Anti-Semitism." *Radical Religion* IV, 1 (Winter, 1938): 34–36. (XIII: 216–220.)

Die politische und geistige Aufgabe der deutschen Emigration. Typescript. (XIII: 200–216.)

Religion und Weltpolitik. Handwritten manuscript. (IX: 139–204.)

"Brief an Thomas Mann." In *Das goldene Buch.* To Thomas Mann from His Friends and Admirers. Hotel Astor, New York, May 9th, 1938. In Thomas Mann Archive, Eidgenössische Technische Hochschule, Zurich. Privately printed.

1939

"History as *the* Problem of Our Period." *Review of Religion* III, 3 (March, 1939): 255–264. (X: 159–169.)

"The Conception of Man in Existential Philosophy." *Journal of Religion* XIX, 3 (July, 1939): 201–215.

"Und die Kirche?" *Press Service of the German-American Writers Association* 5 (1939): 1–2.

"The European War and the Christian Churches." *Direction* (Darien, Conn.) II, 8 (December, 1939): 10–11. (XIII: 269–274.)

1940

"Freedom in the Period of Transformation." In *Freedom: Its Meaning*, edited by Ruth Nanda Anshen. New York: Harcourt, Brace, 1940. (X: 181–201.)

"Has Higher Education an Obligation to Work for Democracy?" *Radical Religion* V, 1 (Winter, 1940): 12–15.

"The Meaning of the Triumph of Nazism." *Christianity and Society* V, 4 (1940): 45–46.

"The Idea of the Personal God." *Union Review* II, 1 (November, 1940): 8–10. Also under the title: "Science and Theology: A Discussion with Einstein." In *Theology of Culture*, edited by Robert C. Kimball. New York: Oxford University Press, 1959. (XII, 300–304.)

Liebe ist stärker als der Tod. Typescript. (XIII: 249–252.)

1941

"Ethics in a Changing World." In *Religion and the Modern World*, by Jacques Maritain and others. Philadelphia: University of Pennsylvania Press, 1941. (III: 70–81.)

"Philosophy and Theology." *Religion in Life* X, 1 (Winter, 1941): 21–30. (V: 100–121.)

"The Permanent Significance of the Catholic Church for Protestantism." *Protestant Digest* III, 10 (February-March, 1941): 23–31. (VII: 124–132.)

"Our Disintegrating World." *Anglican Theological Review* XXIII, 2 (April, 1941): 134–146. (X: 202–212.)

"Religion and Education." *Protestant Digest* III, 11 (April-May, 1941): 58–61. (XIII: 331–335.)

"Symbol and Knowledge." *Journal of Liberal Religion* II, 4 (Spring, 1941): 202–206.

"Existential Thinking in American Theology." *Religion in Life* X (Summer, 1941): 452–455.

"I Am an American." *Protestant Digest* III, 12 (June-July, 1941): 24–26.

"Why War Aims?" ("War Aims—I.") *Protestant Digest* III, 12 (June-July, 1941): 33–38. (XIII: 254–259.)

"What War Aims?" ("War Aims—II.") *Protestant Digest* IV, 1 (August-September, 1941): 13–18. (XIII: 259–264.)

"Whose War Aims?" ("War Aims—III.") *The Protestant* IV, 2 (October-November, 1941): 24–29. (XIII: 264–269.)

"Dr. Richard Kroner." *Alumni Bulletin of the Union Theological Seminary* XVII, 1 (November, 1941): 3–4.

1942

"Love's 'Strange Work.'" *The Protestant* IV, 3 (December-January, 1942): 70–75. (VIII: 199–204.)

"Challenge to Protestantism." *The Protestant* IV, 4 (February-March, 1942): 1–4.

"Marxism and Christian Socialism." *Christianity and Society* VII, 2 (Spring, 1942): 13–18. (XIII: 303–312.)

"Protestant Principles." *The Protestant* IV, 5 (April-May, 1942): 17–19.

"The Word of Religion to the People of This Time." *The Protestant* IV, 5 (April-May, 1942): 43–48. (X: 213–220.)

"Läuterndes Feuer." *Aufbau/Reconstruction* VIII, 22 (May 29, 1942): 10. (XIII: 275–278.)

"Was soll mit Deutschland geschehen?" *Aufbau/Reconstruction* VIII, 29 (July 17, 1942): 6. (XIII: 278–279.)

"Es geht um die Methode." *Aufbau/Reconstruction* VIII, 32 (August 7, 1942): 7–8. (XIII: 279–281.)

"Spiritual Problems of Post-war Reconstruction." *Christianity and Crisis* II, 14 (August 10, 1942): 2–6. (XIII: 282–291.)

"Our Protestant Principles." *The Protestant* IV, 7 (August, September, 1942): 8–14. (VII: 133–140.)

"'Faith' in the Jewish-Christian Tradition." *Christendom* VII, 4 (Autumn, 1942): 518–526. (VIII: 101–110.)

"Kierkegaard in English." *American-Scandinavian Review* XXX, 3 (September, 1942): 254–257. (XII: 327–332.)

"Kierkegaard as Existential Thinker." *Union Review* IV, 1 (December, 1942): 5–7.

1943

"Storms of Our Times." *Anglican Theological Review* XXV, 1/2 (January-April, 1943): 15–32. (X: 221–236.)

"Flight to Atheism." *The Protestant* IV, 10 (February-March, 1943): 43–48.

"Comment" on the report of The Commission on a Just and Durable Peace. *The Witness* XXVI, 45 (April 8, 1943): 4.

"What is Divine Revelation?" *The Witness* XXVI, 46 (April 15, 1943): 8–9.

"Immigrants' Conference." *Aufbau/Reconstruction* IX, 27 (July 2, 1943): 3.

"Man and Society in Religious Socialism." *Christianity and Society* VIII, 4 (Fall, 1943): 10–21.

1944

"Critiques" of articles by F.S.C. Northrup ("Philosophy and World Peace") and John A. Ryan ("Religious Foundations for an Enduring Peace.") In *Approaches to World Peace*. Fourth Symposium, edited by Lyman Bryson, L. Finkelstein, R.M. MacIver. New York: Harper & Brothers, 1944.

"Trends in Religious Thought that Affect Social Outlook." In *Religion and the World Order*, edited by F. Ernest Johnson. New York: Harper and Row, 1944. Also in *Outside Readings in Sociology*, edited by E.A. Schuler. New York: T.Y. Crowell, 1952.

Ostern 1944 Handwritten manuscript. (Radio address over Voice of America.) (XIII: 324–328.)

Address of Chairman Paul Tillich at the Founding of the Council for a Democratic Germany, 17 June 1944. Typescript. (XIII: 318–322.)

"Existential Philosophy." *Journal of the History of Ideas* V, 1 (January, 1944): 44–70. (IV: 145–173.)

"Russia's Church and the Soviet Order." *Think* X, 1 (January, 1944): 22–23.

"The God of History." *Christianity and Crisis* IV, 7 (May 1, 1944): 5–6.

"A Program for a Democratic Germany." *Christianity and Crisis* IV, 8 (May 15, 1944): 3–5. (XIII: 313–318.)

"Depth." *Christendom* IX, 3 (Summer, 1944): 317–325.

"A Statement." *Bulletin of the Council for a Democratic Germany* I, 1 (September 1, 1944): 1, 4. (XIII: 322–323.)

"An Important Letter." *Bulletin of the Council for a Democratic Germany* I, 2 (1944): 1, 4. Answer to Rabbi Stephen S. Wise, Oct. 25, 1944.

"Estrangement and Reconciliation in Modern Thought." *Review of Religion* IX, 1 (November, 1944): 5–19. (IV: 183–199.)

"Now Concerning Spiritual Gifts. . . ." *Union Review* VI, 1 (December, 1944): 15–17.

1945

"Outlook for 1945." *Bulletin of the Council for a Democratic Germany* I, 3 (1945): 1.

"A Telegram." *Bulletin of the Council for a Democratic Germany* I, 3 (1945): 3.

"The Crimea Concept and the Council." *Bulletin of the Council for a Democratic Germany* I, 4 (1945): 1.

"The End of Nazism." *Bulletin of the Council for a Democratic Germany* I, 5 (1945): 1.

"Critiques" of articles by Robert J. Havighurst ("Education for Intergroup Co-operation"), Rudolf Allers ("Some Remarks on the Problems of Group Tensions"), A. Campbell Garnett ("Group Tensions in the Modern World"), and Amos N. Wilder ("Theology and Cultural Incoherence"). In *Approaches to National Unity.* Fifth Symposium, edited by Bryson, Finkelstein, MacIver. New York: Harper & Brothers, 1945.

"The World Situation." In *The Christian Answer*, edited by Henry P. Van Dusen. New York: Charles Scribner's Sons, 1945. (X: 237–279.)

"All Things to All Men." *Union Review* VI, 3 (May, 1945): 3–4.

"Nietzsche and the Bourgeois Spirit." *Journal of the History of Ideas* VI, 3 (June, 1945): 307–309. (XII: 286–288.)

"Der Protestantismus im künftigen Deutschland." *The German American* (May 15, 1945): 8.

"Ehrung für Berthold Viertel." *The German American* (May 15, 1945): 6.

"The Christian Churches and the Emerging Social Order in Europe." *Religion in Life* XIV, 3 (Summer, 1945): 329–339. (XIII: 291–303.)

"The Redemption of Nature." *Christendom* X, 3 (Summer, 1945): 299–305.

"Conscience in Western Thought and the Idea of a Transmoral Conscience." *Crozer Quarterly* XXII, 4 (October, 1945): 289–300. (III: 56–70.)

1946

"The Meaning of the German Church Struggle for Christian Missions." In *Christian World Mission*, edited by William K. Anderson. Nashville: Commission on Ministerial Training, The Methodist Church, 1946.

"Vertical and Horizontal Thinking." *American Scholar* XV, 1 (Winter, 1945–46): 102–105. (V: 32–36.)

"Religion and Secular Culture." *Journal of Religion* XXVI, 2 (April, 1946): 79–86. (IX: 82–93.)

"The Relation of Religion and Health: Historical Considerations and Theoretical Questions." *Review of Religion* X, 4 (May, 1946): 348–384. (IX: 246–286.)

"The Two Types of Philosophy of Religion." *Union Seminary Quarterly Review* I, 4 (May, 1946): 3–13. (V: 122–137.)

"Redemption in Cosmic and Social History." *Journal of Religious Thought* III, 1 (Autumn-Winter, 1946): 17–27. (VIII: 240–251.)

"The Nature of Man." *Journal of Philosophy* XLIII, 25 (December 5, 1946): 675–677.

1947

"The Problem of Theological Method." *Journal of Religion* XXVII, 1 (January, 1947): 16–26.

"Behold, I Am Doing a New Thing." *Union Seminary Quarterly Review* II, 4 (May, 1947): 3–9.

1948

The Protestant Era. Edited by James L. Adams. Chicago: The University of Chicago Press, 1948.

The Shaking of the Foundations. New York: Scribner, 1948.

"The Disintegration of Society in Christian Countries." In *The Church's Witness to God's Design.* New York: Harper & Brothers, 1948. (X: 280–294.)

"Die philosophisch-geistige Lage und der Protestantismus." In *Philosophische Vorträge und Diskussionen,* edited by Georgi Schischkoff. Wurzach/Württ.: Pan Verlag, 1948.

"Martin Buber and Christian Thought: His Threefold Contribution to Protestantism." *Commentary* V, 6 (June, 1948): 515–521. (VII: 141–150.)

"Das geistige Vakuum." *Das sozialistische Jahrhundert* II, 20 (September 15, 1948): 303–305.

"How Much Truth Is In Karl Marx?" *Christian Century* LXV, 36 (September 8, 1948): 906–908. (XII: 265–272.)

"Visit to Germany." *Christianity and Crisis* VIII, 19 (November 15, 1948): 147–149. (XIII: 364–370.)

1949

"A Reinterpretation of the Doctrine of the Incarnation." *Church Quarterly Review* CXLVII, 294 (January-March, 1949): 133–148. (VIII: 205–219.)

"Psychotherapy and a Christian Interpretation of Human Nature." *The Review of Religion* XIII, 3 (March, 1949): 264–268.

"Creative Love in Education." *World Christian Education* IV, 2 (Second Quarter, 1949): 27, 34.

"Das Ja zum Kreuze." *Monatsschrift für Pastoraltheologie* XXXVIII, 6 (June, 1949): 287–289. (XIII: 279–382.)

"The Present Theological Situation in the Light of the Continental European Development." *Theology Today* VI, 3 (October, 1949): 299–310.

"Beyond Religious Socialism." *The Christian Century* LXVI, 24 (June 15, 1949): 732–733.

"Existentialism and Religious Socialism." *Christianity and Society* XV, 1 (Winter, 1949–50): 8–11.

"The Second Focus of the Fellowship." *Christianity and Society* XV, 1 (1949/50): 19–20.

1950

"Anxiety-Reducing Agencies in Our Culture." *In Anxiety*, edited by Paul H. Hoch and Joseph Zubin. New York: Grune and Stratton, 1950. (X: 293–302.)

"The Concept of God." *Perspective* II, 3 (January, 1950): 12.

"The Protestant Vision." *Chicago Theological Seminary Register* XL, 2 (March, 1950): 8–12.

"Religion and the Intellectuals." *Partisan Review* XVII, 3 (March, 1950): 254–256.

"Reply" to Gustave Weigel, S.J.: "Contemporaneous Protestantism and Paul Tillich." *Theological Studies* XI, 2 (June, 1950): 177–201. "Reply," 201–202.

"The New Being." *Religion in Life* XIX, 4 (Autumn, 1950): 511–517.

The Recovery of the Prophetic Tradition in the Reformation. Washington, D.C.: Henderson Services, 1950. (VII: 171–215.)

The Christian Conscience and Weapons of Mass Destruction. New York: The Department of International Justice and Goodwill, December, 1950.

1951

Systematic Theology. Vol. 1. Chicago: University of Chicago Press, 1951.

Christianity and the Problem of Existence. Washington, D.C.: Henderson Services, 1951.

Politische Bedeutung der Utopie im Leben der Völker. Berlin: Gebrüder Weiss, 1951. (VI: 157–210.)

Protestantische Vision. Katholische Substanz, Protestantisches Prinzip, Sozialistische Entscheidung. Düsseldorf: "Schriftenreihe der Evangelischen Arbeitsausschusses Düsseldorf," No. 3, 1951.

1952

The Courage to Be. New Haven: Yale University Press, 1952. (XI: 13–139.)

"Autobiographical Reflections." In *The Theology of Paul Tillich,* edited by Charles W. Kegley and Robert W. Bretall. New York: Macmillan, 1952. (XII: 58–77.)

"Answer." Reply to interpretation and criticism in *The Theology of Paul Tillich,* edited by Charles W. Kegley and Robert W. Bretall. New York: Macmillan, 1952.

"Being and Love." In *Moral Principles of Action,* edited by Ruth Nanda Anshen. New York: Harper & Brothers, 1952.

"Victory in Defeat: The Meaning of History in the Light of Christian Prophetism." *Interpretation* VI, 1 (January, 1952): 17–26. (VI: 126–136.)

"Jewish Influences on Contemporary Christian Theology." *Cross Currents* II, 3 (Spring, 1952): 35–42. (VIII: 292–303.)

"Is There a Judeo-Christian Tradition?" *Judaism* I, 2 (April, 1952): 106–109.

"Authority and Revelation." *Official Register of Harvard University: Harvard Divinity School* XLIX, 8 (April 7, 1952): 27–36. (VIII: 59–69.)

"Communicating the Gospel." *Union Seminary Quarterly Review* VII, 4 (June, 1952): 3–11. (VIII: 265–275.)

"Human Nature Can Change." *American Journal of Psychoanalysis* XII, 1 (1952): 65–67.

"Christian Criteria for Our Culture." *Criterion* I, 1 (October, 1952): 1, 3–4.

"Love, Power and Justice." *The Listener* XLVIII, 1231 (October 2, 1952:) 544–545.

"The Four Levels of the Relationship Between Religion and Art." In *Contemporary Religious Art.* New York: Union Theological Seminary, 1952.

Ansprache zur 425jährigen Gründungsfeier der Universität Marburg. Typescript. (XIII: 359–363.)

1953

"The Conquest of Theological Provincialism." In *The Cultural Migration: The European Scholar in America,* edited by W. Rex Crawford. Philadelphia: University of Pennsylvania Press, 1953. (VIII: 13–27.)

Der Mensch im Christentum und im Marxismus. Düsseldorf: "Schriftenreihe des Evangelischen Arbeitsausschusses Düsseldorf," 5, 1953. (III: 194–209.)

Die Judenfrage, ein christliches und ein deutsches Problem. Berlin: Weiss, 1953. (III: 128–170.)

"The Person in a Technical Society." In *Christian Faith and Social Action,* edited by John A. Hutchinson. New York: Charles Scribner's Sons, 1953.

"The Truth Will Make You Free." *Pulpit Digest* XXXIII, 180 (April, 1953): 17–23.

"Karen Horney." *Pastoral Psychology* IV, 34 (May, 1953): 11–13, 66.

"The Nature of Authority." *Pulpit Digest* XXXIV, 186 (October, 1953): 25–27, 30–32, 34.

"Hermann Schafft zum 70. Geburtstag." *Evangelische Welt* VII, 23 (1953): 703.

Zur Frage christlicher Grundbegriffe. Ein Beitrag in Form eines Briefes." *Das Evangelische Düsseldorf* 58 (December, 1953). (XIII: 335–336.)

1954

Love, Power, and Justice. Ontological Analyses and Ethical Applications. New York, London: Oxford University Press, 1954. (XI: 143–225.)

"Religion in Two Societies." New York: Metropolitan Museum of Art, 1954.

"Authentic Religious Art." Preface (with Theodore W. Greene) to *Masterpieces of Religious Art.* Chicago: Art Institute of Chicago, 1954.

"Ansprache zum Semesterbeginn." *Freies Christentum* VI, 5 (May 1, 1954): 54–57. (XIII: 352–358.)

"The Hydrogen Cobalt Bomb." *Pulpit Digest* XXXIV, 194 (June, 1954): 32, 34. (XIII: 454.)

"The Meaning and Sources of Courage." *Child Study* XXXI, 3 (Summer, 1954): 7–11.

"The Theology of Missions." *Occasional Bulletin of the Missionary Research Library* V, 10 (August 10, 1954): 6. (VIII: 276–284.)

1955

Biblical Religion and the Search for Ultimate Reality. Chicago: University of Chicago Press, 1955. (V: 138–184.)

The New Being. New York: Scribner, 1955.

"Moralisms and Morality from the Point of View of the Ethicist." In *Ministry and Medicine in Human Relations,* edited by Iago Galdston. New York: International Universities Press, 1955.

"Das Neue Sein als Zentralbegriff einer christlichen Theologie." *Eranos-Jahrbuch* XXIII ("Mensch und Wandlung"). Zürich: Rhein, 1955. (VIII: 220–239.)

"Theology and Symbolism." In *Religious Symbolism*, edited by F. Ernest Johnson. New York: Harper & Brothers, 1955.

"Participation and Knowledge: Problems of an Ontology of Cognition." In *Sociologica*, edited by Theodor W. Adorno and Walter Dirks. Frankfurt a. M.: Europäische Verlagsanstalt, 1955. (IV: 107–117.)

"Religion." In *Present Knowledge and New Directions*. New York: Herbert Muschel, 1955. (V: 37–42.)

"Religion and Its Intellectual Critics." *Christianity and Crisis* XV, 3 (March 7, 1955): 19–22. (XIII: 336–344.)

"Schelling und die Anfänge des existentialistischen Protestes." *Zeitschrift für philosophische Forschung* IX, 2 (1955): 197–208. (IV: 133–144.)

"Psychoanalysis, Existentialism and Theology." *Faith and Freedom* IX, 1, 25 (Autumn, 1955): 1–11. (VIII: 304–315.)

"Das christliche Menschenbild im 20. Jahrhundert." *Universitas* X, 9 (September, 1955): 917–920. (III: 181–184.)

"Religious Symbols and Our Knowledge of God." *Christian Scholar* XXXVIII, 3 (September, 1955): 189–197. (V: 213–222.)

"Beyond the Dilemma of Our Period." *The Cambridge Review* 4 (November, 1955): 209–215. (XIII: 345–351.)

"Heal the Sick; Cast Out Demons." *Union Seminary Quarterly Review* XI, 1 (November, 1955): 3–8.

"Theology and Architecture." *Architectural Forum* CIII, 6 (December, 1955): 131–134.

"I'll Always Remember . . . One Moment of Beauty." *Parade* (New York) Sept. 25, 1955, p. 2.

"Comment" on criticisms of Nels F.S. Ferré. *Presbyterian Outlook* CXXXVII, 50 (December 26, 1955): 6.

1956

Die Philosophie der Macht. Berlin: Colloquium Verl., 1956. (IX: 205–232.)

"Existential Analysis and Religious Symbols." In *Contemporary Problems in Religion*, edited by Harold A. Basilius. Detroit: Wayne University Press, 1956. (V: 223–236.)

"Existential Aspects of Modern Art." In *Christianity and the Existentialists*, edited by Carl Michalson. New York: Scribner, 1956.

"Reinhold Niebuhr's Doctrine of Knowledge." In *Reinhold Niebuhr: His Religious, Social, and Political Thought*, edited by Charles W. Kegley and Robert W. Bretall. New York: The Macmillan Co., 1956. (XII: 337–345.)

"Reply to Nels F.S. Ferré: "Where Do We Go from Here in Theology?" *Religion in Life* XXV, 1 (Winter, 1955–56): 19–21.

"Theology and Counseling." *Journal of Pastoral Care* X, 4 (Winter, 1956): 193–200.

"Reply" to Gustave Weigel, S.J.: "The Theological Significance of Paul Tillich." *Gregorianum* XXXVII, 1 (1956): 34–53; "Reply," 53–54.

"Reply" to William Rickel: "Is Psychotherapy a Religious Process?" *Pastoral Psychology* VII, 62 (March, 1956): 39–40.

"Letter" to Reinhold Niebuhr on Picasso's "Guernica" and its Protestant significance. *Christianity and Crisis* XVI, 3 (March 5, 1956): 24.

"The Church and Contemporary Culture." *World Christian Education* XI, 2 (Second Quarter, 1956): 41–43. (IX: 100–109.)

"The Christian Consummation: A Conversation." *The Chaplain* XIII, 2 (April, 1956): 10–13, 18–19. Symposium with Albert T. Mollegen and Nels F.S. Ferré.

"The Beginning of Wisdom." *Pulpit Digest* XXXVI, 218 (June, 1956): 27–31.

"Relation of Metaphysics and Theology." *Review of Metaphysics* X, 1 (September, 1956): 57–63.

"The Nature and the Significance of Existentialist Thought." *Journal of Philosophy* LIII, 23 (November 8, 1956): 739–748. (IV: 174–182.)

"Religiöser Sozialismus." In *Handwörterbuch der Sozialwissenschaften*. Neuauflage des Handwörterbuchs der Staatswissenschaften, edited by Erwin V. Beckerath and others. Vol. 9. Stuttgart: Fischer; Tübingen: Mohr; Göttingen: Vandenhoeck & Ruprecht, 1956.

Das Ewige Jetzt. Heilt die Kranken, treibt die Dämonen aus. Düsseldorf, 1956.

1957

Systematic Theology. Vol. 2. Chicago: University of Chicago Press, 1957.

Dynamics of Faith. New York: Harper & Row, 1957. (VIII: 111–196.)

"Letter to W. Burnet Easton, Jr." In *Basic Christian Beliefs*, edited by W. Burnet Easton, Jr. Philadelphia: Westminster Press, 1957.

"Theology of Education." In *The Church School in Our Time*. Concord: St. Paul's School, 1957. (IX: 236–245.)

"The Word of God." In *Language: An Enquiry Into its Meaning and Function*, edited by Ruth Nanda Anshen. New York: Harper & Row, 1957. (VIII: 70–81.)

"Loneliness and Solitude." *Divinity School News* (University of Chicago) XXIV, 2 (May 1, 1957): 1–7.

"Impressions of Europe—1956." Colgate Rochester Divinity School Bulletin XXIX, 2 (1957): 22–29. (XIII: 370–379.)

"Environment and the Individual." *Journal of the American Institute of Architects* XXVIII, 2 (June, 1957): 90–92. (IX: 333–337.)

"The Dance." *Dance Magazine* XXXI, 6 (June, 1957): 20. (XIII: 134.)

"Discussion" of "The Immortality of Man" by Margaret Mead, in *Pastoral Psychology* VIII, 75 (June, 1957): 17–22; "Discussion," 22–24.

"Conformity." *Social Research* XXIV, 3 (Autumn, 1957): 354–360. (XIII: 459–465.)

"Protestantism and the Contemporary Style in the Visual Arts." *Christian Scholar* XL, 4 (December, 1957): 307–311.

1958

"Kairos." In *A Handbook of Christian Theology*, edited by Marvin Halverson and Arthur A. Cohen. New York: Meridian Books, 1958.

"Do Not Be Conformed." *Pulpit Digest* XXXVIII, 237 (January, 1958): 19–24.

"Beyond the Usual Alternatives." *The Christian Century* LXXV, 19 (May 7, 1958): 553–555.

"The Riddle of Inequality." *Union Seminary Quarterly Review* XIII, 4 (May, 1958): 3–9.

"Conversation with Werner Rode." In *Wisdom*. Conversations with the Elder Wise Men of Our Day. Edited by James Nelson. New York: W.W. Norton & Co., 1958.

"The Theology of Pastoral Care." In *Clinical Education for the Pastoral Ministry*, edited by Ernest E. Bruder and Marian L. Barb. Washington, D.C.: Advisory Committee on Clinical Pastoral Education, 1958. (VIII: 316–324.)

"Humanität und Religion." In *Hansischer Goethe-Preis 1958*. Hamburg: Stiftung F.V.S., 1958. (IX: 110–119.)

"God's Pursuit of Man." *Alumni Bulletin of Bangor Theological Seminary* XXXIII, 2 (April, 1958): 21–25.

"Manifeste und latente Kirche." *Kommunität*. Vierteljahreshefte der Evangelischen Akademie Berlin II, 6 (1958): 94.

"Freedom and the Ultimate Concern." In *Religion in America*, edited by John Cogley. New York: Meridian Books, 1958.

"The Lost Dimension in Religion." *Saturday Evening Post* 230, 50 (June 14, 1958): 29, 76, 78–79. (V: 43–50.)

Contribution to "Theologians and the Moon." *Christianity Today* III, 1 (October 13, 1958): 31. (XIII: 45.)

Contribution to "A Colloquy on the Unity of Learning." *Daedalus* 87 (1958): 160–162.

1959

"Is a Science of Human Values Possible?" In *New Knowledge in Human Values*, edited by Abraham H. Maslow. New York: Harper & Row, 1958. (III: 100–106.)

"Kairos—Theonomie—Das Dämonische." Ein Brief zu Eduard Heimanns 70. Geburtstag. In *Hamburger Jahrbuch für Wirtschafts- und Gesellschaftspolitik*, edited by Heinz-Dietrich Ortlieb. Vol. 4. 1959. Tübingen: Mohr, 1959.

"Das christliche Verständnis des modernen Menschen." In *Das ist der Mensch*. Beiträge der Wissenschaft zum Selbstverständnis des Menschen. Stuttgart: Kröner, 1959. (III: 188–193.)

"The Eternal Now." In *The Meaning of Death*, edited by Hermann Feifel. New York: McGraw-Hill Book Co., 1959.

"Religion in the Intellectual Life of the University." *Harvard Alumni Bulletin* 61, 6 (1959): 298–299. (XIII: 466–470.)

Theology of Culture, edited by Robert C. Kimball. New York: Oxford University Press, 1959.

"Human Fulfillment." In *The Search for America*, edited by Huston Smith and others. Englewood Cliffs, N.J.: Prentice-Hall, 1959.

"The Idea of God as Affected by Modern Knowledge." *Crane Review* I, 3 (1959): 83–90. (XIII: 395–403.)

"What Worries You Most about America Today?" *Esquire* 51, 2 (1959): 51.

"In Thinking Be Mature." *The Washington Diocese* XXVIII, 2 (1959): 16–19.

"The Good I Will, I Do Not." *Union Seminary Quarterly Review* XIV, 3 (1959): 17–23.

Contribution to "The Beat Poets." *Wagner Literary Magazine* (Spring, 1959): 20.

"Between Utopianism and Escape from History." *Colgate Rochester Divinity School Bulletin* XXXI, 2 (1959): 32–40. (VI: 149–156.)

"How We Communicate the Christian Message." *The New Christian Advocate* III, 5 (1959): 12–17.

"The Significance of Kurt Goldstein for Philosophy of Religion." *Journal of Individual Psychology* XV, 1 (1959): 20–23. (XII: 305–309.)

"Religion and the Ethical Norms." *Vox* II, 3 (1959): 4–12.

"Dimensions, Levels, and the Unity of Life." *Kenyon Alumni Bulletin* XVII, 4 (1959): 4–8. (IV: 118–129.)

My Changing Thought on Zionism. Typescript. (XIII: 403–408.)

1960

"Hermann Schafft." In *Hermann Schafft. Ein Lebenswerk*, edited by Werner Kindt. Kassel: Stauda, 1960. (XIII: 27–33.)

"Marx's View of History: A Study in the History of the Philosophy of History." In *Culture and History: Essays Presented to Paul Radin*, edited by Stanley Diamond. New York: Columbia University Press, 1960. (XII: 273–285.)

"The Relationship Today between Science and Religion." In *The Student Seeks an Answer*. Waterville, Maine: Colby College Press, 1960. (XIII: 386–394.)

"The Relevance of the Ministry in Our Time and Its Theological Foundation." In *Making the Ministry Relevant*, edited by Hans Hofmann. New York: Scribner, 1960.

"The Impact of Psychotherapy on Theological Thought." *Pastoral Psychology* XI, 101 (1960): 17–23. (VIII: 325–335.)

"Christentum und Marxismus." *Politische Studien* XI, 119 (1960): 149–154. (III: 170–177.)

"Creative Integrity in a Democratic Society." *Polemic* V (Spring, 1960).

"The Image of Man in Contemporary Art." *Context* (Yale Divinity School) VIII, 2 (1960): 28–40.

"The Divine Name." *Christianity and Crisis* XX, 7 (1960): 55–58.

"Existentialism, Psychotherapy, and the Nature of Man." *Existential Inquiries* I, 6 (1960): 10–18.

"Theology and Philosophy." *Journal of Theology* (Tokyo Union Theological Seminary) 19 (1960): 1–16.

"The Dynamics of Religion and the Structure of the Demonic." *Journal of Theology* (Tokyo Union Theological Seminary) 19 (1960): 17–30.

"Spiritual Foundations of Democracy." *Kokusai Bunka Kaikan Kaiho* (Bulletin of the International House of Japan, Tokyo) 5 (1960).

"Religion and Culture." *Asian Cultural Studies*. (International Christian University, Tokyo) 2 (1960): 1–9.

"Tillich Relates His Impressions of Japanese Political Situation." *The Harvard Crimson Weekly Review* (October 28, 1960): 3. (XIII: 490–517.)

"The Basic Ideas of Religious Socialism." *International House of Japan Bulletin* 6 (1960): 11–15, 32. (XIII: 408–419.)

"Interview with Paul Tillich." *Glamour* December 1960: 104–105.

"The Significance of Existentialism for Theology." *Kirisutokyo Kenkyu/ Studies in the Christian Religion* (Kyoto) XXXII, 1 (1960): 1–13.

"On the Boundary Line." *The Christian Century* 77, 49 (1960): 1435–1437.

"The Philosophical Background of My Theology." *Kirisutokyo Gaku* (Christian Studies) (Tokyo) New Series 2 (1960): 1–13. (XIII: 477–488.)

"Art and Ultimate Reality." *Cross Currents* X, 1 (1960): 1–12. (IX: 356–368.)

On Creative Listening. Typescript. (XIII: 471–477.)

1961

"Die Hoffnung der Christen." In *Juden, Christen, Deutsche*, edited by Hans Jürgen Schultz. Stuttgart: Kreuz-Verlag, 1961. (VIII: 252–256.)

"The Meaning and Justification of Religious Symbols." In *Religious Experience and Truth*, edited by Sidney Hook. New York: New York University Press, 1961, pp. 3–11. (V: 237–244.)

"Science and the Contemporary World in the View of a Theologian." In *Public and Private Association in the International Educational and Cultural Relationship of the United States.* Washington: Office of the Special Assistant to the Secretary for Coordination of International Educational and Cultural Relations. Feb. 15, 1961: 67–70.

"Ein Gruss von Paul Tillich." *Christ und Sozialist* 4 (1961): 7.

"God as Reality and Symbol." *Essays and Studies* (Tokyo) XI, 2 (1961): 101–109.

"Zur Theologie der bildenden Kunst und der Architektur." *Kunst und Kirche* Vol. 24 (1961): 99–103. (IX: 345–355.)

"Tillich Encounters Japan." *Japanese Religions* (Kyoto) II, 2/3 (1961): 48–71.

"The God above God." *The Listener* 66, 1688 (1961): 169, 172.

"The Meaning of Health." *Perspectives in Biology and Medicine* V, 1 (1961): 92–100. (IX: 287–296.)

Contribution to "The Nuclear Dilemma—A Discussion." *Christianity and Crisis* XXI, 19 (1961): 203–204. (XIII: 456–457.)

"Paul Tillich on the Christian Church Today." *The Listener* 66, 1707 (1961): 1025–1026.

"Aphorismen zur Festgabe 'Der Spannungsbogen.'" In *Paul Tillich im Spiegel der Reden und Artikel zu seinem 75. Geburtstag am 20. August 1961.* Stuttgart: Evangelisches Verlagswerk, 1961/62.

"Erst Rückzug—dann Befreiungskrieg?" *Der Spiegel* 49 (1961): 71–73.

The Problem of Birth Control. Typescript. (XIII: 458.)

1962

Auf der Grenze. Aus dem Lebenswerk Paul Tillichs. Stuttgart: EVW, 1962.

Die neue Wirklichkeit. Munich. Deutscher Taschenbuch Verlag, 1962.
Symbol und Wirklichkeit. Göttingen: Vandenhoeck & Ruprecht, 1962.
Die verlorene Dimension. Not und Hoffnung unserer Zeit. Hamburg:
Furche, 1962.
"Can Reliigon Survive?" In *In Albert Schweitzer's Realms. A Sym-
posium,* edited by A.A. Roback. Cambridge, Mass.: Sci-Art Publishers,
1962.
"Carl Gustav Jung." In *Carl Gustav Jung, 1875–1961.* A Memorial
Meeting, New York, Dec. 1, 1961. New York: The Analytic Psychology
Club, 1962. (XII: 316–319.)
"Contemporary Protestant Architecture." In *Modern Church Architec-
ture.* A guide to the form and spirit of 20th century religious buildings.
New York: McGraw-Hill Book Co., 1962. (IX: 338–344.)
"Interview mit Paul Tillich." In *Auszug des Geistes. Bericht über eine
Sendereihe von Radio Bremen,* edited by Lutz Besch. Bremen: Heye &
Co., 1962.
"Sin and Grace in the Theology of Reinhold Niebuhr." In *Reinhold
Niebuhr: A Prophetic Voice in Our Time,* edited by Harold R. Landon.
Greenwich, Conn.: The Seabury Press, 1962.
"Some Questions on Brunner's Epistemology." In *The Theology of Emil
Brunner,* edited by Charles W. Kegley. New York: Macmillan, 1962.
(XII: 346–354.)
"Spiritual Presence." *Union Seminary Quarterly Review* XVII, 2 (1962):
121–128.
"Nuclear Morality." *Partisan Review* XXIX, 2 (1962): 311–312.
"Symbols of Eternal Life." *Harvard Divinity School Bulletin* XXVI, 3
(1962): 1–10.
"Man, the Earth, and the Universe." *Christianity and Crisis* XXII, 11
(1962): 108–112.
"Grenzen." In *Paul Tillich. Vier Ansprachen anlässlich der Verleihung
des Friedenspreises des Deutschen Buchhandels.* Frankfurt/M.: Börsen-
verein des Deutschen Buchhandels e. V., 1962. (XIII: 410–428.)
"The Philosophy of Social Work." *The Social Service Review* XXXVI, 1
(1962): 13–16. (XIII: 221–226.)
"What is Basic in Human Nature." *American Journal of Psychoanalysis*
XXII, 2 (1962): 115–121.

1963

Systematic Theology. Vol. 3. Chicago: University of Chicago Press,
1963.
Christianity and the Encounter of the World Religions. New York:
Columbia University Press, 1963. (V: 51–98.)

"Salvation." *The Princeton Seminary Bulletin* 57, 1 (1963): 4–9.

The Eternal Now. New York: Scribner, 1963.

Morality and Beyond, edited by Ruth Nanda Anshen. New York: Harper and Row, 1963. (III: 13–80.)

"Die christliche Hoffnung und ihre Wirkung in der Welt." In *Die Hoffnungen unserer Zeit,* edited by J. Schlemmer. Munich: Piper, 1963.

"Has Man's Conquest of Space Increased or Diminished His Stature?" In *The Great Ideas Today,* Chicago: Encyclopaedia Britannica, 1963.

"Comment on War within Man." In *War within Man. A Psychological Enquiry into the Roots of Destructiveness,* by Erich Fromm. Philadelphia: American Friends Service Committee, 1963.

"Mit Konflikten Leben." In *Sonderbeilage der Ruhr-Nachrichten.* Zum 11. Deutschen Evangelischen Kirchentag, Dortmund, 24.–28.7.1963.

"The Human Condition." *Criterion* II, 3 (1963): 22–24. (XIII: 429–433.)

"The Prophetic Element in the Christian Message and the Authoritarian Personality." *McCormick Quarterly* XVII, 1 (1963): 16–26.

"Ecumenical Perspectives." *Ecumenical Exchange* (University of Missouri/Kansas City) 1 (1963): 6–8.

1964

"An Afterword. Appreciation and Reply." In *Paul Tillich in Catholic Thought,* edited by Thomas A. O'Meara and Celestin D. Weisser. Dubuque, Iowa: Priory Press, 1964.

"Interrogation of Paul Tillich." Conducted by William L. Reese. In *Philosophical Interrogations,* edited by Sydney and Beatrice Rome. New York: Holt, Rinehart and Winston, 1964.

"Typische Formen des Selbstverständnisses beim heutigen Menschen." In *Jahrbuch des Marburger Universitätsbundes.* Bd. I. Edited by Ludwig Erich Schmitt. Marburg: Elwert, 1962. (III: 184–188.)

"That They May Have Life." *Union Seminary Quarterly Review* XX, 1 (1964): 3–8.

"Address." On the occasion of the opening of the new Galleries and Sculpture Garden of the Museum of Modern Art. May 25, 1964. *Criterion* III, 3 (1964): 39–40. (XIII: 433–436.)

"A Letter from Tillich." *Colby Library Quarterly* VI, 9 (1964): 383. [Impressions from a Journey to Israel.] Typescript. (XIII: 517–528.)

1965

Ultimate Concern. Tillich in Dialogue. Edited by D. Mackenzie Brown. New York: Harper & Row, 1965.

"Heil und Heilen." In *Das kranke Herz*. Munich: Piper, 1965.

"The Right to Hope." *Neue Zeitschrift für Systematische Theologie und Religionsphilosophie* 7 (1965): 371–377.

"Das Recht auf Hoffnung." In *Ernst Bloch zu ehren*. Beiträge zu seinem Werk, edited by Siegfried Unseld. Frankfurt/M.: Suhrkamp, 1965. (XIII: 528–537.)

Contribution to a discussion: "Christianity and other Faiths." *Union Seminary Quarterly Review* XX, 2 (1965): 177–178.

"Pacem in Terris." *Criterion* IV, 2 (1965): 15–18. (XIII: 436–443.)

"Reply" to an article by Leslie H. Farber: "I'm Sorry, Dear." *Commentary* XXXVIII, 5 (1964): 47–64; "Reply" XXXIX, 4 (1965): 16, 18.

"Conversation with Tillich." *Glen Echo* XVI, 3 (1965): 3–8.

"Brief an Thomas Mann. 23.5.43." *Blätter der Thomas-Mann-Gesellschaft* 5 (1965): 48–52. (XIII: 22–27.)

"Martin Buber." In *Martin Buber, 1878–1965, an Appreciation of His Life and Thought*. New York: American Friends of the Hebrew University, 1965. (XII: 320–323.)

"My Belief in Faith." *Réalités* 177 (1965): 68–71. Interview with Tanneguy de Quénétain.

"Honesty and Consecration in Religious Art and Architecture." *Protestant Church Buildings and Equipment* XIII, 3 (1965): 15, 26–29, 32, 33, 36. (XIII: 444–452.)

"A Final Conversation with Paul Tillich." By Albert H. Friedlander. *The Reconstructionist* XXXI, 14 (1965): 21–25.

"How Has Science in the Last Century Changed Man's View of Himself?" *The Current* VI, 1–2 (1965): 85–89. (III: 209–217.)

"Interview mit Paul Tillich." *Priestly Studies* XXXI, 3 (1965): 5–15. Interview with Lorenzo Avila, O.F.M.

1966

The Future of Religions, edited by Jerald C. Brauer. New York: Harper & Row, 1966.

"Words by Paul Tillich." *Harvard Divinity Bulletin* XXX, 2 (1966): 23–28.

"Reply." *The Journal of Religion* 46, 1 Part II (1966): 184–196.

"The Decline and the Validity of the Idea of Progress." *The Ohio University Review* VIII (1966): 5–22.

1967

My Search for Absolutes, edited by Ruth Nanda Anshen. New York: Simon & Schuster, 1967.

Perspectives on 19th and 20th Century Protestant Theology, edited by Carl E. Braaten. New York: Harper & Row, 1967.

1968

A History of Christian Thought, edited by Carl E. Braaten. New York: Harper & Row, 1968.

Friedrich Schleiermacher." In *Religion des konkreten Geistes*. Stuttgart: EVW, 1968.

"Paul Tillich and Carl Rogers: A Dialogue." *Pastoral Psychology* XIX, 181 (1968): 55–62, 64.

"The Problem of Immortality." In *East-West Studies on the Problem of the Self*, edited by P.T. Raju and Alburey Castell. The Hague: Nijhoff, 1968.

1969

What is Religion? Edited by James L. Adams. New York: Harper & Row, 1969.

Für und wider den Sozialismus, edited by Wolf-Dieter Marsch. Munich, Hamburg: Siebenstern Taschenbuch, 1969.

Der Mensch zwischen Bedrohung und Geborgenheit. Ein Tillich-Brevier. Edited by Erhard Seeberger and Gotthold Lasson. Stuttgart: EVW, 1969.

"Letter to Thomas Mann" (1943). In *The Intellectual Legacy of Paul Tillich*, edited by James R. Lyons. Detroit: Wayne State University Press, 1969.

1970

My Travel Diary: 1936. Between Two Worlds. Edited by Jerald C. Brauer. Translated by Maria Pelikan. New York: Harper & Row, 1970.

1971

Political Expectation, edited by James L. Adams. New York: Harper & Row, 1971.

"Paul Tillich in Conversation: Culture and Religion." (Transcribed and edited by James B. Ashbrook.) *Foundations* XIV, 1 (1971): 6–17.

"Paul Tillich in Conversation: Culture and Theology." (Transcribed and edited by James B. Ashbrook.) *Foundations* XIV, 2 (1971): 102–115.

"Paul Tillich in Conversation: History and Theology." (Transcribed and edited by James B. Ashbrook.) *Foundations* XIV, 3 (1971): 209–223.

"Dialogues, East and West: Conversation between Dr. Paul Tillich and Dr. Hisamatsu Shin'ichi. Part 1." *The Eastern Buddhist* (New Series) (Kyoto) IV, 2 (1971): 89–107. Part 2. *Ibid.* V, 2 (1972): 108–128.

1972

"Paul Tillich in Conversation on Psychology and Theology." (Transcribed and edited by James B. Ashbrook.) *The Journal of Pastoral Care* XXVI, 3 (1972): 176–189.

"Paul Tillich Converses with Psychotherapists." Edited by James B. Ashbrook. *Journal of Religion and Health* XI, 1 (1972): 40–72.

1973

Emanuel Hirsch, Paul Tillich. Briefwechsel 1917–1918. Edited by Hans-Walter Schütte. Berlin and Schleswig-Holstein: Die Spur, 1973.

SUBJECT INDEX

NAME INDEX